MW01275516

Health Savings Account Answer Book
Second Edition

by Christine L. Keller, Gary S. Lesser, and Susan D. Diehl

This comprehensive, authoritative volume provides up-to-date coverage of recent legislative and regulatory developments relating to health savings accounts (HSAs). It provides clear and concise guidance on the complex qualification, contribution, administration, and compliance issues that arise in connection with HSAs.

Highlights of the Second Edition

Health Savings Account Answer Book, Second Edition, offers the practitioner in-depth analysis of the full range of issues concerning these plans. Highlights include:

- Discussion of the prohibited transaction exemption under the Pension Protection Act of 2006, which allows HSA providers to offer personalized investment advice to HSA account holders.

- Discussion of the advantages to an employer of allowing employees to contribute to HSAs on a pretax basis through an employer's cafeteria plan.

- Changes and clarifications that were made under the final employer contribution comparability regulations and their significance.

- Discussion of the expansion of the final employer contribution comparability rules and the exceptions from the comparable employer contribution requirements under the new final regulations.

- Comparability issues for independent contractors, sole proprietors, partnerships, former employees, part-time employees, unionized employees, and others.

- Examination of the mechanics of funding, prefunding, testing periods, and categories of coverage relating to comparable contributions.

- Updated 2006 form filing requirements for HSA owners and contributing employers.

- Analysis of the Bush Administration's proposed changes to the HSA rules.

- Examination of the effect of state laws on HSA contribution eligibility and legislative proposals to address these issues.

- Discussion of how the USA Patriot Act affects the establishment of an HSA.

- Expansion and analysis of HSA adoption statistics.

- Discussion of ERISA fiduciary rules and the consequences when an HSA is subject to ERISA, including whether a trust rather than a custodial account is required.
- Discussion of the grace period rules that allow unused contributions in a cafeteria plan to carry over from one plan year to the next and their effect on HSA contribution eligibility.
- Analysis of changes made to the definition of *dependent* for HSA and other purposes by the Working Families Tax Relief Act of 2004 (WFTRA) and the Gulf Opportunity Zone Act of 2005 (GOZA).
- Analysis of the interaction between HSAs and other types of health coverage and available transitional relief.
- Review of the changes made to the transition rules involving state laws for non-calendar-year plans and the additional relief for coverage periods of 12 months or less.

9/06

For questions concerning this shipment, billing, or other customer service matters, call our Customer Service Department at 1-800-234-1660.

For toll-free ordering, please call 1-800-638-8437.

© 2006 Aspen Publishers, Inc.

a Wolters Kluwer business

Health
Savings Account
Answer Book

Health Savings Account Answer Book

Second Edition

Christine L. Keller, Esq.
Gary S. Lesser, Esq.
Susan D. Diehl

ASPEN
PUBLISHERS

76 Ninth Avenue, New York, NY 10011
www.aspenpublishers.com

This publication is designed to provide accurate and authoritative information in regard to the subject matter covered. It is sold with the understanding that the publisher is not engaged in rendering legal, accounting, or other professional services. If legal advice or other professional assistance is required, the services of a competent professional person should be sought.

—From a *Declaration of Principles* jointly adopted by
a Committee of the American Bar Association and
a Committee of Publishers and Associations

© 2006 Aspen Publishers, Inc.
a Wolters Kluwer business
www.aspenpublishers.com

All rights reserved. No part of this publication may be reproduced or transmitted in any form or by any means, electronic or mechanical, including photocopy, recording, or any information storage and retrieval system, without permission in writing from the publisher. Requests for permission to reproduce content should be directed to the Aspen Publishers website at *www.aspenpublishers.com*, or a letter of intent should be faxed to the permissions department at 212-771-0803.

Printed in the United States of America

ISBN 0-7355-5988-0

1 2 3 4 5 6 7 8 9 0

About Aspen Publishers

Aspen Publishers, headquartered in New York City, is a leading information provider for attorneys, business professionals, and law students. Written by preeminent authorities, our products consist of analytical and practical information covering both U.S. and international topics. We publish in the full range of formats, including updated manuals, books, periodicals, CDs, and online products.

Our proprietary content is complemented by 2,500 legal databases, containing over 11 million documents, available through our Loislaw division. Aspen Publishers also offers a wide range of topical legal and business databases linked to Loislaw's primary material. Our mission is to provide accurate, timely, and authoritative content in easily accessible formats, supported by unmatched customer care.

To order any Aspen Publishers title, go to *www.aspenpublishers.com* or call 1-800-638-8437.

To reinstate your manual update service, call 1-800-638-8437.

For more information on Loislaw products, go to *www.loislaw.com* or call 1-800-364-2512.

For Customer Care issues, e-mail CustomerCare@aspenpublishers.com; call 1-800-234-1660; or fax 1-800-901-9075.

Aspen Publishers
a Wolters Kluwer business

SUBSCRIPTION NOTICE

This Aspen Publishers product is updated on a periodic basis with supplements to reflect important changes in the subject matter. If you purchased this product directly from Aspen Publishers, we have already recorded your subscription for the update service.

If, however, you purchased this product from a bookstore and wish to receive future updates and revised or related volumes billed separately with a 30-day examination review, please contact our Customer Service Department at 1-800-234-1660, or send your name, company name (if applicable), address, and the title of the product to:

Aspen Publishers
7201 McKinney Circle
Frederick, MD 21704

Preface

Aspen Publishers' *Health Savings Account Answer Book, Second Edition,* provides an up-to-the-minute tutorial on this emerging form of consumer-directed health plan. It will benefit a wide variety of professional markets, including pension consultants, plan sponsors, health and insurance agents, financial planners and investment advisors, plan administrators, attorneys, custodians, trustees, brokers, and accountants, as well as those institutions that promote, market, service, or provide technical support to health and/or retirement plans, products, and related services.

Health Savings Account Answer Book, Second Edition, is a decision-making tool. Its combination of theory and practice-based advice provides a clear course of action to increase the subscriber's understanding of all aspects of the creation, administration, and operation of Health Savings Accounts (HSAs), as mandated by the Internal Revenue Code, Treasury regulations, and IRS notices, procedures, and announcements.

Written by a team of practicing experts, preeminent in their fields, *Health Savings Account Answer Book, Second Edition,* provides step-by-step guidance on the creation, operation, and administration of HSAs. Topics covered include medical coverage and insurance, contributions and deductions, HSA rollovers and transfers, distributions, administration and compliance, and other federal and state laws that affect HSAs. Subscribers will find answers to such commonly asked questions as the following:

- What is an HSA?
- Who is eligible to establish an HSA?
- What are the differences between an HSA, an HRA, and a health FSA?
- Which federal government agencies regulate HSAs?
- What state laws apply to HSAs?
- How are deductions claimed? How are excludable contributions handled?
- Do the prohibited transaction provisions of ERISA and/or Code Section 4975 apply to an HSA? Does the prohibited transaction penalty tax apply to an HSA?
- What is the HDHP requirement? What is an HDHP?

- What factors should an employer consider before offering an HSA with HDHP coverage? What factors should an individual consider before enrolling?

- How does an HSA protect the owner in the event of catastrophic financial loss due to unforeseen illness or injury?

- How are Medigap policies treated?

Health Savings Account Answer Book, Second Edition, covers the full range of HSA technical issues and concerns and provides a clear course of action on such topics as:

- When are employer HSA contributions deductible, and when are they excluded from income?

- What are "comparable" employer contributions? What is the testing period used to determine "comparable" contributions?

- Are HSA contributions made under a cafeteria plan subject to the comparability rules?

- Do employer contributions count as fringe benefits under the Davis-Bacon Act?

- How are contributions made by a Subchapter S corporation treated by the corporation and the shareholders?

- What are the rules relating to rollovers and transfers? When can a trustee or custodian refuse to accept rollovers and transfers?

- How is Form 8889—*Health Savings Accounts (HSAs)* completed?

- Is an HSA subject to HIPAA privacy regulations? Would the electronic standards apply?

- When is an HSA a security subject to regulation by the Securities and Exchange Commission?

- When are HSA distributions subject to tax—and to penalty?

Among the many rules and procedures discussed in *Health Savings Account Answer Book, Second Edition,* are the following:

- What are the special rules if one or both spouses have family coverage?

- How is the maximum deductible computed when spouses have separate health plans?

- What are the estate and gift tax aspects of an HSA, of key interest to attorneys and CPAs?

- Do community property rules affect the HSA contribution limitations?

- What are the exceptions to the rule that require that the employee not be covered under any other HDHP?

- Are penalty payments or flat dollar charges for failure to obtain provider pre-certification counted toward the $5,250/$10,500 limits for 2006?

- How are Medicare-eligible individuals or those receiving Veteran Affairs benefits treated for contribution purposes?
- What are qualified medical expenses eligible for tax-free treatment?
- When are payments for insurance treated as qualified medical expenses?
- Do the "use it or lose it" rules apply to an HSA or affect eligibility to make contributions?
- Are HSA rollovers and transfers subject to a "one in 12-month" or "60-day" rule?
- How can Archer Medical Savings Accounts be transferred or rolled over to an HSA?

List of Questions. The List of Questions in the front of an Answer Book is comparable to a detailed table of contents. It helps the reader to locate areas of immediate interest. Within each chapter, section headings group and organize questions by topic.

Examples. Numerous examples and practice pointers are interspersed with textual discussion to illustrate important concepts.

Planning Pointers. These paragraphs offer tips and advice to practitioners in the effective design, implementation, and administration of employee benefit plans.

Citations. Case citations and references to statutes and authorities are included to help readers who wish to research specific issues.

Appendixes. Updated appendix material includes charts on state laws affecting HSAs, as well as coverage of pertinent legislation and regulation.

Index. A detailed topical index is provided as a further aid to locating specific information. All references are to question numbers and appendices.

Abbreviations and Acronyms. A number of the terms and statutory references that appear repeatedly in this book are referred to by their abbreviations and/or acronyms after the first mention. The most common of the abbreviations and acronyms are:

- Ann.—IRS Announcement
- C.B.—Cumulative Bulletin of the IRS
- Code; I.R.C.—Internal Revenue Code
- DOL Adv. Op.—Department of Labor Advisory Opinion
- ERISA—Employee Retirement Income Security Act of 1974
- GOZA—Gulf Opportunity Zone Act of 2005
- IR—IRS Information Release
- IRA –Individual retirement arrangement (account and annuity)
- I.R.B.—Internal Revenue Bulletin
- IRS—Internal Revenue Service

- Ltr. Rul.—Private Letter Ruling
- Prop. Treas. Reg.—Proposed Treasury Regulation
- P.T.E.—Prohibited Transaction Exemption
- Pub. L.—Public Law
- Rev. Proc.—Revenue Procedure
- Rev. Rul.—Revenue Ruling
- Temp. Treas. Reg.—Temporary Treasury Regulation
- Treas. Reg.—Treasury Regulation
- WFTRA—Working Families Tax Relief Act of 2004

It is the authors' hope that *Health Savings Account Answer Book, Second Edition*, will become an essential research tool for practitioners in the field of employee benefits.

Christine L. Keller
Gary S. Lesser
Susan D. Diehl
August 2006

About the Authors

Christine L. Keller, Esq., LL.M., is a principal at Groom Law Group. She joined the firm in 2001 after practicing for six years at the Internal Revenue Service, Office of Chief Counsel (Tax-Exempt and Government Entities Division). At the Office of Chief Counsel, Christine worked first in the qualified plans litigation branch and later in the health and welfare branch. She is one of the principal authors of two sets of final cafeteria plan regulations published by the IRS in 2000 and 2001. At Groom Law Group, Christine advises employers, insurers, and plan administrators concerning federal and state laws that affect the administration of welfare benefit plans, cafeteria plans, health savings accounts, and other employee benefit arrangements. She also assists clients with obtaining rulings from the IRS and submitting comments to the IRS and Department of Labor in response to agency guidance. She has experience with drafting various types of plan documents, including defined contribution health plans, summary plan descriptions, welfare plans, and cafeteria plans. She has published articles in *RIA Pension & Benefits Week* on USERRA & The Soldiers' and Sailors' Civil Relief Act (Dec. 2001) and Defined Contribution Health Plans (Sept. 2002) and in *Employee Benefits News* on HSA Funding Issues (January 2006).

Christine earned an LL.M. (Taxation) with distinction and a Certificate in Employee Benefits from Georgetown University Law Center in February 2000. She earned her J.D. from the State University of New York at Buffalo Law School in 1995 and graduated cum laude from Alfred University in 1990 with a B.S. in Business Administration and a minor in Industrial Engineering. She is admitted to practice in New York and the District of Columbia.

Gary S. Lesser, Esq., is the principal of GSL Galactic Consulting, located in Indianapolis, Indiana. Mr. Lesser maintains a telephone-based consulting practice providing services to other professionals and business owners. Mr. Lesser is a nationally known author, educator, and speaker on retirement plans for individuals and smaller businesses. He has broad technical and practical knowledge of both qualified and nonqualified retirement plans.

Mr. Lesser is the technical editor and co-author of *SIMPLE, SEP, and SARSEP Answer Book; Life Insurance Answer Book; Roth IRA Answer Book; 457 Answer Book;* and *Quick Reference to IRAs* (all Aspen Publishers). Mr. Lesser is also the principal author and technical editor of *The CPA's Guide to Retirement Plans for Small Businesses* (American Institute of Certified Public Accountants (AICPA)). He has developed several software programs that are used by financial planners, accountants, and other pension practitioners to design and market retirement plans for smaller businesses. His two software programs—*QP-SEP Illustrator*™ and *SIMPLE Illustrator*^SM—are marketed and distributed nationally. He has also been published in the *EP/EO Digest, Journal of Taxation of Employee Benefits, Journal of Compensation and Benefits, Journal of Pension Benefits, Life Insurance Selling, Rough Notes,* and the *NAPFA Advisor.* Mr. Lesser is an associated professional member of the American Society of Pension Actuaries (ASPA).

In 1974, Mr. Lesser started his employee benefits career with the Internal Revenue Service as a Tax Law Specialist/Attorney in the Employee Plans/ Exempt Organizations (EP/EO) Division. He later managed and operated a pension administration and actuarial service organization, was an ERISA marketing attorney for a national brokerage firm, and was a senior vice-president/director of retirement plans for several nationally known families of mutual funds and variable annuity products. Mr. Lesser graduated from New York Law School and received his B.A. in accounting from Fairleigh Dickinson University. He is admitted to the bars of the state of New York and the United States Tax Court. Mr. Lesser can be reached at GSL Galactic Consulting, 944 Stockton St., Indianapolis, IN 42260-4925, (317) 254-0385, at QPSEP@aol.com, or at http://www.garylesser.com.

Susan D. Diehl is president of PenServ, Inc., a pension consulting firm with headquarters in Horsham, Pennsylvania. PenServ also has offices in the Philadelphia, Dallas, and Columbia (South Carolina) areas and serves a client base of more than 800 organizations. The firm provides retirement plan services, including technical manuals, a monthly news publication, a hotline service, plan administration, plan documents, administrative forms, continuing professional education seminars, and in-house review of plan documents and administrative procedures.

Before establishing PenServ, Ms. Diehl was vice-president and director of Technical Services for a national consulting firm for eight years. She also served as assistant vice-president and administrator of Retirement Services at Abraham Lincoln Federal for six years. In addition she served three terms as president of the Montgomery County Chamber of Commerce. In 1992, she received the Athena Award and is included in the Athena Hall of Fame in Michigan.

Ms. Diehl is a former member of the Department of Labor's Advisory Council on Employee Welfare and Pension Benefit Plans established under ERISA and served as the council's Chairperson in 1995. She also served a two-year term on the IRS's Information Reporting Program Advisory Committee (IRPAC). Ms. Diehl often testifies before the IRS and the Department of Labor's Pension and Welfare Benefits Administration (PWBA) on matters relating to retirement plan regulation. She is past Chairperson of the Board of PACT, Inc.

(Pension Action Council Taskforce), a national organization that presents retirement plan issues to members of Congress, the IRS, and the DOL.

Ms. Diehl is a contributor to *Individual Retirement Account Answer Book* and a co-author of *Roth IRA Answer Book* and *SIMPLE, SEP, and SARSEP Answer Book* (all Aspen Publishers). A graduate of Arcadia University in Glenside, Pennsylvania, she received a bachelor's degree in mathematics and went on to study mathematics at the University of Graz in Austria.

Introduction

There is a significant trend in employer-provided health care: consumer-directed health plans. In these plans, the decision of how to spend health care dollars rests more with the employee, and his or her health care provider, than with the employer or insurance company. Consumer-directed health plans are part of an overall initiative to help reign in the rising costs of health care and health insurance. This policy goal takes on added importance because an increase in the cost of health insurance means a decrease in the number of people covered by insurance. Employees who participate in consumer-driven health plans become wiser consumers of medical services as a result of their enhanced decisionmaking responsibility. Another advantage is that the lower costs associated with consumer-directed health plans provide more coverage options for individuals who wish to purchase health insurance outside of the employment context.

The inclusion of the health savings account (HSA) provision as part of the Medicare Modernization Act in 2003 is an important part of the trend toward consumer-directed health plans. President George W. Bush was very supportive of including HSAs in this important legislation, which modernized Medicare by adding a prescription drug feature to the Medicare program. Many members of Congress were motivated to vote for the Medicare Modernization Act because of its HSA provision. They expressed concern about rising health care costs and believed that making HSAs available to all Americans would help address those spiraling costs.

In terms of developing cost-consciousness in medical spending, it is useful to review how medical insurance operates. Traditional health insurance pays for all medical costs once a deductible is met, usually requiring some sort of co-pay with each visit or prescription drug. Health Maintenance Organizations (HMOs) contain costs by limiting the health care professionals and procedures that the HMO will pay for. HSAs require that the HSA owner participate in a high deductible health plan (HDHP) before he or she can contribute to the HSA, and the amount of the maximum HSA contribution cannot exceed the deductible amount under the HDHP. High deductible health insurance is less expensive than traditional health insurance and HMO coverage because it insures only major catastrophic health care expenses; the consumer pays for all other medical services, either directly or through a vehicle such as an HSA.

Thus there are two ways in which high deductible health insurance reduces costs: the premium for such insurance is lower, and there is more prudent health care spending. By their support of the HSA provision in the Medicare Modernization Act, Congress and the Bush administration expressed their belief that the use of HDHPs and HSAs would result in more cost-conscious decisions by consumers of medical services.

The operation of HDHPs is similar to that of other types of insurance (e.g., automobile insurance or homeowners insurance), which make payments only when there is a major problem (e.g., an automobile accident or a house fire). Traditional health insurance generally starts paying claims for medical care, whether routine or not, after a low deductible is reached. This is analogous to having an automobile insurer pay for changing a car's fluids, in addition to providing coverage in case of accidents. Because traditional health insurance pays for all medical expenses (once the low deductible is reached), the cost of such insurance is higher than the cost of an HDHP, where the consumer pays for routine medical services.

Another important change is that using the HSA with an HDHP provides a tax-effective way to pay for out-of-pocket medical costs, since all contributions made to the HSA that meet the contribution limits are fully tax-deductible by the HSA owner. Compare that to the current system of itemized deduction for out-of-pocket health care expenses. Given the restrictions on the amount of medical deduction (amounts over 7 percent of adjusted gross income), individuals rarely get any tax benefit for paying medical expenses themselves. Clearly, the use of an HSA to pay for these medical expenses benefits everyone, no matter what their tax bracket.

The successful implementation of the HSA legislation was an important priority of the Bush administration. As the former Benefits Tax Counsel at the U.S. Department of the Treasury, I was involved in crafting the guidance to help implement HSAs. Our main objective was to offer guidance, consistent with the legislation, that would facilitate the offering of qualifying high deductible health insurance and the accounts themselves. We asked those individuals in the health care and financial services industry who were considering providing HSAs and HDHPs to tell us what issues needed to be addressed and when such guidance would be needed in order to provide a successful rollout of the these products. We met with many of the stakeholders to determine how to craft helpful, easy-to-understand guidance that could be used by all employees, including those who were not familiar with the process for issuing tax-related guidance. To that end, Treasury and the Internal Revenue Service issued eight pieces of guidance by July 2004 that addressed many of the important issues surrounding HSAs and high deductible health insurance. In addition, we heard that financial institutions were concerned about the forms that were needed for the establishment of HSAs. Treasury and the IRS provided forms that any financial institution would choose to use for their clients to establish an HSA. *Health Savings Account Answer Book* provides an excellent description of all the guidance promulgated by the federal government regarding HSAs and HDHPs.

In addition to the guidance, the Bush administration made a very proactive effort to explain the benefits of HSAs and HDHPs to the American public. President Bush had several town-hall meetings promoting the HSA concept, as did Secretary of the Treasury John Snow. Treasury had a separate Web site that contained all of the information regarding HSAs, and the Department answered and continues to answer questions from the public about HSAs. Doubtless, many subscribers to *Health Savings Account Answer Book* have heard me or my former staff talk at length about the HSA guidance at numerous meetings around the country and on countless conference calls.

It is through HSAs and HDHPs that consumers are most enabled to become cost-conscious regarding health care spending. *Health Savings Account Answer Book* serves as a valuable aid in understanding how these insurance vehicles operate. The more people know and understand these products, the more likely they are to use them, and that is an important step in reducing the steadily increasing costs of health care in America.

William F. Sweetnam, Jr.
Groom Law Group*

---

* Mr. Sweetnam was the Benefits Tax Counsel at the U.S. Department of the Treasury from April 2001 to February 2005 and was Tax Counsel on the majority staff of the U.S. Senate Committee on Finance from January 1998 to February 2001.

Contents

Contents

Contents

List of Questions

Chapter 1 Overview of HSAs

Chapter 2 General HSA Rules

In General

Eligible Individual for Establishing an HSA

Chapter 3 Medical Coverage and Insurance

Chapter 4 Contributions and Deductions

Transitional Relief

Contribution Limitations

Catch-Up Contributions

Computing Annual Contributions

Special Computation Rules for Married Individuals

Tax Treatment of Contributions

IRS Reporting by Individuals

Partnership Considerations

Chapter 5 HSA Rollovers and Transfers

Chapter 6 Distributions

Chapter 7 Administration and Compliance

Chapter 8 Federal and State Laws Affecting HSAs

Chapter 1

Overview of HSAs

The steadily rising cost of health care and premiums for health coverage in the United States presents an economic challenge for many individuals; some struggle to maintain coverage, while others remain uninsured. In addition, employers of all sizes that have traditionally provided health benefits for their workforces have become concerned about their ability to continue to offer such coverage on an affordable basis. This was the climate when, in December 2003, Congress created, as part of the Medicare Prescription Drug, Improvement, and Modernization Act of 2003, a new type of tax-favored savings vehicle for health expenses known as a Health Savings Account (HSA). Chapter 1 provides information about the history of HSAs, including their establishment by Congress and their regulation by government agencies, and explores the pros and cons of HSA arrangements from the perspectives of individuals and employers.

Introduction

Q 1:1   What is a health savings account?

A health savings account (HSA), described in Section 223 of the Internal Revenue Code (Code), is a funded account, similar to an IRA. Contributions may be made within specified limits by individuals who meet certain eligibility requirements and/or by employers or others on behalf of such individuals. Amounts in an HSA grow on a tax-deferred basis and, if used for qualified medical expenses, may be distributed on a tax-free basis. In order to contribute to an HSA, an individual must be covered under a high deductible health plan (HDHP) and may not also participate in a non-HDHP, subject to certain exceptions.

Q 1:2   Is the HSA an entirely new creation by Congress?

No. The HSA is based upon and similar to the Archer Medical Savings Account (MSA) (see Q 2:5), which became available for use by self-employed individuals and employees of small employers (i.e., employers with 50 or fewer employees) in 1996. MSAs have not enjoyed widespread use, however, due in large part to the restriction that prohibits employers with more than 50 employees from making the account available to employees. When MSA legislation was passed, Congress placed a cap on the number of individuals (generally 750,000 taxpayers) who could have an MSA. That number was never reached. [H.R. Conf. Rep. No. 108-391, at 841 (2003)] In addition, MSAs were intended to be temporary and were due to expire in 2000, but Congress has extended that deadline three times. [I.R.S. Ann. 2005-12, 2005-7 I.R.B. 555]

Two substantive differences between MSAs and HSAs relate to the deductible under the HDHP and the funding of the account, as delineated below:

1. With respect to the deductible, there is a required upper limit on the deductible for MSAs under the HDHP, but for HSAs there is only a lower limit.

2. With respect to funding, MSAs are not permitted to be funded by both an employer and an employee during the same plan year, or with pretax salary reductions through an employer's cafeteria plan. HSAs may be funded by both the employer and the employee during the same plan year, as well as by any other individual on behalf of the employee. HSAs may also be funded through an employer's cafeteria plan on a pretax basis.

Q 1:3   What factors contributed to the enactment of the HSA legislation?

In the years immediately preceding the enactment of the HSA legislation, *consumer-driven*, or *defined contribution*, health plans emerged. Through these plans, employers offered employees a defined amount of health care dollars to be spent or saved for future use, at the employees' discretion. Proponents of these alternative arrangements note that they can make costs more predictable and provide incentives to employees to make wiser health care spending decisions. HSAs are consistent with the consumer-driven philosophy. In addition, amounts in the HSA account may be used for nonmedical purposes. With the exception of MSAs, existing vehicles for providing such coverage on a tax-advantaged basis do not allow that flexibility. Finally, because HSAs are based on MSAs, which have already been enacted, there was precedent for the approach.

Q 1:4   Why do proponents of HSAs consider HSAs to be an improvement over the current health insurance system?

In order to participate in an HSA, an individual must be covered by an HDHP. HSA proponents say that participants can save money by participating in an

HDHP, which generally has lower premiums than a non-HDHP. In addition, HSA proponents say that, if participants are given a choice to either save money in an HSA account, which can earn interest tax-free, or spend it on medical goods and services, they will confine their spending to necessary purchases and will demand lower prices and/or value for their dollar. In contrast, the full cost of a service under traditional health plans is not as obvious to a participant because he or she typically is responsible only for the co-payment. Thus, HSA proponents argue that HSAs will re-introduce market forces to the health care system, as well as allowing savings to accumulate on a tax-free basis to pay for future health care expenses.

HSA/HDHP Providers

Q 1:5   Did companies offer HSAs with accompanying HDHPs on January 1, 2004, the date the law became effective?

HSAs with *individual* HDHPs were offered effective January 1, 2004, by a few companies, many of whom had previously offered MSAs. HSAs with group HDHPs were not widely available on January 1, 2004, primarily because most existing HDHPs offered on the group market had to be modified to comply with the requirements under the HSA legislation. For example, many HDHPs offered on the group market were structured to provide pre-scription drug coverage before the deductible was satisfied. These products have been modified, and many group health insurers offered HSAs and HDHPs that satisfied the requirements under the HSA legislation effective January 1, 2005.

Q 1:6   Do some companies offer their services as HSA trustees or custodians only, without offering an accompanying HDHP?

Yes. There are companies that offer services as HSA trustees or custodians only. The number of HSA trustees/custodians has been growing steadily since the HSA legislation passed. The Treasury Department website contains a link to a site that contains lists of HSA insurers and trustees (www.HSAinsider.org). In order to be an HSA trustee, a company must be a bank, an insurance company, or a nonbank trustee (see Qs 2:1, 7:23). Each year the IRS publishes a list of companies that are approved as nonbank trustees. [I.R.S. Ann. 2005-59, 2005-37 I.R.B. 524]

HSAs are expected to continue to attract banks and financial institutions to sponsor the accounts and manage the assets in them. The aggregate amounts held and invested in HSAs are expected to grow steadily each year. In addition, HSA sponsors can charge fees that are applied to set-up, maintenance, and service fees. These factors may make the HSA as lucrative for these institutions as individual retirement arrangements (IRAs), which gained popularity in the mid-70s, have become. [See "Health Savings Accounts Attract Wall Street," by Eric Dash, The New York Times (Jan. 27, 2006)]

Other Defined Contribution Health Care Arrangements

Q 1:7   In addition to HSAs, what types of health accounts are considered defined contribution or consumer-driven arrangements?

Health Reimbursement Arrangements (HRAs), Health Flexible Spending Arrangements (FSAs), and Archer MSAs are considered defined contribution or consumer-driven arrangements because they all allow employees to decide how the dollars credited or deposited to the account are spent. [I.R.S. Notice 2002–45, 2002–2 C.B. 93; Rev. Rul. 2002–41, I.R.C. §§ 106(c), 220; Prop. Treas. Reg. § 1.125–2, Q&A-7]

Q 1:8   What are the main differences among an HSA, an HRA, and a health FSA?

All three vehicles share a common purpose of making dollars available on a tax-advantaged basis for reimbursement of medical expenses. However, there are differences in the way these accounts are required to be structured under federal law. Main differences among an HSA, HRA, and FSA include the following:

1. An HSA is the only arrangement of the three that must be funded through a custodial account or trust and accompanied by an HDHP. An HSA is also the only arrangement of the three for which amounts in the HSA account may be used for nonmedical purposes, although such expenditure requires inclusion for income tax purposes and may result in a 10 percent additional tax.

2. An FSA is the only arrangement of the three in which amounts that are unused at the end of the plan year must be forfeited (subject to the 2½ month extension under Notice 2005-4; see Q 4:11, "Caution").

3. An HRA is the only arrangement of the three that must be paid for solely by the employer; and salary reduction contributions are prohibited.

(See appendix H for a detailed comparison of HRAs, FSAs, and HSAs.)

Regulation

Q 1:9   Which federal government agencies regulate HSAs?

HSAs are governed by Code Section 223 and are therefore regulated by the Internal Revenue Service (IRS). An HSA is also subject to prohibited transaction rules under Code Section 4975 that are regulated by the Department of Labor (DOL). (Under Reorganization Plan Number 4 of 1978, 43 Federal Register 47713 (Oct. 17, 1978), the authority of the Secretary of the Treasury to issue rulings under Code Section 4975 has been transferred, with certain exceptions, to the Secretary of Labor.) The DOL also regulates whether a particular HSA is subject to ERISA (see Qs 8:1–8:7). Finally, to the extent that an HSA invests in securities, or is considered a security itself, the Securities and Exchange Commission (SEC) will regulate (see Q 8:45).

Q 1:10 Are states permitted to regulate HSAs?

Yes. A state may regulate an HSA for state income tax purposes (see Q 8:40), and, to the extent that the HSA is not considered an ERISA plan, state trust law will apply to the HSA (see Q 8:29). In addition, states may regulate insured HDHPs that accompany the HSAs (see Q 8:36). ERISA preemption generally precludes a state from regulating a self-funded health plan.

Q 1:11 Which federal government agencies have issued guidance on HSAs?

The IRS has issued a number of items of guidance in the relatively short period of time since HSAs have been enacted. Most of this guidance is in the form of revenue rulings and notices, with questions and answers, and some guidance provides transitional relief. In addition, the IRS has issued proposed regulations on the comparable contribution requirements under Code Section 4980G that apply to HSAs. [Prop. Treas. Reg. § 54.4980G-1–5; 70 Fed. Reg. 50233 (Aug. 26, 2005)] The proposed regulations were modified and made final on July 31, 2006 & (see Qs, 4:93–4:138). The regulations apply only to employers who make contributions to employee HSAs, and generally require that an employer make similar contributions for all employees who participate in the employer's qualifying HDHP. If the employer's contributions do not satisfy these rules, the employer will be subject to a 35 percent excise tax on all HSA contributions that the employer makes for a year (see Q 4:94).

In addition, the IRS has issued new tax forms and instructions (Form 1040, Form W-2, Form 8889, Form 5498-SA, Form 1099-SA), model trust and custodial account agreements (Forms 5305(c) and 5305(b)), and Publication 969, describing HSA rules.

The DOL has issued Field Assistance Bulletin 2004-1 (involving ERISA) and Advisory Opinion 2004-09A (involving the Prohibited Transaction Rules). (See appendix C.) The Department of Health and Human Services, Centers for Medicare and Medicaid Services (CMS) has issued guidance on account-based plans with respect to Medicare Part D, which includes a discussion of HSAs (see Q 8:34, 8:35). The SEC has not issued any guidance.

Q 1:12 What prompted the IRS to issue so much guidance on HSAs in 2004?

The statute had an extremely short effective date. It was signed into law on December 8, 2003, and the HSA provisions were effective less than a month later, on January 1, 2004.

The IRS indicated in public meetings held shortly after HSAs were enacted that the agency was interested in helping employers clarify outstanding issues as soon as possible in order to facilitate the ability of employers to offer HSAs as part of their array of benefits. During the period that the guidance was being drafted, the IRS requested and received numerous comments from the public.

Advantages and Disadvantages

Q 1:13   What are the primary advantages to an individual of participating in an HSA?

From an individual's perspective, primary advantages of HSA participation include:

- Reduced premiums for health coverage (cost of HDHP coverage will be lower than non-HDHP coverage)
- More control over medical spending
- Ability to set aside money for future use on a tax-favored basis

(See Q 2:41 for a comprehensive list of possible advantages of participating in an HSA.)

Q 1:14   What are the advantages to an employer of offering an HSA option to employees?

Offering an HSA option gives the employer a more predictable financial obligation, as well as the opportunity to restructure cost sharing between the employer and employees. For some employers, particularly small ones, an HSA may provide the opportunity to offer a health plan to employees for the first time. Other employers may offer the HSA as an additional medical coverage option. In addition, an HSA, which is a defined contribution approach to health care rather than a defined benefit approach, may bring an employer's health plans in line with changes that have already been made to the employer's retirement plans. Finally, as noted above, the premium for an HDHP is generally lower than for a non-HDHP health plan, which will result in a cost savings to the employer, to the extent that the employer contributes to this cost.

Q 1:15   What are the advantages to an employer of allowing employees to contribute to an HSA on a pretax basis through the employer's cafeteria plan?

An employer may offer an HSA option as part of its cafeteria plan, allowing an individual to make HSA contributions on a pretax basis. Alternatively, contributions may be made by an individual on an after-tax basis, with a corresponding deduction available to the individual at year-end on the individual's tax return. Similarly, employers may structure employer HSA contributions through a cafeteria plan, or make contributions without using a cafeteria plan.

For an employer, there are several advantages to allowing employees to make HSA contributions through its cafeteria plan:

1. HSA contributions by an employee through a cafeteria plan (provided they are within statutory limits) are treated as employer contributions that are not subject to withholding from wages for income tax or subject to the

Federal Insurance Contributions Act (FICA), the Federal Unemployment Tax Act (FUTA), or the Railroad Retirement Tax Act. Thus, by allowing employees to make HSA contributions through the cafeteria plan, the employer will reduce its liability for these taxes, as long as it is reasonable for an employer to believe at the time a contribution is made that such contribution will not exceed the HSA limits that apply to a particular employee.

2. Offering an HSA through an existing cafeteria plan provides the employer with a convenient way to integrate the HSA into existing benefit options. For example, if the employer currently offers a flex dollar system, the employer could allow employees to use flex dollars to fund the HSA.

3. If the employer wants to use a creative method for establishing its level of HSA contributions (e.g., matching the amounts that an employee contributes or contributing more to employees who participate in wellness programs), an HSA must be offered through a cafeteria plan to avoid violating the comparable contribution rules under Code Section 4980G. In that event, the nondiscrimination requirements of Code Section 125 would have to be satisfied.

Q 1:16 Will the HSA serve as a good vehicle to set aside funds for retiree health?

Although it is possible that funds in an HSA will accumulate and be available for use in retirement, the fact that an individual must generally give up all other health coverage except for HDHP coverage makes it likely that a good portion of the amount deposited to the HSA will be used by the HSA account owner to pay his or her medical expenses each year. This will not be true for individuals who are able to use other assets for ongoing health expenses, allowing the amounts in the HSA to accumulate. However, for many individuals, the amount remaining in the HSA upon retirement may not be significant. There are, however, proposals to increase the HSA contribution limits, which would enhance the ability of individuals to accumulate assets for retiree medical expenses. (See Qs 1:25-1:30.)

Q 1:17 What are the *primary* disadvantages to an individual of participating in an HSA?

The primary disadvantages of an HSA to the individual include the following:

1. An HSA participant who is not accustomed to participating in an HDHP may not feel that he or she has adequate coverage, particularly if the participant is responsible for paying all costs below the deductible from his or her own funds or from the HSA. (However, HDHPs are permitted to offer *preventive care* coverage before the deductible is satisfied, so a participant in an HDHP with generous preventive care coverage may view the coverage level as adequate.)

2. If medical expenses are incurred before money is set aside in the HSA for the year, the participant is required to pay those expenses out-of-pocket.

3. If there are significant medical expenses, it is unlikely that any HSA money will be available to carry over from year to year that could be used for retiree medical or nonmedical expenses, eliminating one of the primary advantages of HSA participation.

(See Q 2:42 for a comprehensive list of possible disadvantages of participating in an HSA.)

Q 1:18   What are the disadvantages to an employer of offering an HSA?

Disadvantages of an HSA to the employer include the following:

1. Employees may view an HSA offering as a reduction of existing benefits, particularly if the employer does not contribute to the HSA on behalf of employees. (This is unlikely to be the case if the employer offers an HSA as part of its array of existing benefits, however.)
2. The employer must invest administrative resources to implement an HSA option and to educate human resources personnel regarding the benefit.
3. An employer that offers an HSA option may discover that the majority of the workforce prefers to maintain existing coverage and is unwilling to switch to an HSA.

Q 1:19   What factors should an individual consider before enrolling in an HSA with HDHP?

Factors that an individual should consider include:

1. The anticipated level of medical expenses for the year,
2. The likelihood that such expenses will be covered under a particular HDHP,
3. The level of resources available to the individual to pay for expenses before the deductible is satisfied, and
4. The existing coverage of such individual's spouse (see Q 1:20) or domestic partner (see Q 1:21).

Q 1:20   How will a spouse's health coverage affect an account owner's ability to contribute to an HSA?

If the spouse of an account owner has separate health coverage, the following special rules may apply:

1. The account owner could be prohibited from contributing to an HSA at all.
2. The account owner could be required to limit the amount contributed to the HSA to the lowest of the two family deductibles.

The account owner could be required to limit the amount contributed to the HSA to the amount of the account owner's family HDHP deductible less the amount that is allocated to the spouse.

These rules, and other variations, are described in chapter 4. Whether or not the account owner's spouse is covered under the HDHP and/or has other coverage, the spouse's medical expenses will be considered "qualified medical expenses," allowing the account owner to take a tax-free distribution from his or her HSA to pay for such expenses, as long as the expenses are not reimbursed by another health plan (see chapter 6).

Q 1:21   How will a domestic partner's health coverage affect the HSA contribution limits?

It appears that a domestic partner's health coverage will generally not affect an account owner's ability to contribute to his or her HSA, even where the employee covers the domestic partner under his or her HDHP. Because no rule requires domestic partners to divide an HSA contribution as married individuals are required to, it appears that a domestic partner who is covered under an account owner's HDHP could open his or her own HSA and contribute the full amount of the deductible or the statutory maximum (whichever is less).

Further, neither Treasury nor the IRS has indicated that there is any problem with an account owner covering a domestic partner under an HDHP and having the domestic partner's expenses count toward satisfying the family deductible under the HDHP, notwithstanding that these individuals are not related. Thus, in the absence of further guidance from IRS or Treasury, this appears permissible.

Note. An account owner may not take a tax-free distribution from his or her HSA to pay for the domestic partner's expenses (as may be done with respect to a spouse), unless the domestic partner is a dependent under Code Section 152 (see Q 2:33).

Q 1:22   What factors should an employer consider before offering an HSA with HDHP coverage?

Before offering an HSA with HDHP coverage, an employer should consider (1) what proportion of its workforce is likely to be receptive to HSAs and (2) the level of resources it wishes to devote to facilitating an HSA arrangement. Employers that wish to assist employees in establishing HSAs have two options:

1. Offer an HDHP that satisfies the HSA requirements and leave it up to employees to establish HSAs on their own, or
2. Offer an HDHP/HSA package, which allows employees one-stop shopping. Also, the employer will have to decide whether to offer employees the flexibiity of making HSA contributions on a pretax basis through the employer's cafeteria plan during the year rather than making contributions on an after-tax basis with an accompanying deduction on the individual's tax return.

Q 1:23   What are the potential consequences to an individual of enrolling in an HSA but failing to follow the applicable rules?

An individual who does not maintain adequate records of medical expenditures may be required to pay income tax and a 10 percent additional tax on amounts distributed from the HSA. In contrast to FSAs and HRAs, HSA account owners are required to maintain their own records of medical expenditures and do not submit claims to their employer for approval. Thus, on audit, an individual would be required to prove that the level of medical expenses matched those on the tax return (Form 1040 and Form 8889) filed by the individual. In addition, if an individual makes excess contributions to an HSA for a given year and fails to withdraw those contributions by April 15 of the following year, the individual will be subject to a 6 percent excise tax on the excess contributions.

Q 1:24   What are the potential consequences to an employer of failing to follow the applicable HSA rules?

An employer that fails to make comparable contributions to the HSAs of employees may be required to pay an excise tax of 35 percent of the aggregate amount contributed by the employer to the HSAs of employees for the year (see Q 4:94). In addition, an employer that excludes HSA contributions from employees' wages without following applicable IRS guidance, or that violates cafeteria plan nondiscrimination rules, may be responsible for paying employment taxes and penalties (see Q 1:24).

An employer could also be found in violation of ERISA rules, which could generate DOL civil penalties or participant lawsuits (see Q 8:20).

Future of HSAs

Q 1:25   What were some of the major issues that commentators to the IRS were concerned about with respect to HSAs in 2004 and continue to be concerned about today?

Issues about which commentators expressed concern to the IRS included the following:

1. HSA participants' eligibility to continue to participate in health FSAs and HRAs (addressed in I.R.S. Notice 2004-45, 2004-28 I.R.B. 1 and I.R.S. Notice 2005-86, 2005-49 I.R.B. 1075 (FSAs with 2½ month grace period) or to make a one-time rollover from an HRA to an HSA.

2. The eligibility of HSA participants to receive prescription drug coverage before the deductible under the HDHP is satisfied (addressed in Rev. Rul. 2004-38, 2004-15 I.R.B. 717, and Rev. Proc. 2004-22, 2004-15 I.R.B. 727).

3. The definition of *preventive care*—not defined by Congress in the HSA legislation and significant because any item that is considered preventive care may be covered under the HDHP before the deductible is satisfied (addressed in I.R.S. Notice 2004-23, 2004-15 I.R.B. 725).

4. The application of the HSA comparable contribution rules, and whether the rules would prohibit employers from making matching contributions or incentive payments to the HSAs of employees (addressed in I.R.S. Notice 2004-50, Q&As 46, 47, 2004-33 I.R.B. 196; Prop. Treas. Reg. § 54.4980G-1–5; 70 Fed. Reg. 50233 (Aug. 26, 2005) (see Qs 4:93–4:133)).

5. State laws that mandate that health insurance policies provide particular benefits, which could preclude an individual in a particular state from participating in an HDHP that satisfies applicable federal rules (see Q 8:36) (addressed in I.R.S. Notice 2004-43, 2004-27 I.R.B. 1 and I.R.S. Notice 2005-83, 2005-49, I.R.B. 1075).

6. The ability of employers to restrict the use of the HSA account to medical expenses (see Q 6:10) and to recoup amounts paid into the HSA of an employee who terminates employment (see Qs 4:134, 6:2) (addressed in I.R.S. Notice 2004-50, Q&As 79, 82, 2004-33 I.R.B. 196).

7. The ability of an employee to contribute to an HSA even if his or her spouse has an FSA. Currently, IRS guidance indicates that an individual may not contribute to an HSA if his or her spouse has an FSA, even if the individual never seeks to be reimbursed for any medical expenses from the spouse's FSA. Commentators have requested that the IRS correct this situation by allowing the individual in the HSA to certify that he or she will not receive reimbursement for any health expenses from the spouse's FSA. The IRS has not provided any guidance on this issue other than I.R.S. Notice 2004-45, 2004-28 I.R.B. 1, which does not adopt this flexible approach.

Earlier indexing of HSA/HDHP cost-of-living adjustments (COLA). Under the current statutory provisions for calculating COLAs, the IRS cannot provide information about the indexed COLA amounts that apply to HSAs and HDHPs earlier than October of each year (see Q 4:21). Commentators would like Treasury to change this rule so that the limits could be announced earlier each year. Treasury has indicated informally that this would require a legislative change.

Q 1:26   Why does the Bush Administration propose budget changes that would expand HSAs in 2007?

The administration believes that such changes would improve access to health care and expand HSAs. The President's budget makes important new proposals that will make health insurance coverage more accessible and affordable to Americans. [General Explanation of the Administration's Fiscal Year 2007 Revenue Proposals ("Blue Book"), Dept. of Treasury (Feb. 2006)]

Q 1:27   What are the reasons for the Administration's proposed changes to the HSA rules?

It is the Administration's position that empowering health care consumers (rather than third-party payers) to play a more direct role in their health care decisions would help to stem the trend of rapidly rising health care costs, and that a more market-oriented and consumer-driven health care system will help control costs and result in more affordable and accessible health care. Furthermore, the U.S. Tax Code does not afford the same treatment to the self-employed, the unemployed, and workers for companies that do not offer health insurance (most of whom are small businesses) as it does to companies that do offer health insurance. Employer-based insurance receives a tax subsidy that individually purchased insurance does not. In addition, employer-based insurance generally receives a tax subsidy, while out-of-pocket spending does not. These large tax subsidies encourage generous health insurance and health spending that is not fully valued and makes labor markets less flexible. The Administration's reasons for the proposed changes are as follows:

1. Because health care purchased through an employer insurance plan is subsidized by the Tax Code, people insure against predictable and routine expenses (not just unpredictable, catastrophic expenses) and are thus insensitive to the cost of the health care they consume.

2. The tax subsidy is generally not available to the uninsured or to individual insurance purchasers, resulting in an underdeveloped individual market.

3. Employer contributions further mask the cost of health care to employees, whose wages tend to be lower when health care costs go up.

4. Employees may be reluctant to leave their jobs for fear of losing their insurance. Portability of health insurance is increasingly important in today's dynamic labor markets, where workers choose to change jobs with increasing frequency.

The Bush Administration believes that these tax distortions would be eliminated if employer insurance, individually purchased insurance, and out-of-pocket health spending were on equal tax footing. [General Explanation of the Administration's Fiscal Year 2007 Revenue Proposals ("Blue Book"), p. 23, Dept. of Treasury (Feb. 2006)]

Q 1:28   What are the proposed changes to HSAs under the Bush Administration's budget proposals?

The general explanation of the Bush Administration's fiscal year 2007 revenue proposals include the following:

1. *Provide an above-the-line deduction and income tax credit for the purchase of HSA-eligible non-group health coverage.* Individuals covered under HSA-eligible HDHPs in the individual insurance market would be allowed an above-the-line deduction for the amount of the premium in determining adjusted gross income (i.e., the taxpayer would receive a deduction regardless of whether the person itemizes deductions). An individual would not qualify for the deduction if, in addition to the high deductible plan for which the deduction is claimed, he or she is covered by other non-high deductible health insurance (except for health insurance that provides only certain limited benefits). Individuals claiming the Health Insurance Tax Credit or Health Coverage Tax Credit or covered by employer plans or public plans or otherwise not eligible to contribute to an HSA would not qualify for the deduction. Premiums deducted by self-employed individuals on Schedule C or F of Form 1040 could not also be deducted above-the-line as HDHP premiums.

    In order to further level the playing field for those purchasing their own individual coverage, individuals covered under HDHPs in the individual insurance market would be allowed a refundable credit (see below).

2. *Increase the amounts that can be contributed to HSAs and provide a refundable income tax credit to offset employment taxes on HSA contributions not made by an employer.* The maximum annual HSA contribution would be increased to the out-of-pocket limit for a participant's HDHP. (For 2006, the statutory maximum out-of-pocket limit is $5,250 for self-only coverage or $10,500 for family coverage.) The maximum HSA contribution would be pro rated for the number of months that the individual is an eligible individual with coverage by the HDHP.

As under current law, a special rule would apply for determining HSA contributions by married individuals with family HDHP coverage. If one spouse has family coverage, both spouses are generally treated as having family coverage. If both spouses have family coverage, the coverage with the lowest bona fide out-of-pocket amount determines the maximum annual HSA contribution by the couple. The maximum annual HSA contribution based on the family HDHP coverage is divided between the spouses equally unless they agree on a different division, which can include allocating the entire contribution to one spouse. If one spouse has family coverage that is not HDHP coverage, neither spouse may contribute to an HSA unless the non-HDHP does not cover both spouses.

Where married couples have non-overlapping coverage, they would be allowed to "stack" the separate maximum contributions up to the out-of-pocket maximum allowed for a family HDHP to determine the amount of the contribution. The contributions to each spouse's HSA would remain subject to that spouse's HSA contribution limit. Family HDHP coverage that covers only a single eligible individual is treated as self-only coverage for purposes of determining the maximum HSA contribution. Thus, if there is only a single eligible individual covered by a family HDHP, the maximum HSA contribution is capped at the out-of-pocket maximum for a self-only plan. With respect to catch-up contributions, if both spouses are eligible individuals, both spouses will be allowed to contribute the contributions to a single HSA owned by one spouse.

In addition, taxpayers making after-tax contributions to an HSA for the year would be allowed a refundable credit equal to a percentage of the after-tax HSA contributions to offset the employment taxes on the contribution. The credit would be the smaller of:

- 15.3 percent of the after-tax contributions to the HSA, or
- 15.3 percent of wages subject to employment taxes.

If the taxpayer has wages above the Social Security wage cap, the credit would be lower to account for the lower employment tax rate on wages above the cap. If the taxpayer is also eligible for a credit based on after-tax HDHP premium payments, the old-age and survivor disability (OASDI) portion of the employment tax in the above calculation would be limited by the combined amount by which the after-tax HDHP premium payments and after-tax HSA contributions exceed the amount of wages above the OASDI cap. (For 2006, the Social Security taxable wage base was $94,200.) In order to recapture the credit relating to employment taxes for contributions that are not used for medical expenses, the additional tax on nonmedical distributions would be increased to 30 percent, with a 15 percent rate on nonmedical distributions after death, disability or attaining the age for Medicare eligibility (i.e., age 65).

3. *Provide a refundable tax credit to lower income individuals for the purchase of HSA-eligible health coverage.* A refundable health insurance tax credit (HITC) would be provided for the cost of an HSA-eligible HDHP purchased by individuals under age 65. The credit would provide a subsidy of up to 90 percent of the health insurance premium, up to a maximum dollar amount described below. The maximum subsidy percentage of 90 percent would apply for low-income taxpayers and would be phased down at higher incomes. Individuals participating in public or employer-provided health plans would generally not be eligible for the tax credit. Individuals would not be allowed to claim the HITC for the same period for which they claim the Health Coverage Tax Credit. In addition, individuals would not be allowed to claim the HITC for the same period for which they claim an above-the-line deduction for their premiums. Individuals with no dependents who file a single return and have modified adjusted gross income (MAGI) up to $15,000 would be eligible for the maximum subsidy rate of 90 percent of the premium (up to $1,111) of the individual's coverage and a maximum tax credit of $1,000. The subsidy percentage for these individuals would be phased down ratably from 90 percent to 50 percent between $15,000 and $20,000 of MAGI, and then phased out completely at $30,000 of MAGI. Thus, for example, a single individual with MAGI of $20,000 would be entitled to a credit of $556 (.50 × $1111).

Other filers with modified AGI up to $25,000 would be eligible for the maximum subsidy rates and the following credit maximums:

- 90 percent of $1,111, or $1,000, for a policy covering only one adult, only one child, or only two or more children,

- 90 percent of $2,222, or $2,000, for a policy or policies covering two adults or one adult and one or more children, and

- 90 percent of $3,333, or $3,000, for a policy or policies covering two adults plus one or more children.

The maximum dollar amounts would be indexed by the medical care component of the Consumer Price Index based on all urban consumers. The subsidy percentage for non-single taxpayers would be phased out ratably between $25,000 and $40,000 of MAGI in the case of a policy covering only one adult or only one child, and between $25,000 and $60,000 of MAGI in the case of a policy or policies covering more than one person. Individuals could claim the HITC for health insurance premiums paid as part of the normal tax filing process. Alternatively, beginning in 2008, the tax credit would be available in advance at the time the insurance is purchased. Individuals would reduce their premium payment by the amount of the credit, and the health insurer would be reimbursed by the IRS for the amount of the advance credit. Eligibility for the advance credit would be based on the individual's prior-year tax return. In addition to the non-group insurance market, qualifying health insurance could also be purchased through private purchasing groups, state-sponsored insurance purchasing pools, and state high-risk pools. Also, at state option, effective after December 31, 2007, the tax credit would be allowed for certain individuals not otherwise eligible for public health insurance programs to buy into privately contracted state-sponsored purchasing groups (e.g., Medicaid or SCHIP purchasing pools for private insurance or state government employee programs for states in which Medicaid or SCHIP does not contract with private plans). States could, under limited circumstances, provide additional contributions to individuals who purchased private insurance through such purchasing groups. The maximum state contribution would be $2,000 per adult for up to two adults for individuals with incomes up to 133 percent of poverty. The maximum state contribution would phase down ratably reaching $500 per adult at 200 percent of poverty. Individuals with income above 200 percent of poverty would not be eligible for a state contribution. States would not be allowed to provide any other explicit or implicit cross-subsidies.

4. *Make other statutory changes to facilitate the formation and administration of HSAs.* For HSA purposes, qualified medical expenses would include any medical expense incurred on or after the first day of HSA-eligible coverage for a year. The reimbursement of the expenses by an HSA established no later than the date for filing the return for that taxable year (not including extension) would be excluded from income. Qualified medical expenses that can be reimbursed by an HSA would be expanded to include the premiums for the purchase of non-group HSA-eligible plans.

   Employers would be allowed to contribute existing HRA balances to the HSAs of employees who would be eligible individuals but for the HRA coverage. The contributions of the HRA balances would not be taken into account for purposes of the comparability rules, or the annual maximum HSA contributions. Only HRAs existing on the date of enactment would qualify for the transfer, and only contributions of HRA balances made in prior taxable years beginning one year after the date of enactment would be covered.

   Contributions to HSAs on behalf of employees who are chronically ill or employees who have spouses or dependents who are chronically ill would be excluded from the comparability rules to the extent the contributions exceed the comparable contributions for other employees.

[General Explanation of the Administration's Fiscal Year 2007 Revenue Proposals ("Blue Book"), p. 23, Dept. of Treasury (Feb. 2006)]

Q 1:29 When would the Bush Administration's fiscal year 2007 budget proposals become effective?

The fiscal year 2007 budget changes relating to HSAs would apply for tax years beginning after December 31, 2006 (see Qs 1:25-1:28).

Q 1:30   What would be the effect of the Bush Administration's fiscal year 2007 budget proposals if they were to become law?

The Treasury Department estimates that these proposals would increase the projected number of Americans with HSAs by 50 percent. In 2010, the Treasury Department projects an increase in the number of HSAs from 14 million to 21 million. [General Explanation of the Administration's Fiscal Year 2007 Revenue Proposals ("Blue Book"), p. 23, Dept. of Treasury (Feb. 2006)]

Q 1:31   What are the leading HSA-related legislative proposals currently in Congress?

The following proposals are currently the leading HSA-related proposals that have been introduced in the 109th Congress:

- *H.R. 2830, the Pension Protection Act, introduced on June 9, 2005, by Congressman John Boehner(R-OH).* A proposal to allow up to $500 of unused health benefits in an employee's FSA to be either (i) carried forward to the employee's FSA for the next plan year or (ii) contributed to the employee's HSA.

- *H.R. 5262, the Tax Free Health Savings Act, introduced on May 2, 2006, by Congressman Eric Cantor (R-VA).* A proposal incorporating the Bush Administration's FY2007 Budget Proposals relating to HSAs (see Q 1:28) that would allow an above-the-line deduction for premiums paid for individual HDHP coverage secured on the individual market and a refundable tax credit that would approximate the FICA taxes paid on the amounts used to pay the premiums. In addition, the proposal would (i) increase the maximum HSA contribution limit to equal the out-of-pocket limit for an HDHP, (ii) provide a refundable tax credit for lower income individuals who purchase HSA-eligible high deductible health coverage, (iii) allow employers to make greater HSA contributions on behalf of chronically ill individuals, and (iv) allow, for a limited time, individuals to roll amounts held in their flexible spending arrangement (FSA) or health reimbursement arrangement (HRA) over to an HSA. The proposal also includes a provision that was not advanced by the Bush Administration which would coordinate FSAs and HRAs to pay for current medical costs, which will allow HSA dollars to be saved for use in future years.

- *H.R. 3873, introduced on September 22, 2005, by Congressman Jeff Fortenberry (R-NE).* A proposal to allow employees to make a one-time tax-free distribution from an eligible retirement plan (e.g., 401(a), 403(b), or 457 plan or an IRA) to an HSA.

Chapter 2

General HSA Rules

Chapter 2 discusses the establishment of Health Savings Accounts (HSAs) under the Internal Revenue Code. This chapter also discusses eligibility rules for establishing an HSA and new definitions of the terms *dependent* and *qualified medical expense.*

In General

Q 2:1   What is an HSA?

An HSA is a trust created or organized in the United States exclusively for the purpose of paying the qualified medical expenses of the account owner, but only if the written governing instrument creating the trust meets all of the following requirements:

1. Regular HSA contributions must be made in cash, although there is an exception for rollovers and trustee-to-trustee transfers (see Qs 4:58, 5:5, 5:39) [I.R.C. § 223(d)(1)(A)(i); I.R.S. Notice 2004-50, Q&A 73, 2004-33 I.R.B. 196];

2. Regular HSA contributions made for a taxable year may not exceed 100 percent of the highest annual deductible amount under the eligible individual's high-deductible health plan (HDHP) for such year (see Q 3:1). For 2006, the maximum contribution is the sum of the monthly allowable amounts for each month the account owner is an eligible individual, up to a maximum of $2,700 ($2,650 for 2005) for individual coverage or $5,450 ($5,250 for 2005) for family coverage (see Q 4:19). [I.R.C. § 223(d)(1)(A)(ii)];

3. The HSA trustee/custodian must be a *bank* as defined in Code Section 408(n), an insurance company as defined in Code Section 816, or an IRS approved nonbank trustee (see Qs 7:23, 7:24). [I.R.C. §§ 223(d)(1)(B), 408(d), 816; Treas. Reg. § 1.408-2(e); I.R.S. Notice 2004-2, Q&A 9, 2004-2 I.R.B. 269];

Note. A financial organization that is authorized to serve as trustee or custodian for an IRA is automatically permitted to serve as trustee or custodian for an HSA without additional approval by the IRS. [I.R.C. § 223(d)(1)(B); I.R.S. Notice 2004-2, 2004-2 I.R.B. 269; I.R.S. Ann. 2003-54, 2003-40 I.R.B. 761; I.R.S. Ann. 2005-59, 2005-37 I.R.B. 524, containing a list of approved nonbank trustees and custodians] An HSA is a new type of financial product and can be offered by various types of financial organizations that qualify as an HSA trustee or custodian (see chapter 7).

4. No part of the HSA assets may be invested in life insurance contracts [I.R.C. § 223(d)(1)(C); I.R.S. Notice 2004-50, Q&A 65, 2004-33 I.R.B. 196];
5. The balance in the participant's HSA account must be nonforfeitable [I.R.C. § 223(d)(1)(E); I.R.S. Notice 2004-50, Q&A 82, 2004-33 I.R.B. 196];
6. The assets of the trust may not be commingled with other property except in a common trust fund as defined in Treasury Regulations Section 1.408-2(b)(5)(ii) or in a common investment fund as defined in Code Section 584(a)(1). [I.R.C. § 223(d)(1)(D); I.R.S. Notice 2004-50, Q&A 66, 2004-33 I.R.B. 196]

[I.R.C. § 223(d)(1)]

Unless these requirements are satisfied, no contributions may be accepted by the trustee or custodian. [I.R.C. § 223(d)(1)(A)]

Q 2:2   Who is the account beneficiary or account owner of an HSA?

The IRS model HSA forms (see Q 7:4) use the term *account owner* to refer to the account beneficiary. [I.R.C. § 223(d)(3)]

Q 2:3   How and when were HSAs created?

Health Savings Accounts were created by the Medicare Prescription Drug, Improvement, and Modernization Act of 2003, which was signed into law on December 8, 2003. [Pub. L. No. 108-173, title XII, § 1201(a), 117 Stat. 2469, (2003) amending Part VII of subchapter B of chapter 1 of the Code by adding § 223, and redesignating former § 223 (a cross-reference) to § 224] See chapter 1 for more information on the history and legislation affecting HSAs.

Q 2:4   When are the HSA rules effective?

The HSA rules are generally effective for taxable years beginning after December 31, 2003. The Medicare Prescription Drug, Improvement, and Modernization Act of 2003, § 1201(k), provides: "The amendments made by this section [amending sections 62, 106, 125, 220, 223, 224, 848, 3231, 3306, 3401, 4973, 4975, 6051, and 6693 and enacting section 4980G of the Code] shall apply to taxable years beginning after December 31, 2003." Thus, the first date that it was permissible for an eligible individual to establish an HSA was January 1, 2004. [I.R.S. Notice 2004-2 Q&A 8, 2004-2 I.R.B. 269]

Q 2:5   Do HSAs replace Archer Medical Savings Accounts?

No. The new Health Savings Account is modeled on the Archer Medical Savings Account (MSA). MSA accounts were permitted under a pilot program effective for years beginning after December 31, 1996. The Archer MSA program will terminate if the number of individuals establishing them exceeds numerical limits. [I.R.C. § 220(i)(2), as amended by § 322(a) of the Working Families Tax Relief Act of 2004 (Pub. L. No. 107–147)] For example, if limits are exceeded in 2005, 2005 will be a "cutoff year" after which, in general, no new Archer MSAs can be established. The IRS has determined that the numerical limits have not been exceeded.

Note. This limit never has been, and is not likely to be, reached.

[I.R.S. Ann. 2005-12, 2005-7 I.R.B. 555]

Regardless, beginning on January 1, 2006, only individuals who already have an Archer MSA or are employees of a participating employer may make new contributions to an MSA unless Archer MSAs are extended again by Congress. [I.R.C. § 220(i)(2)]

> **Note.** An individual will not be treated as an eligible individual for purposes of contributing to an MSA for any tax year beginning after the cutoff year unless (1) the individual was an active MSA participant for a tax year ending on or before the close of the cutoff year or (2) the individual became an active MSA participant for the tax year ending after the cutoff year by reason of coverage under an HDHP of an MSA-participating employer. [I.R.C. § 220(i)] The cutoff year is the year 2005 or the first year before 2005 for which the IRS determines that the numerical limitation for that year has been exceeded. [I.R.C. § 220(i)]

Eligible Individual for Establishing an HSA

Q 2:6   Who is an eligible individual for purposes of establishing an HSA?

The term *eligible individual* means, with respect to any month, any individual who:

- Is covered under an HDHP as of the first day of such month
- Is not covered under any other health plan while being covered by an HDHP that:

— Is not an HDHP, and

— Provides coverage for any benefit provided for under the HDHP, subject to certain exceptions (see Q 2:8)

• Is not enrolled in Medicare (generally, has not reached age 65; see Q 2:15; see Qs 4:26–4:29 regarding catch-up contributions)

• Cannot be claimed as a dependent on another person's tax return

[I.R.C. § 223(c)(1)(A); I.R.S. Notice 2004-2, Q&A 2, 2004-2 I.R.B. 269, as modified by I.R.S. Notice 2004-50, 2004-33 I.R.B. 196, see *Effect on Other Documents*]

However, an individual can be eligible to contribute to an HSA if his or her spouse has non-HDHP *family* coverage, provided the spouse's coverage does not cover the individual. [Rev. Rul. 2005-25, 2005-18 I.R.B. 971]

Example 1. Horace and Wanda are a married couple, and both are age 35. Throughout 2006, Horace has self-only coverage under an HDHP. Horace has no other health coverage, is not enrolled in Medicare, and may not be claimed as a dependent on another taxpayer's return. Wanda has non-HDHP family coverage for herself and for Horace's and Wanda's two dependents, but Horace is excluded from Wanda's coverage. Although Wanda has non-HDHP family coverage, Horace is not covered under that health plan. Horace is, therefore, an eligible individual.

Note. The special rules for married individuals treating both spouses as having family coverage (see Q 4:33) do not apply, because Wanda's non-HDHP family coverage does not cover Horace. Thus, Horace remains an eligible individual. However, Horace may not make the catch-up contribution because he is not age 55 in 2006. Wanda has non-HDHP coverage and is, therefore, not an eligible individual.

Caution. If a spouse has a health FSA that covers an HSA account owner, the HSA account owner's eligiblity to make HSA contributions may be affected (see Q 4:10). [See I.R.S. Notice 2004-45, 2004-28 I.R.B. 1].

Example 2. The same facts as in Example 1, except that Horace has HDHP family coverage for himself and for one of Horace's and Wanda's dependents. Wanda has non-HDHP family coverage for herself and for Horace's and Wanda's other dependent. Horace is excluded from Wanda's coverage. Because the non-HDHP family coverage does not cover Horace, the special rules that treat both spouses as having family coverage do not affect Horace's eligibility to make HSA contributions. Wanda has non-HDHP coverage and is, therefore, not an eligible individual.

Example 3. Horace and Wendy are a married couple, and both are age 35. Throughout 2006, Horace has HDHP family coverage for himself and for Horace's and Wendy's two dependents. In addition, Wendy is not covered under Horace's health plan and has no other health plan coverage. Horace is eligible to make HSA contributions. Because Horace's family coverage does not cover Wendy, the special rules do not apply to treat Wendy as having family coverage. Nonetheless, Wendy has no health plan coverage and is, therefore, not an eligible individual.

Note. A state could have laws that mandate certain benefits be included in an insured HDHP. These laws may, for example, require certain benefits to be covered under an HDHP without regard to whether the deductible is satisfied. Unless a state's mandated benefits satisfy the definition of preventive care for federal purposes (see Qs 3:45, 3:51, 3:52), this would cause the HDHP to fail to satisfy the federal requirements under Code Section 223. If so, an individual in a state with those laws could not contribute to an HSA. Other state laws may require that an insurer or HMO must comply with limits on deductibles, which could similarly conflict with federal requirements.

The IRS has addressed this by issuing transition guidance for months before January 1, 2006, for state requirements in effect on January 1, 2004. The guidance states that during this time period, an HDHP will not be considered to violate federal requirements if the sole reason it does not comply with federal requirements is because it is complying with state benefit mandates. However, after January 1, 2006, individuals who are covered by insured HDHPs or HMOs subject to state laws that conflict with Code Section 223 requirements will not be considered *eligible individuals* who are able to contribute to HSAs. (See appendix E for a list of states with mandates that could cause an HDHP to fail to satisfy applicable requirements.) [Notice 2004-43, 2004-27 IRB 10]

Note. Generally, a health plan may not reduce existing benefits before the plan's renewal date. Thus, even though a state may amend its laws before January 1, 2006, to authorize HDHPs that comply with Code Section 223(c)(2), non-calendar-year plans may still fail to qualify as HDHPs after January 1, 2006. (See transitional relief for non-calendar-year plans in Q 3:21).

Q 2:7   If an employee begins HDHP coverage midmonth, when does the employee become an eligible individual?

An eligible individual must have HDHP coverage as of the first day of the month. An individual with employer-provided HDHP coverage on a payroll-by-payroll basis becomes an eligible individual on the first day of the month on or following the first day of the pay period when HDHP coverage begins. [I.R.C. § 223(b)(2); I.R.S. Notice 2004-50, Q&A 11, 2004-33 I.R.B. 196]

Example. Omar, an employee, begins HDHP coverage on the first day of a biweekly payroll period, which is August 6, 2006, and continues to be covered by the HDHP throughout 2006. For purposes of contributing to an HSA, Omar becomes an eligible individual on September 1, 2006.

Q 2:8   Are there any exceptions to the rule that requires that the employee not be covered under any other non-HDHP?

Yes. There are two exceptions to the rule that requires that the employee not be covered under any other non-HDHP (see Q 2:6). They are:

- Coverage for any benefit provided by "permitted insurance"
- Coverage, whether through insurance or otherwise, for accidents, disability, dental care, vision care, or long-term care

[I.R.C. § 223(c)(2)(3); I.R.S. Notice 2004-2, Q&As 5 and 6, 2004-2 I.R.B. 269]

See chapter 3 for more information related to medical plan coverage, including a description of permitted insurance.

Q 2:9   May an ineligible individual establish an HSA if his or her spouse is an eligible individual?

No. Although the special rule for married individuals in Code Section 223(b)(5) generally allows a married couple to divide the maximum HSA contribution between spouses, if only one spouse is an eligible individual (see Q 2:9), only that spouse may contribute to an HSA. [Rev. Rul. 2005-25, 2005-18 I.R.B. 971; I.R.S. Notice 2004-50, Q&A 31, 2004-33 I.R.B. 196]

Q 2:10   May a joint HSA be established by a married couple?

No. An HSA may be established only on behalf of one individual. Thus, if a husband and wife are eligible to contribute to an HSA, they are both eligible to establish separate HSAs. Only one person may be the account owner of an HSA. [I.R.S. Notice 2004-50, Q&A 63, 2004-33 I.R.B. 196] (See Qs 4:33-4:35, and 4:40 concerning allocating contributions (other than catch-up contributions) between spouses. See Q 6:19 concerning reimbursements from a spouse's HSAs.).

Practice Pointer. If both spouses are age 55 or older and they both want to make "catch-up" contributions, they must each establish an HSA.

Q 2:11   Are HSAs available to residents of the U.S. Virgin Islands, Guam, and the Commonwealth of the Northern Mariana Islands?

Yes. Bona fide residents of the U.S. Virgin Islands, Guam, and the Commonwealth of the Northern Mariana Islands may establish HSAs. However, bona fide residents of Puerto Rico and American Samoa may establish HSAs only after statutory provisions similar to Code Sections 223 (relating to HSAs) and 106(d) (relating to employer-provided medical expense coverage) are enacted. [I.R.S. Notice 2004-50, Q&A 87, 2004-33 I.R.B. 196]

Q 2:12   Are HSAs available to residents of Hawaii?

Hawaiian residents are not prohibited from having HSAs. However, an HDHP offered by an employer in Hawaii would have to satisfy Hawaii's Prepaid Health Care Act (PHCA), which sets forth various requirements concerning plan benefits and cost-sharing, and would have to be approved as a qualified plan by

Hawaii's Prepaid Health Care Council. [Haw. Rev. Stat., ch. 393] Hawaii Department of Labor and Industrial Relations (DLIR) staff has informally indicated that, while Hawaii may be willing to approve HDHP/HSA plans as satisfying PHCA requirements, the state likely would require significant employer HSA contributions as a condition for approval. Accordingly, at the present time, HSAs are generally established only by Hawaian resisidents who do not have employer-provided health coverage (e.g., sole proprietors, self-employed individuals, and those working as part-time employees) (see Q 8:38).

Q 2:13   Will an individual be treated as participating in an HDHP and no other non-HDHP if he or she elected HDHP coverage but also had the option to choose a plan that was not an HDHP?

Yes. To determine if an employee is an eligible individual, the employee's actual health coverage election is controlling, not the choices offered by the employer. [I.R.S. Notice 2004-50, Q&A 1, 2004-33 I.R.B. 196]

Q 2:14   Are individuals who are eligible for Medicare but who are not enrolled in Medicare Part A or B eligible to establish HSAs?

Yes. Individuals who are eligible for Medicare but who are not enrolled in Medicare Part A or B remain eligible to contribute to an HSA. See Qs 4:26–4:28 regarding eligibility to make a catch-up contribution. [I.R.S. Notice 2004-50, Q&A-2, 2004-33 I.R.B. 196]

Q 2:15   When does eligibility to contribute to an HSA end for a Medicare-eligible individual?

Eligibility for making HSA contributions ends beginning with the month the HSA owner becomes eligible for *and* enrolls in either Medicare Part A or Part B. [I.R.C. § 223(b)(7); I.R.S. Notice 2004-50, Q&A 2, 2004-33 I.R.B. 196] Thus, an otherwise eligible individual who is not actually enrolled in Medicare Part A or Part B may contribute to an HSA until the month that he or she actually enrolls in Medicare.

Example 1. Yetta, age 66, is covered under her employer's HDHP. Although Yetta is eligible for Medicare, she is not actually entitled to Medicare because she did not apply for benefits under Medicare (i.e., enroll in Medicare Part A or Part B). If Yetta is otherwise an eligible individual, she may contribute to an HSA.

Note. Enrollment in Medicare Part A is automatic if a person begins receiving Social Security retirement benefits.

Example 2. In August 2006, Xavier attains age 65 and applies for and begins receiving Social Security benefits. Xavier is automatically enrolled in Medicare Part A. As of August 1, 2006, Xavier is no longer an eligible individual and may not contribute to an HSA.

Example 3. Evelyn turned age 65 in July 2006 and enrolled in Medicare. Evelyn had self-only coverage under an HDHP with an annual deductible of $1,050. She is eligible for an additional contribution of $700 because of the catch-up provisions applicable for 2006. Evelyn's contribution limit for 2006 is $875 ($1,750/12 × 6). Evelyn can make contributions for January through June totaling $875, but cannot make any contributions for July through December.

Q 2:16   Are individuals who are eligible for medical benefits through the Department of Veterans Affairs (VA) eligible to make contributions to an HSA?

Possibly. Individuals who are eligible for medical benefits through the VA, who are otherwise eligible for an HSA, may contribute to the HSA as long as they have not received such medical benefits from the VA at any time during the preceding three months. [I.R.S. Notice 2004-50, Q&A 5, 2004-33 I.R.B. 196]

Q 2:17   Is a government retiree who is enrolled in Medicare Part B (but not Part A) an eligible individual for HSA purposes?

No. An individual who is enrolled in Medicare may not contribute to an HSA. [I.R.C. § 223(b)(7); I.R.S. Notice 2004-50, Q&A 4, 2004-33 I.R.B. 196]

Q 2:18   May an otherwise HSA-eligible individual who is age 65 or older and thus eligible for Medicare, but is not enrolled in Medicare Part A or Part B, make the additional catch-up contributions for individuals age 55 or older?

Yes, because an individual who is not enrolled in Medicare (Part A or Part B) may contribute to an HSA and make additional catch-up contributions if age 55 or older. [I.R.S. Notice 2004-50, Q&A 12, 2004-33 I.R.B. 196; I.R.S. Notice 2004-2, Q&A 3, 2004-2 I.R.B. 269]

Q 2:19   May active duty or retired service members receiving medical coverage under TRICARE contribute to an HSA?

No. Active duty or retired service members receiving medical coverage under TRICARE are not eligible individuals and may not contribute to an HSA. [I.R.S. Notice 2004-50, Q&A 6, 2004-33 I.R.B. 196] Should TRICARE offer an HSA-qualified HDHP, individuals who select it and are otherwise eligible would be able to make contributions to an HSA.

Q 2:20   When does an HSA account become *effective*?

Although established, an HSA account cannot be effective before the effective date of the eligible individual's HDHP coverage.

Note. If HDHP coverage begins on any day other than the first day of the month, the HSA account cannot be effective any sooner than the first day of the following month (see Q 2:7).

Q 2:21 Can an HSA be *established* before it becomes effective?

Yes. All of the paperwork may be completed and the minimum contribution deposited prior to the effective date that HDHP coverage begins. However, the account is not officially effective (see Q 2:7) until HDHP coverage begins.

Practice Pointer. Completing the necessary steps before HDHP coverage begins ensures that the HSA will be *established* as early as possible. This is especially important when HDHP coverage is effective on a non-business day.

Q 2:22 If an individual sends in paperwork and an initial deposit to the HSA trustee, is the HSA considered established as of the date of mailing?

Possibly. There is little guidance on this point. The answer may depend upon when the HSA trustee considers the account to be established in accordance with its established procedures. In the case of the IRS model forms, "an HSA is established after the form is fully executed by both the account owner and the trustee" (or custodian). (See *Purpose of Form*, General Instructions, Form 5305-B—Health Savings Trust Account and Form 5305-C—Health Savings Custodial Account.)

Q 2:23 Which rules apply to determine whether a child of divorced parents may be covered under a parent's HSA or HDHP on a tax-free basis?

There are different rules that apply to determine whether a child of divorced parents may be covered under the HSA or HDHP on a tax-free basis. These rules are summarized below.

High Deductible Health Plan (HDHP): A child could receive benefits under his or her divorced parent's health coverage on a tax-free basis—whether or not that parent is the custodial parent—as long as:

1. Both parents, together, provide over half the child's support for the year (other than through multiple support agreements under which a group of contributors provides support for a child); and

2. One or both parents have custody for more than half the calendar year. [I.R.C. § 105(b); 152(e); see, Treas. Reg. § 1.152-4T, Q&A-5] There is no corollary rule in Code Section 106 (which allows exclusion of the premium for employer-provided health coverage); however, the IRS has taken the informal position that the rule described in Code Section 105(b) relating to a child of divorced parents, should apply for purposes of Code Section 106 as well.

Health Savings Account (HSA): Unless the parties agree otherwise, the parent who has custody for the greater part of the year can make a tax-free HSA withdrawal to pay the child's medical expenses for that year. If the child resides with both parents for equal parts of the year, the parent with the highest adjusted gross income is treated as the custodial parent and can make a tax-free HSA withdrawal to pay the child's medical expenses for that year. [I.R.C. § 152(c)(4)(B)] Alternatively, if the custodial parent signs a written declaration that he or she will not take the deduction, and this written declaration is attached to the noncustodial parent's tax return, the noncustodial parent may withdraw funds from his or her HSA on a tax-free basis for the medical expenses of his or her child for that year. [See I.R.C. § 152(e)]

Qualified Medical Expenses

Q 2:24   Which distributions from an HSA are excludable from gross income?

Distributions from an HSA used exclusively to pay for qualified medical expenses of the account owner, his or her spouse, or dependents are excludable from gross income (see chapter 6). In general, amounts in an HSA can be used for qualified medical expenses and will continue to be excludable from the account owner's gross income even if the individual is not currently eligible to make contributions to the HSA.

Q 2:25   What are qualified medical expenses?

Qualified medical expenses include amounts paid with respect to the account owner, his or her spouse, or dependents for medical care as defined in Code Section 213(d), provided such amounts are not compensated for by insurance or otherwise. Qualified medical expenses are more fully discussed in chapter 6.

Q 2:26   What is included in *medical care*?

The term *medical care* includes amounts paid for the diagnosis, cure, mitigation, treatment, or prevention of disease, or for the purpose of affecting any structure or function of the body. [I.R.C. § 213(d)(1); Treas. Reg. § 1.213-1(e)(1)(ii)] An expenditure that is merely beneficial to the general health of an individual, such as an expenditure for a vacation, is not an expenditure for medical care. However, expenditures for "medicines and drugs" are expenditures for medical care (see Q 6:43).

Q 2:27   Are payments for insurance qualified medical expenses?

Generally, qualified medical expenses do not include payment for insurance. Exceptions to this rule include:

1. Coverage under a health plan during any period of continuation coverage required under federal law (i.e., COBRA);

2. Coverage under a qualified long-term care insurance contract as defined in Code Section 7702B(b) (see Q 6:47);

3. Coverage under a health plan during a period in which the individual is receiving unemployment compensation under any federal or state law [I.R.C. § 223(d)(2)(C)(iii)]; and

4. For individuals over age 65, premiums for Medicare Part A or B, Medicare HMO, and the employee share of premiums for employer-sponsored health insurance, including premiums for employer-sponsored retiree health insurance, can be paid from an HSA (see Q 6:38), but not Medigap premiums (e.g., in the case of any account owner who has attained the age specified in Section 1811 of the Social Security Act, any health insurance other than a Medicare supplemental policy (as defined in Section 1882 of the Social Security Act)).

[I.R.S. Notice 2004-2, Q&A-27, 2004-2 I.R.B. 2]

Q 2:28   May qualified medical expenses be incurred before the HSA is established?

No. The qualified medical expenses must be incurred after the HSA has been established. [I.R.S. Notice 2004-2, Q&A 26, 2004-2 I.R.B. 269] The IRS granted transitional relief on this issue for 2004 (see Q 6:17).

Q 2:29   May an HSA be used to pay for an individual's qualified medical expenses on a tax-free basis even if such individual is not covered by an HDHP?

Yes. Distributions from an HSA to pay for qualified medical expenses of the account owner, the account owner's spouse, or dependents may be made without regard to their status as eligible individuals. Thus, it is not necessary for an individual to be covered by an HDHP in order to have his or her qualified medical expenses reimbursed by an HSA on a tax-free basis. [I.R.S. Notice 2004-50, Q&A 36, 2004-33 I.R.B. 196] However, distributions made for expenses reimbursed by another health plan are not excludable from income, whether or not the other health plan is an HDHP (see Qs 6:4, 6:18-6:20).

Dependents

Q 2:30   What is the significance for HSAs of the Gulf Opportunity Zone Act of 2005?

On December 16, 2005, Congress passed the Gulf Opportunity Zone Act of 2005 (GOZA) (H.R. 4440), which was signed into law by President George W.

Bush on December 21, 2005. [Pub. L. No. 109-135] The act contains tax incentives and other relief to businesses and individuals affected by hurricanes Katrina, Rita, and Wilma. It also includes a package of technical corrections to recently enacted tax legislation, including the Working Families Tax Relief Act of 2004. (WFTRA) Pub. L. No. 108-31 The tax technical corrections include a correction to the definition of eligible *dependent* with respect to HSAs and to dependent care flexible spending arrangements (FSAs). This change is retroactive to the effective date of WFTRA, January 1, 2005. (See Qs 2:31-2:38.)

Q 2:31   How did WFTRA change the definition of *dependent*?

Section 201 of WFTRA amended the definition of *dependent* in Code Section 152, effective for taxable years beginning after December 31, 2004. In some regards, the new definition is more restrictive. Under the new definition, an individual must be either a *qualifying child* or a *qualifying relative* to be a dependent. [I.R.C. § 152; WFTRA, § 201, Pub. L. No. 108-311, 118 Stat. 1166]

> **Note.** The definition was intended to provide a uniform definition of *dependent* for purposes of the dependency exemption, the child credit, the earned income credit, the child and dependent care credit, and head-of-household filing status, but not to group health plans or HSAs—to which prior law was to apply. Because of an apparent technical oversight, an exception for employer-sponsored group health plans, HSAs, or dependent care assistance plans was not created. With respect to employer-sponsored group health plans, the IRS came to the rescue in Notice 2004-79 [2004-49 I.R.B. 898], which essentially restored prior law treatment (the pre-WFTRA definition) to employer-sponsored group health plans. However, this guidance did not restore the pre-WFTRA definition for HSAs or dependent care assistance plans.

Q 2:32   How did GOZA change the definition of *dependent*?

The technical corrections contained in GOZA extended the same relief to HSAs and dependent care FSAs that Treasury and IRS extended to health plans through Notice 2004-79 [2004-49 I.R.B. 898], by eliminating the income limitations from the definition of *qualifying relative*. [GOZA § 404(c)] This means that individuals can qualify as dependents for purposes of receiving tax-free HSAs or distributions without regard to gross income. Similarly, individuals can satisfy the definition of *dependent* for purposes of dependent care FSAs without regard to gross income.

The technical correction also specifies that an individual may qualify as a dependent for purposes of an HSA without regard to whether such individual is married and files a joint return with another taxpayer or is a dependent of another taxpayer. Thus, an individual who is treated as a dependent under this rule "is not subject to the general rule that a dependent of a dependent shall be treated as having no dependents. . . ." [Joint Committee Report, WFTRA § 404 (J.C.T. Rep. No. JXC-88-05)]

The changes in GOZA with respect to the definition of dependent are retroactive to the WFTRA effective date of January 1, 2005.

Q 2:33   Who is a dependent for HSA purposes beginning January 1, 2005?

Beginning January 1, 2005, the term *dependent*, for HSA purposes means either a *qualifying child* (see Q 2:35) or a *qualifying relative* (without regard to the gross income limitation under Code Section § 152(d)(1)(B)) or the requirements of Code Section § 152(b)(1) and (b)(2) (see Qs 2:32, 2:39). For years beginning before 2005, see Q 2:40. [I.R.C. § 152(a)(1), 152(a)(2)]

Q 2:34   What relationship must the individual have to the taxpayer to be treated as a dependent?

To be a dependent, the individual must bear one of the following relationships with respect to the taxpayer:

- Son or daughter, or a descendent of either
- Stepson or stepdaughter
- Brother, sister, stepbrother, or stepsister
- Father or mother, or ancestor of either
- Stepfather or stepmother
- Son or daughter of a brother or sister
- Brother or sister of the father or mother
- Son-in-law, daughter-in-law, father-in-law, mother-in-law, brother-in-law, or sister-in-law, or
- An individual (other than an individual who at any time during the year was the taxpayer's spouse) who, for the taxable year of the taxpayer, has as his or her principal place of residence the home of the taxpayer and is a member of the taxpayer's household

[I.R.C. § 152(a)(1), 152(a)(2)]

The terms *brothers* and *sisters* include half-blood relatives. [I.R.C. § 152(f)(4)] A *child* shall include a legally adopted child, a child who is placed in the taxpayer's home by an authorized placement agency for legal adoption, or a foster child. [I.R.C. § 152(f)(B)-(C), 152(f)(6)] Special rules apply to missing children presumed by law enforcement authorities to have been kidnapped. [See I.R.C. § 152(f)(6)(A)-(B)]

A *dependent* does not include an individual who is not a citizen or national of the United States unless the individual is a resident of the U.S. or of a country contiguous to the U.S. However, a child who is legally adopted by a U.S. taxpayer does qualify as a dependent. [I.R.C. § 152((b)(3)]

Q 2:35   Who is a qualifying child?

A *qualifying child* is a daughter, son, stepchild, sibling, or stepsibling (or descendant of any of any of these) who has the same principal place of abode as the taxpayer for more than one-half of the taxable year and who (other than in the case of total disability) has not yet attained a specified age (see Qs 2:35-2:37). [I.R.C. § 152(c)(1)]

Q 2:36   Does an individual's age affect his or her status as a qualifying child?

Yes. In order to be treated as a qualifying child, an individual must not have attained age 19 (age 24 if a student) before the close of the calendar year in which the taxable year of the account owner begins. [I.R.C. § 152(c)(3), as amended]

Q 2:37   Does an individual's disability affect his or her status as a qualifying child?

No. The age requirements of 19 or 24 (see above) do not apply if the child is permanently and totally disabled. *Permanent and total disability* is defined in Code Section 22(e)(3) and need not be for the entire year. [I.R.C. § 152(c)(3)(B), as amended by WFTRA § 201]

> **Note.** Under prior law (before 2004), there was no age requirement, nor was disability an issue.

Q 2:38   When does a child attain a specified age for purposes of the qualifying child definition?

It would appear that a child attains a specific age on the anniversary of the date that the child was born. This uniform definition is used by the IRS for purposes of the dependent care, adoption, child tax, and earned income credits, and it also applies to dependent care assistance programs, foster care payments, adoption assistance programs, and dependency exemptions. [Rev. Rul. 2003-72, 2003-33 I.R.B. 346; I.R.C. §§ 21 (child care credit), 23 (adoption expenses), 24 (child credit), 32 (earned income credit), 129 (dependent care exclusion), 131 (foster care payments), 137 (adoption assistance), and 151 (personal exemptions)]

> **Note.** Code Section 152(c)(3)(A) provides that a child not have attained the specified age (age 19 or age 24) "as of the close of the calendar year in which the taxable year of the taxpayer begins. . . . " Thus, an individual is no longer a qualifying child after the calendar year in which the taxpayer's taxable year began if the individual attained the specified age during the prior calendar year.

Q 2:39   Who is a qualifying relative for purposes of an HSA?

A *qualifying relative* is a person who satisfies all of the following four requirements:

1. Is not a *qualifying child* of the taxpayer or of any other taxpayer for any taxable year beginning in the calendar year in which the taxable year begins [I.R.C. § 152(d)(1)(D)];

2. Bears a relationship to the taxpayer (see Q 2:34) [I.R.C. § 152(d)(1)(A), 152(d)(2)];

3. Receives more than half of his or her support from the taxpayer for the calendar year in which the taxable year begins [I.R.C. § 152(d)(1)(C), 152(d)(3), regarding multiple support agreements]; and

4. Does not have gross income for the calender year in which the taxpayer's taxable year began in excess of the Code Section 151(d) dependency exemption amount ($3,300 in 2006).

Example. Frank's taxable year begins on July 1, 2006. His son Sam, a student, will attain age 24 on December 1, 2006. Sam is not a qualifying child for Frank's 2006-2007 taxable year because Sam was age 24 when Frank's taxable year began.

[I.R.C. § 152(d)(1); I.R.C. § 223(d), as amended by GOZA § 404(c)]

Q 2:40   Who is a dependent for HSA purposes before 2005?

Under the pre-WFTRA Code Section 152 definition, the term *dependent* generally means an individual who bears the relationship described in Q 2:34 and who received more than one-half of his or her support for the year from the taxpayer.

Thus, prior to amendment by WFTRA, there were no income limits or age limitations. [I.R.C. § 152, before amendment by WFTRA 201] The income limit applicable to HSA effective January 1, 2005, was removed retroactively by GOZA. Thus, beginning in 2005, the income limits that would have applied to a qualifying relative *dependent* for HSA purposes in 2005 were retroactively removed. [See I.R.C. § 223(d)(2)(A), as amended by GOZA Section 404(c)]

A similar change (removing the income limitation) was made to Code Section 21(b)(1)(B), defining the term *qualifiying individual* for dependent care services and reimbursement from a dependent care assistance plan.

Advantages and Disadvantages of HSAs

Q 2:41   What are the potential advantages of an HSA to an individual?

There are many advantages that may accrue from the establishment of an HSA, including the following:

1. *No employer involvement.* Eligible individuals can establish an HSA without employer involvement.

2. *Deductions for contributions.* Except for employer contributions, all HSA after-tax contributions (within limits) are deductible. Employer contributions are excluded from income.

3. *Contributions by family members permitted.* Unlike an FSA or an HRA, family members (among others) may make contributions into an eligible individual's HSA.

4. *Deduction or exclusions from gross income.* Employer contributions are generally excludable from gross income. In other cases, contributions made by or on behalf of an eligible individual are generally deductible from gross income.

5. *Itemization.* An eligible individual is not required to itemize deductions on Form 1040, Schedule A—*Itemized Deductions* in order to claim a deduction for his or her allowable HSA contribution.

6. *Tax-exempt status.* Distributions are exempt from federal income tax (tax free) if used to pay for qualified medical expenses. In other cases, the growth in the account is tax deferred (e.g., when payments are not used for qualified medical expenses).

7. *Tax-free distributions.* Distributions from the account of all contributions and earning are tax-free when used to pay for an unreimbursed qualified medical expense.

Example. Harry, an eligible individual, has a health plan through his employer with no annual deductible for 2006. The insurer charges an annual premium of $4,000. If Harry switches to an HDHP with a $1,050 annual deductible, the insurer will charge only $3,200 for the same policy. In addition to saving $800 in premiums, Harry will get a federal income tax deduction for his HSA contribution (see Q 4:43). His account will grow tax free, and he will be able to access the funds in the HSA on a tax-free basis when used to pay for qualified medical expenses. Harry may decide, instead, not to use his HSA and allow his funds to grow on a tax-free basis for future medical expenses.

8. *Vesting.* All account balances are fully vested (nonforfeitable). There are no use-it or lose-it rules, as is the case with FSAs.

9. *Account ownership.* HSA accounts are owned by the individual (even if employer contributions are made into the HSA).

10. *Choice.* The account owner chooses: how much to contribute, when to contribute, the type of financial product(s) to use for investment of account assets, which financial institution will hold the account, how much to use for medical expenses, and whether to pay for medical expenses from the HSA or save the account for future use.

11. *Savings.* HSAs encourage savings for future medical expenses, such as: long-term care expenses, noncovered services under future health insurance coverage, insurance coverage after retirement (and before Medicare coverage begins), medical expenses after retirement (and before Medicare coverage begins), and out-of-pocket expenses incurred when covered by Medicare.

12. *Spousal ownership.* The designated spouse beneficiary is automatically treated as the owner upon the death of the account owner.

13. *Portability.* HSA accounts are portable, regardless of whether the account owner is employed or unemployed, which employer the individual works for, changes in age or marital status, and future medical coverage. An HSA can be rolled over or transferred to another HSA (once per 12-month period). Rollovers and transfers from an Archer MSA into an HSA are permitted (once per 12-month period).

14. *No use-it or lose-it rules.* Unlike FSAs, unused account balances are not forfeited.

15. *Encouragement of thrift.* HSA rules encourage account holders to spend their funds wisely.

16. *Lower health care premiums.* The premium for a health plan with a higher deductible is likely to be less costly than the same health plan with a lower deductible.

17. *Cafeteria plan.* Contributions may be made by the eligible individual, on behalf of an eligible individual, or by the individual's employer (generally through a cafeteria plan).

18. *Higher contribution limits than an Archer MSA.* An Archer MSA limits contributions to 75 percent of the deductible amount (65 percent for self-only coverage).

19. *Catch-up contributions.* Individuals age 55 and older may generally contribute additional "catch-up" amounts ($700 for 2006, $600 for 2005).

20. *Dependent treatment.* The account owner's spouse and dependents need not be covered by the HDHP to receive benefits from an HSA on a tax-free basis (see Q 2:29).

21. *Consumer choice and flexibility.* HSAs give individuals and employers flexibility and choice in coverage.

22. *Protection.* When coupled with an HDHP, an HSA protects against catastrophic financial loss due to unforeseen illness or injury.

23. *No gift tax.* The amount that a beneficiary receives from an HSA is not treated as a taxable gift (see Q 6:74).

24. *Long-term care insurance.* Tax-free distributions from an HSA may be used to pay for long-term care insurance premiums (see Q 6:37) as well as for COBRA continuation coverage and health continuation insurance while the HSA account holder is receiving unemployment compensation (see Q 2:27).

25. *Divisibility.* An HSA account is divisible upon divorce (see Q 5:41).

26. *Mistake of fact.* Distribution made because of a mistake of fact may be returned if the trustee or custodian permits (see Qs 6:66-6:69).

27. *Tax shelter.* High-income individuals are likely to use an HSA as a tax shelter (i.e., for accumulations). These individuals will pay all medical expenses from non-sheltered assets.

28. *Comparability in employer contributions.* Employer contributions (if any are made) to an HSA must be comparable (see Qs 1:24, 4:93–4:128, 4:130, 4:137–4:138), unless offered through a cafeteria plan. This requirement does not apply to an HRA or FSA (but highly compensated/non-highly compensated nondiscrimination requirements apply to health FSAs and HRAs, which are both self-funded health plans). [I.R.C. §§ 105(h), 125, 4980G]

The following examples demonstrate some of the benefits to individuals of having an HSA.

Example 1. The Half-Penny Scale Corporation offers its employees a family health insurance plan with a $5,000 deductible. With its insurance cost savings, Half-Penny contributes $4,000 to each employee's HSA. Newton, an employee, incurs $5,000 of medical expenses during the year. All expenses are qualified medical expenses. Newton's out-of-pocket expenses will not exceed $1,000 for the year.

Example 2. Same facts as in example 1, except that Newton is not an employee of Half-Penny and has a traditional health insurance plan with a 20 percent co-pay and a $500 deductible. Newton would be responsible for $1,400 ($500 + (.20 × $4,500)).

Example 3. Same facts as in example 1, except that Newton incurs no medical expenses for the year. The $4,000 that Half-Penny contributed to his HSA can be carried forward to the next year or can be used in future years when he may no longer have health care coverage.

Q 2:42   What are the potential disadvantages to an individual of an HSA?

Potential disadvantages of an HSA for an individual include:

1. *Increased debt.* HSAs coupled with HDHPs may create a greater risk of accruing medical debts, especially for families with low income levels and few financial resources to draw upon.

2. *Increased out-of-pocket costs for less-healthy individuals.* An HDHP may increase out-of-pocket expenses for individuals with high health care consumption. These individuals would probably benefit more from a health plan that has a low deductible or no deductible.

3. *Decreased quality of health.* An HDHP may have an adverse effect on health if an individual forgoes medication and tests because he or she cannot—or does not want to—pay expenses.

4. *HDHP requirement.* Making contributions to an HSA is dependent on having an HDHP (on the first day of the month).

5. *Excess contribution penalty.* Contributions in excess of annual limits may be subject to a cumulative nondeductible excise tax of 6 percent (see Qs 4:74, 4:78).

6. *Cessation of account.* An account ceases to be an HSA upon the death of the account owner unless the spouse is designated as the beneficiary of the HSA (see Qs 5:26, 5:28, 6:71, 7:48, 7:57, 7:68).

7. *Taxation upon death.* The account is taxable if the beneficiary is not the spouse of the account holder upon the death of the account owner (see Q 6:71).

8. *Taxation in estate.* If a decedent's estate is the beneficiary of the HSA, the estate will have to recognize income in respect to a decedent (see Q 6:71).

9. *No deduction for losses.* Because allowable contributions are deductible, a taxpayer cannot claim a loss from declines in the account value.

10. *Insufficient build-up.* An individual establishing a new HSA might not have sufficient funds accumulated in the account to pay for medical expenses below the deductible under the HDHP.

11. *Income and penalty taxes.* Amounts distributed from an HSA that are not used to pay for qualified medical expenses are subject to federal income tax and, if the individual is under age 65, will be subject to an additional 10 percent penalty, unless another exception applies.

12. *Early distribution penalty.* Unless age 65 or another exception applies, a 10 percent penalty is applied on distributions not used to pay for qualified medical expenses (see Qs 6:60–6:62).

13. *Individual responsibility.* The account owner is responsible for determining that HSA payments are used for qualified medical expenses.

14. *IRS reporting.* An HSA account owner must generally file Form 8889—*Health Savings Accounts (HSAs)*, to report contributions, determine HSA deductions, and report HSA distributions. No reporting forms are required of participants for HRAs and FSAs.

15. *Record retention.* The account owner must keep records to demonstrate to the IRS, if audited, that distributions were used to pay for qualifying medical expenses.

Note. The insurer will require policyholders to submit claims so that it can track the plan's deductible.

16. *Medicare enrollment.* Eligibility to contribute to an HSA ends in the month in which the account owner enrolls in Medicare.

17. *Adverse selection.* Under the theory of adverse selection, healthy people and less-healthy people separate into different insurance arrangements and the cost of insurance for the less-healthy consequently rises. Thus, such individuals may become uninsured or underinsured.

Example. Employers that provide a choice between comprehensive protection and an HDHP may experience a shift of the healthier employees to the HDHP. Those employees who remain in the comprehensive plan will likely cause the average cost (for that group) to increase. Healthy workers might even abandon employer-based coverage completely and establish an HSA on their own, especially if they are paying a substantial amount of the premium for the HDHP.

Q 2:43   Who is best suited for adopting an HSA?

Those individuals who prefer, or already have, a high deductible on their health insurance policies (especially those individuals who are highly compensated) will gain the most benefits—primarily in terms of tax benefits. Conversely, if an individual has an employer-paid health policy with no (or a low) deductible, such individuals would not be good candidates for an HSA (nor would they qualify).

An HSA can provide a method for contributing a stream of tax-favored savings for those who are healthy enough and who can afford to do so. Simply stated, the higher the tax bracket, the greater the benefit. On the other hand, lower-paid employees—who may find it difficult to save—may have little enthusiasm for an HSA, even if they would benefit from one (see Q 2:42).

HSA Adoption Statistics

Q 2:44   Are statistics identifying purchasers of HSAs available?

A recent survey reviewing thousands of HSA-eligible plans sold between January 1 and December 31, 2004, highlighted many of the identifying and key demographics of purchasers of HSA-eligible health insurance plans. The comprehensive survey and report was prepared by eHealthInsurance, the largest online health insurance broker in the United States. In July 2005, the report was updated for HSA-eligible plans sold between January 1 and June 30, 2005, and it compares these latest figures to those provided in the 2004 annual survey, highlighting key changes between the two. The survey focused on the continued adoption of HSA-eligible health insurance plans, as well as trends in costs and plan benefits. For the first half of 2005, and with comparisons to the 2004 data, the survey identifies and compares key demographics of purchasers of HSA-eligible health insurance plans, presents and compares the monthly premiums for HSA-eligible health insurance plans, and outlines the health insurance benefit levels included in the HSA-eligible plans purchased by consumers from January 1 through June 30, 2005.

Highlights from the 2005 eHealthInsurance annual survey and report include the following:

1. Nearly half of the people who purchased HSA-eligible plans were 40 years old or older.
2. The average age of purchasers of HSA-eligible plans is 40, whereas the average age of purchasers of non-HSA-eligible plans is 35.
3. HSA-eligible plans are equally attractive to both individuals and families.

4. Individuals account for 51 percent of purchasers, and 49 percent are families (37 percent of purchasers are families with children; 12 percent are couples without children).

5. HSA-eligible plans are being adopted by all income levels; 40 percent of HSA-eligible plans were purchased by people with incomes of $50,000 or below.

6. HSAs may play a role in helping uninsured people get health insurance. More than two-thirds of HSA-eligible plan purchasers who were previously uninsured for more than six months had incomes of $50,000 or less.

7. HSA-eligible plans are affordable: 89 percent of HSA-eligible plan purchasers paid $200 or less per person per month.

8. Of HSA-eligible plans purchased in 2004, 85.4 percent paid 100 percent of office visits, surgery, hospitalization, and lab/X-ray services after the plan deductible was met.

9. Of HSA-eligible plans purchased in 2004, 99.4 percent included prescription drug benefits.

Other key findings of the report on HSA-eligible health plan purchasers include:

1. More than one-third of HSA-eligible health plan purchasers are families with children; and

2. Of those in the $15,000 to $35,000 income bracket, there was a 161 percent increase of previously uninsured purchasers during all of 2004 compared to the first six months of the year.

> [*Source:* Copyright 2005 © eHealthInsurance Services, Inc., "Health Savings Accounts: The First Year In Review . . ." (Feb. 15, 2004). For reprint permission, contact Emily Fox at (650) 210-3140. Reprinted with permission; see http://images.ehealthinsurance.com/ehealthinsurance/Report-New/0215052004HSA1stYrRev.pdf]

Highlights from the eHealthInsurance survey for the first six months of 2005, which also draws from the previous release of the survey (see above), include the following:

1. In 2005 there was a modest shift toward plan purchasers in lower income levels. The percentage of HSA-eligible plan buyers in the first half of the year with incomes at or below $50,000 increased by 2.5 percentage points from the previous year.

2. The percentage of HSA-eligible plan purchasers with incomes of $15,000 or less who were previously uninsured increased 5.1 percentage points, from 44.4 percent to 49.5 percent.

3. The proportion of people paying $50 or less per month increased by 6.3 percentage points or a 75 percent relative increase over 2004.

4. 62.6 percent of all HSA-eligible plan purchasers in the first half of 2005 paid $100 or less per month for their plans.

5. Overall, monthly premiums for HSA-eligible plans decreased by an average of 15 percent from 2004.

6. 2005 premiums for the 45–64 year old segment decreased most significantly of all age groups, with an average reduction of $38 per month, or $456 annually, from 2004. This is a 17 percent average decrease over 2004 plan premiums.

7. 2005 showed a shift toward younger buyers compared with those who purchased HSA-eligible plans in 2004. The segment of 21–29 year olds grew by 5.9 percentage points and is the primary driver of this change.

8. Individuals (rather than families) made up a larger portion of all HSA-eligible plan purchasers in the first six months of 2005 compared to all of 2004. The segment increased 5.8 percentage points to 57.1 percent.

9. Overall, HSA-eligible plans purchased in 2005 cost on average $29 per month, or $348 per year, less than HSA-eligible plans purchased in 2004.

10. Of the HSA-eligible plans purchased in 2005, nearly 80 percent had prescription drug benefits and half paid 100 percent of the coverage after the deductible was met.

11. Among HSA-eligible plans purchased in the first half of 2005, 78.5 percent covered hospitalization and lab/X-ray services at full cost once the plan's annual deductible was met.

12. 80.8 percent of the HSA-eligible plans paid for 100 percent of emergency room visits, after the deductible was met.

13. Two-thirds of plans purchased in the first half of 2005 covered office visits at full cost once the plan's annual deductible was met.

[**Source:** Copyright 2005 © eHealthInsurance Services, Inc., "Health Savings Accounts: The First Six Months of 2005" (July 27, 2005). For reprint permission, contact Emily Fox at (650) 210-3140. Reprinted with permission; see www.image.ehealthinsurance.com/content/ReportNew/072705HSA6mosReportFinal.pdf]

Other reports and surveys have reported the following:

1. America's Health Insurance Plans (AHIP) reported, in preliminary results of a 2006 study, that at least three million consumers currently receive health coverage through HDHPs offered in conjunction with HSAs. According to the study, enrollment in the new insurance policies eligible for HSAs has roughly tripled since March 2005 (when a similar AHIP survey found that 1,031,000 people were covered by HSA-compatible insurance policies). Thus, coverage under HSA-compatible insurance policies (HDHP) has nearly tripled in the last ten months.

[**Source:** A copy of the press release is available at www.ahip.org/content/pressrelease.aspx?docid=14641]

2. In 2005, Assurant Health, an individual and small-group health insurer, reported that "37 percent of its new individual medical sales have been HSAs." The report shows that as of September 16, 2005:

   • 70 percent of HSA purchasers are families with children

- 61 percent of HSA purchasers are over age 40
- 29 percent of HSA purchasers are from households of four or more people
- 31 percent of all HSA purchasers have high school or technical school training as their highest level of education
- 44 percent of HSA applicants did not indicate having prior health insurance coverage on their application
- 29 percent of HSA purchasers have family incomes of less than $50,000
- 20 percent of HSA purchasers have family incomes of less than $40,000
- 19 percent of HSA purchasers have a net worth of less than $25,000

[*Source:* Assurant Health, "Quick Facts: Health Savings Accounts" (Sept. 16, 2005). The release is available at www.assuranthealth.com/about/factsheet.shtml]

3. A survey by Deloitte Center for Health Solutions shows why HSA plans are attractive to employers. The cost of the average health insurance plan increased by 7.3 percent in 2005, while the cost of HSA and other consumer-driven health plans went up by only 2.8 percent.

[*Source:* Deloitte Center for Health Solutions, "Survey: Consumer-Driven Health Plan Cost Growth Significantly Slower Than Other Plans" (Jan. 24, 2006). The survey is available at www.bizjournals.com/orlando/stories/2006/02/06/newscolumn1.html?from_rss=1]

4. The Commonwealth Fund and the Employee Benefit Research Institute (EBRI) released the results of a survey in December 2005, reporting that "individuals with more comprehensive health insurance were more satisfied with their health plan than individuals in high deductible plans" and that people with consumer-directed plans spent more out of pocket and were more likely to forgo care. The survey had a small sample size of 1,204 participants, and only 1 percent of the sample size had a consumer-directed health plan. The results may also have been skewed by other factors.

[*Source:* "Early Experience With High-Deductible and Consumer-Driven Health Plans: Findings From the EBRI/Commonwealth Fund Consumerism in Health Care Survey," Paul Fronstin, Ph.D., and Sara R. Collins, Ph.D., The Commonwealth Fund, Dec. 2005. A multimedia presentation of the findings is available at: www.cmwf.org/usr_doc/site_docs/webcast/Articulate/EBRI/player.html. A similar presentation, but without video for a slower connection, may be accessed at www.cmwf.org/usr_doc/site_docs/webcast/Articulate/EBRI_56k/player.html]

5. *Blue Cross Blue Shield* found that HSA-eligible enrollees are of all ages and of no different health status than people enrolled in traditional coverage. In addition, the August 2005 survey shows that:
   - The number of previously uninsured people currently enrolled in an HSA-eligible product (12 percent) is double that of enrollees in traditional insurance products (6 percent);

- HSA-eligible enrollees are far more likely to use wellness programs and online tools to track costs than are people in a non-consumer-directed health plan; and
- HSA-eligible enrollees are more likely to access information and services available to assist them in decision making than are individuals with traditional insurance.

[*Source:* "Blue Shield Blue Cross Presentation, Health Savings Accounts—The Consumer Prospective" (Nat. Press Club, Sept. 28, 2005). The presentation is available at: www.bcbshealthissues.com/events/consumer/sullivan_presentation.ppt]

Q 2:45   How might an HSA work for an individual?

An individual may be healthy today, or have a condition requiring regular medication, or be faced with an unexpected medical condition. The following examples demonstrate how an HSA could work under specific circumstances. Most people cannot recoup the amount of their premium payment for health insurance unless they have a large, catastrophic-type claim. HDHP policies with an HSA may make sense for some individuals because these types of policies allow the individual to be covered for large health care expenses at a reduced premium, while "self-insuring" themselves for the small ones with tax-free dollars.

Note. In the following examples, if contributions are made through an employer's cafeteria plan, there will be a FICA tax savings for both HDHP premium payments and HSA contributions. If the HSA is established outside of the employer's plan, the individual will have an income tax deduction but will get no FICA tax savings (unless the Bush Administration proposal goes through, see Q 1:28). HSA administrative fees and account earnings are not considered.

Example 1. Sam, who earns $28,000 per year, is young, healthy, and single. Sam was covered by an HDHP (self-only coverage) during the entire 2006 calendar.

As a preventive measure, Sam goes to his doctor's office in November and receives a routine annual exam. In December, Sam established an HSA and deposited $650 into an HSA for the year. Sam also uses the dollars in his HSA to reimburse himself on a tax-free basis for the prescription sunglasses he purchased earlier in the year. In this example, Sam saves over $200 ($1,870 − $1,668) with an HDHP and an HSA compared to a traditional health plan with a lower deductible; $320 ($650 − $330) rolls over and remains in Sam's HSA for future use.

Plan Benefits	Traditional Plan	HDHP Plan with an HSA
Deductible/person	$250	$1,200
Coinsurance (percentages)	80/20	80/20

Plan Benefits	*Traditional Plan*	*HDHP Plan with an HSA*
Out-of-pocket limit[1]	$1,000	$3,000
Office copays	$20	none
Drug copays	$10/$20	none
A. Annual Premium:	**$1,700**	**$1,200**
Medical Expenses:		
Office visit/exam (1 @ $200)	$20	$180
Eyeglasses (1 @ $150)	$150	$150
B. Total Expenses:	**$400**	**$1,380**
C. HSA Contribution:	**$0**	**$2,000**
D. Tax Savings on Contribution (assume 28%)	**$0**	**$560**
Total Cost:[2]	$1,870	$1,668
Less HSA Account Balance	$0	$320 ($650 − $330)
Net Result:	$1,870	$1,348
Savings ($5,200 − $4,820):		**$522**[3]

---

[1] Includes deductible and coinsurance
[2] "Total Cost" equals A + (greater of B or C) minus D
[3] The "savings" are only an approximation. Result will vary from person to person depending upon individual tax circumtances and actual premium costs.

Example 2. Holly earns $45,000. Holly goes to her doctor twice during 2006 for a back condition and takes medication for pain. Holly was covered by an HDHP (self-only coverage) during the entire year and contributed $2,000 into her HSA—the amount of the deductible under the HDHP—for the 2006 year. In this example, Holly saves $380 ($5,200 − $4,820) with an HDHP and an HSA compared to a traditional health plan with a lower deductible;. $620 remains in her HSA for future use.

Plan Benefits	**Traditional Plan**	**HDHP Plan with an HSA**
Deductible	$250	$2,000
Coinsurance (percentages)	80/20	80/20
Out-of-pocket limit[1]	$1,000	$3,000
Office copays	$20	none
Drug copays	$10/$20	none
A. Annual Premium:	**$4,800**	**$4,000**
Medical Expenses:		
Office visit/exam (2 @ $150)	$40	$300
Medication (12 @ $90)	$360	$1,080
B. Total Expenses:	**$400**	**$1,380**
C. HSA Contribution:	**$0**	**$2,000**

D. Tax Savings on Contribution
(assume 28%): $0 $560

Total Cost:[2] $5,200 $5,440
Less HSA Account Balance $0 $620 ($2,000 − $1,380)
Net Result: $5,200 $4,820

Savings ($5,200 − $4,820):   **$380[3]**

---

[1] Includes deductible and coinsurance
[2] "Total Cost" equals A + (greater of B or C) minus D
[3] The "savings" are only an approximation. Result will vary from person to person depending upon individual tax circumtances and actual premium costs.

Example 3. Holly has an accident and requires surgery on her knee. The surgery costs $7,000. The deductible and coinsurance are applied, and the out-of-pocket maximums are exceeded. In this example, Holly will have to pay an additional $160 ($6,490 − $6,430). Nothing is left in Holly's HSA account.

Plan Benefits	_Traditional_	_HDHP Plan with an HSA_
A. Annual Premium:	$4,800	$4,000
Medical Expenses:		
Office visit/exam (2 @ $150)	$40	$300
Medication (12 @ $90)	$240	$1,080
Surgery	$1,250	$1,620
B. Total Expenses:	**$1,530**	**$3,000**
C. HSA Contribution:	$0	$2,000
D. Tax Savings on Contribution (assume 28%)	$0	$560
Total Cost:[2]	$6,330	$6,440
Less HSA Account Balance	$0	$0 (used $2000)
Net Result:	$6,300	$6,490
Additional Cost:	**$160**	

---

[1] Includes deductible and coinsurance
[2] "Total Cost" equals A + (greater of B or C) minus D
[3] The "savings" are only an approximation. Result will vary from person to person depending upon individual tax circumtances and actual premium costs.

Practice Pointer. Instead of using the funds in the HSA to pay for the medical expenses in the above examples, the funds could remain in the HSA and accumulate on a tax-free basis for qualified medical expenses incurred in subsequent years. Alternatively, if no deduction was claimed for the current year qualified medical expenses, the expenses could be reimbursed tax-free in a subsequent year. The taxpayer should be sure to keep proper documentation.

Chapter 3

Medical Coverage and Insurance

Chapter 3 examines medical coverage and insurance for purposes of determining whether the individual is treated as being covered by a high deductible health plan (HDHP) and no other plan that is not a high deductible health plan. Annual deductibles and out-of-pocket expenses are also addressed. Chapter 3 also explains the exceptions (e.g., for "permitted insurance") and transitional rules that may apply in determining whether the minimum annual deductible requirement is met and whether out-of-pocket limits are exceeded in a given year. Contributions to HSAs are discussed in chapter 4.

HDHP Requirements

Q 3:1   What is a high deductible health plan?

Generally, a high deductible health plan (HDHP) is a health plan that satisfies certain requirements with respect to minimum annual deductibles and maximum annual out-of-pocket expenses (see Q 3:16). [I.R.C. § 223(c)(2)] (See appendix D.) For HSA contribution purposes, a health plan must meet two main requirements to be considered an HDHP:

1. *Minimum annual deductible.* The HDHP's annual deductible for the 2006 tax year must be at least $1,050 for self-only coverage (see Q 3:35) and at least $2,100 for family coverage (see Q 3:36). [I.R.C. §§ 223(c)(2)(A)(i)(I), 223(c)(2)(A)(i)(II)] Table 3-1 shows the minimum annual deductibles for 2006 and earlier years.

Table 3-1. Minimum Annual Deductible

Year Coverage	2006	2005	2004
Self-Only	$1,050	$1,000	$1,000
Family	$2,100	$2,000	$2,000

2. *Out-of-pocket expenses.* The annual out-of-pocket expenses—including expenses incurred in satisfying the deductible under the HDHP and co-payments required to be paid under the HDHP for covered benefits (other than premiums)—may not exceed specified limits. Special rules apply to deductibles for services performed out-of-network (see Qs 3:11, 3:17). Table 3-2 shows the maximum out-of-pocket expenses (including co-payments) for 2006 and earlier years. [I.R.C. §§ 223(c)(2)(A)(ii)(I), 223(c)(2)(A)(ii)(II); Rev. Proc. 2005-70, § 3.22, 2005-37 I.R.B. 979; see also Treasury Press Release, JS-2996 (Nov. 22, 2005); Rev. Proc. 2004-71, § 3.22(2), 2004-50 I.R.B. 1]

Table 3-2. Maximum Out-of-Pocket Expenses

Year Coverage	2006	2005	2004
Self-Only	$ 5,250	$ 5,100	$ 5,000
Family	$10,500	$10,200	$10,000

Example 1. A plan provides health coverage for Albert and his family in 2006. The plan provides for the payment of covered medical expenses of any member of Albert's family once the member has incurred covered medical

expenses during the year in excess of $1,050 even if the minimum family deductible of $2,100 has not been satisfied. If Albert incurred covered medical expenses of $1,500 in a year and no other family member incurred medical expenses during the year, the plan would pay $450. Thus, benefits are potentially available under the plan even if the family's covered medical expenses do not exceed $2,100. Because the plan provides family coverage with an annual deductible of less than $2,100, the plan is not an HDHP for 2006.

Example 2. Same facts as in the preceding example, except that the plan has a $5,250 family deductible and only provides payment for covered medical expenses if any member of Albert's family has incurred covered medical expenses during the year in excess of $2,100. The plan satisfies the requirements for an HDHP with respect to the deductibles.

Example 3. Perseus has self-coverage under his employer's HDHP for 2006 with a $2,000 annual deductible. This means that Perseus will pay the first $2,000 of any medical expenses incurred during the year before the health plan will pay any benefits. The HDHP then provides that it will pay 80 percent of the next $3,000 in medical expenses incurred by Perseus during the year and Perseus will pay 20 percent of the next $3,000, or $600. The HDHP will then pay 100 percent of the covered medical expenses over $5,000. Perseus's total annual out-of-pocket expenses (not counting any premiums Perseus might have to pay) is $2,600, which is within the 2006 out-of-pocket limit of $5,250 ($5,100 for 2005) for self-coverage and the HDHP deductible of $2,000 is greater than the minimum of $1,050 for self-only coverage. Therefore, the plan is an HDHP.

Q 3:2   Can an insured or self-insured medical reimbursement plan sponsored by an employer be an HDHP?

Yes. An HDHP can be an insured or a self-insured plan. [I.R.S. Notice 2004-2, Q&A 7, 2004-2 I.R.B. 269]

Q 3:3   Is a limited coverage plan treated as an HDHP?

No. An HDHP does not include a plan where substantially all of the coverage is for accidents, disability, dental care, vision care, or long-term care (see Qs 3:4, 3:39).

Q 3:4   Must an HDHP provide meaningful medical coverage in order to be considered an HDHP under Code Section 223?

Yes. The fact that Congress clearly specified that a plan that primarily covers "permitted insurance" or accidents, disability, dental care, vision care, or long-term care would not be considered an HDHP for purposes of the HSA rules indicates that the HDHP accompanying the HSA must provide meaningful medical coverage for participants. This is consistent with IRS Notice 2004-50

[2004-33 I.R.B. 196], which allows an HDHP to exclude certain benefits as long as significant benefits remain (see Qs 3:30). However, there is no bright line to determine when HDHP coverage will be considered meaningful and when it will be considered merely a sham. Some employers and insurers may be interested in offering reduced benefits under the HDHP in exchange for lower premiums. However, there is a limit to how much the benefits can be reduced. It would appear that, in order to be considered an HDHP for purposes of the HSA rules, an HDHP must, at a minimum, exhibit risk-shifting and risk distribution characteristics of insurance and cover major medical and hospital benefits. [I.R.S. Notice 2004-50, Q&As 14, 15, 2004-33 I.R.B. 196]

> **Note.** An HDHP does not include a plan if substantially all of its coverage is for permitted insurance (see Q 3:40) and/or coverage for accidents, disability, dental care, vision care, or long-term care (see Qs 2:8, 3:30). [I.R.C. § 223 (c)(2)(B)]

Q 3:5   Does a state high-risk health plan qualify as an HDHP?

Yes. A state high-risk health plan (high-risk pool) will qualify as an HDHP for 2006 if the plan does not pay benefits below the minimum annual deductible of $1,050 ($1,000 for 2005 and 2004) for self-only coverage and $2,100 ($2,000 for 2005) for family coverage (see Q 3:1). [I.R.S. Notice 2004-50, Q&A 13, 2004-33 I.R.B. 196]

Q 3:6   Would a health plan that negotiates discounted prices for services qualify as an HDHP if an HSA owner receives services at a discount?

Yes. Health plans that negotiate discounted prices for services do not fail to meet the HDHP requirements merely because an HSA owner receives services at the discounted rate before satisfying the plan deductible. [I.R.S. Notice 2004-50, Q&A 25, 2004-33 I.R.B. 196]

Q 3:7   Are the minimum annual deductible and maximum out-of-pocket expense amounts applicable to the HDHP under Code Section 223 adjusted for inflation?

Yes. These annual amounts, as well as the maximum HSA contribution/ deduction, are indexed for inflation using annual cost-of-living adjustments. Any increase is rounded to the nearest multiple of $50 (see Table 3-1). [I.R.C. § 223(g)(1)-(2); for 2006, see Rev. Proc. 2005-70, § 3.22, 2005-47 I.R.B. 973; Treas. Press Rel., JS-2996 (Nov. 22, 2005); for 2005, see Rev. Proc. 2004-71, § 3.22(2), 2004-50 I.R.B. 1]

The dollar amounts in Code Section 223(b)(2) (i.e., the $2,250 and $4,500 limitations) are adjusted to reflect cost-of-living increases relative to the consumer price index (CPI) for 1997. The CPI for a year is the average for the 12-month period ending on August 31 for such year. The $2,250 and

$4,500 base amounts used to compute the monthly limitation on deductions for 2006 can be computed as follows (to the nearest multiple of $50):

(a) $2,700 = \dfrac{\$2,250 \times \text{Average CPI Sept. 2004 to Aug. 2005}}{\text{Average CPI Sept. 1996 to Aug. 1997}}$

(b) $5,450 = \dfrac{\$4,500 \times \text{Average CPI Sept. 2004 to Aug. 2005}}{\text{Average CPI Sept. 1996 to Aug. 1997}}$

For the dollar amounts in Code Section 223(c)(2)(A) (i.e., the $1,000 and $5,000 figures), the adjustment uses 2003 instead of 1997. The $1,000 and $5,000 base amounts used to determine whether a health plan is an HDHP (minimum deductible and maximum out-of-pocket expenses) for 2006 can be computed as follows (to the nearest multiple of $50):

(a) $1,050 = \dfrac{\$1,000 \times \text{Average CPI Sept. 2004 to Aug. 2005}}{\text{Average CPI Sept. 2002 to Aug. 2003}}$

(b) $5,250 = \dfrac{\$5,000 \times \text{Average CPI Sept. 2004 to Aug. 2005}}{\text{Average CPI Sept. 2002 to Aug. 2003}}$

Q 3:8 Must an HDHP be offered on a calendar year basis?

No. The HDHP need not be offered on a calendar year basis. Code Section 223(c), which defines a high deductible health plan, states only that a high deductible health plan must have a minimum annual deductible. Neither the statute nor any Treasury guidance indicates that the deductible must be based on a calendar year. In fact, Notice 2004-50, Q&A-22 (see example) suggests the opposite by including as part of the facts an HDHP that begins on July 1. [See also, I.R.S. Notice 2005-83, 2005-49 I.R.B. 1075]

Q 3:9 How are changes to the deductibles and out-of-pocket expense limits applied?

Any required change to the deductibles and out-of-pocket expense limits may be applied as of the renewal date of the plan in cases where the renewal date occurs after the beginning of the calendar year, but in no event longer than a 12-month period ending on the renewal date. Thus, a fiscal-year plan that satisfies the minimum annual deductible on the first day of the first month of its fiscal year may apply that deductible for the entire fiscal year, even if the minimum annual deductible increases on January 1 of the next calendar year. [I.R.S. Notice 2004-50, Q&A 86, 2004-33 I.R.B. 196; rule also mentioned in Treas. Press Rel. JS-2996 (Nov. 11, 2005)]

Example. An individual obtains self-only coverage under an HDHP on June 1, 2005, the first day of the plan year, with an annual deductible of $1,000— the minimum annual deductible allowed for 2004 and 2005 for self-only coverage. Assume that the cost-of living adjustment requires the minimum deductible amount to be increased for 2006 to $1,050 (which it was). The plan's deductible is not increased to comply with the increased minimum deductible amount until the plan's renewal date of June 1, 2006. The plan satisfies the requirements for an HDHP with respect to deductibles through May 30, 2006.

Plan Deductible

Q 3:10   What is the plan deductible?

The plan deductible is the amount of covered medical expenses that must be paid by the HSA owner before the health plan will begin to cover medical expenses.

Q 3:11   Are plan deductibles for out-of-network services taken into account when determining the HDHP maximum out-of-pocket limitation?

No. In the case of a health plan using a network of providers, such plan's annual deductible for services provided outside of such network is disregarded when determining whether the maximum out-of-pocket limit ($5,250 for self-only coverage for 2006 and $10,500 for family coverage) under an HDHP is satisfied. [I.R.C. § 223(c)(2)(D), 223(c)(2)(D)(ii)].

> **Practice Pointer.** Although separate in-network and out-of-network deductibles appear to be permitted, an HDHP is not required to have separate deductibles for in-network and out-of-network services. If there is a separate out-of-network deductible, however, that deductible will be disregarded in determining an HSA account owner's maximum annual contribution or deduction for the year pursuant to the Code (see Q 3:17). [I.R.C. § 223(c)(2)(D)(ii)]

Q 3:12   Can a health plan's deductible period last longer than 12 months?

Yes. However, if the health plan's deductible period is longer than 12 months, the plan's limit must be adjusted to determine whether the maximum annual deductible is exceeded. If that limit is exceeded, the plan is not an HDHP.

Q 3:13   How is the plan's annual deductible limit adjusted when the deductible period lasts longer than 12 months?

In the case of self-coverage, the HDHP's annual deductible for the 2006 tax year is $1,050 ($1,000 for 2004 and 2005). For family coverage, the deductible must be at least $2,100 ($2,000 for 2005). For plans that define the deductible period over a period longer than 12 months, the limits must generally be adjusted to determine whether a plan satisfies the HSA requirements (see Q 3:1). [I.R.S. Notice 2004-50, Q&A 24, 2004-33 I.R.B. 196] The limit is adjusted by taking the following steps:

1. Multiply the minimum annual deductible by the number of months allowed to satisfy the deductible.

2. Divide the amount in Step 1 by 12. This is the adjusted deductible for the longer period that is used to test for compliance.

3. Compare the amount in Step 2 to the plan's deductible. If the plan's deductible equals or exceeds the amount in Step 2, the plan satisfies the requirements for the minimum deductible.

Note. For months before January 1, 2006, a health plan that would otherwise qualify as an HDHP except for an annual deductible that does not satisfy the rules above for periods of more than 12 months may be treated as an HDHP under the transitional rule (see Q 3:14).

Example 1. For 2006, a health plan takes into account medical expenses incurred in the last three months of 2005 to satisfy its deductible for calendar year 2006. The plan's deductible for self-only coverage is $1,500 and covers 15 months (the last three months of 2005 and 12 months of 2006). To determine whether the health plan's deductible satisfies the $1,050 for self-coverage annual deductible limits for 2006, the following calculations are performed:

1. Minimum annual deductible (self-only coverage): $1,050

2. Multiplied by the number of months in which expenses incurred are taken into account to satisfy the deductible: 15 = $15,750

3. Divide the result ($15,750) by 12: = $1,312.50

The HDHP minimum deductible for self-only coverage for 15 months must be at least $1,312.50. Because the plan's deductible, $1,500, exceeds $1,312.50, the plan's self-only coverage satisfies the plan deductible rule. The maximum annual HSA contribution for an eligible individual with self-only coverage under these facts is $1,200: the lesser of (1) ($1,500/15) × 12 = $1,200 or (2) $2,700 for 2006.

Example 2. Same facts as in the preceding example, except the family deductible for the 15-month period is $3,000. To determine whether the health plan's deductible satisfies the $2,100 for family coverage annual deductible limits for 2006, the following calculations are performed:

1. Minimum annual deductible (family coverage): $2,100

2. Multiplied by the number of months in which expenses incurred are taken into account to satisfy the deductible: 15 = $31,500

3. Divide the result ($31,500) by 12: $2,625

The HDHP minimum deductible for family coverage for 15 months must be at least $2,625. Because the plan's deductible, $3,000 exceeds $2,625, the plan's family coverage satisfies the plan deductible rule. The maximum annual HSA contribution for an eligible individual with family coverage under these facts is $2,400: the lesser of (1) ($3,000/15) × 12 = $2,400 or (2) $5,250 for 2006.

Transitional Rule

Q 3:14   Can a health plan that would otherwise qualify as an HDHP but for an annual deductible that does not satisfy the rules for periods of more than 12 months be treated as an HDHP?

Possibly. For months before January 1, 2006, a health plan that would otherwise qualify as an HDHP but for an annual deductible that does not satisfy the rules stated in Q 3:13 for periods of more than 12 months will be treated as an HDHP if the plan was in effect or submitted for approval to state insurance regulators by August 16, 2004 (the date of publication of Notice 2004-50 in the Internal Revenue Bulletin). Individuals covered under these health plans will continue to be eligible to contribute to HSAs before January 1, 2006. [I.R.S. Notice 2004-50, 2004-33 I.R.B. 196, see "Transition Relief" on last page]

Note. The transitional guidance was provided to allow policy providers time to modify HDHP policies to include prescription drug benefits that meet the HDHP requirements.

Out-of-Pocket Expenses

Q 3:15   What are out-of-pocket expenses?

The term *out-of-pocket expenses* includes the plan's annual deductible, co-payments, and any co-insurance payments required by the plan, but does not include premiums for covered benefits. [I.R.C. § 223(c)(2)(A)(ii); I.R.S. Notice 2004-2, Q&A 3, 2004-2 I.R.B. 269; see also I.R.S. Notice 2004-50, Q&A 21, 2004-33 I.R.B. 196]

Q 3:16   What are the limits for out-of-pocket expenses?

The annual out-of-pocket expenses for covered benefits for 2006 may not exceed $5,250 ($5,100 for 2005 and $5,000 for 2004) for self-only coverage and $10,500 ($10,200 for 2005 and $10,000 for 2004) for family coverage. [Rev. Proc. 2005-70, § 3.22, 2005-47 I.R.B. 979; see also Treas. Press Rel. JS-2996 (Nov. 22, 2005); Rev. Proc. 2004-71, § 3.22 (2), 2004-50 I.R.B. 970]

Q 3:17   Are amounts paid by the HSA owner toward covered medical expenses for non-network services required to be applied toward the out-of-pocket limit?

No. Amounts paid by the HSA owner toward covered medical expenses for non-network services are *not* required to be applied toward the out-of-pocket limit. Rather, the annual out-of-pocket limit need only include amounts spent for covered services within the network.

Note. A network plan is a plan that generally provides more favorable benefits for services provided by its network of providers than for services provided outside of the network. In the case of a plan using a network of providers, the plan does not fail to be an HDHP (if it would otherwise meet the requirements of an HDHP) solely because the out-of-pocket expense limits for services provided outside of the network exceed the maximum annual out-of-pocket expense limits allowed for an HDHP (see Q 3:16). However, the plan's annual deductible for out-of-network services is not taken into account in determining the annual contribution limit (see Q 4:19). [I.R.C. § 223(c)(2)(D)(ii)] In other words, if there are two separate deductibles (one for network and one for non-network), only the network deductible is used to determine the HSA deduction and contribution limit.

Q 3:18   Must a plan specify an out-of-pocket maximum in order to be considered an HDHP?

Generally, a plan that does not specify an out-of-pocket maximum is not an HDHP. However, if a plan is structured in such a way that the account owner would never exceed the out-of-pocket limitation, then the plan could be considered an HDHP. [I.R.S. Notice 2004-50, Q&A 17, 2004-33 I.R.B. 196]

Example 1. A plan requires an HSA owner with self-only coverage to satisfy a $2,000 deductible, and then pays 100 percent of covered benefits above the deductible. This plan would never violate the out-of-pocket maximum limitation.

Example 2. A plan provides self-only coverage with a $2,000 deductible. The plan imposes a lifetime limit on reimbursements for covered benefits of $1 million. For expenses for covered benefits incurred above the deductible, the plan reimburses 80 percent of the usual and customary (UCR) costs. Because there is no express limit on out-of-pocket expenses, the plan does not qualify as an HDHP because it is possible that the out-of-pocket maximum limitation will be exceeded.

Example 3. Same facts as in the preceding example, except that after the 20 percent co-insurance paid by the covered individual reaches $3,000, the plan pays 100 percent of the UCR costs until the $1 million limit is reached (see Q 3:30). For the purpose of determining the individual's out-of-pocket expenses, the plan takes into account only the 20 percent of UCR paid by the individual, up to $3,000. This plan satisfies the out-of-pocket maximum limitation even though no express maximum is stated.

Transitional Rule

Q 3:19   What transitional relief was granted by the IRS to HDHPs relative to out-of-pocket expenses when the health plan does not provide any maximum on payments above the deductible?

For months before January 1, 2005, a health plan that would qualify as an HDHP but for the lack of an express maximum on payments above the deductible that complies with the out-of-pocket requirement (see Q 3:18) will be treated as an HDHP. Individuals covered under these health plans will continue to be eligible to contribute to HSAs before January 1, 2005. [I.R.S. Notice 2004-50, 2004-33 I.R.B. 196, see "Transitional Rule" of notice on last page]

Q 3:20   What transitional relief was provided for a health plan that complies with state laws that mandate benefits without regard to a deductible or a deductible below the minimum annual deductible?

Several states currently require that health plans provide certain benefits without regard to a deductible that is below the minimum (e.g., first-dollar coverage or coverage with a low deductible). These health plans are not HDHPs. An individual covered under this type of health plan is not eligible to contribute to an HSA. However, because of the short period between the enactment of HSAs and the effective date of Code Section 223, these states did not have sufficient time to modify their laws to conform to the standards of Code Section 223. When a plan is not an HDHP solely because of state-mandated benefits, an otherwise eligible individual covered under this type of plan will be treated as an eligible individual and may contribute to an HSA for months before January 1, 2006 (the transition period) for state-mandated benefits in effect on January 1, 2004. [I.R.S. Notice 2004-43, 2004-27 I.R.B. 10] This transitional rule was extended for certain non-calendar-year health plans (see Q 3:21).

Q 3:21   Why was the transitional relief provided in Notice 2005-83 extended for non-calendar-year health plans?

Generally, a health plan may not reduce existing benefits before the plan's renewal date. Thus, even though a state may amend its laws before January 1, 2006, to authorize HDHPs that comply with Code Section 223(c)(2), non-calendar-year plans may still fail to qualify as HDHPs after January 1, 2006, because existing benefits cannot be changed until the next renewal date.

Example. A state amends its statute effective July 30, 2005, to comply with HDHP requirements under federal law. A fiscal year plan with a year that begins on July 1, 2005, is required to retain the state-mandated low deductible coverage for the plan year July 1, 2005, through June 30, 2006, because the benefits can be modified only on the renewal date. As a result, although the state has amended its statute, the health plan will fail to be an HDHP for months after January 1, 2006 (i.e., for the months of January through June 2006). (See, however, Q 3:22.)

Q 3:22   When does the additional transitional relief for a coverage period of 12 months or less in a non-calendar-year health plan expire?

The transition relief in Notice 2004-43 [2004-27 I.R.B. 10] (see Q 3:19) was modified to provide that, for any coverage period of 12 months or less beginning before January 1, 2006, a health plan that otherwise qualifies as an HDHP as defined in Code Section 223(c)(2), except that it complied on its most recent renewal date before January 1, 2006, with state-mandated requirements (in effect on January 1, 2004) to provide certain benefits without regard to a deductible or with a deductible below the minimum annual deductible (see Q 3:1), will be treated as an HDHP. The additional transitional relief does not apply after the earlier of the health plan's next renewal date or December 31, 2006. [I.R.S. Notice 2005-83, 2005-49 I.R.B. 1075]

Other Out-of-Pocket Issues

Q 3:23 Must a penalty payment or flat-dollar charge paid by the covered individual for failure to obtain pre-certification for a specific provider be treated as an out-of-pocket expense?

No. Penalty payments or flat-dollar charges incurred because of a failure to obtain pre-certification for covered expenses are not required to be treated as out-of-pocket expenses. Therefore, an HDHP need not count such amounts toward the $5,250/$10,500 maximum out-of-pocket limits for 2006 (see Q 3:16). [I.R.S. Notice 2004-50, Q&As 18-19, 2004-33 I.R.B. 196]

> **Example.** A health plan that otherwise qualifies as an HDHP generally requires a 10 percent co-insurance payment after a covered individual satisfies the deductible. However, if an individual fails to get pre-certification for a specific provider, the plan requires a 20 percent co-insurance payment. Only the generally applicable 10 percent co-insurance payment is included in computing the maximum out-of-pocket expenses paid. [I.R.S. Notice 2004-50, Q&A 19, 2004-33 I.R.B. 196; see too I.R.S. Notice 2004-2, Q&A 4, 2004-2 I.R.B. 269] The plan satisfies the maximum out-of-pocket limitation requirements for an HDHP. The result in this example would be the same if the plan imposed a higher co-insurance amount for an out-of-network provider.

Q 3:24 Are cumulative embedded deductibles under family coverage subject to the out-of-pocket maximum?

Yes. In general, an HDHP must limit the out-of-pocket expenses paid by the covered individuals, either by design or by its express terms (see Qs 3:16, 3:26).

> **Example.** In 2006, a plan which otherwise qualifies as an HDHP provides family coverage with a $2,100 deductible for each family member. The plan pays 100 percent of covered benefits for each family member after that family member satisfies the $2,100 deductible. The plan does not provide any express limit on out-of-pocket expenses. The maximum out-of-pocket expense limit for family coverage is $10,500 ($10,200 for 2005). The plan is not an HDHP for a family with six or more covered individuals because the amount that these individuals pay in out-of-pocket expenses exceeds the maximum out-of-pocket threshold under Code Section 223 ($2,100 × 6 ($12,600) exceeds $10,500). However, the out-of-pocket expense limit of $10,500 for any family with two to five covered individuals is not exceeded because the amount that these individuals pay in out-of-pocket expenses

would not exceed the maximum out-of-pocket threshold under Code Section 223 ($2,100 × 5 ($10,500) equals, but does not exceed $10,500). [I.R.S. Notice 2004-50, Q&A 20 (ex. 1), 2004-33 I.R.B. 196]

Q 3:25   Are cumulative embedded deductibles under family coverage subject to the out-of-pocket maximum if the plan contains an umbrella deductible of $10,500 or less for 2006?

No. The plan qualifies as an HDHP for the family, regardless of the number of covered individuals. The out-of-pocket maximum of $10,500 for 2006 ($10,200 for 2005) cannot be exceeded.

Example. In 2006, a plan which otherwise qualifies as an HDHP provides family coverage with a $2,100 deductible for each family member. The plan pays 100 percent of covered benefits for each family member after that family member satisfies the $2,100 deductible. The plan includes an umbrella deductible of $10,500. The plan reimburses 100 percent of covered benefits if the family satisfies the $10,500 in the aggregate, even if no single family member satisfies the $2,100 embedded deductible. The out-of-pocket maximum ($10,500 for 2006) is not exceeded and the plan qualifies as an HDHP for the family, regardless of the number of covered individuals. [I.R.S. Notice 2004-50, Q&A 20 (ex. 2), 2004-33 I.R.B. 196]

Q 3:26   Are amounts incurred by an individual for medical care for noncovered expenses included in computing the plan's out-of-pocket expenses?

No. Amounts incurred for noncovered benefits (including amounts in excess of UCR and financial penalties) are not counted toward the $1,050/$2,100 ($1,000/$2,000 for 2005) deductible or the $5,250/$10,500 ($5,150/$10,200 for 2005) out-of-pocket limits for 2006. Note, however, that a health plan's out-of-pocket limit includes the deductible, co-payments, and other amounts (but not premiums). [I.R.S. Notice 2004-2, Q&A 3, 2004-2 I.R.B. 269; I.R.S. Notice 2004-50, Q&A 21, 2004-33 I.R.B. 196]

Note. If a plan does not take co-payments into account in determining whether the deductible is satisfied, the co-payments must still be taken into account in determining whether the out-of-pocket maximum is exceeded.

Example. In 2006, a health plan has a $1,050 deductible for self-only coverage. After the deductible is satisfied, the plan pays 100 percent of UCR for covered benefits. In addition, the plan pays 100 percent for preventive care, minus a $20 co-payment per screening. The plan does not take into account co-payments in determining whether the $1,050 deductible has been satisfied. The co-payments must be included in determining whether the plan meets the out-of-pocket maximum of $5,250 (the 2006 limit for self-only coverage). Unless the plan includes an express limit on out-of-pocket expenses taking into account the co-payments, or limits the co-payments to $4,200 (for 2006), the plan is not an HDHP. If co-payments were limited to $4,200, the $5,250 limit would not be exceeded with a $1,050 deductible.

Q 3:27 If an employer changes health plans midyear, is the minimum annual deductible of $1,050/$2,100 (for 2006) satisfied if the new HDHP provides a credit toward the deductible for expenses incurred during the previous health plan's short plan year?

Yes. If the period during which expenses are incurred for purposes of satisfying the deductible is 12 months or less and the plan satisfies the requirements for an HDHP, the new plan's taking into account expenses incurred during the prior plan's short plan year (whether or not the prior plan is an HDHP) and not reimbursed does not violate the minimum $1,050/$2,100 annual deductible requirement of an HDHP for 2006. [I.R.S. Notice 2004-50, Q&A 22, 2004-33 I.R.B. 196]

Example. An employer with a calendar-year health plan switches from a non-HDHP plan to a new plan with coverage effective on July 1. The annual deductible under the new plan satisfies the $1,050/$2,100 (for 2006) annual deductible limits for an HDHP. The new plan counts expenses incurred under the prior plan during the first six months of the year in determining whether the new plan's annual deductible is satisfied. The new plan satisfies the HDHP deductible limit.

Q 3:28 If an eligible individual changes coverage during the plan year from self-only HDHP coverage to family HDHP coverage, does the individual fail to be covered by an HDHP merely because the family HDHP coverage takes into account expenses incurred while the individual had self-only coverage?

No. The family plan does not fail to be an HDHP because it takes into account expenses incurred while an individual had self-only coverage under an HDHP. [I.R.S. Notice 2004-50, Q&A 23, 2004-33 I.R.B. 196]

Example. Melody, an eligible individual, has self-only qualifying HDHP coverage from January 1 through April 30, marries in April, and from May 1 through December 31 has family qualifying HDHP coverage. The family coverage plan applies expenses incurred by Melody from January through April toward satisfying the family deductible. Melody's coverage satisfies the HDHP requirements for family coverage. Melody's contribution to an HSA is based on four months of the self-only coverage (i.e., 4/12 of the deductible for the self-only coverage) and eight months of family coverage (8/12 of the deductible for family coverage).

Limitation on Benefits

Q 3:29 May an HDHP impose a lifetime limit on benefits?

Yes. An HDHP may impose a reasonable lifetime limit on benefits provided under the plan.

Q 3:30 Are amounts paid by a covered individual above a lifetime limit treated as out-of-pocket expenses?

No. Amounts paid by a covered individual above the lifetime limit are not treated as out-of-pocket expenses in determining the annual out-of-pocket maximum. However, a lifetime limit on benefits designed to circumvent the maximum annual out-of-pocket amount is not reasonable (see Q 3:33). [I.R.S. Notice 2004-50, Q&A 14, 2004-33 I.R.B. 196]

Example. Assume a health plan has an annual deductible that satisfies the $1,050 deductible for self-only coverage and the $2,100 deductible for family coverage for 2006. After satisfying the deductible, the plan pays 100 percent of covered expenses, up to a lifetime limit of $1 million. The lifetime limit of $1 million is reasonable, and the health plan is not disqualified from being an HDHP because of the lifetime limit on benefits.

Q 3:31 If a plan imposes reasonable annual or lifetime limits on specific benefits, are amounts paid by covered individuals beyond these annual or lifetime limits subject to the maximum out-of-pocket limitations?

No. The out-of-pocket maximums ($5,250/$10,500 for 2006) apply to covered benefits only. [I.R.S. Notice 2004-50, Q&A 15, 2004-33 I.R.B. 196]

Q 3:32 May a plan limit covered benefits?

Generally, yes. A plan may be designed with reasonable benefit restrictions limiting the plan's covered benefits.

Q 3:33 When is a restriction or exclusion on benefits reasonable?

A restriction or exclusion on benefits is reasonable only if significant other benefits remain available under the plan in addition to the benefits subject to the restriction or exclusion. [I.R.S. Notice 2004-50, Q&A 14, 2004-33 I.R.B. 196]

Example 1. In 2006, a self-only health plan with a $1,050 deductible includes a $1 million lifetime limit on covered benefits. The plan provides no benefits for experimental treatments, mental health, or chiropractic care visits. Although the plan provides benefits for substance abuse treatment after the deductible is satisfied, it limits payments to 26 treatments per year. Although the plan provides benefits for fertility treatments, it limits lifetime reimbursements to $10,000, after the deductible is satisfied. Other than these limits on covered benefits, the plan pays 80 percent of major medical expenses incurred after satisfying the deductible. When the 20 percent co-insurance paid by the covered individuals reaches $4,000, the plan pays 100 percent. Under these facts, the plan is an HDHP and no expenses incurred by a covered individual other than the deductible and the 20 percent co-insurance are treated as out-of-pocket expenses subject to the maximum out-of-pocket limitation.

Example 2. In 2006, a self-only health plan with a $1,050 deductible imposes a lifetime limit on reimbursements for covered benefits of $1 million. Although the plan pays 100 percent of expenses incurred for covered benefits after satisfying the deductible, the plan imposes a $10,000 annual limit on benefits for any single condition. The $10,000 annual limit under these facts is not reasonable because significant other benefits do not remain available under the plan. Under these facts, any expenses incurred by a covered individual after satisfying the $1,050 deductible are treated as out-of-pocket expenses.

Q 3:34   If a plan limits benefits to UCR amounts, are amounts paid by covered individuals in excess of UCR included in determining the out-of-pocket expenses paid for purposes of calculating the maximum out-of-pocket limit?

No. Restricting benefits to UCR is a reasonable restriction on benefits. Thus, amounts paid by covered individuals in excess of UCR that are not paid by an HDHP are not included in determining maximum out-of-pocket expenses. [I.R.S. Notice 2004-50, Q&A 16, 2004-33 I.R.B. 196]

Family Coverage vs. Self-Only Coverage

Q 3:35   What is self-only coverage under an HDHP?

Self-only coverage under an HDHP means a health plan that covers only one eligible individual. [I.R.S. Notice 2004-50, Q&A 12, 2004-33 I.R.B. 196]

Q 3:36   What is family coverage under an HDHP?

Family coverage under an HDHP is defined as any coverage that is not self-only coverage. [I.R.C. § 223(c)(4)] Thus, family HDHP coverage is a health plan covering one eligible individual and at least one other individual (whether or not the other individual is an eligible individual). [I.R.S. Notice 2004-50, Q&A 12, 2004-33 I.R.B. 196] However, an individual can be eligible to contribute to an HSA if his or her spouse has non-HDHP *family* coverage, provided the spouse's coverage does not cover the individual. [Rev. Rul. 2005-25, 2005-18 I.R.B. 971]

Q 3:37   May a family-coverage HDHP plan cover only the eligible individual?

No. Family coverage under an HDHP is a health plan that covers an eligible individual and at least one other person (see Q 3:36).

Q 3:38   Can benefits under a family-coverage plan be paid before the family incurs annual covered medical expenses in excess of the minimum annual deductible under Code Section 223?

No, except for preventive care. In general, a plan is a family-coverage HDHP only if nothing is payable under the HDHP until the family incurs annual covered medical expenses in excess of the minimum annual deductible of the plan. However, an exception applies to expenses for preventive care (see Q 3:45). It does not matter which family member incurs the expenses. [I.R.S. Notice 2004-2, Q&A 3, 2004-2 I.R.B. 269]

Other Health Plan Coverage

Q 3:39   Are there exceptions to the rule requiring that the eligible individual not be covered under any other health plan?

Generally, an eligible individual may not be covered under any other non-HDHP (see Q 2:6). [I.R.C. § 223(c)(1)(A)(ii)] However, there are two exceptions that permit other coverage to be disregarded. [I.R.C. § 223(c)(1)(B)] Disregarded coverage includes:

1. Coverage for any benefit provided by *permitted insurance* (see Q 3:40). [I.R.C. § 223(c)(1)(B)(i)]
2. Coverage, whether through insurance or otherwise, for accidents, disability, dental care, vision care, or long-term care (see Q 2:8). [I.R.C. § 223(c) (1)(B)(ii)]

An HDHP does not include a plan if substantially all of its coverage is for coverage described in (1) or (2) above. [I.R.C. § 223(c)(2)(B)]

Permitted Insurance

Q 3:40   What is permitted insurance?

For eligibility purposes, certain types of insurance coverage—referred to as *permitted insurance*—is disregarded in determining if an individual is an eligible individual (see Qs 2:8, 3:39). [I.R.C. § 223(c)(3)]

Q 3:41   What does permitted insurance include?

Permitted insurance includes insurance if substantially all of the coverage provided under such insurance relates to any of the following:

- Liabilities incurred under workers' compensation laws [I.R.C. § 223(c)(3)(A)(i)–(iv)]

- Tort liabilities [I.R.C. § 223(c)(3)(A)(i)–(iv)]
- Liabilities relating to ownership or use of property [I.R.C. § 223(c)(3)(A)(i)–(iv)]
- Such other similar liabilities as the Secretary of Treasury may specify [I.R.C. § 223(c)(3)(A)(i)–(iv)]
- Insurance for a specified disease or illness [I.R.C. § 223(c)(3)(B)]
- Insurance paying a fixed amount per day (or other period) of hospitalization [I.R.C. § 223(c)(3)(C)]

Note. Medicare supplemental insurance is not on the permitted insurance list.

Note. A plan that provides coverage substantially all of which is for a specific disease or illness is not an HDHP.

Q 3:42   May an otherwise eligible individual who is covered by both an HDHP and insurance contracts for one or more specific diseases or illnesses contribute to an HSA if the insurance provides benefits before the deductible of the HDHP is satisfied?

Yes, provided that the principal health coverage is provided by the HDHP. An eligible individual covered under an HDHP may be covered "for any benefit provided by permitted insurance" (see Qs 3:40, 3:41) The term *permitted insurance* includes "insurance for a specified disease or illness." Therefore, an eligible individual may be covered by an HDHP and also by permitted insurance for one or more specific diseases, "such as cancer, diabetes, asthma or congestive heart failure," as long as the principal health coverage is provided by the HDHP. [I.R.S. Notice 2004-50, Q&A 7, 2004-33 I.R.B. 196]

Q 3:43   Must coverage for permitted insurance be provided under an insurance contract?

Generally, yes. Benefits for permitted insurance—liabilities incurred under workers' compensation laws, tort liabilities, liabilities relating to ownership or use of property, insurance for a specified disease or illness, and insurance paying a fixed amount per day (or other period) of hospitalization—must generally be provided through insurance contracts and not on a self-insured basis. However, where benefits (such as workers' compensation benefits) are provided in satisfaction of a statutory requirement and any resulting benefits are secondary or incidental to other benefits, the benefits will qualify as permitted insurance even if self-insured. [I.R.S. Notice 2004-50, Q&A 8, 2004-33 I.R.B. 196]

The IRS has provided additional clarification on how the following affect eligibility for an HSA: prescription drug programs (see Q 3:44), medical discount cards (see Q 3:53), employer-provided employee assistance (see Q 3:54), and wellness and disease management programs (see Q 3:56). Also, the IRS has provided guidance on when other account-based plans (e.g., health FSA, HRA) may be used with an HSA.

Prescription Drug Coverage

Q 3:44   May an individual who is covered by a health plan that provides prescription drug benefits before the deductible of the HDHP is satisfied contribute to an HSA?

Generally, no. An individual who is covered by a health plan that provides prescription drug benefits (separately or through a rider) before the deductible of the HDHP is satisfied cannot normally contribute to an HSA. [Rev. Rul. 2004-38, 2004-15 I.R.B. 717]

Transitional relief. To allow policy providers time to modify HDHP policies to include prescription drug benefits that meet the HDHP requirements, the IRS issued transitional guidance specific to prescription drug coverage.

Under this transitional guidance, for months before January 1, 2006, if an otherwise eligible individual has both an HDHP and another health plan that provides for prescription coverage before the minimum HDHP deductible has been satisfied, the individual will continue to be considered an eligible individual and may make HSA contributions. [Rev. Proc. 2004-22, 2004-15 I.R.B. 727]

Preventive Care Safe Harbor

Q 3:45   What is the preventive care safe harbor?

The safe harbor for preventive care allows certain benefits to be provided by an HDHP without satisfying the $1,050/$2,100 minimum deductible for 2006 ($1,000/$2,000 for 2005 and 2004). [I.R.S. Notice 2004-23, 2004-15 I.R.B. 725]

In Notice 2004-23 [2004-15 I.R.B. 725] the IRS provides a list of services and benefits that qualify as *preventive care* under Code Section 223(c)(2)(C). That section states: "[a] plan shall not fail to be treated as a high deductible health plan by reason of failing to have a deductible for preventive care (within the meaning of section 1871 of the Social Security Act, except as otherwise provided by the Secretary)." [I.R.C. § 223(c)(2)(C)] An HDHP may, therefore, provide preventive care benefits without a deductible or with a deductible below the minimum annual deductible.

Q 3:46   What benefits and services are permitted under the preventive care safe harbor?

The IRS defined the following medical procedures as safe harbor items that could be provided as preventive care before the HDHP deductible is met. The list of allowed preventive care includes, but is not limited to, the following:

- Periodic health evaluations, including tests and diagnostic procedures ordered in connection with routine examinations (e.g., annual physicals)

- Routine prenatal and well-child care
- Child and adult immunizations
- Tobacco cessation programs
- Obesity weight-loss programs
- Screening services specified in Table 3-3

Table 3-3. Preventive Care Safe-Harbor Screening Services

Cancer Screening
    Breast cancer (e.g., mammogram)
    Cervical cancer (e.g., pap smear)
    Colorectal cancer
    Prostate cancer (e.g., PSA test)
    Skin cancer
    Oral cancer
    Ovarian cancer
    Testicular cancer
    Thyroid cancer

Heart and Vascular Diseases Screening
    Abdominal aortic aneurysm
    Carotid artery stenosis
    Coronary heart disease
    Hemoglobinopathies
    Hypertension
    Lipid disorders

Infectious Diseases Screening
    Bacteriuria
    Chlamydial infection
    Gonorrhea
    Hepatitis B virus infection
    Hepatitis C
    Human immunodeficiency virus (HIV) infection
    Syphilis
    Tuberculosis infection

Mental Health Conditions and Substance Abuse Screening
    Dementia

Depression

Drug abuse

Problem drinking

Suicide risk

Family violence

Metabolic, Nutritional, and Endocrine Conditions Screening

Anemia, iron deficiency

Dental and periodontal disease

Diabetes mellitus

Obesity in adults

Thyroid disease

Musculoskeletal Disorders Screening

Osteoporosis

Obstetric and Gynecologic Conditions Screening

Bacterial vaginosis in pregnancy

Gestational diabetes mellitus

Home uterine activity monitoring

Neural tube defects

Preeclampsia

Rh incompatibility

Rubella

Ultrasonography in pregnancy

Pediatric Conditions Screening

Child developmental delay

Congenital hypothyroidism

Lead levels in childhood and pregnancy

Phenylketonuria

Scoliosis, adolescent idiopathic

Vision and Hearing Disorders Screening

Glaucoma

Hearing impairment in older adults

Newborn hearing

[I.R.S. Notice 2004-23, 2004-15 I.R.B. 725]

Note. The IRS requests comments on the appropriate standard for preventive care and, in particular, recommendations concerning any benefit or service that should be added to Notice 2004-23.

Q 3:47 Are prescription drugs or medications that are used to prevent a disease or recurrence of a disease from which an HSA owner, spouse, or dependent has recovered eligible for safe-harbor treatment?

Yes. Prescription drugs or medications that are used to prevent a disease or recurrence of a disease from which an HSA owner, spouse, or dependent has recovered are eligible for safe-harbor treatment as preventive care benefits. Thus, coverage for these items may be provided under the HDHP before the HSA deductible is satisfied (see Qs 3:45, 3:48). [I.R.S. Notice 2004-50, Q&A 27, 2004-33 I.R.B. 196]

Q 3:48 To what extent do drugs or medications come within the safe harbor for preventive care services as "preventive care"?

Notice 2004-23 [2004-15 I.R.B. 725] sets out a preventive care safe harbor, which describes those benefits that can be covered before the HDHP deductible is satisfied (see Q 3:46). [I.R.C. § 223(c)(2)(C)] Solely for this purpose, drugs or medications are preventive care when taken by an individual who has developed risk factors for a disease that has not yet manifested itself or not yet become clinically apparent (i.e., asymptomatic) or to prevent the reoccurrence of a disease from which an individual has recovered.

For example, the treatment of high cholesterol with cholesterol-lowering medications (e.g., statins) to prevent heart disease, or the treatment of recovered heart attack or stroke victims with angiotensin-converting enzyme (ACE) inhibitors to prevent a reoccurrence, constitute preventive care. In addition, drugs or medications used as part of procedures providing preventive care services (see Q 3:46) are eligible for safe-harbor treatment. [I.R.S. Notice 2004-50, Q&A 27, 2004-33 I.R.B. 196]

Q 3:49 Must an HDHP provide preventive care benefits?

No. There is no requirement in the Code that an HDHP provide benefits for preventive care or provide preventive care with a deductible below the minimum annual deductible. [I.R.S. Notice 2004-23, 2004-15 I.R.B. 725]

Q 3:50 Does preventive care include the treatment of an existing illness?

Generally, no. Preventive care does not generally include any service or benefit intended to treat an existing illness, injury, or condition (but see Q 3:51). [I.R.S. Notice 2004-50, Q&A 27, 2004-33 I.R.B. 196]

Q 3:51   Does a preventive care service or screening that also includes the treatment of a related condition during that procedure come within the safe harbor for preventive care in Notice 2004-23?

Although Notice 2004-23 [2004-15 I.R.B. 725] states that preventive care generally does not include any service or benefit intended to treat an existing illness, injury, or condition, in situations where it would be unreasonable or impracticable to perform another procedure to treat the condition, any treatment that is incidental or ancillary to a preventive care service or screening as described in Notice 2004-23 also falls within the safe harbor for preventive care. For example, removal of polyps during a diagnostic colonoscopy is preventive care that can be provided before the deductible in an HDHP has been satisfied. [I.R.S. Notice 2004-50, Q&A 26, 2004-33 I.R.B. 196]

Q 3:52   Does the characterization of a benefit required by state law determine whether health care is preventive?

No. The determination of whether health care that is required by state law to be provided by an HDHP without regard to a deductible is "preventive" for purposes of the exception for preventive care is to be based on the standards set forth in Notice 2004-23 [2004-15 I.R.B. 725] and other guidance issued by the IRS, rather than on how that care is characterized by state law.

> **Note.** State insurance laws often require health plans to provide certain health care benefits without regard to a deductible or on terms no less favorable than other benefits provided by the health plan (see Qs 3:20, 8:36.)

> **Note.** Code Section 220(c)(2)(B)(ii) allows an HDHP for purposes of an Archer MSA to provide preventive care without a deductible if required by state law. However, that section does not define preventive care for HSA purposes.

Medical Discount Cards

Q 3:53   May an individual who is covered by an HDHP, and also has a discount card that enables the user to obtain discounts for health care services or products, contribute to an HSA?

Yes. Discount cards that entitle the holder to obtain discounts for services or products at managed care market rates will not disqualify an individual from making an HSA contribution as long as the individual is required to pay the discounted cost of health care until the deductible of the HDHP is satisfied. [I.R.S. Notice 2004-50, Q&A 9, 2004-33 I.R.B. 196]

> **Example.** An employer provides its employees with a pharmacy discount card. For a fixed annual fee (paid by the employer) each employee receives a card that entitles the holder to choose any participating pharmacy. During the one-year life of the card, the cardholder receives a 15 to 50 percent discount off the usual and customary fees charged by the pharmacy, with no dollar cap on the amount of discounts received during the year. The

cardholder is responsible for paying the discounted costs of any drugs until the deductible of any other health plan covering the individual is satisfied. An employee who is otherwise eligible for an HSA will not become ineligible solely as a result of having this benefit.

Employee Assistance, Disease Management, and Wellness Programs

Q 3:54 Does coverage under an Employee Assistance Program (EAP), disease management program, or wellness program make an individual ineligible to contribute to an HSA?

Coverage under an employer-provided EAP, disease management program, or wellness program does not make an individual ineligible to contribute to an HSA, provided that the program does not provide significant benefits in the nature of medical care or treatment. If it does not, the EAP, disease management program, or wellness program will not be considered a *health plan* for HSA purposes. [I.R.S. Notice 2004-50, Q&A 10, 2004-33 I.R.B. 196]

Q 3:55 Would services provided by a nurse practitioner at an employer's on-site clinic be considered a health plan that makes an individual ineligible to contribute to an HSA?

Probably not. It is likely that a significant component of the services provided by the nurse practitioner will be preventive, and can therefore be provided without regard to the deductible under an HDHP (see Q 3:45). Further, to the extent that clinical services are provided, it is likely that such services will be minor in nature (e.g., treatment of minor injuries, illness, or first aid) and not significant benefits in the nature of medical care or treatment.

> **Practice Pointer.** There are exceptions under ERISA (DOL Reg. § 2510.3-1(c)) and COBRA (Treas. Reg. § 54.4980B-2, Q&A-1(d)) to exempt on-site facilities from the definition of medical care. If the services of a nurse practitioner are treated as outside of ERISA and not subject to COBRA, that would provide additional support for the conclusion that such services are not a disqualifying "health plan" for purposes of an HSA.

Q 3:56 May the safe-harbor screening and preventive care services be disregarded in determining whether an EAP provides significant benefits for medical care or treatment?

Yes. To determine whether a program provides significant medical benefits, screening, and preventive care services described in Notice 2004-23 are disregarded (see Q 3:46).

Example 1. Jupiter Corporation offers a program that provides employees with benefits under an EAP, regardless of enrollment in a health plan. The EAP is specifically designed to assist Jupiter in improving productivity by helping employees identify and resolve personal and work concerns that affect job performance and the work environment. The benefits consist primarily of free or low-cost confidential short-term counseling to identify an employee's problem that may affect job performance and, when appropriate, make referrals to an outside organization, facility, or program to assist the employee in resolving the problem. The issues addressed during the short-term counseling include, but are not limited to, substance abuse, alcoholism, mental health or emotional disorders, financial or legal difficulties, and dependent care needs. Jupiter's EAP is not a *health plan* under Code Section 223(c)(1) because it does not provide significant benefits in the nature of medical care or treatment.

Example 2. Saturn Corporation maintains a disease management program that identifies employees and their family members who have, or are at risk for, certain chronic conditions. The disease management program provides evidence-based information, disease-specific support, case monitoring, and coordination of the care and treatment provided by a health plan. Typical interventions include monitoring laboratory or other test results, telephone contacts or Web-based reminders of health care schedules, and providing information to minimize health risks. Saturn's disease management program is not a *health plan* under Code Section 223(c)(1) because it does not provide significant benefits in the nature of medical care or treatment.

Example 3. Venus Corporation offers a wellness program for all employees regardless of participation in a health plan. The wellness program provides a wide range of education and fitness services designed to improve the overall health of the employees and prevent illness. Typical services include education; fitness, sports, and recreation activities; stress management; and health screenings. Any costs charged to the individual for participating in the services are separate from the individual's coverage under the health plan. Venus's wellness program is not a *health plan* under Code Section 223(c)(1) because it does not provide significant benefits in the nature of medical care or treatment.

Health Reimbursement Arrangements

Q 3:57 May an account owner who participates in an HDHP and a post-deductible health reimbursement arrangement (HRA) be an eligible individual?

Yes. An account owner who participates in an HDHP and a post-deductible HRA may still be an eligible individual. The deductible for the HRA does not need to be the same as the deductible for the HDHP. However, in no event may the HDHP or other health coverage provide benefits before the minimum annual deductible for the HDHP is satisfied (see Q 4:10). [Rev. Rul. 2004-45, 2004-22 I.R.B. 971]

Note. If the HDHP and the other coverage do not have identical deductibles, the HSA contribution is limited to the lowest deductible amount (see chapter 4).

Example. In 2006, an individual has self-only coverage under an HDHP with a deductible of $2,500. The individual is also covered under a post-deductible HRA that pays or reimburses qualified medical expenses after $2,000 of the HDHP deductible has been satisfied. In this case, if the individual incurs covered medical expenses of $2,250, the HRA will pay $250. Because the HRA deductible of $2,000 is less than the HDHP deductible of $2,500, the individual's HSA contribution limit is $2,000 (see Q 4:10).

Long-Term Care Insurance

Q 3:58   May an account owner pay for long-term care premiums from an HSA?

Yes. An account owner may pay for long-term care premiums from an HSA, as long as such premiums are within the limits necessary to be considered qualified medical expenses (see Qs 6:47–6:49). [I.R.S. Notice 2004-50, Q&A 41, 2004-33 I.R.B. 196]

Q 3:59   May an account owner pay for long-term care services from an HSA (i.e., services that are provided without regard to insurance)?

Yes. An account owner may pay for long-term care services from an HSA, as long as such services are qualified medical expenses (see Q 6:39). [I.R.S. Notice 2004-50, Q&A 42, 2004-33 I.R.B. 196]

Practice Pointer. Although Code Section 106(c) generally prohibits payment of coverage for long-term care benefits under a Code Section 125 plan (cafeteria plan), this prohibition does not apply to distributions from HSAs. [I.R.S. Notice 2004-50, Q&A 42, 2004-33 I.R.B. 196]

HSAs Under a Code Section 125 Cafeteria Plan

Q 3:60   May an HSA be funded by salary reduction contributions through a cafeteria plan?

Yes. An HSA may be funded by salary reduction contributions through a cafeteria plan described in Code Section 125. [I.R.S. Notice 2004-2, Q&A 33, 2004-2 I.R.B. 269] Thus, an employee may elect to have amounts contributed on a pretax basis as employer contributions to an HSA.

Caution. The initial release of the 2005 version of Publication 15-B, which provides information on the employment tax treatment of fringe benefits, incorrectly included HSAs in a list of benefits that cannot be offered under a cafeteria plan. The IRS has now posted a corrected version on its Web site. [www.irs.ustreas.gov/pub/irs-pdf/p15b.pdf; see also, www.irs. gov/formspubs/article/0,,id=109875,00.html regarding changes to tax forms and publications]

Q 3:61   Must a cafeteria plan document be amended to allow employees to fund an HSA with salary reduction contributions?

Yes. A cafeteria plan must be in writing and must, among other things, describe the benefits offered under the plan and the periods during which the benefits are provided. The HSA should, therefore, be described as a benefit in the cafeteria plan. [Prop. Treas. Reg. § 1.125-1, Q&A-3 (1984)] In addition, there is more flexibility to change an HSA salary reduction election than for other cafeteria plan benefits (see Qs 3:60, 3:64). Accordingly, a rule regarding when the election for HSA salary reduction elections may be changed (e.g., prospectively, at any time) should be added.

> **Practice Pointer.** Although the IRS does not review cafeteria plan documents and issue determination letters as it does for Section 401(a) qualified retirement plans, on audit, the IRS would expect an employer to be able to produce a written cafeteria plan that satisfies the requirements specified in the regulations.

Q 3:62   May the employer offer negative elections for an HSA if offered through a cafeteria plan?

Yes. An employer's cafeteria plan may provide for negative elections to enroll employees. Negative elections may be used to enroll employees as described in Revenue Ruling 2002-27. [I.R.S. Notice 2004-50, Q&A 61, 2004-33 I.R.B. 196; Rev. Rul. 2002-27, 2002-20 I.R.B. 925]

Q 3:63   Which requirements that apply to health flexible spending arrangements (FSAs) under a Code Section 125 cafeteria plan do not apply to HSAs?

The following requirements for health FSAs under a Code Section 125 cafeteria plan (which are generally imposed so that health FSAs operate in a manner similar to "insurance-type" accident or health plans under Code Section 105) are not applicable to HSAs:

1. The general prohibition against a benefit that defers compensation by permitting employees to carry over unused elective contributions or plan benefits from one plan year to another plan year. See Q 4:11 regarding the 2½ month grace period rules established in 2005 that may affect an individual's eligibility to make HSA contributions. [I.R.C. § 125(d)(2)(D); Treas. Reg. § 1.125-2, Q&A-7];

2. The requirement that the maximum amount of reimbursement must be available at all times during the coverage period [Treas. Reg. § 1.125-2, Q&A-7];

3. The mandatory 12-month period of coverage.

[I.R.S. Notice 2004-50, Q&A 57, 2004-33 I.R.B. 196]

Q 3:64   Do the Code Section 125 change-in-status rules apply to elections of HSA contributions through a cafeteria plan?

No. A cafeteria plan may permit an employee to revoke an election during a period of coverage with respect to a qualified benefit and make a new election for the remaining portion of the period only as specified in regulations under Code Section 125. [See Treas. Reg. § 1.125-4; I.R.S. Notice 2004-50, Q&A 58, 2004-33 I.R.B. 196] Because the eligibility requirements and contribution limits for HSAs are determined on a month-by-month basis (see Q 4:19), rather than on an annual basis, an employee who elects to make HSA contributions under a cafeteria plan may start or stop the election or increase or decrease the election at any time as long as the change is effective after the request for the change is received (i.e., prospectively).

Q 3:65   Can an employer place additional restrictions on the election of HSA contributions under a cafeteria plan?

Yes. However, if an employer places additional restrictions on the election of HSA contributions under a cafeteria plan, the same restrictions must apply to all employees. [I.R.S. Notice 2004-50, Q&A 58, 2004-33 I.R.B. 196]

Q 3:66   Can an employer permit employees to elect an HSA midyear if offered as a new benefit under the employer's cafeteria plan?

Yes, provided the election for the HSA is made on a prospective basis. However, the HSA election does not permit a change or revocation of any other coverage under the cafeteria plan unless the change is permitted by regulations under Code Section 125. [See Treas. Reg. § 1.125-4; I.R.S. Notice 2004-50, Q&A 59, 2004-33 I.R.B. 196] This may affect the employees' eligibility to establish an HSA (see Q 3:64).

Q 3:67   When the HSA is offered as a new benefit under the employer's cafeteria plan midyear, are there circumstances that will prevent the employee from being an eligible individual?

Yes. While an HSA may be offered to and elected by an employee midyear, the employee may have other coverage under the cafeteria plan that cannot be changed or limited, (e.g., coverage under a health FSA), which may prevent the employee from being an eligible individual (see, too, Qs 4:10, 4:119). [See Rev. Rul. 2004-45, 2004-22 I.R.B. 971]

Q 3:68   If an employee elects to make contributions to an HSA through the employer's cafeteria plan, may the employer contribute amounts to an employee's HSA to cover qualified medical expenses incurred by an employee that exceed the employee's current HSA balance?

Yes. Where an employee elects to make contributions to an HSA through a cafeteria plan, the employer may, but is not required to, contribute amounts to an employee's HSA up to the maximum amount elected by the employee. While any accelerated contribution made by the employer must be equally available to all participating employees throughout the plan year and must be provided to all participating employees on the same terms, the employee must repay the amount of the accelerated contribution by the end of the plan year. [I.R.S. Notice 2004-50, Q&A 60, 2004-33 I.R.B. 196] An employer may not recoup contributions made to an HSA from an employee's HSA (see Qs 2:1, 6:2). [I.R.S. Notice 2004-50, Q&A 82, 2004-33 I.R.B. 196]

Retiree Health Coverage

Q 3:69   Are HSA distributions qualified medical expenses if used to pay for the retiree portion of health care coverage once the account owner reaches age 65?

Yes. This exception applies regardless of whether the plan is insured or self-insured (see Q 6:40). [I.R.C. § 223(d)(2)(C)(iv)]

Miscellaneous Issues

Q 3:70   Is an HSA a group health plan under Code Section 5000(b)(1) for purposes of the 25 percent excise tax on nonconforming group health plans?

Under Code Section 5000, the term *group health plan* means a plan (including a self-insured plan) of, or contributed to by, an employer (other than a government entity, but including a self-employed person) or employee organization to provide health care (directly or otherwise) to the employees, former employees, the employer, others associated or formerly associated with the employer in a business relationship, or their families. Unless certain participation requirements are satisfied, the plan is treated as a "nonconforming group health plan." However, if no contributions are made to the HSA by an employer (including a self-employed individual) or employee organization, the HSA is not a group health plan. In other cases, it is unclear whether the HSA would be treated as a group health plan under Code Section 5000, which imposes a 25 percent excise tax on "nonconforming" group health plans, because distributions may be used for nonmedical purposes. [I.R.C. § 5000(b)(1),(c)]

Q 3:71   Do HIPAA privacy and security rules apply to an HSA?

It depends. This issue is more fully discussed in chapter 8.

Chapter 4

Contributions and Deductions

Contributions and their deductibility or exclusion from gross income are discussed in chapter 4. The limitations on contributions and special rules for married individuals are explained. Chapter 4 also explains the contribution rules and restrictions relating to employer contributions to HSAs either directly or through a cafeteria plan. The tax treatment of contributions, IRS reporting by individuals, as well as partnership and S corporation considerations are also discussed. The cafeteria plan grace period rules (up to 2½ months), exceptions, and the transitional rule (for plan years ending before June 5, 2006) and their affect on HSA eligibility are discussed in this chapter. This chapter also examines the comparability rules for employer contributions. Rollover contributions and trustee-to-trustee transfers are more fully discussed in chapter 5; distribution taxation is discussed in chapter 6. See appendix D for a chart containing annual HSA limitations amounts.

On July 31, 2006, the proposed employer contribution comparability requirements were modified and finalized. Structurally, the final regulations follow the form of the proposed regulations that were issued in 2005. Chapter 4 discusses the changes and clarifications that were made under the final regulations and their significance (see Qs 4:52, 4:55, 4:56, 4:93–4:97, 4:100, 4:107, 4:111, 4:115, 4:121, 4:123, 4:125, 4:128).

Making HSA Contributions

Q 4:1   In what form must contributions be made to an HSA?

Annual contributions to an HSA must be made in cash. Contributions may not be made in the form of stock or other property. [I.R.S. Notice 2004-2, Q&A 16, 2004-2 I.R.B. 269] An exception is made for rollovers and transfers from an Archer MSA or another HSA (see Qs 5:6, 5:39). Rollovers and transfers are more fully discussed in chapter 5.

For purposes of an HSA, an Archer MSA is a trust or custodial account as described in Code Section 220. [I.R.C. § 223(c)(5)]

Q 4:2   May an HSA be fully funded in the beginning of a year?

Yes. The maximum annual contribution may be made at the beginning of the year, but not before the start of the year for which the contribution is being made (see Q 4:73 regarding excess contributions). To contribute the maximum annual contribution, an individual must have the same coverage during the entire year (see also Q 4:112 regarding pre-funding of employer contributions).

Note. There is no actual "monthly limit" (see Q 4:15). Although the annual HSA contribution deduction limit is the sum of the monthly limits (see Q 4:19), contributions may be made at any time. For example, if an individual has disqualifying coverage and is said to be ineligible for three months ending on March 31, the individual may contribute 9/12ths of the 2006 HSA contribution limit (at any time).

Caution. If the HSA account owner's HDHP coverage changes during the year, (e.g., to coverage with a lower deductible, or coverage that is not an HDHP), an HSA that was fully funded at the beginning of the year based upon the assumption that the original HDHP would remain in place for the full year may have excess contributions that will have to be withdrawn prior to April 15 of the following year to avoid the 6 percent excise tax.

Q 4:3   What is the last date for making annual contributions to an HSA?

In general, contributions must be made by the due date of the individual's federal income tax return not including extensions. Thus, a 2006 HSA contribution may generally be made at any time in 2006 and before the due date of the 2006 return (generally April 15 of the following year). [I.R.C. § 223(d)(4)(B)]

Note. Farmers must file their federal income tax returns by March 1 (rather than the general April 15 due date), unless estimated taxes are paid by January 18.

Tax-free distributions may be received from the HSA only for qualified medical expenses incurred on or after the date the HSA is established. However, for 2004, if an HSA was established by the due date (generally April 15, 2005), tax-free distributions could have been received from the HSA for qualified medical expenses incurred on or after the first day of the month in which the taxpayer became an eligible individual under a transitional rule that applied only for calendar year 2004. [I.R.S. Notice 2004-2, Q&A-26, 2004-2 I.R.B. 269, modified by I.R.S. Notice 2004-25, 2004-15 I.R.B. 727 (the "transitional relief")] However, the transitional relief was not extended beyond 2004. For 2005 and thereafter, tax-free distributions may be received from the HSA only for qualified medical expenses incurred on or after the date the HSA is established. [I.R.S. Notice 2004-2, 2004-2 I.R.B. 269]

Caution. A contribution postmarked after December 31 will be treated as a current-year contribution by the trustee or custodian unless the taxpayer has designated that the contribution is for the prior year. For example, if an individual is making a contribution in 2007 with respect to the prior year, the contribution form (and preferably the check) should indicate "2006 contribution."

Q 4:4   For contributions to be made on behalf of an eligible individual, is the individual required to have compensation?

No. HSA contributions may be made regardless of whether the eligible individual (see Q 2:6) has compensation. However, the employee's deduction for contributions made under an HDHP established by an employer may not exceed the individual's compensation or earned income. [I.R.C. § 223(b)(4)(A), 223(b)(4)(B)]

Practice Pointer. Unlike Archer MSAs, contributions may be made by or on behalf of eligible individuals even if the individuals have no compensation or if the contributions exceed their compensation.

Q 4:5   May HSA contributions be made into an individual retirement account (IRA)?

No. Although an HSA is similar to an IRA in many respects, an IRA cannot be used as an HSA, nor can an HSA be combined with an IRA. [See I.R.S. Notice 96-53, A-9, A-10, 1996-2 C.B. 219, regarding Archer Medical Savings Accounts]

Q 4:6   Must contributions be made into an HSA established at the same institution that provides the HDHP?

No contributions may be made into any HSA that the individual may have established. The HSA can be established through a qualified trustee or custodian that is different from the HDHP provider. [I.R.S. Notice 2004-2, Q&A 10, 2004-2 I.R.B. 269]

Eligibility for HSA Contributions

Q 4:7   Who may contribute to an HSA?

Any eligible individual or any other person on an eligible individual's behalf (see Q 2:6) may contribute to an HSA. For example, if the HSA is established by an employee, the employee, the employee's employer, or both may contribute to the HSA of the employee in a given year. If the HSA is established by a self-employed (or unemployed) individual, the individual may contribute to the HSA. In addition, any other individual (e.g., a family member) may also make contributions to an HSA on behalf of an individual. [I.R.S. Notice 2004-50, Q&A 28, 2004-33 I.R.B. 196]

Contributions may also be made through a cafeteria plan (see Q 4:8). In addition, a partnership may also contribute to a partner's HSA (see Q 14:142), and an S corporation may contribute to the HSA of a 2 percent shareholder-employee (see Q 14:154).

Practice Pointer. Although Notice 2004-2 refers only to contributions by employers or family members, the IRS subsequently clarified that any person (an employer, a family member, or any other person) may make contributions to an HSA on behalf of an eligible individual. [I.R.S. Notice 2004-2, Q&A

11, 2004-2 I.R.B. 269; I.R.S. Notice 2004-50, Q&A 28, 2004-33 I.R.B. 196] The individual who makes the contribution does not qualify for the HSA deduction, however. Rather, the account owner may generally take the deduction, or an exclusion from gross inome if the contributions are made under a cafeteria plan, for contributions made on his or her behalf (see Qs 4:43, 4:53).

Note. The DOL has approved certain cash bonus incentives paid in connection with the establishment of HSAs and HDHPs by banks and insurance companies to individuals' HSAs (see Q 6:59).

Q 4:8   May contributions to an HSA be made through a cafeteria plan?

Yes. Payments for an HDHP and contributions to an HSA can be made through a cafeteria plan. [I.R.S. Notice 2004-2, Q&As 16 and 33, 2004-2 I.R.B. 269]

Q 4:9   May a state government make an HSA contribution on behalf of an eligible individual?

Yes (see Q 4:7). In addition, a state government's HSA contribution on behalf of an eligible individual insured under the state's comprehensive health insurance programs for high-risk individuals (state high-risk pool) may qualify as an HDHP if it does not pay benefits below the minimum annual deductible of an HDHP ($1,050 for self-only coverage and $2,100 for family coverage for 2006 ($1,000/$2,000 for 2005)) (see Q 3:10). [I.R.S. Notice 2004-50, Q&A 29, 2004-33 I.R.B. 196]

Other Employee Health Plans

Q 4:10   May an employee covered by an HDHP and a health FSA or an HRA make contributions to an HSA?

Generally not. An employee covered by an HDHP and a health FSA or an HRA that pays or reimburses qualified medical expenses generally cannot make contributions to an HSA (see Q 3:67). However, an employee can make contributions to an HSA while covered under an HDHP for periods during which the individual is covered under any of the arrangements discussed below.

Limited-purpose health FSA or HRA. The FSA and/or HRA are limited-purpose arrangements if they pay or reimburse only vision and dental expenses (i.e., permitted coverage), or preventive care benefits. An HRA, because it can be used to reimburse premiums, could also reimburse long-term care premiums, premiums for a specified disease or illness, or premiums for a fixed amount per day or other period of hospitalization (i.e., permitted insurance) as well. In certain circumstances (i.e., when an HRA does not satisfy the definition of an FSA under Code Section 106(c)), the HRA may also reimburse long-term care services. If the covered benefits are limited in this manner, it does not matter whether the FSA and/or HRA pay benefits without imposing a deductible.

The following examples present situations where an individual is covered by an HDHP and an FSA or HRA. The individual's eligibility to make HSA contributions is examined.

Example 1. Stuart is covered by an HDHP. The HDHP has an 80/20 percent co-insurance feature above the deductible. Stuart is also covered by a health FSA under a Code Section 125 cafeteria plan and an HRA. The health FSA and HRA pay or reimburse all of his medical expenses (within the meaning of IRC Section 213) that are not covered by the HDHP (e.g., co-payments, co-insurance, expenses not covered due to the deductible, and other medical expenses not covered by the HDHP). The health FSA and HRA coordinate the payment of benefits under the ordering rules of Notice 2002-45. [2002-28 I.R.B. 93] Stuart is not entitled to benefits under Medicare and may not be claimed as a dependent on another person's tax return.

Here, Stuart is covered by an HDHP and by a health FSA and HRA that pay or reimburse medical expenses incurred before the minimum annual HSA deductible of $1,050 (the 2006 limit) has been satisfied. The health FSA and HRA pay or reimburse medical expenses that are not limited to the exceptions for permitted insurance, permitted coverage, or preventive care. As a result, Stuart is not an eligible individual for the purpose of making contributions to an HSA. This result would be the same if Stuart were covered by a health FSA or HRA sponsored by his spouse's employer. [Rev. Rul. 2004-45, 2004-22 I.R.B. 971; see also Rev. Rul. 2004-38, 2004-15 I.R.B. 717]

Example 2. Same facts as in Example 1, except that the health FSA and HRA are limited-purpose arrangements that pay or reimburse, pursuant to the written plan document, only vision and dental expenses (whether or not the minimum annual deductible of the HDHP has been satisfied). In addition, the health FSA and HRA pay or reimburse preventive care benefits as described in Notice 2004-23 [2004-15 I.R.B. 725] (see Q 3:46). Although Stuart is covered by an HDHP and by a health FSA and HRA that pay or reimburse medical expenses incurred before the minimum annual HSA deductible ($1,050 for 2006) has been satisfied, the medical expenses paid or reimbursed by the health FSA and HRA include only vision and dental benefits (which are permitted coverage) and preventive care. All of these benefits may be covered as a separate health plan, as a separate or optional rider, or as part of the HDHP, whether or not the minimum annual HSA deductible has been satisfied. Stuart is an eligible individual for the purpose of making contributions to an HSA. [Rev. Rul. 2004-45, 2004-22 I.R.B. 971]

Example 3. Same facts as in Example 1, except that Stuart is not covered by a health FSA. Under his employer's HRA, Stuart elects, before the beginning of the HRA coverage period, to forgo the payment or reimbursement of medical expenses incurred during that coverage period. The decision to forgo the payment or reimbursement of medical expenses does not apply to permitted insurance, permitted coverage, and preventive care (*excepted medical expenses*) (see Q 3:46; Notice 2004-23, 2004-15 I.R.B. 725). Medical expenses incurred during the suspended HRA coverage period (other than the excepted medical expenses, if otherwise allowed to be paid or reimbursed by an HRA) cannot be paid or reimbursed by the HRA currently or later (i.e., after the HRA suspension ends). However, the employer decides to continue to make employer contributions to Stuart's HRA during the suspension period.

Here, however, Stuart elected to forgo the payment or reimbursement of medical expenses incurred during an HRA coverage period. The suspension of payments and reimbursements by the HRA does not apply to permitted insurance, permitted coverage, and preventive care (if otherwise allowed to be paid or reimbursed by the HRA). Stuart is an eligible individual for the purpose of making contributions to an HSA until the suspension period ends, and he is again entitled to receive, from the HRA, payments or reimbursements of Code Section 213(d) medical expenses incurred after the suspension period.

Example 4. Same facts as in Example 1, except that the health FSA and HRA are post-deductible arrangements that pay or reimburse only Stuart's medical expenses (including the 20 percent co-insurance responsibility for expenses above the deductible) after the minimum annual deductible of the HDHP has been satisfied. Because Stuart's health FSA and HRA pay or reimburse medical expenses (including the 20 percent co-insurance not otherwise covered by the HDHP) only after the HDHP's minimum annual deductible has been satisfied, he is an eligible individual for the purpose of making contributions to an HSA.

Example 5. Same facts as in Example 1, except that Stuart is not covered by a health FSA. The employer's HRA is a retirement HRA that reimburses only those medical expenses incurred after the individual retires. Stuart is an eligible individual for the purpose of making contributions to an HSA before retirement because the HRA will pay or reimburse only medical expenses incurred after retirement.

Note. In addition, combinations of these arrangements that are consistent with these requirements would not disqualify an individual from being an eligible individual. For example, if an employer offers a combined post-deductible health FSA and a limited-purpose health FSA, this would not disqualify an otherwise eligible individual from contributing to an HSA.

Caution. In Notice 2005-42 [2005-23 I.R.B. 1204], the IRS announced that it is permissible for a Code Section 125 plan to provide for a 2½ month "grace period" after the end of a plan year during which a participant with a remaining balance in an FSA (at the end of the plan year) may be reimbursed for eligible expenses incurred up to 2½ months after the plan year's end. If a plan is not amended to include a grace period, unused FSA balances are forfeited at the end of the plan year under the so-called "use-it-or-lose-it" rule. The adoption of a grace period might prevent a participant from contributing to an HSA for the period (generally three months) that the employee had disqualifying "other coverage" (see Qs 4:11-4:16).

Example 6. Xavier is a participant in a pretax Code Section 125 cafeteria plan. The plan year is the calendar year. In 2005, Xavier signs up for an election of $1,500, but only uses $1,000 during the year. He makes no election

for 2006 and has no other health coverage. The plan contains a grace period of
2½ months (pursuant to Notice 2005-42) during which Xavier may submit
additional claims for expenses that occurred during the 2½ month grace
period. Xavier is not an HSA eligible individual during 2005 and the months
that include the grace period (January through March, 2006). The result
would be different if the FSA were a limited-purpose FSA (see above). In
addition, depending upon the deductible amount (e.g., $2,500 under the
FSA) and how it is applied with respect to 2005 and 2006, if Xavier were a
participant in a post-deductible health FSA (see below), he might not be
disqualified from being treated as an eligibile individual during the
2½ month period in 2006 (and being permitted to make a contribution).

Example 7. Same facts as in the preceeding example, except the cafeteria
plan year ends on June 5, 2006 (or earlier) and Xavier uses the entire $1,500
during the year and has no unused balance, although the plan contains a
general purpose health FSA (i.e., not a limited-purpose FSA or a post-deductible FSA). Xavier may be HSA eligible under a transitional rule for months
starting in July 2006 (see Q 4:18) because he has a zero balance in his health
FSA and does not have any other impermissible health coverage for months
ending after June 2006

Example 8. Same facts as in the preceeding example, except Xavier only uses
$500 during the year and the health FSA plan year ends on March 31, 2006.
Xavier is not HSA eligible (January through June 2006) because he has general pupose health FSA coverage (January through March) and an unused
balance in his health FSA account (April through June). The result would be
different if Xavier's employer were to amend the health FSA to make the grace
period unavailable for individuals who elect HDHP coverage under the transitional rule (see Q 4:18). In such case, Xavier would be eligible starting in
April 2006, when the impermissible coverage under his health FSA ended.
Otherwise, he is not eligible until July 2006 (the month after the grace period
ended).

[I.R.C. §§ 125(a), 125(d), 125(f), 223(a), 223(b), 223(c)(1)(A), 223(c)(1)(A)(ii),
223(b)(2)(A), 223(b)(2)(B), 223(c)(1)(B), 223(c)(2)(A), 223(c)(2)(C); Rev. Rul.
2004-45, 2004-22 I.R.B. 971; Rev. Rul. 2004-38, 2004-15 I.R.B. 717; I.R.S. Notices
2005-42, 2005-23 I.R.B. 1204, 2004-23, 2004-15 I.R.B. 725: 2002-45, 2002-2 C.B.
93; see also H.R. Conf. Rep. No. 108–391, at 841 (2003); regarding examples 7
and 8, see I.R.S. Notice 2005-86, 2005-49 I.R.B. 1075]

Suspended HRA. A suspended HRA is an HRA that, pursuant to an election
made before the beginning of the HRA coverage period, does not pay or
reimburse, at any time, any medical expense incurred during the suspension
period except preventive care, permitted insurance, and permitted coverage (if
otherwise allowed to be paid or reimbursed by the HRA). During the suspension
period, the individual participating in the HRA is an eligible individual for the
purpose of making contributions to an HSA. When the suspension period ends,
the individual is no longer an eligible individual because the individual is again
entitled to receive payment or reimbursement of Code Section 213(d) medical
expenses from the HRA. An individual who does not forgo the payment or

reimbursement of medical expenses incurred during an HRA coverage period is not an eligible individual for HSA purposes during that HRA coverage period.

Caution. If an HSA is funded through salary reduction under a cafeteria plan during the suspension period, the terms of the salary reduction election must indicate that the salary reduction is used only to pay for the HSA offered in conjunction with the HRA, not to pay for the HRA itself. Thus, the mere fact that an individual participates in an HSA funded pursuant to a salary reduction election does not necessarily result in attributing the salary reduction to the HRA.

Post-deductible health FSA or HRA. A post-deductible health FSA or HRA does not pay or reimburse any medical expense incurred before the $1,050/$2,100 (for 2006) minimum annual deductible is satisfied. The participating individual is an eligible individual for the purpose of making contributions to the HSA. The deductible for the HRA or health FSA ("other coverage") need not be the same as the deductible for the HDHP, but in no event may the HDHP or other coverage provide benefits before the minimum annual deductible. Where the HDHP and the other coverage do not have identical deductibles, contributions to the HSA are limited to the lower of the deductibles. In addition, although the deductibles of the HDHP and the other coverage may be satisfied independently by separate expenses, no benefits may be paid before the minimum annual deductible, $1,050/$2,100 (for 2006) has been satisfied.

Retirement HRA. A retirement HRA pays or reimburses only those medical expenses incurred after retirement (and no expenses incurred before retirement). In this case, the participating individual is an eligible individual for the purpose of making contributions to the HSA before retirement, but loses eligibility for coverage periods when the retirement HRA may pay or reimburse Code Section 223(d) medical expenses. Thus, after retirement, the individual is no longer an eligible individual for the purpose of the HSA.

[I.R.C. § 223(c)(3); Rev. Rul. 2004-45, 2004-22 I.R.B. 971]

Cafeteria Plan Grace Period Rules

Q 4:11   May a cafeteria plan permit employees to carry over unused contributions to a subsequent year?

Yes. Although the IRS generally takes the position that allowing cafeteria plan salary reduction contributions to carry over from one plan year to the next is a prohibited deferral of compensation [I.R.C. § 125(d)(2)(A); Prop. Treas. Reg. § 1.125-1, 1.125-2], this position was modified by Notice 2005-42. [2005-23 I.R.B. 1204]. Under the notice, an employer may adopt a grace period in a cafeteria plan so that the "forfeitures" of unused benefits that might otherwise occur at the end of the plan year under the so called "use-it-or-lose-it rule" can be avoided. (see Q 4:14).

Caution. Because the *annual* limitation for HSA contributions is determined on a monthly basis (see Qs 4:19, 4:32), the adoption of a grace period may have an affect upon an individual's eligibility to fully fund his or her HSA. For example, an individual who is participating in a health FSA with a grace period of 2½ months may only be permitted to contribute 9/12 of the full annual contribution amount because such individual may be considered an *"ineligible individual"* who has non-HDHP health coverage for the first three months of the year. [I.R.S. Notice 2005-86, 2005-49 I.R.B. 1075, amplifying Notice 2005-42, 2005-42 I.R.B. 1204 and Rev. Rul. 2004-45, 2004-22 I.R.B. 971; Treas. Press Release JS-3022 (Nov. 11, 2005)].

Q 4:12   How can an employer provide a grace period in a cafeteria plan?

A cafeteria plan document may, at the employer's option, be amended to provide for a grace period immediately following the end of each plan year. Expenses for qualified benefits incurred during the grace period may be paid or reimbursed from benefits or contributions remaining unused at the end of the immediately preceding plan year. To incorporate this rule, the cafeteria plan document must be amended prior to the end of its plan year (either calendar or fiscal) for which the change will be effective and must identify the benefits under the cafeteria plan to which the extended period will apply. As a practical matter, health and dependent care FSAs are the only benefits for which an extension of this type appears to make sense, and the extension could be limited to just one of these benefits. The new rule cannot be applied retroactively to earlier plan years.

The IRS has indicated informally that it would be permissible for a plan to impose a cap on the amount of benefits that are subject to the grace period as long as the cap is applied uniformly to all plan participants. Further, if an employer has more than one cafeteria plan, the extension can be limited to only one cafeteria plan.

Q 4:13   How long may the grace period last?

The grace period must not extend beyond the 15th day of the third calendar month after the end of the immediately preceding plan year to which it relates (i.e., "the 2½ month rule"). A plan is not required to adopt this rule, or to provide the full 2½ month extension (i.e, a lesser period is acceptable). If a cafeteria plan document is amended to include a grace period, a participant who has unused benefits or contributions relating to a particular qualified benefit from the immediately preceding plan year, and who incurs expenses for that same qualified benefit during the grace period, may be paid or reimbursed for those expenses from the unused benefits or contributions as if the expenses had been incurred in the immediately preceding plan year. The effect of the grace period is that the participant may have as long as 14 months and 15 days (the 12 months in the current cafeteria plan year plus the grace period) to use the benefits or contributions for a plan year before those amounts are "forfeited" under the "use-it-or-lose-it" rule. [I.R.S. Notice 2005-42, 2005-23 I.R.B. 1204]

Q 4:14   May unused benefits be cashed out or converted?

No. During the grace period, a cafeteria plan may not permit unused benefits or contributions to be cashed out or converted to any other taxable or nontaxable benefit. Unused benefits or contributions relating to a particular qualified benefit may be used only to pay or reimburse expenses incurred with respect to that particular qualified benefit. For example, unused amounts elected to pay or reimburse medical expenses in a health FSA may not be used to pay or reimburse dependent care or other expenses incurred during the grace period. To the extent any unused benefits or contributions from the immediately preceding plan year exceed the expenses for the qualified benefit incurred during the grace period, those remaining unused benefits or contributions may not be carried forward to any subsequent period (including any subsequent plan year) and are "forfeited" under the "use-it-or-lose-it" rule.

> **Practice Pointer.** As under current practice, employers may continue to pro-
> vide a "run-out" period after the end of the grace period, during which
> expenses for qualified benefits incurred during the cafeteria plan year and
> the grace period may be paid or reimbursed.

Q 4:15   How may an employer adopt a grace period?

An employer may adopt a grace period for the current cafeteria plan year (and subsequent cafeteria plan years) by amending the cafeteria plan document before the end of the current plan year. [I.R.S. Notice 2005-42, 2005-23 I.R.B. 1204]

> **Example 1.** An employer with a cafeteria plan year ending on December 31,
> 2005, amended the plan document before the end of the plan year to permit a
> grace period that allows all participants to apply unused benefits or contribu-
> tions remaining at the end of the plan year to qualified benefits incurred
> during the grace period immediately following that plan year. The grace pe-
> riod adopted by the employer ends on the fifteenth of the third calendar
> month after the end of the plan year March 15, 2006, for the plan year ending
> December 31, 2005). Benny, an employee, timely elected salary reduction of
> $1,000 for a health FSA for the plan year ending December 31, 2005. As of
> December 31, 2005, Benny has $200 remaining unused in his health FSA.
> Benny timely elected salary reduction for a health FSA of $1,500 for the plan
> year ending December 31, 2006. During the grace period from January 1
> through March 15, 2006, Benny incurs $300 of unreimbursed medical
> expenses. The unused $200 from the plan year ending December 31, 2005,
> is applied to pay or reimburse $200 of Benny's $300 of qualified medical
> expenses incurred during the grace period. Therefore, as of March 16,
> 2006, Benny has no unused benefits or contributions remaining for the
> plan year ending December 31, 2005. The remaining $100 of medical
> expenses incurred between January 1 and March 15, 2006 is paid or reim-
> bursed from Benny's health FSA for the plan year ending December 31, 2006.
> As of March 16, 2006, Benny has $1,400 remaining in the health FSA for the
> plan year ending December 31, 2006.

Example 2. Same facts as in the preceding example, except that Benny incurs $150 of qualified medical expenses during the grace period (January 1 through March 15, 2006). As of March 16, 2006, Benny has $50 of unused benefits or contributions remaining for the plan year ending December 31, 2005. The unused $50 cannot be cashed out, converted to any other taxable or nontaxable benefit, or used in any other plan year (including the plan year ending December 31, 2006). The unused $50 is subject to the "use-it-or-lose-it" rule and is "forfeited." As of March 16, 2006, Benny has the entire $1,500 elected in the health FSA for the plan year ending December 31, 2006.

Q 4:16   How long does a grace period remain in effect?

If adopted by an employer, the grace period remains in effect for the entire period even though the participant may terminate employment on or before the last day of the grace period. However, an employer may limit the availability of the grace period to certain cafeteria plan benefits and not others. For example, a cafeteria plan offering both a health FSA and a dependent care FSA may limit the grace period to the health FSA. In no event, may the grace period extend beyond the fifth day of the third calendar month after the end of the immediately preceding plan year to which it relates, but it may be adopted for a shorter period. [I.R.S. Notice 2005-42, 2005-23 I.R.B. 1204]

Eligibility Issues Regarding HSAs and Health FSAs

Q 4:17   May an individual who is otherwise eligible for an HSA be covered under certain types of health FSAs and remain eligible to contribute to an HSA?

Yes. An individual who is otherwise eligible for an HSA may be covered under certain types of health FSAs and remain eligible to contribute to an HSA. This result is the same even if the individual is covered by a health FSA sponsored by a spouse's employer.

As discussed in Q 4:10, one HSA-compatible arrangement is a limited-purpose health FSA, which pays or reimburses expenses only for preventive care and "permitted coverage" (e.g., dental care and vision care). Another HSA-compatible arrangement is a post-deductible health FSA, which pays or reimburses preventive care and other qualified medical expenses only if incurred after the minimum annual deductible for the HDHP ($1,050/$2,100 for 2006) is satisfied. This means that qualified medical expenses incurred before the HDHP deductible is satisfied may not be reimbursed by a post-deductible FSA even after the HDHP deductible had been satisfied. Thus, an otherwise HSA eligible individual will remain eligible if covered under a limited-purpose health FSA or a post-deductible FSA, or a combination of both. [Rev. Rul. 2004-45, 2004-1 C.B. 971]

Example 1. *General purpose health FSA during grace period.* Constellation amends its cafeteria plan document to provide a grace period, but takes no other action with respect to its general purpose health FSA. Because a health FSA that pays or reimburses all qualified medical expenses constitutes impermissible "other coverage" for HSA eligibility purposes, an individual who participated in the health FSA (or a spouse whose medical expenses are eligible for reimbursement under the health FSA) for the immediately preceding cafeteria plan year and who is covered by the grace period is not eligible to contribute to an HSA until the first day of the first month following the end of the grace period. For example, if the health FSA grace period ends March 15, 2006, an individual who did not elect a general health FSA or other disqualifying coverage for 2006 is HSA eligible on April 1, 2006, and may conribute 9/12ths of the 2006 HSA contribution limit. The result is the same even if a participant's health FSA has no unused contributions remaining at the end of the immediately preceding cafeteria plan year.

Example 2. *Mandatory conversion from health FSA to HSA-compatible health FSA for all participants.* Asteroid amends its cafeteria plan document to provide for both a grace period and a mandatory conversion of the general purpose health FSA to a limited-purpose or post-deductible FSA (or combined limited-purpose and post-deductible health FSA) during the grace period. The amendments do not permit an individual participant to choose between an HSA-compatible FSA or an FSA that is not HSA-compatible. The amendments apply to the entire grace period and to all participants in the health FSA who are covered by the grace period. Coverage of these participants by the HSA-compatible FSA during the grace period does not disqualify participants who are otherwise eligible individuals from contributing to an HSA during the grace period.

Note. As a practical matter, in the absence of transitional relief, an employer who offers both a health FSA and an HSA option to employees and wishes to make the grace period available under the health FSA has two choices:

1. Limit the 2½ month grace period to dental, vision, and preventive care expenses for all employees, or
2. Offer an unrestricted grace period to all employees.

Under choice (2), FSA participants who have HSAs during the year of the grace period will have limited contributions.

Transitional Relief

Q 4:18   When may an individual participating in a general purpose health FSA that provides coverage during a grace period be eligible to contribute to an HSA during the grace period?

For cafeteria plan years ending before June 5, 2006, an individual participating in a general purpose health FSA that provides coverage during a grace period will be eligible to contribute to an HSA during the grace period if the following requirements are met:

1. If not for the coverage under a general purpose health FSA, the individual would be an *eligible individual* during the grace period (i.e., in general, is covered under an HDHP and is not, while covered under an HDHP, covered under any impermissible other health coverage); and

2. Either the individual's (and the individual's spouse's) general purpose health FSA has no unused contributions or benefits remaining at the end of the immediately preceding cafeteria plan year; or

3. In the case of an individual who is not covered during the grace period under a general purpose health FSA maintained by the employer of the individual's spouse, the individual's employer amends its cafeteria plan document to provide that the grace period does not provide coverage to an individual who elects HDHP coverage (see Q 4:11).

[I.R.S. Notice 2005-86, 2005-49 I.R.B. 1075, amplifying Notice 2005-42, 2005-42 I.R.B. 1204 and Rev. Rul. 2004-45, 2004-22 I.R.B. 971; Treas. Press Release JS-3022 (Nov. 11, 2005)]

Contribution Limitations

Q 4:19   What is the maximum annual contribution that can be made to an HSA?

In general, the maximum annual contribution to an HSA is the sum of the limits determined separately for each month, based on status, eligibility, and health plan coverage as of the first day of the month (see Q 4:30). Special rules apply in the case of married individuals (see Q 4:33), ineligible individuals (see Q 4:39), embedded deductibles (see Qs 4:36–4:38), and post-deductible HRA (see Q 4:25). See annual contribution limit chart at Q 4:32.

Self-only coverage (statutory limits). The maximum annual contribution for eligible individuals with self-only coverage under an HDHP is the lesser of:

1. The annual deductible under the HDHP (see Qs 3:1, 3:16), or

2. $2,250 (base amount, as indexed) (see Q 4:21).

For 2006, the maximum annual HSA contribution for an eligible individual with self-only coverage is $2,700.

[I.R.C. § 223(b); I.R.S. Notice 2004-2, Q&A 12, 2004-2 I.R.B. 269]

Family coverage (statutory limits). For eligible individuals with family coverage under an HDHP, the maximum annual contribution is the lesser of:

1. The annual deductible under the HDHP (see Qs 3:6, 3:16), or

2. $5,150 (base amount, as indexed) (see Q 4:21).

For 2006, the maximum annual HSA contribution for an eligible individual with family coverage is $5,450.

In addition to the maximum contribution amount, catch-up contributions may be made by or on behalf of individuals age 55 or older who are also not enrolled in Medicare (see Qs 2:6, 2:14, 2:15, 4:12–4:29). [I.R.S. Notice 2004-2, Q&A 12, 2004-2 I.R.B. 269, as modified by I.R.S. Notice 2004-50, 2004-33 I.R.B. 196]

Note. The base amounts ($2,250/$5,150) are the amounts from which the initial 2004 and subsequent years HSA limits are derived (see Q 4:21).

Q 4:20   Are the HSA annual contribution limitations coordinated with contributions made to an Archer MSA?

Yes. The HSA contribution limitations are reduced (but not below zero) by the aggregate amounts contributed by the account owner to an Archer MSA. [I.R.C. § 223(b)(4)(A)] The family coverage limit is also reduced further by any contribution to an Archer MSA. [I.R.C. § 223(b)(5)(B)(i)]

Q 4:21   Are the maximum annual contribution amounts indexed for inflation?

Yes. The dollar amounts specified in Code Section 223(b) are indexed for inflation from 1997. [I.R.C. § 223(g)(1)] Thus, the statutory limit of $2,250 (for self-only coverage) was increased to $2,700, and the $4,500 (for family coverage) statutory limit was increased to $5,450 (for 2006). [Rev. Proc. 2005-70, § 3.22, 2005-47 I.R.B. 979; see also Treas. Press Release, JS-2996 (Nov. 22, 2005)] The amounts are adjusted to the nearest multiple of $50. [I.R.C. § 223(g)(2)] The maximum annual HSA contribution amounts (since HSAs were permitted for taxable years beginning in 2004) are shown in Table 4-1. The catch-up contribution limits are adjusted through 2009 (see Q 4:28).

Table 4-1. Maximum Annual HSA Contributions (Excluding Catch-Up Contributions) for Self-Only and Family Coverage

Coverage	2004	2005	2006
Self-only coverage ($2,250)	$2,600	$2,650	**$2,700**
Family coverage ($4,500)	$5,150	$5,250	**$5,450**

The same annual contribution limit applies whether the contributions are made by an employee, an employer, a self-employed person, or a family member. Table 4-1 shows the maximum HSA contribution for single and family coverage for 2004–2006, and Table 4-2 shows the maximum out-of-pocket expense under an HDHP, at specified plan deductibles under an HDHP for 2005 and 2006.

**Table 4-2. Maximum HSA Contributions and Out-of-Pocket Expenses
at Specified Plan Deductibles Under an HDHP**

	HDHP Maximum	Out-of-Pocket Contribution		Maximum HSA Coverage Deductible	
		2006	**2005**	2006	**2005**
Single	$1,000	$ 5,250	**$ 5,100**	$1,000	**$1,000**
	$1,500	$ 5,250	**$ 5,100**	$1,500	**$1,500**
	$2,000	$ 5,250	**$ 5,100**	$2,000	**$2,000**
	$2,500	$ 5,250	**$ 5,100**	$2,500	**$2,500**
	$3,000	$ 5,250	**$ 5,100**	$2,700	**$2,650**
	$4,000	$ 5,250	**$ 5,100**	$2,700	**$2,650**
	$5,000	$ 5,250	**$ 5,100**	$2,700	**$2,650**
Family	$2,000	$10,500	**$10,200**	$2,000	**$2,000**
	$3,000	$10,500	**$10,200**	$3,000	**$3,000**
	$4,000	$10,500	**$10,200**	$4,000	**$4,000**
	$5,000	$10,500	**$10,200**	$5,000	**$5,000**
	$6,000	$10,500	**$10,200**	$5,450	**$5,250**
	$7,000	$10,500	**$10,200**	$5,450	**$5,250**
	$8,000	$10,500	**$10,200**	$5,450	**$5,250**

Q 4:22 May an eligible individual have more than one HSA, and do contribution limits apply?

Yes. An eligible individual may establish more than one HSA and may contribute to more than one HSA. The same rules governing HSAs apply (e.g., maximum contribution limit), regardless of the number of HSAs established by an eligible individual. [I.R.S. Notice 2004-50, Q&A 64, 2004-33 I.R.B. 196]

Example. Yuri, an eligible individual, has a maximum contribution limit of $2,700 for 2006. Yuri's employer contributes $1,000 to an HSA on behalf of Yuri. Yuri opens a second HSA and contributes $1,700. If additional contributions are made for 2006 to either of the HSAs, those additional contributions will be excess contributions to Yuri's HSAs.

Q 4:23 How are contributions treated if the eligible individual has more than one HSA?

If an individual has more than one HSA, the aggregate annual contributions to all the HSAs are subject to the limit. [I.R.S. Notice 2004-2, Q&A 12 2004-2 I.R.B. 269]

Q 4:24 How is the contribution limit computed for an individual who begins coverage under an HDHP midyear and continues to be covered under the HDHP for the rest of the year?

The annual contribution limit is based upon the number of months in the year that an individual is covered by a qualifying HDHP. [I.R.S. Notice 2004-2, Q&A 13, 2004-2 I.R.B. 269]

> **Example.** On June 1, 2006, Carmen, an eligible individual, begins self-only coverage under an HDHP with an annual deductible of $3,000. If the annual deductible is $3,000 for the HDHP, then the lesser of the annual deductible and $2,700 (the 2006 limit) is $2,700. The monthly contribution limit is $225 ($2,700/12). The annual contribution limit is $1,575 (7 × $225).

> **Note.** Although "monthly limit" is used in calculating the annual HSA contribution, as noted in Qs 4:2 and 4:3, all of an HSA contribution may be contributed on the first day of eligibility, or otherwise as the account owner decides, up the due date of the federal income tax return (generally April 15 of the following year). Thus, there is no actual "monthly limit."

Q 4:25 What is the contribution limit for an eligible individual covered by an HDHP and also by a post-deductible HRA?

A post-deductible HRA that does not pay or reimburse any medical expense incurred before the minimum annual deductible is satisfied is described in Revenue Ruling 2004-45. The ruling states that the deductible for the HRA need not be the same as the deductible for the HDHP, but in no event may the HDHP or other coverage provide benefits before the minimum annual deductible is satisfied (generally the lesser of the plan's deductible or $2,700 for self-coverage for 2006). Where the HDHP and the other coverage do not have identical deductibles, contributions to the HSA are limited to the lower of the deductibles. In addition, although the deductibles of the HDHP and the other coverage may be satisfied independently by separate expenses, no benefits may be paid by the HDHP or the other coverage before the minimum annual deductible has been satisfied. [I.R.C. § 223(c)(2)(A)(i); Rev. Rul. 2004-45, § 4, 2004-22 I.R.B. 971]

> **Example.** In 2006, Roberta has self-only coverage under an HDHP with a deductible of $2,500. She is also covered under a post-deductible HRA (as

described in Rev. Rul. 2004-45) that pays or reimburses qualified medical expenses only after $2,100 of the HDHP's deductible has been satisfied (i.e., if Roberta incurs covered medical expenses of $2,250, the HRA will pay $150). Because the HRA's deductible of $2,100 is less than the HDHP's deductible of $2,500, Roberta's HSA contribution limit is $2,100.

Catch-Up Contributions

Q 4:26   Are catch-up contributions permitted?

Yes. For individuals (and their spouses covered under an HDHP) who have attained age 55 and who are also not enrolled in Medicare, the HSA contribution limit is increased by $700 in calendar year 2006. [I.R.S. Notice 2004-2, Q&A 14, 2004-2 I.R.B. 269, as modified by I.R.S. Notice 2004-50, 2004-33 I.R.B. 196] The 2007 catch-up limit is $800 (see Q 4:28).

After an individual has enrolled in Medicare (generally, at age 65, the Medicare eligibility age), contributions, including catch-up contributions, are no longer permitted to be made to an HSA (see Q 4:27).

Practice Pointer. If both spouses are age 55 or older and they both want to make "catch-up" contributions, they must each establish an HSA. Catch-up contributions may not be allocated between spouses. [I.R.C. § 223(b)(5)(B), 223(b)(5)(B)(ii)]

Q 4:27   May an otherwise HSA-eligible individual who is age 65 or older and thus eligible for Medicare, but is not enrolled in Medicare Part A or Part B, make the additional catch-up contributions for individuals age 55 or older?

Yes. An individual who is 65 or older but who is not enrolled in Medicare (Part A or Part B) may contribute to an HSA and make additional catch-up contributions if age 55 or older. [I.R.S. Notice 2004-50, Q&A 13, 2004-33 I.R.B. 196; I.R.S. Notice 2004-2, Q&A 14, 2004-2 I.R.B. 269, as corrected by I.R.S. Ann. 2004-67, 2004-36 I.R.B. 459]

Q 4:28   What are the catch-up contribution limits?

The catch-up contribution limit for 2004 was $500. The amount will increase in $100 increments annually until it reaches $1,000 in calendar year 2009 and thereafter (see Table 4-3). For 2006, the HSA catch-up limit is $700. [I.R.C. § 223(b)(3)(B); I.R.S. Notice 2004-50, Q&A 14, 2004-33 I.R.B. 196]

Table 4-3. Catch-Up Limits for Years 2004 through 2009

For Taxable Years	Catch-Up Limit
2004	$500
2005	$600
2006	$700
2007	$800
2008	$900
2009 and thereafter	$1000

Example 1. Mable, an eligible individual for the full year, is single, age 55, and not enrolled in Medicare in 2006. Her HSA contribution limit is increased by $700. For example, if Mable has self-only coverage, she can contribute up to the amount of her annual health plan deductible plus $700, but not more than $3,400 ($2,700 plus $700) for 2006.

Example 2. Same facts as in the preceding example, except that Mable is married to an older individual who is also not enrolled in Medicare. They have family coverage for the entire year. Because both spouses meet the age requirement, the total contribution under family coverage cannot be more than $6,850 ($5,450 + $700 + $700).

Example 3. For 2006, Mr. Biaggi and his wife both have family coverage under separate HDHPs. Mr. Biaggi is 58 years old, and Mrs. Biaggi is 53. Mr. Biaggi has a $6,000 deductible under his HDHP, and Mrs. Biaggi has a $2,000 deductible under her HDHP. Mr. and Mrs. Biaggi are both treated as being covered under the HDHP with the $2,000 deductible. Mr. Biaggi can contribute $1,700 to an HSA (one-half of the $2,000 deductible plus $700 additional contribution), and Mrs. Biaggi can contribute $1,000 to an HSA (unless Mr. and Mrs. Biaggi agree to a different division of the $2,000 deductible) for 2006.

Q 4:29 Are the maximum catch-up amounts indexed for inflation?

No. The catch-up limit amount for a calendar year is determined by statute (see Q 4:28). [I.R.C. 223(b)93)(B)]

Computing Annual Contributions

Q 4:30 How are catch-up contributions computed?

As with the annual contribution limit, the catch-up contribution limit is computed on a monthly basis, taking into account the number of months an individual was an eligible individual covered by an HDHP and a non-HDHP (see Q 4:19). [I.R.S. Notice 2004-2, Q&A 14, 2004-2 I.R.B. 269]

Example. Samantha had been participating in self-only coverage under an HDHP with an annual deductible of $1,100. She attains age 65, becomes eligible for Medicare benefits in July 2006 and is enrolled in Medicare. Samantha is no longer eligible to make HSA contributions (including catch-up contributions) after June 2006. Samantha's monthly contribution limit can be computed as follows:

$1,100 (the deductible)/12 + $700 (the 2006 catch-up limit)/12 = $150

Samantha may make contributions for January through June totaling $900 (6 × $150), but may not make any contributions with respect to July through December 2006 (see Q 4:32).

Q 4:31   Is there a simple method to determine the annual contribution limit if under age 55?

If an individual was under age 55 at the end of 2006, and was an eligible individual on the first day of every month during 2006 with the same annual deductible and coverage, the HDHP's annual contribution limit is the smaller of the following amounts:

- The HDHP's annual deductible, or
- $2,600 for 2004 ($5,150 for family coverage), or
- $2,650 for 2005 ($5,250 for family coverage), or
- $2,700 for 2006 ($5,450 for family coverage)

To determine the annual contribution in more complex instances, the following rules may be used:

1. Use the family coverage amount ($5,450 for 2006) if the individual and his or her spouse had more than one HDHP and one of the plans provided family coverage. Disregard any plans with self-only coverage.
2. If the individual and his or her spouse had more than one HDHP with family coverage, use the plan with the lowest annual deductible.
3. If the individual had family coverage with both an umbrella deductible and an embedded deductible for each individual covered by the plan, the annual contribution (and annual deduction for individuals making pretax contributions) is the smaller of $5,450 (for 2006) or the:
   a. Umbrella deductible, or
   b. Embedded individual deductible multiplied by the number of family members covered by the plan.

Example. In 2006, Jim and Nancy both had family coverage under an HDHP and were under age 55 at the end of 2006. The HDHP will pay benefits for (1) any family member whose covered expenses exceed $2,000 (the embedded individual deductible) and (2) all family members after the covered expenses exceed $5,000 (the umbrella deductible). The annual contribution is $4,000 (the smaller of $5,000 or $4,000 ($2,000 × 2)). Jim and Nancy's maximum contribution and HSA deduction is $4,000 (the smaller of $4,000 or $5,450 for 2006). This amount is entered on line 3 of Form 8889—*Health Savings Accounts (HSAs)*.

Q 4:32 How can the annual contribution limit be computed if the individual did not have the same coverage on the first day of every month during 2006 or was age 55 or older at the end of 2006?

If the individual did not have the same coverage on the first day of every month during 2006, or was age 55 or older at the end of 2006, the annual contribution limit can be computed by completing the chart in Table 4-4 for each month of 2006. A copy of the chart should be kept with the taxpayer's records. Enter the result on the worksheet next to the corresponding month. The amount entered is used to determine allowable HSA contributions, excess contributions, and deductions for contributions on Form 8889—*Health Savings Accounts (HSAs)*.

Practice Pointer. If eligibility and coverage did not change from one month to the next, enter the same number entered for the previous month.

Table 4-4. Annual Contribution Limit Computation

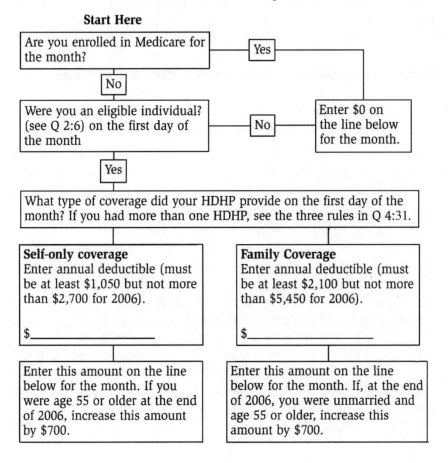

January	$_____
February	$_____
March	$_____
April	$_____
May	$_____
June	$_____
July	$_____
August	$_____
September	$_____
October	$_____
November	$_____
December	$_____
Total for all months	$_____
Limitation. Divide the total by 12.	$_____

This amount is the contribution limit for the year. The amount is entered on line 3 of Form 8889—*Health Savings Accounts (HSA)* and is used in computing contribution limits, excess contributions, and deduction amounts.

Special Computation Rules for Married Individuals

Q 4:33   If one or both spouses have family coverage, how is the contribution limit computed?

In the case of individuals who are married to each other, if either spouse has family coverage, generally both are treated as having family coverage. [I.R.C. § 223(b)(5)(A)]

Where both spouses have family HDHP coverage, but one spouse has other coverage, the contribution limits for the spouses vary depending on the specific circumstances. See the following examples:

Practice Pointer. A married couple's tax filing status (i.e., joint or separate) does not affect a particular spouse's contribution.

Example 1. Fred and Marcy, both age 35, are married and have family HDHP coverage with a $5,000 deductible. Fred has no other coverage. Marcy also has self-only coverage with a $200 deductible. Marcy, who has coverage under a low-deductible plan, is not eligible and cannot contribute to an HSA. Fred may contribute up to $5,000 to an HSA.

Example 2. Arnold and Beth, both age 35, are married and have family HDHP coverage with a $5,000 deductible. Arnold has no other coverage. Beth also has self-only HDHP coverage with a $2,000 deductible. Both Arnold and Beth are eligible individuals. Arnold and Beth are treated as having only family coverage. The combined HSA contribution by Arnold and Beth cannot exceed $5,000, to be divided between them by agreement.

Example 3. Quark and Monna, both age 35, are married and have family HDHP coverage with a $5,000 deductible. Quark has no other coverage. Monna has a disability and is enrolled in Medicare. Monna is not an eligible individual and cannot contribute to an HSA, but Quark may contribute up to $5,000 to an HSA.

Example 4. Kareem and Alicia are married. Kareem and Alicia will both turn age 55 by the end of 2006. Kareem has self-only coverage under an HDHP with a $1,500 deductible, and Alicia has family coverage under a separate HDHP with a $5,000 deductible. Since one of the spouses has family coverage, they are both treated as having family coverage for purposes of determining the annual contribution limit. Kareem can contribute $3,200 to an HSA (one-half of the deductible of $5,000 plus $700 catch-up) for 2006. Alicia can contribute $3,200 to an HSA (one-half of the deductible of $5,000 plus $700 catch-up) for 2006. Kareem and Alicia could agree on a different division of the $5,000 (see Q 4:40).

However, an individual may be eligible to contribute to an HSA if his or her spouse has non-HDHP *family* coverage, provided the spouse's coverage does not cover the individual. [Rev. Rul. 2005-25, 2005-18 I.R.B. 971]

Example 5. Harold and Wanda are a married couple, and both are age 35. Throughout 2006, Harold has self-only coverage under an HDHP with an annual deductible of $2,000 (see Q 3:1). Harold has no other health coverage, is not enrolled in Medicare, and may not be claimed as a dependent on another taxpayer's return. Wanda has non-HDHP family coverage for Wanda and for Harold's and Wanda's two dependents, but Harold is excluded from Wanda's coverage. Although Wanda has non-HDHP family coverage, Harold is not covered under that health plan. Harold is, therefore, an eligible individual.

Note. The special rules for married individuals treating both spouses as having family coverage do not apply, because Wanda's non-HDHP family coverage does not cover Harold. Thus, Harold remains an eligible individual and may contribute up to $2,000 to an HSA (the lesser of the HDHP deductible for self-only coverage or $2,700) for 2006. Harold may not make the catch-up contribution because he is not age 55 in 2006. Wanda has non-HDHP coverage and is, therefore, not an eligible individual.

Example 6. The same facts as in Example 5, except that Harold has HDHP family coverage for Harold and for one of Harold's and Wanda's dependents, with an annual deductible of $5,000. Wanda has non-HDHP family coverage for Wanda and for Harold's and Wanda's other dependent. Harold is excluded from Wanda's coverage. Because the non-HDHP family coverage does not cover Harold, the special rules that treat both spouses as having family coverage do not affect Harold's eligibility to make HSA contributions up to Harold's annual HSA contribution limit. Harold may, therefore, contribute up to $5,000 to an HSA (the lesser of the family HDHP deductible or

$5,450). Wanda has non-HDHP coverage and is, therefore, not an eligible individual.

Example 7. Horace and Wendy are a married couple, and both are age 35. Throughout 2006, Horace has HDHP family coverage for Horace and for Horace's and Wendy's two dependents, with an annual deductible of $5,000. In addition, Wendy is not covered under Horace's health plan and has no other health plan coverage. Horace may contribute up to $5,000 to an HSA (the lesser of the family HDHP deductible or $5,450). Because Horace's family coverage does not cover Wendy, the special rules do not apply to treat Wendy as having family coverage. Wendy has no health plan coverage and is, therefore, not an eligible individual.

Q 4:34   Which plan deductible limit is used for computing contributions when each spouse has family coverage under a separate health plan?

If each spouse has family coverage under a separate health plan, both spouses are treated as covered under the plan with the lowest deductible.

Example 1. Xavier and Christina, both age 35, are married and have family HDHP coverage with a $5,000 deductible. Xavier has no other coverage. Christina also has family HDHP coverage with a $3,000 deductible. Both Xavier and Christina are eligible individuals. Xavier and Christina are treated as having family HDHP coverage with the lowest annual deductible ($3,000). Thus, the maximum combined HSA contribution by Xavier and Christina is $3,000, to be divided between them by agreement.

Example 2. Paul and Pauleen, both age 58, are married and have family HDHP coverage with a $5,000 deductible. Paul has no other coverage. Pauleen also has family coverage with a $200 deductible. Paul and Pauleen are treated as having family coverage with the lowest annual deductible ($200), which is below the minimum required deductible amount of $2,000 for 2006 (see Q 3:1). Neither Paul nor Pauleen is an eligible individual, and neither may contribute to an HSA.

Example 3. Ike and Tina are married. Ike is 57, and Tina is 52. Ike and Tina both have family coverage under separate HDHPs. Ike has a $3,000 deductible under his HDHP, and Tina has a $2,000 deductible under her HDHP. Ike and Tina are treated as covered under the plan with the $2,000 deductible. Ike can contribute $1,700 to an HSA (one-half of the deductible of $2,000 plus $700 (the 2006 catch-up contribution)), and Tina can contribute $1,000 to an HSA (unless they agree to a different division) (see Q 4:40).

Example 4. Herbert and Neptune are married. Herbert is 40, and Neptune is 33. Herbert and Neptune each have a self-only HDHP. Herbert has a $1,500 deductible under his HDHP and Neptune has a $2,000 deductible under her HDHP. Herbert can contribute $1,000 to an HSA and Neptune can contribute $1,500 to an HSA.

Q 4:35   What is the contribution limit for spouses?

If either spouse has family coverage, the contribution limit for the spouses is the lowest deductible amount, divided equally between the spouses unless they agree on a different division (see Q 4:40). [I.R.C. § 223(b)(5)(A), 223(b)(5)(B)(ii)] However, both spouses may make the catch-up contributions for individuals age 55 or over without exceeding the family coverage limit. [I.R.C. § 223(b)(3)(A); I.R.S. Notice 2004-50, Q&A 15, 2004-33 I.R.B. 196] Special rules apply if an individual is excluded from his or her spouse's non-HDHP (see Q 4:33).

> **Example 1.** Tom and Jaxx are married. Tom has a family-coverage HDHP with a deductible of $2,000. The contribution limit is $1,000 for Tom and $1,000 for Jaxx, unless they agree on a different division. However, if eligible, Tom and Jaxx may make each make catch-up contributions to their HSA in addition to the $2,000 (as allocated) limit (see Q 4:26).

> **Note.** The family coverage limit is reduced further by any contribution to an Archer MSA. [I.R.C. § 223(b)(5)(B)(i)]

The following examples illustrate the contribution limits for married individuals completing Form 8889—*Health Savings Accounts (HSAs)* for 2006.

> **Example 2.** In 2006, Claudia has an HDHP for her family for the months of July through December. The annual deductible of the HDHP is $4,000. Claudia attains age 55 on September 5, 2006. On the worksheet for line 3, Claudia would show $4,000 for the three months July through September) and $4,700 for the three months October through December. She would divide the total of those amounts ($26,100) by 12 to determine her contribution limit ($2,175) for 2006.

> **Example 3.** In 2006, Tom has an HDHP for his family for the months of July through December (six months). The annual deductible of Tom's HDHP is $4,000. Tom is under age 55. On the worksheet for line 3 in the Form 8889 instructions, Tom enters $4,000 for each month (July through December) that he is an eligible individual. Tom divides the total of those amounts ($24,000) by 12 to determine his contribution limit ($2,000) for 2006.

> **Example 4.** For 2006, Bruce is an eligible individual with self-only HDHP coverage. His annual deductible is $1,200. Bruce gets married in March, and, beginning April 1, 2006, Bruce and his spouse have family HDHP coverage with a $2,400 deductible. Both Bruce and his wife, Linda, are under age 55. Linda is not an eligible individual. On the worksheet for line 3, Bruce would show $1,200 for the first three months and $2,400 for the last nine months. He would divide the total of those amounts ($25,200) by 12 to determine his contribution limit ($2,100) for the year. If Linda became an eligible individual during 2006, Bruce would have to allocate the deductible for the family HDHP coverage for the period they were both eligible individuals equally between him and his spouse unless they agree on a different allocation, including allocating nothing to one spouse. Bruce would not allocate the self-only deductible between himself and his spouse.

Q 4:36   What is an embedded individual deductible?

Although an HDHP may have an umbrella deductible (see Q 4:37), it may also provide payments for covered medical expenses if any individual member of the family incurs medical expenses in excess of the minimum annual deductible (see Q 4:34). That limit, which is applied to each family member, is referred to as the *embedded individual deductible*. [I.R.S. Notice 2004-50, Q&A 30, 2004-33 I.R.B. 196]

Q 4:37   What is an umbrella deductible?

An umbrella deductible is the stated maximum amount of expenses the family could incur before receiving benefits under the HDHP. [I.R.S. Notice 2004-50, Q&A 30, 2004-33 I.R.B. 196]

Q 4:38   How is the maximum annual HSA contribution limit determined for an eligible individual with family coverage under an HDHP that includes embedded individual deductibles and an umbrella deductible?

Generally, the maximum annual HSA contribution limit for an eligible individual with family coverage under an HDHP (without regard to catch-up contributions) is the lesser of:

- The annual deductible under the HDHP, or
- The statutory limit on family coverage contributions ($5,450 for 2006 or $5,250 for 2005; see Q 4:10).

[I.R.C. § 223(b)(2)(B), 223(g); I.R.S. Notice 2004-50, Q&A 30, 2004-33 I.R.B. 196]

However, the maximum annual HSA contribution limit for an eligible individual who has family coverage under an HDHP with embedded individual deductibles and an umbrella deductible is the least of the following amounts:

- The maximum annual contribution limit for family coverage ($5,450 for 2006; $5,250 for 2005);
- The umbrella deductible (see Q 4:37); or
- The embedded individual deductible (see Q 4:36) multiplied by the number of family members covered by the plan.

Note. The embedded individual deductible must satisfy the minimum annual deductible for an HDHP ($2,100 for 2006; $2,000 for 2004 and 2005). [I.R.S. Notice 2004-2, Q&A 3, 2004-2 I.R.B. 269]

Example 1. In 2006, Clyde and Morra, a married couple, have HDHP coverage for themselves and their two dependent children. The HDHP will pay benefits for (1) any family member whose covered expenses exceed $2,000 (the embedded individual deductible) and for (2) all family members after their covered expenses exceed $5,000. The umbrella deductible is $5,000.

The maximum annual statutory contribution limit is $5,250. The embedded deductible multiplied by the number of family members covered is $8,000 (4 × $2,000). Accordingly, the maximum annual contribution that Clyde and Morra can make to their HSAs is $5,000 (the least of $5,000, $5,450, or $8,000). The $5,000 limit is divided equally between Clyde and Morra ($2,500 each) unless they agree to a different division.

Example 2. The same facts as in the preceding example, except that the HDHP provides coverage only for Clyde and Morra. The maximum annual statutory contribution limit is $5,450 (the 2006 limit). The umbrella deductible is $5,000. The embedded individual deductible multiplied by the number of family members covered is $4,000 (2 × $2,000). The maximum annual contribution that Clyde and Morra can make to their HSAs for 2006 is $4,000 (the least of $5,000, $5,450, or $4,000).

Q 4:39   How do the maximum annual HSA contribution limits apply to family HDHP coverage that may include an ineligible individual?

If only one spouse is an eligible individual, only that spouse may contribute to an HSA, notwithstanding the special rule for married individuals that generally allows a married couple to divide the maximum HSA contribution between spouse and the treatment of both spouses having family coverage (see Q 4:33).

For 2006, the maximum annual HSA contribution for a married couple with family HDHP coverage is the lesser of (1) the lowest HDHP family deductible applicable to the family (minimum $2,100) or (2) the statutory maximum of $5,450 ($5,250 for 2005). [I.R.S. Notice 2004-50, Q&A 31, 2004-33 I.R.B. 196] (See Q 4:38 for an HDHP with embedded individual deductibles.)

Example 1. In 2006, Sandy and Darleen are a married couple, and neither is eligible to make catch-up contributions. Sandy and Darleen have family HDHP coverage with a $5,000 deductible. Sandy is an eligible individual and has no other coverage. Darleen also has self-only coverage with a $200 deductible. Darleen, who has coverage under a low-deductible plan, is not an eligible individual. Sandy may contribute $5,000 (the lesser of $5,000 or $5,450) to an HSA, while Darleen may not contribute to an HSA for 2006.

Example 2. The same facts as in the preceding example, except that, in addition to the family HDHP with a $5,000 deductible, Darleen has self-only HDHP coverage with a $2,000 deductible rather than self-only coverage with a $200 deductible. Both Sandy and Darleen are eligible individuals. Sandy and Darleen are treated as having only family coverage (see Q 4:33). The maximum combined HSA contribution by Sandy and Darleen is $5,000 (the lesser of $5,000 or $5,450 (the 2006 limit), to be divided between them by agreement.

Example 3. The same facts as Example 1, except that, in addition to the family HDHP with a $5,000 deductible, Darleen has family HDHP coverage with a

$3,000 deductible rather than self-only coverage with a $200 deductible. Both Sandy and Darleen are eligible individuals. Sandy and Darleen are treated as having family HDHP coverage with the lowest annual deductible (see Q 4:31). The maximum combined HSA contribution by Sandy and Darleen is $3,000 (the lesser of $3,000 or $5,450) for 2006, to be divided between them by agreement.

Example 4. The same facts as Example 1, except that, in addition to family coverage under the HDHP with a $5,000 deductible, Darleen has family coverage with a $500 deductible rather than self-only coverage with a $200 deductible. Sandy and Darleen are treated as having family coverage with the lowest annual deductible ($500). Neither Sandy nor Darleen is an eligible individual, and neither may contribute to an HSA for 2006.

Example 5. The same facts as Example 1, except that, in addition to the family HDHP with a $5,000 deductible, Darleen is enrolled in Medicare rather than having self-only coverage with a $200 deductible. Darleen is not an eligible individual. Sandy may contribute $5,000 to an HSA, while Darleen may not contribute to an HSA for 2006.

Example 6. Cory, a single individual, does not qualify for catch-up contributions. Cory is an eligible individual and has a dependent, Lorri. Cory and his dependent have family HDHP coverage with a $5,000 deductible. The dependent also has self-only coverage with a $200 deductible. Cory may contribute $5,000 to an HSA, while Lorri may not contribute to an HSA.

Q 4:40　How may spouses agree to divide the annual HSA contribution limit between themselves?

Code Section 223(b)(5) provides special rules for married individuals and states that HSA contributions (without regard to the catch-up contribution) "shall be divided equally between them unless they agree on a different division." Thus, spouses can divide the annual HSA contribution in any way they want, including allocating nothing to one spouse. [I.R.C. § 223(b)(5); I.R.S. Notice 2004-50, Q&A 32, 2004-33 I.R.B. 196; see also I.R.S. Notice 2004-2, Q&A 15, 2004-2 I.R.B. 269]

Example. In 2006, Tiger, an eligible individual, has self-only HDHP coverage with a $1,200 deductible from January 1 through March 31. In March, Tiger and Lola marry. Neither Tiger nor Lola qualifies for the catch-up contribution. From April 1 through December 31, 2006, Tiger and Lola have HDHP family coverage with a $2,400 deductible. Lola is an eligible individual from April 1 through December 31, 2006. Tiger and Lola's contribution limit for the nine months of family coverage is $1,800 (nine months of the deductible for family coverage, 9/12 × $2,400). Tiger and Lola divide the $1,800 between them. Tiger's contribution limit to his HSA for the three months of single coverage is $300 (three months of the deductible for self-only coverage, 3/12 × $1,200). The $300 limit is not divided between Tiger and Lola (see Q 4:33).

Q 4:41   How does an employer report HSA contributions?

Employer contributions to an HSA generally must be reported on the employee's Form W-2—*Wage and Tax Statement*. [I.R.C. § 6051] The IRS has released forms and instructions, similar to those required for Archer MSAs, on how to report HSA contributions, deductions, and distributions. [I.R.S. Notice 2004-2, Q&A 34, 2004-2 I.R.B. 269] Special considerations apply to partners and a more than 2 percent shareholder of an S Corporation (see Qs 4:142, 4:154). The report (form W-2) must be received by January 31 of the following year.

Q 4:42   How is an employer's contribution to an HSA reflected on Form W-2—*Wage and Tax Statement*?

An employer's contribution to an HSA is entered in box 12 of Form W-2 with code W. This applies regardless of whether the contributions are (1) made from employee contributions deducted pursuant to a cafeteria plan election or (b) made by the employer outside of Code Section 125 under the comparability requirements. The amount is entered by the HSA owner on Form 8889, *Health Savings Accounts (HSAs)*. Administration and compliance issues are more fully discussed in chapter 7. [I.R.S. Ann. 2004-2, 2004-2 I.R.B. 322]

Deductions for Individual Contributions

Q 4:43   Are an eligible individual's HSA contributions deductible?

Contributions made by an eligible individual to an HSA (which are subject to the limits described previously in this chapter) are deductible by the eligible individual in determining adjusted gross income. [I.R.C. § 223(a)] For an eligible individual, a deduction is permitted for the taxable year equal to an amount that is the aggregate amount paid in cash during such taxable year to an HSA by either the account owner or any other person. Employer contributions, including any pretax contributions through the employer's cafeteria plan, are not deductible, but instead are generally excludable from the employee's gross income (see Qs 4:44–4:51).

Q 4:44   How is the deduction taken on the individual's federal income tax return?

Generally, contributions made to an HSA, within permissible limits, by or on behalf of a taxpayer who is an eligible individual are deductible by a taxpayer under Code Section 223(a). The deduction is an adjustment to gross income (i.e., an above-the-line deduction) under Code Section 62(a)(19). [I.R.S. Notice 2004-2, Q&A 17, 2004-2 I.R.B. 269] However, if an employer makes a contribution, within permissible limits, to the HSA on behalf of an employee who is an eligible individual, the contribution is generally excluded from the employee's gross income and wages. [I.R.C. §§ 106(d), 223(a)] Special rules apply to partners and to a 2 percent or more shareholder of an S Corporation (see Qs 4:142–4:162). [See I.R.C. § 1372(b) (defining the term *2 percent shareholder*)]

Q 4:45 Is the deduction for contributions to a self-employed individual's own HSA taken into account in determining net earnings from self-employment under Code Section 1402(a)?

No. The deduction for making the contribution to the self-employed's own HSA is an adjustment to income on his or her personal income tax return. Because it is not a deduction attributable to a trade or business expense, the deduction is not taken on Form 1040, Schedule C—*Profit or Loss From Business* and is not taken into account when completing Schedule SE—*Self-Employment Tax*. (See Qs 4:142–4:162 regarding the tax treatment of partners and 2 percent shareholders of an S Corporation.) [I.R.S. Notice 2004-50, Q&A 84, 2004-33 I.R.B. 196]

Q 4:46 If a C corporation makes a contribution to the HSA of a shareholder who is not an employee of the C corporation, what are the tax consequences to the shareholder and to the C corporation?

If a C corporation makes a contribution to the HSA of a shareholder who is not an employee of the C corporation, the contribution will be treated as a distribution under Code Section 301, regarding distributions of property. The distribution is treated as a dividend to the extent the C corporation has earnings and profits. The portion of the distribution that is not a dividend is applied against and reduces the adjusted basis of the stock. To the extent the amount of the distribution exceeds the adjusted basis of the stock, the balance is treated as gain from a sale or exchange of property. [I.R.S. Notice 2004-50, Q&A 88, 2004-33 I.R.B. 196]

Q 4:47 Must an individual itemize deductions in order to claim a deduction for HSA contributions?

No. Allowable contributions are deductible whether or not an eligible individual itemizes deductions. [I.R.S. Notice 2004-2, Q&A 17, 2004-2 I.R.B. 269]

Q 4:48 Can HSA contributions be claimed as an itemized expense on the federal income tax return?

No. The deduction is taken "above the line" (see Q 4:43). The eligible individual cannot also deduct the contribution as a medical expense deduction under Code Section 213. [I.R.S. Notice 2004-2, Q&A 17, 2004-2 I.R.B. 269]

Q 4:49 Are contributions made by a family member or other person on behalf of an eligible individual deductible?

Yes. Contributions made by a family member (or other person) on behalf of an eligible individual to an HSA (which are subject to the limits described in Qs 4:19–4:29) are deductible by the eligible individual in computing adjusted gross income (whether or not the eligible individual itemizes deductions). [I.R.S. Notice 2004-2, Q&A 18, 2004-2 I.R.B. 269]

Q 4:50   May an individual who may be claimed as a dependent on another person's tax return deduct contributions to an HSA?

No. An individual who may be claimed as a dependent on another person's tax return is not an eligible individual and may not deduct contributions to an HSA. [I.R.C. § 223(b)(6); I.R.S. Notice 2004-2, Q&A 18, 2004-2 I.R.B. 269]

Q 4:51   Do community property rules apply in determining limitations on contributions or their deductibility?

No. HSA limitations are determined without regard to community property rules. [I.R.C. § 223(d)(4)(D)]

Employer Contributions in General

Q 4:52   May employer contributions exceed the maximum allowable amount for the individual?

No. The combined contribution limit to an HSA from all sources (i.e.,the account owner, a family member or other individual, or an employer) cannot exceed the maximum allowable amount for the eligible individual.

Note. If the employer chooses to make HSA contributions, then the employer is required to make comparable HSA contributions for all participating employees (i.e., eligible employees with comparable coverage) during the same period unless contributions are made through a cafeteria plan (see Q 4:93).

Practice Pointer. The IRS final comparability regulations (final rules) governing employer contributions to HSAs were issued on July 31, 2006. [Treas. Reg. § 54.4980G-1 through 5; 71 Fed. Reg. 43056] The final rules clarify the steps employers need to take in order to fall within the "cafeteria plan exception," allowing the employer's HSA contributions to be subject to the cafeteria plan nondiscrimination rules under Code Section 125 rather than the comparability rules. In addition, the final regulations add some important flexibility, such as providing an exception for collectively bargained employees and expanding the categories of HDHP coverage for which employers may vary HSA contributions.

Q 4:53   How are employer payments to an HSA treated?

Employer payments to an HSA are generally excluded from an employee's gross income (see Q 4:43). Any amount paid by an employer to an HSA that exceeds the statutory contribution limits (see Q 4:19) is treated as the payment of compensation to the employee (other than a self-employed individual who is an employee within the meaning of Code Section 401(c)(1)). The payment is included in the individual's gross income in the taxable year for which the amount was contributed, whether or not the employee is allowed to deduct the HSA contribution. [I.R.C. §§ 106(d)(1), 223(d)(4)(C)]

Q 4:54　What tax advantages does an employer receive by allowing employees to make HSA contributions through the employer's cafeteria plan?

HSA contributions by an employee through a Section 125 cafeteria plan (provided they are within statutory limits) are not counted as wages for purposes of the Federal Insurance Contributions Act (FICA), the Federal Unemployment Tax Act (FUTA), or the Railroad Retirement Tax Act. Thus, by allowing employees to make HSA contributions through the cafeteria plan, the employer will reduce its liability for these taxes because the employee will have lower wages for purposes of calculating these taxes. [See, I.R.S. Notice 2004-2, Q&A-19, 2004-2 I.R.B. 269] In addition, the employee will not be required to pay his or her share of FICA tax on such contributions.

As a practical matter, the FUTA savings is limited, as the employer pays only 6.2 percent on the first $7,000 of an employee's wages, so unless the HSA contribution reduces the employee's wages below $7,000, it will not have an impact. [I.R.C. § 3306(b)(1)] The FICA savings is more significant: the employer's share for Medicare hospital coverage is 1.45 percent of all of an employee's wages, and the employer's share for Social Security is 6.2 percent on the employee's wages up to $94,200 (the 2006 limit.) [I.R.C. § 3111(a)-(b)] So, any reduction of wages will directly reduce the amount of FICA an employer is required to pay. Similarly, the employee share of FICA is the same as the employer share, so any reduction in wages will also save the employee money in FICA tax. [I.R.C. § 3101(a)-(b)]

Q 4:55　Can an employer make higher contributions to the HSA accounts of participants with chronic health conditions?

Possibly. If the contribution is made "through the cafeteria plan," the comparable contribution rule under Code section 4980E does not apply, and the employer has flexibility to vary contributions as long as the nondiscrimination rules of Code Section 125 are satisfied. Notice 2004-50, Q&A-47 and 49 [2004-33 I.R.B. 196], states that the comparable contribution rule does not apply to contributions made through a cafeteria plan. If the contribution is not made through the cafeteria plan, it would violate the comparable contribution requirements under Code Section 4980E and proposed regulations.

Final Regulations Note. In perhaps the most significant change from the proposed regulations, the final regulations clarify what requirements are necessary to "make contributions through a cafeteria plan." In the proposed regulations, it was not clear whether employees must be given the option to receive cash instead of contributions with respect to *all* employer HSA contributions in order for such contributions to be considered "made through a cafeteria plan." The final regulations make clear that an employer's contributions will be considered made through a cafeteria plan if (1) employees are permitted to make their own contributions to an HSA by salary reduction through a cafeteria plan and (2) all contributions are made pursuant to a written cafeteria plan document.

The significance of this clarification is that contributions made through a cafeteria plan are subject to the nondiscrimination requirements of Code Section 125 rather than the comparable contribution requirements of Code Section 4980G. This means that an employer is prohibited from favoring highly compensated employees or key employees with respect to cafeteria plan eligibility or benefits, including HSA contributions, but the employer is not required to contribute similar amounts to the HSAs of employees. This should allow employers more flexibility and creativity in benefit design structures. For example, by using a cafeteria plan, employers can provide contributions to match employees' contributions to their HSAs. Employers can also provide various incentives (e.g., by contribution to HSAs of employees who participate in health risk assessment, disease management programs, or wellness programs). None of these contribution structures would pass the comparable contribution requirement under Code Section 4980G without this exception.

Note. The Bush Administration supports creating a specific exception that would allow employers to make higher contributions to the HSAs of chronically ill employees (see Q 1:28).

Q 4:56 Are contributions to an HSA subject to the nonqualified deferred compensation rules under Code Section 409A?

No. An HSA is not subject to the nonqualified deferred compensation plan rules under Code Section 409A, even though all contributions are fully vested and nonforfeitable (see Q 2:1). Code Section 409A provides that all amounts deferred under a nonqualified deferred compensation plan for all taxable years are currently includible in gross income to the extent not subject to a substantial risk of forfeiture and not previously included in gross income, unless certain requirements are met. These rules are not limited to arrangements between an employer and employee. However, there is a specific exemption for HSAs under IRS guidance, which provides that the term *nonqualified deferred compensation plan* does not include an HSA under Code Section 223. Thus, an HSA is not treated as a nonqualified deferred compensation plan under Code Section 409A(d)(1)(B). [See, I.R.S. Notice 2005-1, Q&A 3(c), 2005-2 I.R.B. 274; Prop. Treas. Reg. § 1.409A-1(a)(5)]]

> **Practice Pointer.** IRS guidance similarly provides that an Archer MSA under Code Section 220 and a medical reimbursement arrangement, including a Health Reimbursement Arrangement, that satisfies the requirements of Code Sections 105 and 106 is not treated as a nonqualified deferred compensation plan under Code Section 409A(d)(1)(B).

Employer Responsibility

Q 4:57 Is the employer responsible for determining employee eligibility for an HSA?

To some extent. With respect to specific employee HSA eligibility, the employer is only responsible for determining:

1. Whether the employee is covered under an HDHP (and the amount of the deductible) or low-deductible health plan or plans (including health FSAs and HRAs) sponsored by that employer; and

2. The employee's age (for catch-up contributions).

[I.R.S. Notice 2004-50, Q&A 81, 2004-33 I.R.B. 196]

> **Note.** If the employer chooses to make HSA contributions, then the employer is required to make comparable HSA contributions for all participating employees (i.e., eligible employees with comparable coverage) during the same period (see Qs 4:93–4:100).

Q 4:58   May the employer rely on an employee's representation of their age?

Yes. The employer may rely on the employee's representation as to his or her date of birth. [I.R.S. Notice 2004-50, Q&A 81, 2004-33 I.R.B. 196]

Q 4:59   Is the employer responsible for determining whether HSA distributions are used exclusively for qualified medical expenses?

No. The individual who establishes the HSA is responsible for determining whether the distributions are used exclusively for the payment of qualified medical expenses—so as to be excludable from gross income (see Q 6:4). [I.R.S. Notice 2004-2, Q&A 30, 2004-2 I.R.B. 269]

Q 4:60   Is an employer permitted to structure cafeteria plan elections for HSAs as negative elections?

Yes. An employer is permitted to structure cafeteria plan elections for all cafeteria plan benefits as negative elections. [See Rev. Rul. 2002-27, 2002-20 I.R.B. 925] HSA salary reduction elections should be governed by this revenue ruling.

> **Example.** J Corporation holds an annual open enrollment period and communicates that employees who elected to make salary reduction contributions to the HSA for 2005 through J Corporation's cafeteria plan, and want to keep the same election and contribution for 2006, need not take any action at open enrollment (i.e., their 2005 election carries over to 2006 unless they make a different election). Sally elected to contribute $1,000 to her HSA through J Corporation's cafeteria plan in 2005, and wishes to make this same election for 2006. Sally takes no action at open enrollment, and J Corporation treats Sally as having made a $1,000 cafeteria plan election to the HSA for 2006. J Corporation has satisfied applicable cafeteria plan requirements.

Exclusion and Deductibility of Employer Contributions

Q 4:61   What is the tax treatment of employer contributions on behalf of an eligible individual?

In the case of an employee who is an eligible individual, employer contributions (provided they are within the limits described in Q 4:19) to an employee's HSA are treated as an employer-provided coverage for medical expenses under an accident or health plan and are excludable under Code Section 106(d). [I.R.S. Notice 2004-2, Q&A 19, 2004-2 I.R.B. 269]

Q 4:62   Are employer contributions on behalf of an eligible individual excluded from the employee's income?

Yes. In the case of an employee who is an eligible individual, employer contributions (provided they are within the limits described in Q 4:19) to an employee's HSA are excludable from the employee's gross income under Code Section 106(d). [I.R.S. Notice 2004-2, Q&A 19, 2004-2 I.R.B. 269]

Note. An employee does not get a deduction for employer contributions to his or her HSA or to amounts the employee contributes on a pretax basis through the employer's cafeteria plan. [I.R.S. Notice 2004-2, Q&A 19, 2004-2 I.R.B. 269]

Q 4:63   Are contributions to an employee's HSA through a cafeteria plan treated as made by the employer or employee?

Contributions to an employee's HSA through a cafeteria plan are treated as employer contributions. Thus, as noted above, an employee does not get a deduction for these contributions when made to his or her HSA. [I.R.S. Notice 2004-2, Q&A 19, 2004-2 I.R.B. 269]

Q 4:64   Are employer contributions subject to Railroad Retirement taxes?

No. Employer contributions are not generally subject to the Railroad Retirement Tax Act. For purposes of the Railroad Retirement Act, the term *compensation* does not include any payment made to or for the benefit of an employee if, at the time of such payment, it is reasonable to believe that the employee will be able to exclude such payment from income under Code Section 106(d), regarding the exclusion of employer contributions to accident and health plans, from an employee's gross income. [I.R.C. §§ 106(b)(2), 106(d), 3231(e)(11); I.R.S. Notice 2004-2, Q&A 19, 2004-2 I.R.B. 269]

Q 4:65   Are employer contributions subject to income withholding from wages?

No. Employer contributions are not subject to withholding from wages for federal income tax purposes if it is reasonable to believe, at the time of payment, that the employee will be able to exclude such payment from income under Code Section 106(d), regarding the exclusion of employer contributions to HSAs, from an employee's gross income. [I.R.C. §§ 3401(a)(21), 3401(a)(22); I.R.S. Notice 2004-2, Q&A 19, 2004-2 I.R.B. 269]

Q 4:66   Are employer contributions subject to FICA taxes?

No. Employer contributions are not subject to FICA taxes. [I.R.S. Notice 2004-2, Q&A 19, 2004-2 I.R.B. 269]

Q 4:67   Are employer contributions made under a cafeteria plan subject to FICA taxes?

No. Employer contributions made under a cafeteria plan are not subject to FICA taxes if (1) such payment would not be treated as wages without regard to such plan and (2) it is reasonable to believe that, if Code Section 125 applied, that section would not treat any wages as constructively received. [I.R.C. § 3121(a)(5)(G); I.R.S. Notice 2004-2, Q&A 19, 2004-2 I.R.B. 269]

Q 4:68   Are employer contributions subject to taxes under the FUTA?

No. Employer contributions are not subject to FUTA taxes if it is reasonable to believe at the time of payment that the employee will be able to exclude such payment from income under Code Section 106(d) regarding the exclusion of employer contributions to accident and health plans from an employee's gross income. [I.R.C. §§ 106(b)(2), 106(d), 3306(b)(18); I.R.S. Notice 2004-2, Q&A 19, 2004-2 I.R.B. 269]

Q 4:69   May an employee deduct employer contributions made on his or her behalf on his or her federal income tax return?

No. An employee may not deduct employer contributions made on his or her behalf on his or her federal income tax return, either as HSA contributions or as medical expense deductions under Code Section 213. [I.R.S. Notice 2004-2, Q&A 19, 2004-2 I.R.B. 269]

Q 4:70   What is the tax treatment of an HSA?

An HSA is generally exempt from tax (as is an IRA or Archer MSA), unless it has ceased to be an HSA (see Q 6:51). Earnings on amounts in an HSA are not includible in gross income while held an HSA (i.e., inside buildup is not taxable). [I.R.C. § 223(e)(1); I.R.S. Notice 2004-2, Q&A 20, 2004-2 I.R.B. 269] (See Q 6:4 regarding the taxation of distributions from the HSA.)

An HSA is, however, subject to tax on its unrelated business taxable income under Code Section 511. Although there is a specific exemption of $1,000, this tax may apply if the account is used for purposes inconsistent with its exempt purpose (e.g., an HSA engaged in the operation of a grocery store, as opposed to an investment in a grocery store). [I.R.C. §§ 223(e)(1), 511, 512]

Note. An employer identification number (EIN) is required for an HSA that must file a return to report taxable unrelated business income.

Timing of Contributions

Q 4:71   When may HSA contributions be made?

Contributions for the taxable year can be made in one or more payments, at the convenience of the individual or the employer, at any time prior to the time prescribed by law (without extensions) for filing the eligible individual's federal income tax return for that year, but not before the beginning of that year.

Q 4:72   Is there a deadline for contributions to an HSA for a taxable year?

Yes. Contributions for the taxable year can be made in one or more payments, at the convenience of the individual or the employer, at any time prior to the time prescribed by law (without extensions) for filing the eligible individual's federal income tax return for that year, but not before the beginning of that year. For calendar-year taxpayers, the deadline for contributions to an HSA is generally April 15 following the year for which the contributions are made. Although the annual contribution is determined monthly, the maximum contribution may be made on the first day of the year. [I.R.S. Notice 2004-2, Q&A 21, 2004-2 I.R.B. 269] (See Qs 4:73–4:85 regarding excess contributions.)

Example. Fanny has self-only coverage under an HDHP with a deductible of $1,500, and she also has an HSA. Fanny's employer contributes $200 to her HSA at the end of every quarter in 2006 and at the end of the first quarter in 2007 (March 31, 2007). Fanny can exclude from income in 2006 all of the employer contributions of $1,000 (5 × $200) because Fanny's exclusion for all contributions does not exceed the maximum annual HSA contributions.

Excess Contributions

Q 4:73   How may an excess HSA contribution be created?

In general, an excess contribution results when contributions to all of an individual's HSAs exceed the maximum amount that may be deducted under Code Section 223(a) or excluded from gross income under Code Section 106(d) in a taxable year. [I.R.C. § 223(f)(3)(B)] An excess could also result from an unqualified direct transfer or rollover.

Q 4:74   What is an excess contribution for purposes of the 6 percent excise tax?

For any year, the term *excess contribution* to an HSA means the sum of:

1. The aggregate amount contributed for the taxable year to the accounts (other than rollover contribution and direct transfers, see Q 4:73) that is neither excludable from gross income under Code Section 106(d) regarding employer-provided coverage nor allowable as an HSA deduction for such year; and

2. The amount of any excess contribution for the preceding taxable year, reduced by the sum of:

    a. Distributions from accounts that were included in gross income because they were not used for qualified medical expenses [I.R.C. § 223(f)(2)], and

    b. The excess (if any) of:

        — The maximum amount allowable as an HSA deduction without regard to the source of contributions, over

        — The amount contributed to the accounts for the taxable year.

[I.R.C. §§ 220(f)(5), 223(f)(5), 4973(g)(1)-(2)]

> **Note.** A contribution that is distributed from the HSA in a correcting distribution of an excess contribution before the due date (including extensions) of an individual's federal income tax return is not treated as an amount contributed for the current year. [I.R.C. § 4973(g)]

Q 4:75   Is it permissible to deduct an HSA contribution by an individual that exceeds the maximum amount that may be contributed in a taxable year?

No. Contributions made by an individual, or on behalf of an individual, to an HSA are not deductible to the extent they exceed the limits described in Q 4:19. [I.R.S. Notice 2004-2, Q&A 22, 2004-2 I.R.B. 269]

Q 4:76   Is it permissible to deduct an HSA contribution by an employer that exceeds the maximum amount that may be deducted or excluded from the individual's gross income in a taxable year?

No. Contributions made to an HSA by an employer, or made on behalf of an individual to an HSA by an employer, are not deductible by the individual to the extent they exceed the limits described in Q 4:19. [I.R.C. § 223(a); I.R.S. Notice 2004-2, Q&A 22, 2004-2 I.R.B. 269]

Q 4:77   May an employer's HSA contribution to an ineligible individual be deducted by the employee?

No. A contribution by an employer on behalf of an employee who is not an eligible individual (or that exceeds the amount allowed to be contributed to the HSA) is not deductible by the employee (see Q 4:78). [I.R.C. § 223(a); I.R.S. Notice 2004-2, Q&A 22, 2004-2 I.R.B. 269] Unless the excess contribution is corrected by the employee, the employee may be subject to an excess contribution penalty tax (see Q 4:64).

Q 4:78   Are excess contributions subject to penalty?

Yes. In general, an excise tax of 6 percent for each taxable year is imposed on the account owner for excess individual and employer contributions (see Q 4:74). [I.R.C. § 4973(a)(5); I.R.S. Notice 2004-2, Q&A 22, 2004-2 I.R.B. 269]

Q 4:79   Can the excess contribution penalty be avoided?

Yes. The 6 percent cumulative penalty can be avoided if the excess contributions for a taxable year (and the net income attributable to such excess contributions) are paid to the account owner before the last day prescribed by law (including extensions) for filing the account owner's federal income tax return for the taxable year. [I.R.C. § 223(f)(3)(A)(i)]

Q 4:80   When is the net income attributable to the excess contribution taxable?

The net income attributable to the excess contribution is included in the account owner's gross income for the taxable year in which the distribution is received. However, the 6 percent excise tax is not imposed on the excess contribution, and the distribution of the excess contributions is not taxed. [I.R.C. § 223(f)(3)(A); I.R.S. Notice 2004-2, Q&A 22, 2004-2 I.R.B. 269]

Q 4:81   What is the result if the net income is not distributed in a correcting distribution?

If there is any net income on the excess contribution, it must be distributed in the correcting distribution. If the net income is not distributed, the amount is treated as a regular distribution and the 6 percent tax applies (see Q 4:74). [I.R.C. § 223(f)(3)(A)(ii)]

Q 4:82   Is the excess contribution distributed in a correcting distribution subject to tax?

No. Although the net income in a correcting distribution is taxable, the distribution of an excess contribution (timely corrected) is not subject to tax as long as such contribution was made on an after-tax basis by the individual. [I.R.C. § 223(f)(3)(A); I.R.S. Notice 2004-2, Q&A 22, 2004-2 I.R.B. 269]

Q 4:83   May an excess contribution be corrected after the extended due date of the individual's federal income tax return?

Yes. However, unless the amount received in the correcting distribution (not timely completed) is used to pay for qualified medical expenses, the amount distributed will be taxable and subject to a 10 percent additional tax, unless an exception applies (see Q 6:62). The 6 percent penalty, however, will no longer apply to the excess contribution after a correcting distribution is made.

> **Example.** Marleen, an eligible individual, made an excess contribution into an HSA of $300 for 2006. She removes $310 (the excess contribution plus gain) on February 10, 2007. The gain of $10 is taxable in 2007. The returned excess of $300 is not subject to income tax or the 10 percent additional tax (see Q 6:66). The gain ($10), however, may be subject to the 10 percent additional tax. The 6 percent penalty does not apply for 2006 because the excess amount was withdrawn (with gain) before the due date of Marleen's federal income tax return (including extensions).

> **Example.** Hank, an eligible individual, made an excess contribution into an HSA of $500 for 2006. His federal income tax return is due on April 15, 2007 (actually April 16, 2007, because the 15th is a Sunday). He does not have a filing extension. Assume Hank removes $600 on April 25, 2007. The correcting distribution (made after April 17) was not timely made. Hank must pay a 6 percent penalty tax on the $500 excess contribution. Unless the amount is used to pay for qualified medical expenses, the amount distributed ($600) will also be taxable and, unless an exception applies, also subject to a 10 percent penalty tax (see Qs 6:4, 6:60). Assuming no excess contributions are made for 2007, the 6 percent excess contribution penalty tax will no longer apply with respect to 2006.

Q 4:84   How are earnings attributable to the excess HSA contribution calculated?

Earnings attributable to excess HSA contributions are computed in exactly the same manner as excess IRA contributions under Treasury Regulations Section 1.408-11. [I.R.S. Notice 2004-50, Q&A 34, 2004-33 I.R.B. 196; see also I.R.S. Notice 2004-2, Q&A 22, 2004-2 I.R.B. 269]

Q 4:85   May an individual who has not made excess HSA contributions treat a distribution from an HSA other than for qualified medical expenses as the withdrawal of excess HSA contributions?

No. An individual may not elect to treat a distribution as a correction of an excess contribution unless the individual's contribution limit is exceeded. [I.R.S.

Notice 2004-50, Q&A 35, 2004-33 I.R.B. 196] Any such withdrawal is deemed a withdrawal for nonqualified medical expenses and includible in the individual's gross income. The 10 percent additional tax also applies, unless otherwise excepted (see Q 6:62). [I.R.S. Notice 2004-50, Q&A 35, 2004-33 I.R.B. 196]

Rollovers and Direct Transfers

Q 4:86 Are rollover contributions and transfers to an HSA permitted?

Generally, yes. Rollover contributions from Archer MSAs and other HSAs into an HSA are permitted (see chapter 5).

Q 4:87 Are rollovers and direct transfers subject to the annual contribution limits?

No. Rollovers are not subject to the annual contribution limits.

Note. Rollovers from an IRA, from an HRA, or from a health FSA to an HSA are not permitted. Rollover and trustee-to-trustee transfers are more fully discussed in chapter 5.

Employer Contributions and ERISA

Q 4:88 Is an HSA established in connection with an employment-based group health plan treated as an employee welfare benefit plan under Title I of ERISA?

Generally, no. An employer can make contributions to the HSA of an eligible individual without being considered to have established or maintained the HSA as an ERISA-covered plan, provided that the employer's involvement with the HSA is limited. ERISA issues are more fully discussed in chapter 8.

[C.F.R. § 2510.3-1(j)(1)-(4); see also C.F.R. § 2509.99-1 relating to payroll deduction IRAs]

Q 4:89 Is an employer required to make COBRA continuation coverage available with respect to an HSA?

No. An employer's contribution to an HSA is not considered to be part of a group health plan. [I.R.C. § 106(b)(5), 106(d)(2); see also Treas. Reg. § 54.4980B-2, A-1, regarding Archer MSAs] Thus, an employer is not required to make COBRA continuation coverage available with respect to an HSA. [I.R.S. Notice 2004-2, Q&A 35, 2004-2 I.R.B. 269] It should be noted, however, that an ERISA-covered HSA (i.e., an employee welfare benefit plan) may be subject to COBRA (see Qs 8:19, 8:21). [ERISA § 607(i)]

Q 4:90   Do the rules under Code Section 419 regarding funded welfare benefit plans affect contributions by an employer to an HSA?

No. Contributions by an employer to an HSA are not subject to the rules under Code Section 419 regarding funded welfare benefit plans. An HSA is a trust or custodial account that is exempt from tax under Code Section 223. Thus, an HSA is not a *fund* under Code Section 419(e)(3) and, therefore, is not a *welfare benefit fund* under Code Section 419(e)(1). [I.R.S. Notice 2004-2, Q&A 36, 2004-2 I.R.B. 269] Neither are contributions subject to the excise tax with respect to funded welfare benefit plans that provide disqualified benefits. [I.R.C. § 4976(a)(1)]

Q 4:91   Do the minimum funding standards under Code Section 412 apply to an HSA?

No. Code Section 412 applies only to certain types of qualified plans under Code Sections 401(a) or 403(a). [I.R.C. § 412(a)] Thus, an employer HSA is not subject to the excise tax relating to minimum funding standards. [I.R.C. § 412(a), 4971(a)]

Q 4:92   Are employer contributions to an HSA subject to the 10 percent tax on nondeductible employer contributions?

No. The excise tax under Code Section 4972 on nondeductible employer contributions does not apply to an HSA. [I.R.C. § 4972(a), 4972(d)] It should be noted that employer contributions to an HSA are generally excluded from an employee's gross income (see Q 4:43).

Comparability of Employer Contributions

Q 4:93   What is the HSA comparability rule?

In general, if an employer chooses to make HSA contributions, then the employer is required to make comparable HSA contributions for all eligible employees with the same category of coverage. Thus, comparable participating employees must receive comparable contributions if any are made. [I.R.C. § 4980E(d) 4980G; Prop. Treas. Reg. § 54.4980G-1, Q&A 1, 54.4980G-4, Q&A-1.]

> **Final Regulations Note.** Final regulations were issued on July 31, 2006. These regulations contain helpful clarifications and additional flexibility that the proposed regulations lacked. [Treas. Reg. § 54.4980G-1 through 5; 71 Fed. Reg. 43056 (July 31, 2006)]

Q 4:94   What are the consequences of violating the comparability rules?

If the employer violates the comparability rules, then the sum of *all* the contributions that the employer made to HSAs for the year are subject to the 35 percent excise tax. There is no exception for an individual based on different coverage status or employment status. All contributions are subject to the excise tax, even if the failure was limited to one coverage status. Presumably, the employer should still be able to take a deduction for such contributions under Code Section 162, however, as long as such compensation is reasonable. The regulations also state that the excise tax can be waived in situations where the excise tax imposed is excessive relative to the failure involved. [I.R.C. § 4980G(b); 4980E(c); Prop. Treas. Reg. § 54.4980G-5, Q&A 5; I.R.S. Notice 2004-2, Q&A 32, 2004-2 I.R.B. 269]

Practice Pointer. The final rules are consistent with the proposed rules concerning the consequences for violating the rules.

Q 4:95   Can an employer correct a violation of the comparability rules?

Possibly. If the employer wants to correct a violation of the comparability rules, the employer cannot reduce the contributions already made to an HSA; additional contributions to an HSA must be made to employees who did not receive a comparable contribution. The additional contributions must be made by April 15 of the following year. A reasonable interest factor must be included on these correcting contributions; however, there is no requirement that the contribution be in excess of the maximum limit on HSA contributions. [I.R.C. § 4980G; Prop. Treas. Reg. § 54.4980G-4, Q&A 12]

The final regulations contain a new Q&A stating that the determination of whether interest is "reasonable" will be based on all of the facts and circumstances but that the federal short-term rate as determined by the Secretary in accordance with Code Section 1274(d) will be deemed reasonable.

Q 4:96   When are the regulations on HSA employer comparable contributions effective?

The IRS proposed regulations issued on August 26, 2005, regarding employer comparable contributions to an HSA are proposed to be effective for all employer contributions made on or after the date of publication as final regulations. However, taxpayers may rely on the proposed regulations for guidance pending the issuance of final regulations. Final regulations were issued on July 31, 2006.

Before adopting the proposed regulations as final regulations, however, the IRS considered written comments that were submitted prior to November 25, 2005. The IRS specifically requested comments on the following:

- The clarity of the proposed rules and how they can be made easier to understand
- The application of the proposed rules to employees on FMLA leave, and
- The application of the proposed rules to employer matching HSA contributions made through a cafeteria plan, such as whether an employer's matching contributions should be limited.

[Preamble, Prop. Treas. Reg. § 54-4980G, 70 Fed. Reg. 165, 50233 (Aug. 26, 2005)]

Final Regulations Note. The final regulations were issued on July 31, 2006, and are effective for employer contributions to HSAs made on or after January 1, 2007. [Treas. Reg. § 54.4980G-1 through 5; 71 Fed. Reg. 43056 (July 31, 2006)] Employers who currently make or plan to make contributions to their employees' HSAs should review their health benefit arrangements and cafeteria plans in light of this new guidance.

Q 4:97   Do the proposed regulations follow previously issued guidance on comparability?

Yes. The proposed regulations generally follow the previously issued guidance on comparability rules. [I.R.S. Notices 2004-2 (Q&A-32) and 2004-50 (Q&As-46–54); see also I.R.C. § 4980G] The rules also provide additional clarification with respect to a few issues not previously addressed, including an exception from the comparability rules for employer contributions to HSAs made through cafeteria plans. The proposed regulations significantly expand upon earlier IRS guidance. Major changes and clarifications include the following:

1. New rules and examples confirming that employers are prohibited from varying contributions for levels of coverage other than self-only and family (e.g., employee plus one), unless such contributions are equal to a percentage of the HDHP deductible (see Q 4:115);

2. Clarification that it is possible to provide contributions for management employees without making contributions for nonmanagement employees by making the employer's HDHP available only to management employees (see Q 4:110);

3. New rules concerning contribution methods, including pre-funding of contributions before the beginning of the calendar year (see Qs 4:125, 4:126);

4. New rules regarding the frequency of contributions during the year, which provide that employer contributions must be made on the same schedule for all employees, with exceptions for employees with different payrolls (see Q 4:127);

5. New rules concerning contributions for former employees, which provide that contributions need not be made for former employees, but, if contributions are made for former employees, those contributions must be similar (see Q 4:122);

6. A new rule regarding employer contributions through a cafeteria plan (see Q 4:135) (earlier IRS guidance provided that an employer could avoid the comparable contribution rules by making a contribution under the employer's cafeteria plan, but did not specify what, if any, requirements had to be satisfied for an employer to do this);

7. An example of how to calculate the 35 percent excise tax that applies if an employer does not make comparable contributions, and a new rule that all or a portion of this excise tax may be waived if it is deemed to be excessive relative to the failure of compliance (see Q 4:118).

Although the proposed regulations clarify many issues, they do not allow as much flexibility in plan design as employers will likely want. For example, under the proposed regulations, an employer cannot vary HSA contributions for employees who have different categories of family HDHP coverage (e.g., employee plus one versus employee plus family) without linking the contributions to a percentage of the deductible (see Q 4:123, examples 6 and 7). Similarly, an employer cannot make additional contributions for employees who exhibit healthy behavior, such as completing a health risk assessment, or even make additional contributions for employees who suffer from illness or chronic conditions (see Q 4:131).

Final Regulations Note. The final regulations generally contain the same provisions as the proposed regulations. However, the final regulations clarify and expand the proposed regulations as noted throughout the chapter.

Q 4:98   Is an employer required to contribute to the HSAs of its employees?

No. An employer is not required to contribute to the HSAs of its employees. However, in general, if an employer makes contributions to any employee's HSA, the employer must make comparable contributions to the HSAs of all comparable participating employees.

Q 4:99   Are employer contributions to an HSA subject to highly compensated employee nondiscrimination rules?

No. Unlike many other employer-provided tax-favored benefits, the HSA rules do not have nondiscrimination rules restricting the amount of benefits provided to highly compensated employees. Instead, the HSA statute requires that all employer pretax contributions to employee HSAs be comparable. Note however, that if HSA contributions are made through cafeteria plan, nondiscrimnation rules do apply.

Q 4:100   Is there an exception to the comparability rules for contributions made through a cafeteria plan?

Yes. An exception from the comparability rules applies for employer contributions to HSAs made through cafeteria plans (see Q 4:121).

Comparability Testing

Final Regulations Note. Except as specifically noted in this section, the final regulations [Treas. Reg. § 54.4980G-1 through 5; 71 Fed. Reg. 43056 (July 31, 2006)] retain the rule described in the proposed regulations.

Q 4:101   What is the testing period for making comparable contributions to employees' HSAs?

To satisfy the comparability rule in Code Section 4980G, an employer must make comparable contributions for the calendar year to HSAs of employees who are eligible individuals (i.e., comparable participating employees) (See Q 4:116).

Employees for Comparability Testing

Q 4:102   Do the comparability rules apply to contributions that an employer makes to the HSA of an independent contractor?

No. The comparability rules apply only to contributions that an employer makes to the HSAs of employees. [Prop. Treas. Reg. § 54.4980G-2, Q&A-1] Because an independent contractor is not an employee, the comparability rules do not apply. However, an employer has to make comparable contributions to all affected employees within the related, controlled, or affiliated group.

Q 4:103   May a sole proprietor who is an eligible individual contribute to his or her own HSA without contributing to the HSAs of his or her employees who are eligible individuals?

Yes. The comparability rules apply only to contributions made by an employer to the HSAs of employees. Because a sole proprietor is not an employee, the comparability rules do not apply to contributions he or she makes to his or her own HSA. [Prop. Treas. Reg. § 54.4980G-2, Q&A-2.]

Example. In a calendar year, Bill, a sole proprietor, is an eligible individual and contributes $1,000 to his own HSA. Bill also contributes $500 for the same calendar year to the HSA of each employee who is an eligible individual. The comparability rules are not violated by Bill's $1,000 contribution to his own HSA.

Q 4:104   May a sole proprietor contribute to the HSAs of employees?

Yes. However, if a sole proprietor contributes to any employee's HSA, he or she must make comparable contributions to the HSAs of all comparable participating employees. In determining whether the comparability rules are satisfied, contributions that a sole proprietor makes to his or her own HSA are not taken into account. [Prop. Treas. Reg. § 54.4980G-2, Q&A-2]

Q 4:105   Do the comparability rules apply to contributions by a partnership to a partner's HSA?

No. Contributions by a partnership to a bona fide partner's HSA are not subject to the comparability rules, because the contributions are not contributions by an employer to the HSA of an employee. The contributions are treated as either guaranteed payments under Code Section 707(c) or distributions under

Code Section 731 (see Qs 4:97–4:108) However, if a partnership contributes to the HSAs of employees who are not partners, the comparability rules apply to those contributions. [Prop. Treas. Reg. § 54.4980G-2, Q&A-3(a)]

> **Example.** The Xavier Partnership is a limited partnership with three equal individual partners, Abe (a general partner), Bob (a limited partner), and Carla (a limited partner). Carla is to be paid $300 annually for services rendered to Xavier in her capacity as a partner without regard to partnership income (i.e., a Code Section 707(c)) guaranteed payment). Dave and Ed are the only employees of Xavier and are not partners in Xavier. Abe, Bill, Carla, Dave, and Ed are eligible individuals, and each has an HSA. During Xavier's year one taxable year, which is also a calendar year, Xavier makes the following contributions:
>
> 1. A $300 contribution to each of Abe's and Bob's HSAs, which are treated as Code Section 731 distributions to Abe and Bob;
> 2. A $300 contribution to Carla's HSA in lieu of paying Carla the guaranteed payment directly; and
> 3. A $200 contribution to the HSAs of Dave and Ed who are comparable participating employees.

Xavier's contributions to Abe's and Bob's HSAs are Code Section 731 distributions, which are treated as cash distributions. Xavier's contribution to Carla's HSA is treated as a guaranteed payment under Code Section 707(c). The contribution is not excludable from Carla's gross income under Code Section 106(d) because the contribution is treated as a distributive share of partnership income for purposes of all Code sections other than Code Sections 61(a) and 162(a), and a guaranteed payment to a partner is not treated as compensation to an employee. Thus, Xavier's contributions to the HSAs of Abe, Bob, and Carla are not subject to the comparability rules. Xavier's contributions to Dave's and Ed's HSAs are subject to the comparability rules because Dave and Ed are employees of Xavier and are not partners in Xavier. Xavier's contributions to its employees, Dave and Ed, satisfy the comparability rules.

Q 4:106   How are members of controlled groups treated when applying the comparability rules?

All persons or entities that are related, controlled, or affiliated are treated as a single employer. [I.R.C. §§ 414 (b), (c), (m), (o); I.R.C. § 4980G(b), 4980E(e); Prop. Treas. Reg. § 54.4980G-2, Q&A-4]

Q 4:107   Do the comparability rules apply separately to unionized employees or groups of collectively bargained employees?

No. The comparability rules do not apply separately to collectively bargained and non-collectively bargained employees. Similarly, the comparability rules do not apply separately to different groups of collectively bargained employees. [Prop. Treas. Reg. § 54.4980G-2, Q&A-5(c)] Therefore, an employer needs to make comparable contributions to collectively bargained and non-collectively bargained employees.

> **Final Regulations Note.** The final regulations include a new provision regarding collectively bargained employees. If health benefits were the subject of good-faith bargaining between employee representatives and the employer, then employees (and former employees) covered by such collective bargaining agreement are not subject to the comparability rules. Therefore, an employer who makes HSA contributions to any of its non-collectively bargained employees may agree to (1) not make HSA contributions to any collectively bargained employees, (2) make HSA contributions under some collective bargaining agreements and not others, or (3) provide different levels of HSA contributions under different collective bargaining agreements.

Coverage Requirements Under HDHPs

Q 4:108   Is an employer permitted to make comparable contributions only to the HSAs of comparable participating employees who have coverage under the employer's HDHP?

Possibly. If, during a calendar year, an employer contributes to the HSA of any employee who is an eligible individual covered under an HDHP provided by the employer, the employer is required to make comparable contributions to the HSAs of all comparable participating employees with coverage under any HDHP provided by the employer. An employer that contributes only to the HSAs of employees who are eligible individuals with coverage under the employer's HDHP is not required to make comparable contributions to HSAs of employees who are eligible individuals but are not covered under the employer's HDHP. However, an employer that contributes to the HSA of any employee who is an eligible individual with coverage under any HDHP, in addition to the HDHPs provided by the employer, must make comparable contributions to the HSAs of all comparable participating employees whether or not covered under the employer's HDHP. [I.R.S. Notice 2004-50, Q&A 53, 2004-33 I.R.B. 196; see also I.R.S. Notice 2004-2, Q&A 32, 2004-2 I.R.B. 269; Prop. Treas. Reg. § 54.4980G-2, Q&A-6(a)]

> **Example 1.** Matrix offers an HDHP to its full-time employees. Most full-time employees are covered under Matrix's HDHP, and Matrix makes comparable contributions only to the HSAs of its employees who are also covered under the HDHP sponsored by Matrix. Daniel, a full-time employee and an eligible individual (see Q 2:6), is covered under his spouse's HDHP and not under the Matrix HDHP. Matrix is not required to make comparable contributions to Daniel's HSA.

> **Example 2.** Jet Away does not offer an HDHP. Several full-time employees, who are eligible individuals, have HSAs. Jet Away contributes to these employees' HSAs. Jet Away must make comparable contributions to the HSAs of all full-time employees who are eligible individuals.

Example 3. Catnip offers an HDHP to its full-time employees. Most full-time employees are covered under Catnip's HDHP, and Catnip makes comparable contributions to these employees' HSAs and also to HSAs of full-time employees not covered under the employer's HDHP. Felicia, a full-time employee and an eligible individual, is covered under her spouse's HDHP and not Catnip's HDHP. Catnip must make comparable contributions to Felicia's HSA.

Q 4:109   If an employee and his or her spouse are eligible individuals who work for the same employer and one employee-spouse has family coverage for both employees under the employer's HDHP, must the employer make comparable contributions to the HSAs of both employees?

Possibly. If the employer makes contributions only to the HSAs of employees who are eligible individuals covered under its HDHP, the employer is generally not required to contribute to the HSAs of both employee-spouses. The employer is required to contribute to the HSA of the employee-spouse with coverage under the employer's HDHP, but is not required to contribute to the HSA of the employee-spouse covered under the employer's HDHP by virtue of his or her spouse's coverage. However, if the employer contributes to the HSA of any employee who is an eligible individual with coverage under any HDHP, the employer must make comparable contributions to the HSAs of both employee spouses if they are both eligible individuals. If an employer is required to contribute to the HSAs of both employee-spouses, the employer is not required to contribute amounts in excess of the annual contribution limits (see Q 4:19). [I.R.C. § 223(b); Prop. Treas. Reg. § 54.4980G-2, Q&A-7(a)]

Example 1. In a calendar year, Electron offers an HDHP to its full-time employees. Most full-time employees are covered under Electron's HDHP, and Electron makes comparable contributions only to these employees' HSAs. George, a full-time employee of Electron and an eligible individual, has family coverage under Electron's HDHP for himself and Gloria, his spouse, who is also a full-time employee of Electron and an eligible individual. Electron is required to make comparable contributions to George's HSA, but is not required to make comparable contributions to Gloria's HSA.

Example 2. In a calendar year, Galaxy offers an HDHP to its full-time employees. Most full-time employees are covered under Galaxy's HDHP and Galaxy makes comparable contributions to these employees' HSAs and to the HSAs of full-time employees who are eligible individuals but are not covered under Galaxy's HDHP. Walter, a full-time employee of Galaxy and an eligible individual, has family coverage under Galaxy's HDHP for himself and his spouse, Wilma, who is also a full-time employee of Galaxy and an eligible individual. Galaxy must make comparable contributions to Walter's HSA and to Wilma's HSA.

Comparability and Management Employees

Q 4:110 Does an employer satisfy the comparable contribution requirements if it makes HSA contributions for nonmanagement employees who are eligible individuals, but not for management employees who are eligible individuals, or if it makes HSA contributions for management employees who are eligible individuals, but not for nonmanagement employees who are eligible individuals?

Possibly. If management employees and nonmanagement employees have HDHP coverage through the employer, the comparability rules are not satisfied unless the employer makes equal contributions or contributes an equal percentage of the HDHP deductibles to the HSAs of these employees. However, if management employees do not have HDHP coverage through the employer, but nonmanagement employees do, nonmanagement employees are comparable participating employees and management employees are not comparable participating employees. In that case, the comparability rules may be satisfied even if the employer makes different contributions to these groups (but see Q 4:121 regarding contributions made through a cafeteria plan). [Prop. Treas. Reg. § 54.4980G-2, Q&A-8(a)]

Example 1. In a calendar year, Global maintains an HDHP covering all management and nonmanagement employees. Global contributes $1,000 for the calendar year to the HSA of each nonmanagement employee who is an eligible individual covered under its HDHP. Global does not contribute to the HSAs of any of its management employees who are eligible individuals covered under its HDHP. The comparability rules are not satisfied.

Example 2. In a calendar year, Network maintains an HDHP for nonmanagement employees only. Network does not maintain an HDHP for its management employees. Network contributes $1,000 for the calendar year to the HSA of each nonmanagement employee who is an eligible individual with coverage under its HDHP. Network does not contribute to the HSAs of any of its nonmanagement employees not covered under its HDHP or to the HSAs of any of its management employees. The comparability rules are satisfied.

Example 3. In a calendar year, Krypton maintains an HDHP for management employees only. Krypton does not maintain an HDHP for its nonmanagement employees. Krypton contributes $1,000 for the calendar year to the HSA of each management employee who is an eligible individual with coverage under its HDHP. Krypton does not contribute to the HSAs of any of its management employees not covered under its HDHP or to the HSAs of any of its nonmanagement employees. The comparability rules are satisfied.

Comparability and Former Employees

Q 4:111   If an employer contributes to the HSAs of former employees who are eligible individuals, do the comparability rules apply to these contributions?

Yes. The comparability rules apply to contributions an employer makes to former employees' HSAs. Therefore, if an employer contributes to any former employee's HSA, it must make comparable contributions to the HSAs of all comparable participating former employees (i.e., former employees who are eligible individuals with the same category of HDHP coverage). However, an employer is not required to make comparable contributions to the HSAs of former employees with coverage under the employer's HDHP because of an election under a COBRA continuation provision. The comparability rules apply separately to former employees because they are a separate category of covered employee (see Q 4:102). [Prop. Treas. Reg. § 54.4980G-2, Q&A-9(a)]

> **Example 1.** In a calendar year, Lattice contributes $1,000 for the calendar year to the HSA of each current employee who is an eligible individual with coverage under any HDHP. Lattice does not contribute to the HSA of any former employee who is an eligible individual. Lattice's contributions satisfy the comparability rules.

> **Example 2.** In a calendar year, Metropolis contributes to the HSAs of current employees and former employees who are eligible individuals covered under any HDHP. Metropolis contributes $750 to the HSA of each current employee with self-only HDHP coverage and $1,000 to the HSA of each current employee with family HDHP coverage. Metropolis also contributes $300 to the HSA of each former employee with self-only HDHP coverage and $400 to the HSA of each former employee with family HDHP coverage. Metropolis's contributions satisfy the comparability rules.

> **Final Regulations Note.** The final regulations provide that where the employer is required to make comparable contributions to former employees, the employer must take "reasonable actions" to locate such eligible former employees. Reasonable actions include the use of certified mail, the Internal Revenue Service Letter Forwarding Program, or the Social Security Administration's Letter Forwarding Service. The final regulations do not provide guidance regarding how an employer would go about determining whether any former employees might be covered under an HDHP other than one sponsored by that employer.

Q 4:112   Is an employer permitted to make comparable contributions only to the HSAs of comparable participating former employees who have coverage under the employer's HDHP?

If, during a calendar year, an employer contributes to the HSA of any former employee who is an eligible individual covered under an HDHP provided by the employer, the employer is required to make comparable contributions to the

HSAs of all former employees who are comparable participating former employees with coverage under any HDHP provided by the employer. An employer that contributes only to the HSAs of former employees who are eligible individuals with coverage under the employer's HDHP is not required to make comparable contributions to the HSAs of former employees who are eligible individuals and who are not covered under the employer's HDHP. However, an employer that contributes to the HSA of any former employee who is an eligible individual with coverage under any HDHP, even if that coverage is not the employer's HDHP, must make comparable contributions to the HSAs of all former employees who are eligible individuals whether or not covered under an HDHP of the employer. [Prop. Treas. Reg. § 54.4980G-2, Q&A-10]

Q 4:113   If an employer contributes only to the HSAs of former employees who are eligible individuals with coverage under the employer's HDHP, must the employer make comparable contributions to the HSAs of former employees who are eligible individuals with coverage under the employer's HDHP because of an election under a COBRA continuation provision?

No. An employer that contributes only to the HSAs of former employees who are eligible individuals with coverage under the employer's HDHP is not required to make comparable contributions to the HSAs of former employees who are eligible individuals with coverage under the employer's HDHP because of an election under a COBRA continuation provision (as defined in Code Section 9832(d)(1)). [Prop. Treas. Reg. § 54.4980G-2, Q&A-11]

Comparability Relating to Archer MSAs

Q 4:114   How do the comparability rules apply if some employees have HSAs and other employees have Archer MSAs?

The comparability rules apply separately to employees who have HSAs and employees who have Archer MSAs. However, if an employee has both an HSA and an Archer MSA, the employer may contribute to either the HSA or the Archer MSA, but not to both. [Prop. Treas. Reg. § 54.4980G-2, Q&A-12(a)]

Example 1. In a calendar year, Nutcracker contributes $600 to the Archer MSA of each employee who is an eligible individual and who has an Archer MSA. Nutcracker contributes $500 for the calendar year to the HSA of each employee who is an eligible individual and who has an HSA. If an employee has both an Archer MSA and an HSA, Nutcracker contributes to the employee's Archer MSA and not to the employee's HSA. Marcy, an employee, has an Archer MSA and an HSA. Nutcracker contributes $600 for the calendar year to Marcy's Archer MSA but does not contribute to Marcy's HSA. Nutcracker's contributions satisfy the comparability rules.

Note. An Archer MSA may be rolled over to an HSA (see Q 5:2).

Example 2. Assume the same facts as in Example 1, except that if an employee has both an Archer MSA and an HSA, Nutcracker contributes to the employee's HSA and not to the employee's Archer MSA. Nutcracker contributes $500 for the calendar year to Marcy's HSA but does not contribute to Marcy's Archer MSA. Nutcracker's contributions satisfy the comparability rules.

Categories of Coverage Relating to Comparability

Q 4:115 What are the categories of HDHP coverage for purposes of applying the comparability rules?

The categories of coverage are self-only HDHP coverage and family HDHP coverage. [I.R.C. § 4980G(b), 4980E(d)(3)(B); Prop. Treas. Reg. § 54.4980G-1, Q&A-2] This means that an employer may provide a different level of contributions to individuals with self-only coverage than to individuals with family coverage and that the contributions do not have to be equal between the two groups.

> **Final Regulations Note.** The final regulations allow the category of family HDHP coverage to be subdivided into self plus one, self plus two, and self plus three or more. These categories give employers additional flexibility in their benefit designs. However, the final regulations specify that contributions with respect to the self plus two category cannot be less than contributions made under the self plus one category. Likewise, contributions with respect to the self plus three category cannot be less than those made under the self plus two category. The final regulations retain the rule from the proposed regulations that an employer who makes HSA contributions to employees with self only HDHP coverage is not required to make any contributions to employees with family HDHP coverage, and vice versa.

Testing Period for Comparability

Q 4:116 What is the testing period for making comparable contributions to employees' HSAs?

To satisfy the comparability rules, an employer must make comparable contributions (see Qs 4:123–4:125) for the calendar year to the HSAs of employees who are comparable participating employees. [I.R.C. § 4980G(a); Prop. Treas. Reg. § 54.4980G-1, Q&A-3]

The Excise Tax and Comparability

Q 4:117 How is the excise tax computed if employer contributions to an HSA do not satisfy the comparability rules for a calendar year?

If employer contributions do not satisfy the comparability rules for a calendar year, the employer may be subject to an excise tax equal to 35 percent of the aggregate amount contributed by the employer to HSAs for that period. [Prop. Treas. Reg. § 54.4980G-1, Q&A-4]

> **Example.** Nutrino has an HDHP that satisfies the definition of an HDHP for the 2007 calendar year. During the 2007 calendar year, Nutrino has eight employees who are eligible individuals with self-only coverage under an HDHP provided by Nutrino. The deductible for the HDHP is $2,000. For the 2007 calendar year, Nutrino contributes $2,000 each to the HSAs of two employees and $1,000 each to the HSAs of the other six employees, for total HSA contributions of $10,000. Nutrino's contributions do not satisfy the comparability rules. Therefore, Nutrino is subject to an excise tax of $3,500 (i.e., 35% × $10,000) for its failure to make comparable contributions to its employees' HSAs.

Q 4:118   May all or part of the excise tax imposed under Code Section 4980G be waived?

Yes. In the case of a failure that is due to reasonable cause and not to willful neglect, all or a portion of the excise tax imposed under Code Section 4980G may be waived to the extent that the payment of the tax would be excessive relative to the failure involved. [I.R.C. § 4980G(b) and 4980E(c); Prop. Treas. Reg. § 54.4980G-5, Q&A-5]

Special Issues Relating to Comparability

Q 4:119   Do the comparability rules apply to amounts rolled over from an employee's HSA or Archer Medical Savings Account?

No. The comparability rules do not apply to amounts rolled over from an employee's HSA or Archer MSA. Such amounts are not treated as employer contributions to an HSA. [I.R.S. Notice 2004-2, Q&A 32, 2004-2 I.R.B. 269; Prop. Treas. Reg. § 54.4980G-2, Q&A-1]

Q 4:120   Do the comparability rules apply to after-tax contributions made to an HSA at the request of an employee?

No. If an employee requests that his or her employer deduct after-tax amounts from the employee's compensation and forward these amounts as employee contributions to the employee's HSA, the Code Section 4980G comparability rules do not apply. Code Section 106(d) provides that amounts contributed by an employer to an eligible employee's HSA shall be treated as employer-provided coverage for medical expenses and excludable from the employee's gross income up to the annual limit (see Q 2:10). After-tax employee contributions to the HSA are not subject to Code Section 4980G because they are not employer contributions under Code Section 106(d). [I.R.S. Notice 2004-50, Q&A 54, 2004-33 I.R.B. 196; Prop. Treas. Reg. § 54.4980G-2, Q&A-2]

Q 4:121 Do the comparability rules apply to contributions made through a cafeteria plan?

No. An exception from the comparability rules applies for employer contributions to HSAs made through cafeteria plans (see Q 4:135). [Prop. Treas. Reg. § 54.4980G-2, Q&A-2] Other rules may apply (see Qs 4:135–4:138).

Practice Pointer. The final regulations make clear that an employer's contributions will be considered made through a cafeteria plan if (1) employees are permitted to make their own contributions to an HSA by salary reduction through a cafeteria plan and (2) all contributions are made pursuant to a written cafeteria plan document.

Comparable Contributions

Q 4:122 What are the categories of covered employees for comparability testing?

In general, the categories of employees listed below are the exclusive categories for comparability testing. An employer must make comparable contributions to the HSAs of all comparable participating employees (i.e., eligible individuals who are in the same category of employees with the same category of HDHP coverage) during the calendar year without regard to any classification other than these categories. The categories of employees for comparability testing are as follows:

1. Current full-time employees (customarily employed for 30 or more hours per week);
2. Current part-time employees (customarily employed for fewer than 30 hours per week); and
3. Former employees (except for former employees with coverage under the employer's HDHP because of an election under a COBRA continuation provision (see Code Section 9832(d)(1)).

[Prop. Treas. Reg. § 54.4980G-2, Q&A-5(a)(1)-(3), (b); I.R.C. § 4980G(b), 4980E(d)(4)(A)-(B)]

Q 4:123 What is a comparable HSA employer contribution under Code Section 4980G?

Contributions are comparable if they are either the same amount or the same percentage of the deductible under the HDHP for employees who are eligible individuals with the same category of coverage. Employees with self-only HDHP coverage are tested separately from employees with family HDHP coverage. An employer is not required to contribute the same amount or the same percentage of the deductible for employees who are eligible individuals with self-only HDHP coverage that it contributes for employees who are eligible individuals with family HDHP coverage. An employer that satisfies the comparability rules by contributing the same amount to the HSAs of all employees who are eligible individuals with self-only HDHP coverage is not required to contribute any amount to the HSAs of employees who are eligible individuals with family HDHP coverage, or to contribute the same percentage of the family HDHP deductible as the amount contributed with respect to self-only HDHP coverage. Similarly, an employer that satisfies the comparability rules by contributing the same amount to the HSAs of all employees who are eligible individuals with family HDHP coverage is not required to contribute any amount to the HSAs of employees who are eligible individuals with self-only HDHP coverage, or to contribute the same percentage of the self-only HDHP deductible as the amount contributed with respect to family HDHP coverage. [IRC § 4980G(b), 4890E(d); Prop. Treas. Reg. § 54.4980G-4, Q&A-1]

> **Example 1.** In the 2007 calendar year, Pumpkin offers its full-time employees three health plans, including an HDHP with self-only coverage and a $2,000 deductible. Pumpkin contributes $1,000 for the calendar year to the HSA of each employee who is an eligible individual electing the self-only HDHP coverage. Pumpkin makes no HSA contributions for employees with family HDHP coverage or for employees who do not elect the employer's self-only HDHP. Pumpkin's HSA contributions satisfy the comparability rules.

> **Example 2.** In the 2007 calendar year, Alpha offers its employees an HDHP with a $3,000 deductible for self-only coverage and a $4,000 deductible for family coverage. Alpha contributes $1,000 for the calendar year to the HSA of each employee who is an eligible individual electing the self-only HDHP coverage. Alpha contributes $2,000 for the calendar year to the HSA of each employee who is an eligible individual electing the family HDHP coverage. Alpha's HSA contributions satisfy the comparability rules.

> **Example 3.** In the 2007 calendar year, Electron offers its employees an HDHP with a $1,500 deductible for self-only coverage and a $3,000 deductible for family coverage. Electron contributes $1,000 for the calendar year to the HSA of each employee who is an eligible individual electing the self-only HDHP coverage. Electron contributes $1,000 for the calendar year to the HSA of each employee who is an eligible individual electing the family HDHP coverage. Electron's HSA contributions satisfy the comparability rules.

> **Example 4.** In the 2007 calendar year, Interociter offers its employees an HDHP with a $1,500 deductible for self-only coverage and a $3,000 deductible for family coverage. Interociter contributes $1,500 for the calendar year to the HSA of each employee who is an eligible individual electing the self-only HDHP coverage. Interociter contributes $1,000 for the calendar year to the HSA of each employee who is an eligible individual electing the family HDHP coverage. Interociter's HSA contributions satisfy the comparability rules.

> **Example 5.** In the 2007 calendar year, Enterprise maintains two HDHPs. Plan X has a $2,000 deductible for self-only coverage and a $4,000 deductible for

family coverage. Plan Y has a $2,500 deductible for self-only coverage and a $4,500 deductible for family coverage. For the calendar year, Enterprise makes contributions to the HSA of each full-time employee who is an eligible individual covered under Plan X of $600 for self-only coverage and $1,000 for family coverage. Enterprise satisfies the comparability rules, if it makes either of the following contributions for the 2007 calendar year to the HSA of each full-time employee who is an eligible individual covered under Plan Y:

- $600 for each full-time employee with self-only coverage and $1,000 for each full-time employee with family coverage, or

- $750 for each employee with self-only coverage and $1,125 for each employee with family coverage (the same percentage of the deductible Enterprise contributes for full-time employees covered under Plan X, 30 percent of the deductible for self-only coverage and 25 percent of the deductible for family coverage).

Enterprise also makes contributions to the HSA of each part-time employee who is an eligible individual covered under Plan X of $300 for self-only coverage and $500 for family coverage. Enterprise satisfies the comparability rules, if it makes either of the following contributions for the 2007 calendar year to the HSA of each part-time employee who is an eligible individual covered under Plan Y:

- $300 for each part-time employee with self-only coverage and $500 for each part-time employee with family coverage, or

- $375 for each part-time employee with self-only coverage and $563 for each part-time employee with family coverage (the same percentage of the deductible Enterprise contributes for part-time employees covered under Plan X, 15 percent of the deductible for self-only coverage and 12.5 percent of the deductible for family coverage).

Example 6. In the 2007 calendar year, Flagship maintains an HDHP. The HDHP has a $2,500 deductible for self-only coverage and the following family coverage options:

- A $3,500 deductible for self plus one dependent,
- A $3,500 deductible for self plus spouse,
- A $3,500 deductible for self plus two or more dependents,
- A $3,500 deductible for self plus spouse and one dependent, and
- A $3,500 deductible for self plus spouse and two or more dependents.

Flagship makes the following contributions for the calendar year to the HSA of each full-time employee who is an eligible individual covered under the HDHP:

- $750 for self-only coverage,
- $1,000 for self plus one dependent,

- $1,000 for self plus spouse,
- $1,000 for self plus two or more dependents,
- $1,000 for self plus spouse and one dependent, and
- $1,000 for self plus spouse and two or more dependents.

Flagship's HSA contributions satisfy the comparability rules.

Example 7. In the 2007 calendar year, Matrix maintains an HDHP. The HDHP has an $1,800 deductible for self-only coverage and the following family coverage options:

- A $3,500 deductible for self plus one dependent,
- A $3,800 deductible for self plus spouse,
- A $4,000 deductible for self plus two or more dependents,
- A $4,500 deductible for self plus spouse and one dependent, and
- A $5,000 deductible for self plus spouse and two or more dependents.

Matrix makes the following contributions for the calendar year to the HSA of each full-time employee who is an eligible individual covered under the HDHP:

- $360 for self-only coverage,
- $875 for self plus one dependent,
- $950 for self plus spouse,
- $1,000 for self plus two or more dependents,
- $1,125 for self plus spouse and one dependent, and
- $1,250 for self plus spouse and two or more dependents.

Matrix's HSA contributions satisfy the comparability rules because Matrix has made contributions that are the same percentage of the deductible for eligible employees with the same category of coverage (20% percent of the deductible for eligible employees with self-only coverage and 25% percent of the deductible for eligible employees with family coverage). Matrix could also satisfy the comparability rules by contributing the same dollar amount for each category of coverage.

Example 8. In a calendar year, Optimize offers its employees an HDHP and a health flexible spending arrangement (health FSA). The health FSA reimburses employees for qualified medical expenses (see Q 2:25). Some of Optimize's employees have coverage under the HDHP and the health FSA. For the calendar year, Optimize contributes $500 to the HSA of each of employee who is an eligible individual, but does not contribute to the HSAs of employees who have coverage under the health FSA or under a spouse's health FSA. In addition, some of Optimize's employees have coverage under the HDHP and are enrolled in Medicare. Optimize does not contribute to the HSAs of employees who are enrolled in Medicare. The employees who have coverage under the health FSA or under a spouse's health FSA are not comparable participating employees because they are not eligible individuals (see Q

2:6). Similarly, the employees who are enrolled in Medicare are not comparable participating employees because they are not eligible individuals (see Qs 2:14, 2:17). Therefore, employees who have coverage under the health FSA or under a spouse's health FSA and employees who are enrolled in Medicare are excluded from comparability testing. [I.R.C. § 4980G(b), 4980E] Optimize's contributions satisfy the comparability rules.

Final Regulations Note. As the above examples demonstrate, the proposed regulations permit different levels of contributions to be made based on an employee's category of coverage. However, the only categories of coverage recognized were self only HDHP coverage and family HDHP coverage. This restricted employers from varying HSA contributions to correspond with common coverage categories such as employee plus one or employee plus children. The final regulations allow the category of family HDHP coverage to be subdivided into self plus one, self plus two, and self plus three or more. These categories give employers additional flexibility in their benefit designs. However, the final regulations specify that contributions with respect to the self plus two category cannot be less than contributions made under the self plus one category. Likewise, contributions with respect to the self plus three category cannot be less than those made under the self plus two category. The final regulations retain the rule from the proposed regulations that an employer who makes HSA contributions to employees with self only HDHP coverage is not required to make any contributions to employees with family HDHP coverage, and vice versa.

The Comparability Rules in Relation to Full-Time and Part-Time Employees

Q 4:124   **How do the comparability rules apply to employer contributions to employees' HSAs if some employees work full-time during the entire calendar year, and other employees work full-time for less than the entire calendar year?**

Employer contributions to the HSAs of employees who work full time for less than 12 months satisfy the comparability rules if the contribution amount is comparable when determined on a month-to-month basis. For example, if the employer contributes $240 to the HSA of each full-time employee who works the entire calendar year, the employer must contribute $60 to the HSA of a full-time employee who works three months of the calendar year. These rules apply to employer contributions made on a pay-as-you-go basis or on a look-back basis (see Q 4:125). [I.R.C. § 4980G(b) and 4980E(d)(2)(B); I.R.S. Notice 2004-2, Q&A 32, 2004-2 I.R.B. 269; Prop. Treas. Reg. § 54.4980G-4, Q&A-2]

Funding Comparable Contributions

Q 4:125 How does an employer comply with the comparability rules when some employees who are eligible individuals do not work for the employer during the entire calendar year?

In general, in determining whether the comparability rules are satisfied, an employer must take into account all full-time and part-time employees who were employees and eligible individuals for any month during the calendar year. Full-time and part-time employees are tested separately. [Prop. Treas. Reg. § 54.4980G-3, Q&A-5] There are two methods used to comply with the comparability rules when some employees who are eligible individuals do not work for the employer during the entire calendar year; contributions may be made on a pay-as-you-go basis or on a look-back basis. (See Q 4:111 regarding comparable contributions to the HSAs of former employees.)

Contributions on a pay-as-you-go basis. An employer may comply with the comparability rules by contributing amounts at one or more times for the calendar year to the HSAs of employees who are eligible individuals, if contributions are the same amount or the same percentage of the HDHP deductible for employees who are eligible individuals as of the first day of the month with the same category of coverage and are made at the same time. Contributions made at the employer's usual payroll interval for different groups of employees are considered to be made at the same time. For example, if salaried employees are paid monthly and hourly employees are paid biweekly, an employer may contribute to the HSAs of hourly employees on a biweekly basis and to the HSAs of salaried employees on a monthly basis. An employer may change the amount that it contributes to the HSAs of employees at any point. However, the changed contribution amounts must satisfy the comparability rules.

[Prop. Treas. Reg. § 54.4980G-4, Q&A-3]

> **Example 1.** Beginning on January 1, Jelly contributes $50 per month on the first day of each month to the HSA of each employee who is an eligible individual. Jelly does not contribute to the HSAs of former employees. In mid-March of the same year, Joan, an employee and an eligible individual, terminates employment after Jelly has contributed $150 to Joan's HSA. After Joan terminates employment, Jelly does not contribute additional amounts to her HSA. In mid-April of the same year, Jelly hires another employee, Greg, an eligible individual, and contributes $50 to Greg's HSA in May and $50 in June. Effective in July of the same year, Jelly stops contributing to the HSAs of all employees and makes no contributions to the HSA of any employee for the months of July through December. In August, Jelly hires another employee, Betty, who is an eligible individual. Jelly does not contribute to Betty's HSA. After Betty is hired, Jelly does not hire additional employees. As of the end of the calendar year, Jelly has made the following HSA contributions to its employees' HSAs:
>
> • Jelly contributed $150 to Joan's HSA,
> • Jelly contributed $100 to Greg's HSA,
> • Jelly did not contribute to Betty's HSA, and

• Jelly contributed $300 to the HSA of each employee who was an eligible individual and employed by Jelly from January through June.

Jelly's contributions satisfy the comparability rules.

Example 2. In a calendar year, Neptune offers its employees an HDHP and contributes on a monthly pay-as-you go basis to the HSAs of employees who are eligible individuals with coverage under Neptune's HDHP. In the calendar year, Neptune contributes $50 per month to the HSA of each of employee with self-only HDHP coverage and $100 per month to the HSA of each employee with family HDHP coverage. From January 1 through March 31 of the calendar year, Albert is an employee and an eligible individual with self-only HDHP coverage. From April 1st through December 31 of the calendar year, Albert is an eligible individual with family HDHP coverage. For the months of January, February, and March of the calendar year, Neptune contributes $50 per month to Albert's HSA. For the remaining months of the calendar year, Neptune contributes $100 per month to Albert's HSA. Neptune's contributions to Albert's HSA satisfy the comparability rules.

Contributions on a look-back basis. An employer may also satisfy the comparability rules by determining comparable contributions for the calendar year at the end of the calendar year, taking into account all employees who were eligible individuals for any month during the calendar year and contributing the correct amount (i.e., a percentage of the HDHP deductible or a specified dollar amount for the same categories of coverage) to the employees' HSAs.

Example. In a calendar year, Kitten offers its employees an HDHP and contributes on a look-back basis to the HSAs of employees who are eligible individuals with coverage under Kitten's HDHP. Kitten contributes $600 (i.e., $50 per month) for the calendar year to the HSA of each of employee with self-only HDHP coverage and $1,200 (i.e., $100 per month) for the calendar year to the HSA of each employee with family HDHP coverage. From January 1 through June 30 of the calendar year, Frank is an employee and is an eligible individual with family HDHP coverage. From July 1 through December 31, Frank is an eligible individual with self-only HDHP coverage. Kitten contributes $900 on a look-back basis for the calendar year to Frank's HSA ($100 per month for the months of January through June and $50 per month for the months of July through December). Kitten's contributions to Frank's HSA satisfy the comparability rules.

Final Regulations Note. The final regulations retain and expand on the rules in the proposed regulations concerning the timing of employer contributions for employees who do not work for the employer during the entire calendar year. As described above, under the proposed regulations, employers could use either the pay-as-you-go or look-back method of contributions to satisfy the comparability requirements for employees who work for less than a full year. The final regulations retain this rule but clarify that for the pay-as-you-go and look-back methods, an employer may establish, on a reasonable and consistent basis, periods for which contributions will be made, such as quarterly, as well as a specific date, such as the first day of the quarter. Presumably, these rules are intended to clarify that employers are not required to deviate from their scheduled funding of HSA accounts to accommodate employees who begin work after the start of the year (as long as the contributions attributable to that employee are made as part of the next scheduled funding) or who terminate employment before the end of the year.

Pre-funding Employer Contributions

Q 4:126 May an employer make all of its contributions to the HSAs of its employees who are eligible individuals at the beginning of the calendar year (i.e., on a pre-funded basis) instead of contributing on a pay-as-you-go or on a look-back basis?

Yes. An employer may make all of its contributions to the HSAs of its employees who are eligible individuals at the beginning of the calendar year. An employer that pre-funds the HSAs of its employees will not fail to satisfy the comparability rules because an employee who terminates employment prior to the end of the calendar year has received more contributions on a monthly basis than employees who have worked the entire calendar year (see Q 4:134). Under Code Section 223(d)(1)(E), an account beneficiary's interest in an HSA is nonforfeitable. An employer must make comparable contributions for all employees who are comparable participating employees for any month during the calendar year, including employees who are eligible individuals hired after the date of initial funding. An employer that makes HSA contributions on a pre-funded basis may also contribute on a pre-funded basis to the HSAs of employees who are eligible individuals hired after the date of initial funding. Alternatively, an employer that has pre-funded the HSAs of comparable participating employees may contribute to the HSAs of employees who are eligible individuals hired after the date of initial funding on a pay-as-you-go basis or on a look-back basis. An employer that makes HSA contributions on a pre-funded basis must use the same contribution method for all employees who are eligible individuals hired after the date of initial funding. [Prop. Treas. Reg. § 54.4980G-4, Q&A-4]

> **Example 1.** On January 1, Mercury contributes $1,200 for the calendar year on a pre-funded basis to the HSA of each of employee who is an eligible individual. In mid-May, Mercury hires Victor, a new employee and an eligible individual. Therefore, Mercury is required to make comparable contributions to Victor's HSA beginning in June. Mercury satisfies the comparability rules with respect to contributions to Victor's HSA if it makes HSA contributions in any one of the following ways:
>
> - Pre-funding Victor's HSA by contributing $700 to Victor's HSA,
> - Contributing $100 per month on a pay-as-you-go basis to Victor's HSA, or
> - Contributing to Victor's HSA at the end of the calendar year taking into account each month that Victor was an eligible individual and employed by Mercury.

If Mercury hires additional employees who are eligible individuals after initial funding, it must use the same contribution method for these employees that it used to contribute to Mercury's HSA.

Example 2. Angelina started her employment with Orion Corporation in March 2006. For all of 2006, Angelina has a private health insurance policy that is not connected with her employment. The policy has a $500 annual deductible limit. Orion pre-funds HSA contributions—with prorated contributions made for employees who enroll later in the year to meet the employer comparability requirements (see Qs 3:60, 4:93). Angelina terminates employment in October. As a result, pre-funded contributions exceed Angelina's deductible limit based on her months of coverage. What is the impact on Angelina and Orion?

Impact on Orion

Excess removal not possible. The nonforfeitability rule prevents Orion from removing the excess from Angelina's HSA.

Liability for withholding taxes. If Orion had a reasonable belief when the amounts were contributed that its contributions to the HSA would be excluded from *wages* for employment (FICA) and federal income tax withholding purposes, there would be no withholding liability (see Qs 4:64–4:68). If not, the excess is taxable compensation subject to the wage withholding and reporting requirements for federal income and FICA taxes reported on Form W-2. If Orion has not withheld the appropriate withholding taxes from the employee, it may have to fund the tax liability.

Impact on Angelina

Contribution deductibility. Angelina is not HSA eligible because she has disqualifying health coverage. The amount is not deductible, nor was it excluded from income by her employer.

Inclusion in income. Angelina is responsible for withdrawing the excess. Angelina must include the excess contribution in her taxable income for 2006.

Avoiding the penalty tax. If not refunded from the HSA prior to her income tax filing deadline, the excess contribution may be subject to the 6 percent excise tax (see Qs 4:73, 4:74, 4:78). This result would not necessarily flow from the current presentation on Form 8889-*Health Savings Accounts (HSAs)* (but see pages 4 and 5 of the instructions).

Contribution Method Consistency

Q 4:127 May an employer vary the contribution method for any month during the calendar year?

No. If an employer makes comparable HSA contributions on a pay-as-you-go basis, it must do so for each employee who is a comparable participating employee during the pay period. If an employer makes comparable contributions on a look-back basis, it must do so for each employee who was a comparable participating employee for any month during the calendar year. If an employer makes HSA contributions on a pre-funded basis, it must do so for all employees who are comparable participating employees at the beginning of the calendar year. An employer that contributes on a pre-funded basis must make comparable HSA contributions for all employees who are comparable participating employees for any month during the calendar year, including employees who are eligible individuals hired after the date of initial funding (but see Q 4:126 for rules regarding contributions for employees hired after initial funding). [Prop. Treas. Reg. § 54.4980G-4, Q&A-5]

Q 4:128   How does an employer comply with the comparability rules if an employee has not established an HSA at the time the employer contributes to its employees' HSAs?

If an employee has not established an HSA at the time the employer funds its employees' HSAs, the employer complies with the comparability rules by contributing comparable amounts to the employee's HSA when the employee establishes the HSA, taking into account each month for which the employee was a comparable participating employee. However, an employer is not required to make comparable contributions for a calendar year to an employee's HSA if the employee has not established an HSA by December 31st of the calendar year. [Prop. Treas. Reg. § 54.4980G-4, Q&A-6]

> **Example.** Beginning on January 1, Riverboat contributes $500 per calendar year on a pay-as-you-go basis to the HSA of each employee who is an eligible individual. An employee, Allison, is an eligible individual during the entire calendar year but does not establish an HSA until March. Notwithstanding Allison's delay in establishing an HSA, Riverboat must make up the missed HSA contributions for January and February by April 15th of the following calendar year.

> **Example.** Beginning on January 1 of year one, Sand contributes $500 per calendar year on a pay-as-you-go basis to the HSA of each employee who is an eligible individual. An employee, Myrtle, is an eligible individual during the entire calendar year but does not establish an HSA until January of the following year. Sand is not required to make comparable contributions for Myrtle with respect to year one.

> **Final Regulations Note.** Under the proposed regulations, if an employee has not established an HSA at the time the employer funds its employees' HSAs, the employer must contribute comparable amounts plus reasonable interest to the employee's HSA when the employee does establish the HSA, taking into account each month that the employee was a comparable participating employee. The proposed regulations contain an exception to this rule for employees who do not establish an HSA by December 31 of the calendar year. The final regulations retain this rule regarding retroactive contributions but do not adopt the December 31 exception. Instead, the final regulations contain a new reserved subsection under the heading "Employee has not

established an HSA by the end of the calendar year." It is unclear why this subsection was reserved rather than drafted and included. Perhaps the IRS is reconsidering its earlier position that comparable contributions do not have to be made for such employees.

Computing Contributions

Q 4:129 If an employer bases its contributions on a percentage of the HDHP deductible, how is the correct percentage or dollar amount computed?

The correct percentage is determined by rounding to nearest 1/100th of a percentage point and the dollar amount is determined by rounding to the nearest whole dollar. [Prop. Treas. Reg. § 54.4980G-4, Q&A-7]

> **Example.** The HDHP provided by Quagmire satisfies the definition of an HDHP for the 2007 calendar year. In the 2007 calendar year, Quagmire maintains two HDHPs. Plan Q has a deductible of $3,000 for self-only coverage. Quagmire contributes $1,000 for the calendar year to the HSA of each employee covered under Plan Q. Plan R has a deductible of $3,500 for self-only coverage. Quagmire satisfies the comparability rules if it makes either of the following contributions for the 2007 calendar year to the HSA of each employee who is an eligible individual with self-only coverage under Plan R:
>
> • $1,000, or
> • $1,167 (33.33 percent times the $3,500 deductible, rounded to the nearest whole dollar amount).

Q 4:130 Is the rule that all comparable participating employees receive comparable contributions satisfied if the employer makes matching contributions to the HSA of each comparable participating employee in an amount equal to the employee's HSA contribution or a percentage of the employee's HSA contribution?

Probably not. If all comparable participating employees do not contribute the same amount to their HSAs and, consequently, do not receive comparable contributions to their HSAs, the comparability rules are not satisfied, notwithstanding that the employer offers to make available the same contribution amount to each comparable participating employee (but see Q 4:126 regarding comparability under a cafeteria plan). [I.R.S. Notice 2004-50, Q&A 46, 2004-33 I.R.B. 196; Prop. Treas. Reg. § 54.4980G-4, Q&A-8]

> **Example 1.** Sample Company honors a request by an employee to make after-tax contributions to Don's HSA. Don contributes $1,000, and John contributes $500 on an after-tax basis through the payroll deduction program. No employer contributions are being made, therefore, the comparability rules do not apply (see Q 4:120).

Example 2. Same facts as in the preceding example, except that Sample offers to match employee contributions on a dollar-for-dollar basis. The contributions are not comparable; thus, the comparability rules are not satisfied.

Example 3. Same facts as in example 2, except that Don and John both contribute $1,000 and there are no other employees eligible to make HSA contributions. The comparability rules are satisfied because all eligible employees are making identical contributions and receive identical matching contributions.

Conditions for Receiving Contributions

Q 4:131 Do employer contributions to employees' HSAs satisfy the comparability rules if they are conditional on an employees's participation in health assessments, disease management programs, and wellness programs and the employer makes the same contributions available to all employees who participate in the programs?

Possibly. If all eligible employees do not elect to participate in all the programs and, consequently, all employees who are eligible individuals do not receive comparable contributions to their HSAs, the employer contributions fail to satisfy the Code Section 4980G comparability rules (but see Q 4:126 regarding comparable contributions made through a cafeteria plan). [I.R.S. Notice 2004-50, Q&A 48, 2004-33 I.R.B. 196; Prop. Treas. Reg. § 54.4980G-4, Q&A-9]

Q 4:132 If an employer makes additional contributions to the HSAs of all comparable participating employees who have attained a specified age or who have worked for the employer for a specified number of years, do the contributions satisfy the comparability rules?

Possibly. If all comparable participating employees do not meet the age or length of service requirement, all comparable participating employees do not receive comparable contributions to their HSAs and the employer contributions fail to satisfy the comparability rules. [I.R.S. Notice 2004-50, Q&A 50, 2004-33 I.R.B. 196; Prop. Treas. Reg. § 54.4980G-4, Q&A-10]

Q 4:133 If an employer makes additional contributions to the HSAs of all comparable participating employees who qualify for catch-up contributions, do the contributions satisfy the comparability rules?

No. If all comparable participating employees do not qualify for the additional HSA catch-up contributions (see Q 4:26), all comparable participating employees do not receive comparable contributions to their HSAs, and the employer contributions fail to satisfy the comparability rules. [Prop. Treas. Reg. § 54.4980G-4, Q&A-11]

Employer Reversions

Q 4:134   If an employer's contributions to an employee's HSA result in noncomparable contributions, may the employer recoup the excess amount from the employee's HSA?

No. An employer may not recoup from an employee's HSA any portion of the employer's contribution to the employee's HSA. Under Code Section 223(d)(1)(E), an account beneficiary's interest in an HSA is nonforfeitable. However, an employer may make additional HSA contributions to satisfy the comparability rules. An employer may contribute up until April 15 following the calendar year in which the noncomparable contributions were made. An employer that makes additional HSA contributions to correct noncomparable contributions must also contribute reasonable interest. However, an employer is not required to contribute amounts in excess of the annual contribution limits (see Q 4:19). [Prop. Treas. Reg. § 54.4980G-4, Q&A-12]

Comparability Exceptions for Cafeteria Plans

Q 4:135   Are contributions made through a Code Section 125 cafeteria plan subject to the Code Section 4980G comparability rules?

No. The Code Section 4980G comparability rules do not apply to contributions made through a cafeteria plan. [Medicare Prescription Drug, Improvement, and Modernization Act of 2003, Pub. L. No. 109–173 (see Conf. Rep. No. 391, 108th Cong., 1st Sess. 843 (2003), 2004 U.S.C.C.A.N. 1808)] In general, a cafeteria plan is a written plan under which all participants are employees and participants may choose among two or more benefits consisting of cash and qualified benefits. Unlike the cafeteria plan nondiscrimination rules, the comparability rules are not based upon discrimination in favor of highly compensated or key employees. Therefore, an employer that maintains an HDHP only for highly compensated or key employees and makes HSA contributions through a cafeteria plan only for those eligible employees does not violate the comparability rules but may violate the cafeteria plan nondiscrimination rules (see Q 4:136).

Q 4:136   Which nondiscrimination rules apply to HSA contributions made through a cafeteria plan?

The nondiscrimination rules in Code Section 125 apply to HSA contributions (including matching contributions) made through a cafeteria plan. Generally, a cafeteria plan is a written plan under which all participants are employees and participants may choose among two or more benefits consisting of cash and qualified benefits. Unlike the cafeteria plan nondiscrimination rules, the comparability rules are not based upon discrimination in favor of highly compensated or key employees. Therefore, an employer that maintains an HDHP only for highly compensated or key employees and makes HSA contributions through a cafeteria plan only for those eligible employees, does not violate the comparability rules, but may violate the cafeteria plan nondiscrimination rules. Thus, for example, where matching contributions (i.e., employer contributions that are equal to or a percentage of the employee's contribution) are made by an employer through a cafeteria plan, the contributions are not subject to the comparability rules of Code Section 4980G. However, contributions, including matching contributions, to an HSA made under a cafeteria plan are subject to nondiscrimination rules (i.e., eligibility rules, contributions and benefits tests and key employee concentration tests) of Code Section 125. [I.R.S. Notice 2004-50, Q&A 46, 2004-33 I.R.B. 196; see also I.R.C. § 125(b), (c) and (g); see also Prop. Treas. Reg. § 1.125-1, Q&A 19]

Q 4:137   If an employer provides HDHP coverage through a cafeteria plan, but the employer's HSA contributions are not provided through the cafeteria plan, do the cafeteria plan nondiscrimination rules or the comparability rules apply to the HSA contributions?

The comparability rules in Code Section 4980G apply to the HSA contributions. The cafeteria plan nondiscrimination rules apply only to HSA contributions made through a cafeteria plan irrespective of whether the HDHP is provided through a cafeteria plan.

Example. Aardvark provides HDHP coverage through its cafeteria plan. Aardvark automatically contributes to the HSA of each employee who is an eligible individual with HDHP coverage through the cafeteria plan. Employees make no election with respect to Aardvark's HSA contributions and have no right to receive cash or other taxable benefits in lieu of the HSA contributions. Aardvark contributes only to the HSAs of employees who have elected HDHP coverage through the cafeteria plan. The comparability rules apply to Aardvark's HSA contributions because the HSA contributions are not made through the cafeteria plan.

Q 4:138   If, under the employer's cafeteria plan, employees who are eligible individuals and who participate in health assessments, disease management programs, or wellness programs, receive an employer contribution to an HSA, unless the employees elect cash, are the contributions subject to the comparability rules?

No. The comparability rules do not apply to employer contributions to an HSA made through a cafeteria plan. [See Prop. Treas. Reg. § 54.4980G-5, Q&A-3]

Tax Treatment of Contributions

Q 4:139   What are the main areas to consider relative to taxation of contributions?

There are three general areas of consideration for taxation of contributions:

1. Tax reporting by individuals (see Qs 4:140, 4:146),
2. Partnership considerations (see Qs 4:142–4:153), and
3. S corporation considerations (see Qs 4:154–4:162).

IRS Reporting by Individuals

Q 4:140   How are HSA contributions reported to the IRS by the taxpayer?

Form 8889—*Health Savings Accounts (HSAs)* is used to report HSA contributions (including those made on the account owner's behalf and employer contributions) and distributions. Form 8889 is also used to report distributions from an HSA. The taxpayer's deduction for contributions to an HSA is claimed on Form 1040 (line 28 on the 2005 version of the form).

Note. The maximum HSA contribution deduction is effectively reduced on Form 8889 for employer contributions to an HSA that are excluded from the employee's gross income.

Form 8889 is filed as an attachment to the taxpayer's federal income tax return, Form 1040. All contributions, including cafeteria plan pretax contributions, made for the year (including those made after the end of the year designated as made for the prior year) must be included on Form 8889. Contributions made by an employer, although generally excluded from an employee's gross income, must also be reflected on the form.

Note. The amount contributed during the year will be reflected on Form 5498-SA—*HSA, Archer MSA, or Medicare+Choice MSA Information*, which is received from the trustee or custodian of the HSA. An employer's contribution (if any) will be shown in box 12 of Form W-2—*Wage and Tax Statement* and coded W.

Q 4:141   Who must file Form 8889—*Health Savings Accounts (HSAs)*?

Form 8889—*Health Savings Accounts (HSAs)* must be filed by an individual if any of the following circumstances apply:

1. The individual made contributions for the year.
2. Someone (including an employer) made contributions on the individual's behalf for the year.
3. The individual received distributions from an HSA during the year.

4. The individual acquired an interest in an HSA because of the death of the account owner (the account holder).

Partnership Considerations

Q 4:142   May a partnership make HSA contributions on behalf of a partner or guaranteed payment partner?

Yes. A partnership may make contributions to an HSA on behalf of a partner or guaranteed payment partner (see example in Q 4:153).

Q 4:143   Are contributions by a partnership that are treated as distributions to the partner under Code Section 731 treated as a contribution to an HSA?

No. Generally, when an employer makes a contribution, within permissible limits, to the HSA on behalf of an employee who is an eligible individual, the contribution is excluded from the employee's gross income and wages. [I.R.C. § 106(d)] However, contributions by a partnership to a bona fide partner's HSA are not treated as contributions by an employer to the HSA of an employee. [Rev. Rul. 69-184, 1969-1 C.B. 256]

Q 4:144   What is the tax treatment of contributions to an HSA by a partnership that are considered distributions to the partner under Code Section 731?

Contributions by a partnership to a partner's HSA that are treated as distributions to the partner under Code Section 731 (regarding the extent of recognition or gain or loss on partnership distributions) are not deductible by the partnership and do not affect the distributive shares of partnership income and deductions. [Rev. Rul. 91-26, 1991-1 C.B. 184 (analysis of situation 1, last paragraph)]

Q 4:145   How are contributions by a partnership that are treated as distributions to the partner under Code Section 731 reported to the partner?

Contributions by a partnership that are treated as distributions to the partner under Code Section 731 are reported by the partnership as distributions of money on Form 1065, Schedule K-1—*Partner's Share of Income, Credits, Deductions, etc.*

Q 4:146   Are contributions by a partnership that are treated as distributions to the partner under Code Section 731 included in a partner's net earnings from self-employment (NESE)?

No. Contributions by a partnership that are treated as distributions to the partner under Code Section 731 are not included in the partner's NESE under

Code Section 1402(a) because the distributions under Section 731 do not affect a partner's distributive share of partnership income or loss under Code Section 702(a)(8).

Q 4:147   Are contributions by a partnership that are treated as distributions to the partner under Code Section 731 deductible by the partner?

Yes. The partner, if an eligible individual (see Q 2:6), may deduct the amount of the allowable contributions made to the partner's HSA during the taxable year as an adjustment to gross income on his or her federal income tax return. [I.R.C. §§ 62(a)(19), 223(a)]

Q 4:148   Are contributions by a partnership that are treated as guaranteed payments under Code Section 707(c), are derived from the partnership's trade or business, and are for services rendered to the partnership treated as contributions to an HSA?

No. Contributions by a partnership to a bona fide partner's HSA are not contributions by an employer to the HSA of an employee. [Rev. Rul. 69-184, 1969-1 C.B. 256]

Q 4:149   Are contributions by a partnership that are treated as guaranteed payments under Code Section 707(c) deductible by the partnership?

Yes. Contributions by a partnership to a partner's HSA for services rendered to the partnership that are treated as guaranteed payments under Code Section 707(c) are deductible by the partnership under Code Section 162 regarding trade or business expenses, provided the requirements of that section are satisfied, taking into account the rules of Code Section 263 (regarding capital expenditures). [I.R.C. §§ 162(a), 707(c); I.R.S. Notice 2005-8, Q&A 2, 2005-4 I.R.B. 368]

Q 4:150   Are contributions by a partnership that are treated as guaranteed payments under Code Section 707(c), are derived from the partnership's trade or business, and are for services rendered to the partnership included in a partner's gross income?

Yes. Contributions by a partnership that are treated as guaranteed payments under Code Section 707(c) are included in a partner's gross income. The contributions are not excludable from the partner's gross income under Code Section 106(d) because the contributions are treated as a distributive share of partnership income under Treasury Regulations Section 1.707-1(c) for purposes of all Code Sections other than Code Sections 61(a) and 162(a). [I.R.C. §§ 106(d), 707(c); See Rev. Rul. 91-26, 1991-1 C.B. 184; I.R.S. Notice 2005-8, Q&A 2, 2005-4 I.R.B. 368]

Q 4:151   How are contributions by a partnership to a partner's HSA that are treated as guaranteed payments under Code Section 707(c) reported by the partnership to the partner?

Contributions by a partnership to a partner's HSA that are treated as guaranteed payments under Code Section 707(c) are reported as guaranteed payments on Form 1065, Schedule K-1—*Partner's Share of Income, Credits, Deductions, etc.* [I.R.S. Notice 2005-8, Q&A 1, 2005-4 I.R.B. 368]

Q 4:152   Are contributions by a partnership that are treated as guaranteed payments under Code Section 707(c), are derived from the partnership's trade or business, and are for services rendered to the partnership treated as net earnings from self-employment?

Yes. Because the contributions are guaranteed payments that are derived from the partnership's trade or business, and are for services rendered to the partnership, the contributions are included in the partner's net earnings from self-employment under Code Section 1402(a) on the partner's Schedule SE (Form 1040). [I.R.S. Notice 2005-8, Q&A 2, 2005-4 I.R.B. 368]

Q 4:153   How are contributions by a partnership that are treated as guaranteed payments under Code Section 707(c), are derived from the partnership's trade or business, and are for services rendered to the partnership included in a partner's gross income?

The partner, if an eligible individual (see Q 2:6), is entitled to deduct the amount of the allowable contributions made to the partner's HSA during the taxable year as an adjustment to gross income on his or her federal income tax return. [I.R.C. §§ 62(a)(19), 223(a), 223(c)(1); I.R.S. Notice 2005-8, Q&A 2, 2005-4 I.R.B. 368]

The following example illustrates the answers in Qs 4:142 through 4:152.

Example. ABC Partnership is a limited partnership with three equal individual partners: Garth (a general partner), Lou (a limited partner), and Laszlo (a limited partner). Laszlo is to be paid $500 annually for services rendered to ABC Partnership in his capacity as a partner and without regard to ABC Partnership income (a guaranteed payment under Code Section 707(c)). The $500 payment to Laszlo is derived from ABC Partnership's trade or business. ABC Partnership has no employees. Garth, Lou, and Laszlo are eligible individuals (as defined in Code Section 223(c)(1)), and each has an HSA. During ABC Partnership's Year 1 taxable year, ABC Partnership makes the following contributions: a $300 contribution to Garth's HSA and a $300 contribution to Lou's HSAs, which are treated by ABC Partnership as Code Section 731 distributions to Garth and Lou; and a $500 contribution to Laszlo's HSA in lieu of paying Laszlo the guaranteed payment directly.

ABC Partnership's contributions to Garth's and Lou's HSAs are not deductible by ABC Partnership and, therefore, do not affect ABC Partnership's calculation of its taxable income or loss. [Rev. Rul. 91-26, 1991-1 C.B. 184] Garth and Lou are entitled to an above-the-line deduction, under Code Sections 223(a) and 62(a)(19), for the amount of the contributions made to their individual HSAs. The Section 731 distributions to Garth's and Lou's individual HSAs are reported as cash distributions to Garth and Lou on Garth's and Lou's Schedule K-1 (Form 1065). The distributions to Garth's and Lou's HSAs are not includible in Garth's and Lou's net earnings from self-employment under Code Section 1402(a), because distributions under Code Section 1402(a) do not affect a partner's distributive share of the partnership's income or loss under Code Section 702(a)(8).

ABC Partnership's contribution to Laszlo's HSA, which is treated as a guaranteed payment under Code Section 707(c) for services rendered to the partnership, is deductible by ABC Partnership under Code Section 162 (if the requirements of that section are satisfied, taking into account the rules of Code Section 263) and is includible in Laszlo's gross income. The contribution is not excludable from Laszlo's gross income under Code Section 106(d) because (1) the contribution is treated as a distributive share of partnership income for purposes of all code sections other than sections 61(a) and 162(a), and (2) a guaranteed payment to a partner is not treated as compensation to an employee. [Rev. Rul. 91-26, 1991-1 C.B. 184] The payment to Laszlo's HSA should be reported as a guaranteed payment on Schedule K-1 (Form 1065). Because the contribution is a guaranteed payment that is derived from the partnership's trade or business and is for services rendered to the partnership, the contribution constitutes net earnings from self-employment to Laszlo under Code Section 1402(a), which should be reported on Schedule SE (Form 1040). Laszlo is entitled, under Code Sections 223(a) and 62(a)(19), to deduct as an adjustment to gross income the amount of the contribution made to his HSA.

S Corporation Considerations

Q 4:154 How is an S corporation treated with respect to contributions made by the S corporation to the HSA of a 2 percent shareholder, who is also an employee (2 percent shareholder-employee) in consideration for services rendered to the S corporation?

Under Code Section 1372, for purposes of applying the provisions of Subtitle A that relate to fringe benefits, an S corporation is treated as a partnership. [I.R.C. § 1372(a)(1), 1372(b)]

Q 4:155   How is a 2 percent shareholder treated with respect to contributions made by the S corporation to the HSA of a 2 percent shareholder, who is also an employee (2 percent shareholder-employee) in consideration of services rendered to the S corporation?

Under Code Section 1372, for purposes of applying the provisions of Subtitle A that relate to fringe benefits, a 2 percent shareholder of the S corporation is treated as a partner of such partnership. [I.R.C. § 1372(a)(2), 1372(b); I.R.S. Notice 2005-8, Q&A 3, 2005-4 I.R.B. 368]

Practice Pointer. The term *2 percent shareholder* means any person who owns, or is considered to own through attribution, on any day during the taxable year of the S corporation, more than 2 percent of the outstanding stock of such corporation or stock possessing more than 2 percent of the total combined voting power of all stock of such corporation. [I.R.C. § 1372(b)] The attribution rules of Code Section 318 are used for the purpose of determining ownership.

Q 4:156   What is the tax treatment of an S corporation's contributions to an HSA of a 2 percent shareholder who is also an employee (2 percent shareholder-employee)?

When an S corporation, which is treated as a partnership (see Q 4:109), makes contributions to an HSA of a 2 percent shareholder-employee in consideration for services rendered, such contributions are treated as guaranteed payments under Code Section 707(c). [I.R.C. §§ 707(c), 1372(a)]

Q 4:157   Are contributions by an S corporation to an HSA of a 2 percent shareholder-employee in consideration for services rendered deductible by the S corporation?

Yes. Contributions by an S corporation, which is treated as a partnership (see Q 4:154), to an HSA of a 2 percent shareholder-employee in consideration for services rendered are deductible by the S corporation under Code Section 162, provided the requirements of that section are satisfied, taking into account the rules of Code Section 263 (regarding capital expenditures). [I.R.C. §§ 162(a), 707(c); I.R.S. Notice 2005-8, Q&A 3, 2005-4 I.R.B. 368]

Q 4:158   Are contributions by an S corporation to an HSA of a 2 percent shareholder-employee in consideration of services rendered excluded from a 2 percent shareholder-employee's gross income?

No. Contributions by an S corporation, which is treated as a partnership (see Q 4:154), to an HSA of a 2 percent shareholder-employee in consideration of services rendered are includible in the 2 percent shareholder-employee's gross income. A 2 percent shareholder-employee is not entitled to exclude these contributions from gross income under Code Section 106(d). [Rev. Rul. 91-26, 1991-1 C.B. 184]

Q 4:159   Are contributions made by an S corporation to an HSA of a 2 percent shareholder-employee subject to FICA tax?

Maybe. For employment tax purposes, when contributions are made by an S corporation to an HSA of a 2 percent shareholder-employee, the 2 percent shareholder-employee generally is treated as an employee subject to FICA tax (see Q 4:160). [I.R.S. Notice 2005-8, Q&A 3, 2005-4 I.R.B. 368]

Q 4:160   Is there an exception relative to FICA taxes for a contribution made by an S corporation to an HSA of a 2 percent shareholder-employee?

Yes. If the requirements for the exclusion under Code Section 3121(a)(2)(B) are satisfied, the S corporation's contributions to an HSA of a 2 percent shareholder-employee are not wages subject to FICA tax, even though the amounts must be included in wages for income tax withholding purposes on the 2 percent shareholder-employee's Form W-2—*Wage and Tax Statement.* [I.R.S. Notice 2005-8, Q&A 3, 2005-4 I.R.B. 368]

> **Practice Pointer.** Code Section 3121 does not generally include as *wages* payments for "medical or hospitalization expenses in connection with sickness or accident disability." [I.R.C. § 3121(a)(2)(B)]

Q 4:161   Are contributions made by an S corporation to an HSA of a 2 percent shareholder-employee subject to SECA taxes?

No. Contributions made by an S corporation to an HSA of a 2 percent shareholder-employee are not subject to the SECA tax. (See I.R.S. Ann. 92-16, 1992-5 I.R.B. 53, clarifying the FICA (Social Security and Medicare) tax treatment of accident and health premiums paid by an S corporation on behalf of a 2 percent shareholder-employee.)

Q 4:162   May a 2 percent shareholder-employee who is an eligible individual deduct the amount of the contributions made to an HSA by his or her employer during the taxable year as an adjustment to gross income on his or her federal income tax?

Yes. The 2 percent shareholder-employee, if an eligible individual (see Q 2:6), is entitled under Code Sections 223(a) and 62(a)(19) to deduct the amount of the employer's contributions to the 2 percent shareholder-employee's HSA during the taxable year as an adjustment to gross income on his or her federal income tax return. [I.R.S. Notice 2005-8, Q&A 3, 2005-4 I.R.B. 368; see I.R.S. Notice 2004-2, Q&A 19, 2004-2 I.R.B. 269, for employment tax rules concerning employer contributions to HSAs of employees other than 2 percent shareholder-employees (see Q 4:165).]

Chapter 5

HSA Rollovers and Transfers

Rollovers and trustee-to-trustee transfers are generally permitted to be made between health savings accounts (HSAs) of an account owner or between HSAs of a designated surviving spouse beneficiary. Rollovers and trustee-to-trustee transfers from an Archer Medical Savings Account (Archer MSA) to an HSA are also permitted. Nontaxable transfers of an HSA to a surviving spouse under a divorce or separation instrument are also allowed. Special rules apply to a non-spouse beneficiary of an HSA. (See charts in appendix D.)

General Rules

Q 5:1 Are rollovers permitted between HSA accounts?

Yes. If the account owner receives a distribution from an HSA account, he or she may generally roll over the distribution to an HSA (see Q 5:26). The HSA used to receive the distribution may be the same HSA that made the distribution, or a different HSA may be used. [I.R.C. § 223(f)(5); I.R.S. Notice 2004-2, Q&A 23, 2004-2 I.R.B. 269; I.R.S. Notice 2004-50, Q&A 77, 2004-33 I.R.B. 196] A distribution from an Archer MSA may generally be rolled over to an HSA (see Q 5:2). Trustee-to-trustee transfers between HSAs are also permitted (see Qs 5:37–5:40).

Q 5:2 Are rollovers permitted from an Archer MSA to an HSA?

Yes. If a taxpayer receives a distribution from an Archer MSA, he or she may generally roll over the distribution into an HSA for his or her own benefit.

[I.R.C. § 223(f)(5); I.R.S. Notice 2004-2, Q&A 23, 2004-2 I.R.B. 269] A non-spouse beneficiary may not roll over a distribution from an Archer MSA. [I.R.C. § 220(f)(5), 220(f)(8)]

Q 5:3 May distributions from an individual retirement account (IRA), a health reimbursement arrangement (HRA), or a health care flexible spending account (FSA) be rolled over into an HSA?

No. Rollovers from a traditional IRA, Roth IRA, HRA, or health care FSA to an HSA are not permitted. [I.R.S. Notice 2004-2, Q&A 23, 2004-2 I.R.B. 269] This restriction also applies to trustee-to-trustee transfers (see Q 5:36).

Note. There is a legislative proposal in Congress that would allow a one-time rollover from an HRA to an HSA. President Bush supports this proposal, but it is not clear if it will be enacted (see Q 1:28).

Q 5:4 May an individual claim a deduction for the amount rolled over?

No. Although the amount rolled over is generally not included in gross income, an individual may not claim a deduction for an amount that is rolled over. [I.R.C. §§ 219(d)(2), 223(d)(4)(A)]

Q 5:5 Must rollover contributions be made in cash?

No. Rollover contributions need not be in cash. [I.R.C. § 223(d)(1)(A); I.R.S. Notice 2004-50, Q&A 73, 2004-33 I.R.B. 196]

Q 5:6 Must the same property received in a distribution from an HSA or Archer MSA be rolled over?

Yes. The same property distributed from the HSA or Archer MSA must be rolled over. Proceeds from the sale of the property distributed may not be rolled over. [I.R.C. §§ 220(f)(5)(A), 223(f)(5)(A)]

Q 5:7 Must all of the cash or property received in a distribution from an HSA or Archer MSA be rolled over?

No. There is no requirement that the entire amount of cash or other property distributed from an HSA to an account owner (or Archer MSA) be rolled over (see Q 5:8). (See Q 5:27 regarding spouses.) Form 8889—*Health Savings Accounts (HSAs)* is used to calculate the taxable portion of an HSA distribution and any penalties that may apply. (For more information, see chapter 6.)

Q 5:8 Is an HSA trustee or custodian required to accept rollover contributions?

No. An HSA trustee or custodian is not required to accept rollover contributions. [I.R.S. Notice 2004-50, Q&A 78, 2004-33 I.R.B. 196]

Q 5:9   What are the tax consequences with respect to the portion of an HSA distribution that is not rolled over to an HSA?

The portion of a distribution that is not rolled over to an HSA may be subject to tax and penalty if not used to pay for qualified medical expenses. (For more information, see chapter 6.)

Q 5:10   Are rollovers subject to the annual contribution limits?

No. Rollovers are not subject to the annual contribution limits (see Q 4:73). [I.R.S. Notice 2004-2, Q&A 23, 2004-2 I.R.B. 269]

Q 5:11   May an HSA holder make a rollover contribution more than once during a one-year period?

No. In general, an account owner may make only one rollover contribution to an HSA during a one-year period. [I.R.C. § 223(f)(5)(B); I.R.S. Notice 2004-23, Q&A 55, 2004 I.R.B. 725] The one-year period ends on the date that an amount distributed from an HSA, not included in income by reason of a prior rollover, was received. Thus, if a rollover is made from one HSA to another HSA, another rollover cannot be made from either of those HSAs until 12 months have passed from the date the individual received the distribution that was rolled over. [I.R.S. Notice 2004-50, Q&A 55, 2004-33 I.R.B. 196]

Practice Pointer. The one-year rule applicable to an HSA is more restrictive than the one-year rule applicable to a traditional IRA (see examples below). The traditional IRA rules limit the number of distributions from the same IRA that may be rolled over. The IRA rules are based on proposed regulations issued in 1984. [Prop. Treas. Reg. § 1.408-4(b)(4)(ii)]

Example 1. Kayla established two traditional IRAs in 2003, IRA-A and IRA-B. She has never received a distribution from either IRA. On January 5, 2006, she rolls IRA-A to IRA-C. On February 5, 2006, she rolls IRA-B to IRA C. The one year rule has not been violated because the rule applies separately to each IRA. IRA-C may not be rolled over until the 12-month period has elapsed.

Example 2. Same facts as in the preceding example, except Kayla established two HSAs instead of traditional IRAs. The rollover of HSA-B to HSA-C violates the one-year rule, because only one rollover may be made to an HSA by an owner during the one-year period ending on the date that an amount distributed from an HSA, not included in income by reason of a prior rollover, was received.

Q 5:12   How is a second rollover treated if it is made before the one-year period has expired?

If a second rollover is made before the one-year period has expired, such subsequent rollover cannot be treated as a tax-free rollover and may be subject to tax and penalty if not used to pay for qualified medical expenses. [I.R.C. § 223(f)(5)] (For more information, see chapter 6.)

> **Example.** Wanda received a distribution from HSA-1 on January 15, 2006, and rolled it over to HSA-2 within the 60-day period (see Q 5:15). On January 14, 2007, Wanda received another distribution from HSA-1 (or HSA-2) and rolled the entire amount distributed into HSA-3. Wanda may have to include the amount she received on January 14, 2007, in income because it was received within the one-year period that ended on the date the amount initially rolled over was received (January 15, 2005). An excess contribution to the HSA has been made (see Q 4:73).

Q 5:13   Does a rollover of a distribution from an Archer MSA into another Archer MSA affect eligibility to roll over a distribution from an HSA?

No. Although rollovers between Archer MSAs are also subject to a one-year rule, the rule applies separately to rollovers between Archer MSAs. [I.R.C. § 220(f)(5)(B)]

> **Example.** Radcliff received distributions from an HSA and an Archer MSA during the same year. Subject to the 60-day rules, both the HSA and the Archer MSA may be rolled over into an HSA. [I.R.C. §§ 220(f)(5), 223(f)(5)] The same HSA may be used to receive both rollovers.

> **Example.** Jill received a rollover eligible distribution from an Archer MSA (MSA-1) and promptly rolled it over to an HSA (HSA-1). Because the one-year rule applies separately to HSAs and Archer MSAs, she may roll over the resulting amount from HSA-1 to another HSA (or back into HSA-1). The one-year period will commence when amounts are distributed from or rolled over from HSA-1.

Q 5:14   If an Archer MSA is rolled over into an HSA, when does the one-year rule pertaining to HSAs apply?

The one-year period applicable to an HSA begins when an amount in the HSA that is subsequently rolled over is withdrawn.

> **Example 1.** Gloria has only one HSA, from which no distributions have been made. She receives a distribution from an Archer MSA and promptly rolls it over into an HSA. Three weeks later, she withdraws the balance in her HSA and promptly rolls the amount into another HSA. The one-year requirement applicable to rollovers between HSAs has not been violated because the first rollover from the Archer MSA to the HSA is not counted (see Q 5:11).

> **Example 2.** Same facts as in the preceding example, except Gloria subsequently received another distribution from her Archer MSA within the one-year period. She may not roll over any portion of this distribution into either an HSA or another Archer MSA because the one-year period applicable to Archer MSAs has expired. [I.R.C. § 220(f)(5)]

Q 5:15   Must the rollover be completed within 60 days?

Yes. To qualify as a rollover, any amount paid or distributed to the account holder must be paid to an HSA within 60 days after the date of receipt of the payment or distribution. [I.R.C. § 223(f)(5)(A); I.R.S. Notice 2004-23, Q&A 55, 2004 I.R.B. 725] This requirement also applies to a spouse beneficiary (see Q 5:28). Similar rules apply to the rollover of an Archer MSA into an HSA. [I.R.C. § 220(f)(5)(A)]

Q 5:16   Must the total amount be distributed in order to roll over an HSA to another HSA?

No. A total distribution is not required from the distributing HSA or MSA in order to make a rollover contribution into another HSA. [I.R.C. § 223(f)(5)(A)]

Q 5:17   Must the same property received in a distribution be rolled over?

Yes. The identical property received in a distribution must be rolled over. There is no provision that permits property distributed from the HSA to be sold and the proceeds rolled over in its place. [I.R.C. § 223(f)(5)(B); see also I.R.C. § 408(d)(3)(A)]

Q 5:18   May an HSA trust or custodial agreement restrict the account owner's ability to roll over amounts from that HSA?

No. The HSA rules under Code Section 223 permit the rollover of amounts in an HSA to another HSA, and transfers from one trustee to another trustee. Thus, the trust or custodial agreement may not contain restrictions on the right to transfer from one HSA to another HSA. [I.R.C. § 223(f)(5); I.R.S. Notice 2004-50, Q&A 77, 2004-33 I.R.B. 196]

Note. An HSA trustee is not, however, required to accept a rollover contribution. [I.R.S. Notice 2004-50, Q&A 78, 2004-33 I.R.B. 196]

Q 5:19   How does a taxpayer report a rollover contribution?

The total of all distributions, including rollover contributions, is reported in Part II, line 12(a), of Form 8889—*Health Savings Accounts (HSAs)*. Any distributions received in 2005 that qualified as a rollover contribution to another HSA should be included. These amounts should be shown in box 1 of Form 1099-SA. Form 8889 is attached to Form 1040—*U.S. Individual Income Tax Return*.

Practice Pointer. It may be necessary to complete Form 8853—*Archer MSAs and Long-Term Care Insurance*, if required, before completing Form 8889.

Practice Pointer. A separate Part II must be completed when a joint return is filed and each spouse has a "separate HSA." [See Form 8889—*Health Savings Accounts (HSAs)*, Part II. It does not appear that separate forms are required when a spouse, as designated beneficiary, is treated as the account owner (see Q 5:30).

Q 5:20   How are rollover contributions reported by the trustee or custodian of the distributing HSA on Form 1099-SA?

A trustee or custodian that distributes a rollover contribution will report the contribution on Form 1099-SA—*Distributions From an HSA, Archer MSA, or Medicare Advantage MSA* in box 1. A code identifying the distribution is to be entered in box 3.

Q 5:21   What are the distribution codes that are used in box 3 of Form 1099-SA?

The following distribution codes are used for identifying and reporting HSA distributions in box 3 of Form 1099-SA—*Distributions From an HSA, Archer MSA, or Medicare Advantage MSA* (see Q 7:57):

- Normal distribution
- Excess contributions
- Disability
- Death other than code 6
- Prohibited transaction
- Death distribution after year of death to non-spouse beneficiary

Q 5:22   When must Form 1099-SA be filed with the IRS and copies provided to the holder of an HSA?

Form 1099-SA—*Distributions From an HSA, Archer MSA, or Medicare Advantage MSA* must be filed with the IRS and sent to each person for whom the trustee or custodian maintained an HSA for the year by May 31.

Q 5:23   How are HSA rollover contributions reported by the receiving trustee or custodian on Form 5498-SA?

The trustee or custodian that receives a rollover contribution must report the amount on line 4 of Form 5498-SA—*HSA, Archer MSA, or Medicare Advantage MSA Information*.

Note. For reporting purposes, trustee-to-trustee transfers to an HSA from an Archer MSA or another HSA are not reported.

Q 5:24   When must Form 5498-SA be filed with the IRS?

For 2005, Form 5498-SA—*HSA, Archer MSA, or Medicare Advantage MSA Information* must be filed with the IRS by May 31, 2006, for each person for whom the trustee or custodian maintains an HSA. A separate Form 5498 is required for each type of plan.

Q 5:25   When must Form 5498-SA be provided to participants?

If a trustee or custodian is required to file Form 5498-SA—*HSA, Archer MSA, or Medicare Advantage MSA Information*, a statement (generally Copy B) must be provided to the participant by May 31, 2005. This form may also be used to report the December 31, 2006, fair market value of the HSA if provided by January 31, 2007.

Inherited HSAs

Q 5:26   How is an HSA treated when the HSA account holder dies?

If the spouse is a designated beneficiary of the HSA, the spouse is automatically treated as the account owner thereafter. [I.R.C. § 223(f)(8)(A)] The rollover rules now apply to that spouse as the HSA account owner.

Q 5:27   May an inherited HSA be rolled over?

Maybe. If an HSA is inherited due to the death of the account holder, no rollover of that HSA is permitted unless the spouse of the decedent is the sole designated beneficiary. [I.R.C. § 223(f)(8)(A)]

Q 5:28   How is an HSA treated when the surviving spouse is not the sole designated beneficiary?

If a person other than the surviving spouse acquires an interest in an HSA, the account ceases to be an HSA as of the date of death (see Q 6:70). The fair market value of the HSA becomes taxable to the (non-spouse) beneficiary.

Example. Paul and Paula are married. Paul has an HSA designating his wife, Paula, and daugher, Sarah, as equal-share beneficiaries of his HSA. Paul dies. Neither Paula or Sarah may roll over their shares into an HSA. Paula and Sarah must include the value of Paul's HSA in their respective gross incomes.

Q 5:29   How is Form 8889 completed by a surviving spouse beneficiary upon the death of the account owner?

If the account owner's surviving spouse is the sole designated beneficiary, the HSA is treated as if the surviving spouse were the account owner. The surviving spouse completes Form 8889 as though the HSA belonged to him or her.

Q 5:30   If there is a non-spouse beneficiary, or if there is no designated beneficiary, how is Form 8889 completed upon the death of the account owner?

If the designated beneficiary is not the account owner's surviving spouse, or there is no designated beneficiary, the account ceases to be an HSA as of the date of death. The beneficiary completes Form 8889 as follows:

1. Enter "Death of HSA account owner" across the top of Form 8889.
2. Enter the name(s) and SSN as shown on federal tax return in the spaces provided at the top of Form 8889 and skip Part I.
3. On line 12a, enter the fair market value of the HSA as of the date of death.
4. On line 13, for a beneficiary other than the estate, enter qualified medical expenses incurred by the account owner before the date of death that are paid within one year after the date of death.
5. Complete the remainder of Part II of Form 8889.

Q 5:31 How is Form 8889 completed if the account owner's estate is the beneficiary?

If the account owner's estate is the beneficiary, the value of the HSA as of the date of death is included on the account owner's final income tax return. Complete Form 8889 as described in Q 5:30 above, except that Part I of Form 8889 should be completed if applicable.

Q 5:32 How is the value of an HSA reported if the account owner's estate is the beneficiary?

If the account owner's estate is the beneficiary, the value of the HSA as of the date of death is included on the account owner's final income tax return.

Q 5:33 How are earnings after the date of death treated?

Earnings on the account after the date of death are reported as income by the holder of the account (unless the spouse is the sole designated beneficiary; see Q 5:28).

Q 5:34 Are earnings after death subject to the additional 10 percent tax?

No. Earnings on the account after death are not subject to the 10 percent additional tax (see Q 6:60).

HSA Transfers

Q 5:35 Is there a limit on the number of trustee-to-trustee transfers permitted between HSAs?

No. The rules under Code Section 223(f)(5) limiting the number of rollover contributions to one a year do not apply to trustee-to-trustee transfers. Thus, there is no limit on the number of trustee-to-trustee transfers allowed during a year. [I.R.S. Notice 2004-50, Q&As 56 and 77, 2004-33 I.R.B. 196]

Q 5:36   How are trustee-to-trustee transfers between HSAs treated?

Trustee-to-trustee transfers between HSAs are not treated as distributions so long as there is no payment to the account owner or to any medical services provider. The amount transferred directly from one trustee or custodian to another trustee or custodian is not included in income, nor is it deducted as a contribution or included as a contribution on line 12(a) of Form 8889—*Health Savings Accounts (HSAs)*.

Q 5:37   Are HSA trustees or custodians required to accept trustee-to-trustee transfers?

No. HSA trustees are not required to accept trustee-to-trustee transfers from an HSA (or an Archer MSA). [I.R.S. Notice 2004-50, Q&A 78, 2004-2 I.R.B. 196]

Q 5:38   May the trust or custodial agreement contain restrictions concerning transfers from one HSA to another?

No. The HSA rules under Code Section 223 permit trustee-to-trustee transfers from one HSA to another HSA. Thus, the trust or custodial agreement may not contain restrictions on the right to transfer from one HSA to another HSA. [I.R.C. § 223(f)(5); I.R.S. Notice 2004-50, Q&A 77, 2004-33 I.R.B. 196]

Q 5:39   Must trustee-to-trustee transfers be made in cash?

No. Trustee-to-trustee transfers need not be made in cash. [I.R.C. § 223(d)(1)(A); I.R.S. Notice 2004-50, Q&A 73, 2004-33 I.R.B. 196]

Transfer Incident to Divorce

Q 5:40   May an HSA be transferred to a spouse or former spouse?

Yes. A transfer incident to divorce or separation agreement can occur between HSA accounts in a manner similar to IRAs. The transfer must take the form of a trustee-to-trustee transfer. [I.R.C. § 223(f)(7)]

Q 5:41   Is a transfer incident to divorce or a separation agreement treated as a taxable distribution?

No. Code Section 223(f)(7) provides that the transfer of all or a portion of the IRA holder's interest in an IRA to his or her spouse or former spouse under a divorce or separation instrument (see Q 5:43) is not considered a taxable distribution.

Q 5:42   What is a divorce or separation instrument?

For HSA purposes, a divorce or separation instrument must be:

- A decree of divorce or separate maintenance or a written instrument incident to such a decree,
- A written separation agreement, or
- A decree requiring a spouse to make payments for the support or maintenance of the other spouse

Consequently, if an individual divides his or her HSA under a private separation agreement that is not incident to either a divorce or a legal separation, the individual will be taxed pursuant to the general rule under Code Section 223(f). [I.R.C. §§ 71(b)(2)(A), 223(f)(7)]

Q 5:43   Is a transfer incident to divorce or a separation agreement treated as a distribution?

No. The transfer of an individual's interest in an HSA to an individual's spouse or former spouse under a divorce or separation instrument described in Code Section 71(b)(2)(A) will not be considered a taxable transfer. The transfer must be a direct trustee-to-trustee or custodian-to-custodian transfer. A rollover of a distribution does not qualify "as a transfer incident. . . ." Thus, it is not possible for a spouse or former spouse to retain any cash or property that is directly transferred.

Q 5:44   How is an HSA treated after a transfer incident to divorce?

After a transfer incident to divorce, the HSA is treated as an HSA with respect to which the spouse to whom the HSA was transferred is the account owner. [I.R.C. § 223(f)(7)]

Note. If such transfer is done properly (e.g., not transferred by rollover), it is not treated as a taxable distribution and the transferee spouse becomes the account owner of the HSA account with respect to the portion transferred pursuant to the divorce.

Q 5:45   May a trustee-to-trustee transfer be made to an HSA from an IRA, an HRA, or a health care FSA?

No. Direct transfers to an HSA from a traditional IRA, Roth IRA, HRA, or health care FSA to an HSA are not permitted. [I.R.S. Notice 2004-2, Q&A 23, 2004-2 I.R.B. 269] Only distributions from an HSA or an Archer MSA may be directly transferred into an HSA.

Other Issues

Q 5:46   May the health coverage tax credit be claimed for premiums paid with tax-free distributions from an HSA?

No. The health coverage tax credit under Code Section 35 regarding health insurance costs of eligible individuals is not available for premiums paid with tax-free distributions from an HSA. [I.R.C. § 35(g)(3); Rev. Proc. 2004-12, 2004-9 I.R.B. 528]

The health coverage tax credit is available to certain individuals who receive a pension benefit from the Pension Benefit Guaranty Corporation (PBGC) or are eligible to receive certain Trade Adjustment Assistance (TAA) or who are eligible for the Alternate Trade Adjustment Assistance (ATAA) program. (See Pub. 502—*Medical and Dental Expenses (Including the Health Coverage Tax Credit)*.)

Chapter 6

Distributions

Chapter 6 examines distributions made from an HSA and the taxation of those distributions. The treatment of the account and distributions of the account to the spouse, estate, or other beneficiary after death is discussed, as well as the income tax withholding rules. This chapter also discusses the return of contributions mistakenly made and the coordination of HSAs with the medical expense deduction. Finally, this chapter discusses distributions resulting from prohibited transactions or upon the account's ceasing to be an HSA due to a pledge of security for a loan.

Taxation of HSA Distributions

Q 6:1 When is an individual permitted to receive distributions from an HSA?

An individual is permitted to receive distributions from an HSA at any time. [I.R.S. Notice 2004-2, Q&A 24, 2004-2 I.R.B. 269]

Q 6:2 May an employer request a distribution from an employee's HSA?

No. Because the account owner's interest in an HSA is nonforfeitable, an employer may never request a distribution from an employee's HSA, even to recoup a portion of a contribution that the employer made to the employee's HSA. [I.R.C. § 223(d)(1)(E); I.R.S. Notice 2004-50, Q&A 82, 2004-33 I.R.B. 196]]

Example. On January 2, 2006, Starship Corporation makes the maximum annual contribution to the HSA of Edward, its only employee, with the expectation that Edward will work for the entire 2006 calendar year. On February 1, 2006, Edward terminates employment. The employer may not recoup from Edward's HSA any portion of the contribution it previously made.

Example. Western held an open enrollment period in fall of 2005 for plan year 2006 during which time employees were given the opportunity to elect either an HDHP/HSA option or, alternatively, an indemnity option under Western's Code Section 125 cafeteria plan. On January 1, 2006, the effective date of HDHP coverage, Western Corporation made $500 contributions to the HSAs of all employees who had elected the HDHP option during open enrollment and completed the HSA paperwork timely. On January 2, 2006, Steve, a Western employee, notified the human resources department that he had changed his mind and wanted to switch to the indemnity option. Under these facts, Western may not permit Steve to change his election for HDHP coverage, because it was made on a pretax basis through Western's cafeteria plan and none of the midyear change events in Treasury Regulations Section 1.125-4 has occurred. Further, even if Western were able to allow Steve to change to the indemnity option on a pretax basis, Western could not withdraw the $500 contribution made to Steve's HSA because such contribution is nonforfeitable.

Note. If Steve had alleged that a "mistake" was made in electing the HSA/HDHP coverage, there is still no direct authority that would allow Western to recover the $500 contribution. However, see Qs 6:64-6:65 regarding mistaken distributions.

Q 6:3 Must HSA distributions commence when the account owner attains a specified age?

No. An HSA is not subject to any required minimum distributions when the account owner reaches a stated age (e.g., 70½).

Q 6:4 How are distributions from an HSA taxed?

Distributions from an HSA used exclusively to pay for qualified medical expenses of the account owner, his or her spouse, or dependents generally are excludable from gross income. [I.R.C. § 223(f)(1)] Distributions used for other purposes are includible in the account owner's gross income and may also be subject to a 10 percent additional tax (see Qs 6:60; 6:62).

Caution. Distributions from an HSA for expenses that have been previously paid or otherwise reimbursed from another source or that have been taken as an itemized deduction must be included in the account owner's gross income and may be subject to a 10 percent additional tax. [I.R.S. Notice 2004-50, Q&A 39, 2004-33 I.R.B. 196]

Practice Pointer. The taxation of reimbursements from an HSA are governed by Code Section 223, and not by Code Section 105 (regarding amounts received under employer-sponsored accident and health plans) or Code Section 106 (regarding contributions by employers to accident and health plans). Thus, it is not necessary to rely on Code Section 105(b) to exclude from income an HSA distribution for medical care.

Q 6:5 May an account owner claim an investment loss if his or her HSA declines in value?

No. The account owner is entitled to a deduction (or exclusion in the case of an HSA funded through a cafeteria plan) for the allowable HSA contributions when made; therefore, no claim for loss on investments is permitted (even if the account is closed). The basis in an HSA is zero. It could also be argued that amounts when distributed would not necessarily have been taxable and, therefore, that no tax loss would have resulted and none can be recognized. [I.R.C. § 212; Treas. Reg. § 1.212-1]

Example. Jo-Ann establishes an HSA on January 1, 2006, and invests her HSA contribution of $3,000 in one of the riskier options offered by the HSA trustee. Before Jo-Ann withdraws any of the funds, her investment is declared worthless and her HSA account reflects a zero balance. Jo-Ann terminates her HSA. Jo-Ann may not claim an investment loss; she has already received a tax benefit in the form of a deduction for the contributions previously made.

Q 6:6 Can tax-free distributions be received by an individual who is not an HSA eligible individual (e.g., an individual who does not have HDHP coverage)?

Yes. Tax-free distribution status does not depend upon being an eligible individual (see Q 2:29). Thus, tax-free distributions may still be made from an HSA to pay or reimburse the qualified medical expenses of an account owner, spouse, or dependent within the meaning of Code Section 152, whether or not such individuals are currently *eligible individuals*.

Responsibility

Q 6:7 Is the trustee responsible for determining whether HSA distributions are used exclusively for qualified medical expenses?

No. Trustees are not responsible for determining whether the distributions are used exclusively for the payment of qualified medical expenses and thus are excludable from gross income (see Q 6:8). [I.R.S. Notice 2004-2, Q&A 29, 2004-2 I.R.B. 269]

Q 6:8   Who is responsible for determining whether HSA distributions are used exclusively for qualified medical expenses?

The individual who establishes the HSA is responsible. Individuals who establish HSAs make that determination and should maintain records of their medical expenses sufficient to show that the distributions have been made exclusively for qualified medical expenses and are, therefore, excludable from gross income. [I.R.S. Notice 2004-2, Q&A 29, 2004-2 I.R.B. 269] It should be noted that employers are not responsible for making medical expense determinations, either.

> **Practice Pointer.** HSA trustees or custodians are not required to determine whether HSA distributions are used for qualified medical expenses.

Restrictions on Distributions

Q 6:9   May a trustee or custodian place reasonable restrictions on withdrawals from an HSA?

Yes. As a general rule, an account owner must have the ability to request a withdrawal from the HSA at any time and for any reason (see Q 6:1). However, a trustee or custodian may place reasonable restrictions on both the frequency and the minimum amount of distributions from an HSA. For example, the trustee may prohibit distributions for amounts of less than $50 or allow only a certain number of distributions per month. Generally, the terms regarding the frequency or minimum amount of distributions from an HSA are matters of contract between the trustee and the account owner and should be specified in the Trust/Custodial agreement. [I.R.S. Notice 2004-50, Q&A 80, 2004-33 I.R.B. 196]

Q 6:10   May an HSA trust or custodial agreement restrict HSA distributions to pay or reimburse only the account owner's qualified medical expenses?

No. An HSA trust or custodial agreement may not contain a provision that restricts HSA distributions to pay or reimburse only the account owner's qualified medical expenses. Thus, the account owner is entitled to distributions for any purpose and distributions can be used to pay or reimburse qualified medical expenses or other, nonmedical expenditures. Only the account owner can determine how the HSA distributions will be used. (See Q 6:9 regarding reasonable restrictions on the frequency or minimum amount of HSA distributions.)

Q 6:11   Must distributions from an HSA that are not used exclusively for qualified medical expenses be included in the account owner's gross income?

Yes. Any amounts distributed from an HSA account that are not used to pay exclusively for qualified medical expenses of the account owner, spouse, and dependent (within the meaning of Code Section 152) are included in the gross income of the account owner and may be subject to an additional 10 percent tax (see Q 6:60). [I.R.S. Notice 2004-50, Q&A 25, 2004-33 I.R.B. 196]

Q 6:12   How are distributions from an HSA that are not used exclusively for qualified medical expenses reported by the account owner to the IRS?

The account owner must report all distributions from an HSA on Form 8889—*Health Savings Accounts (HSAs)*. The taxable portion is to be included in the total on Form 1040, line 21, with "HSA" entered on the dotted line next to line 21.

Q 6:13   How are distributions from an HSA that are subject to the 10 percent additional tax reported to the IRS by the account owner?

The 10 percent additional tax is reported on Form 8889—*Health Savings Accounts (HSAs)* that is filed with Form 1040. The additional tax is reported on line 63, with "HSA" entered on the dotted line next to line 63.

Q 6:14   Are amounts distributed to an individual not currently eligible to make contributions excluded from gross income if used exclusively for qualified medical expenses?

Yes. In general, amounts in an HSA can be used for qualified medical expenses of the account owner, his or spouse, or a dependent and will be excludable from gross income even if the individual receiving the payment is not currently eligible for contributions to the HSA (e.g., the individual is over age 65 and entitled to Medicare benefits or no longer has an HDHP). [I.R.S. Notice 2004-2, Q&A 25, 2004-2 I.R.B. 269] Amounts not used for qualified medical expenses may be subject to a 10 percent additional tax (see 6:60).

Q 6:15   Will tax-free treatment apply to a distribution made directly from the HSA to a third party that is used exclusively to pay for qualified medical expenses incurred by the account owner, spouse, or dependent?

Yes. This tax-free treatment applies to payments made directly from the HSA to the medical service provider, to payments from the HSA to the account owner as reimbursement for qualified medical expenses incurred, or to payments that the account owner uses to pay the service provider. [I.R.C. § 223(b)]

Q 6:16   May qualified medical expenses incurred before establishment of an HSA be reimbursed from an HSA?

In general, qualified medical expenses may be paid or reimbursed by an HSA only if they were incurred after the HSA was established. [I.R.S. Notice 2004-2,

Q&A 26, 2004-2 I.R.B. 269] A transitional rule was established for 2004 (see Q 6:17).

> **Example 1.** Fenway, an eligible individual, establishes and contributes $1,000 to an HSA in October 2006. Shortly thereafter, on December 1, 2006, Fenway incurs a $1,500 qualified medical expense and has a balance in his HSA of $1,025. On January 3, 2007, he contributes another $1,000 to his HSA, bringing the balance in the HSA to $2,025. In June 2007, Fenway receives a distribution of $1,500 as reimbursement for the $1,500 medical expense incurred in the prior year (2006). If Fenway can show that the $1,500 HSA distribution in 2007 is a reimbursement for a qualified medical expense that has not been previously paid for by a health insurance plan or otherwise reimbursed and has not been taken as an itemized deduction, the distribution is excludable from the account owner's gross income.

> **Example 2.** Same facts as in the preceding example, except that Fenway established the HSA on December 2, 2006. The expense was incurred before the HSA was established. The $1,500 distributed to Fenway is includable in Fenway's gross income and may be subject to a 10 percent additional tax (see Q 6:60).

Q 6:17   Why was transitional relief provided in 2004?

Because of the short time period between the enactment of HSAs and the effective date of Code Section 223 (see Q 2:4), many taxpayers who otherwise would be eligible to establish and contribute to HSAs (i.e., generally, individuals covered by an HDHP) were unable to do so early in 2004 because they were unable to locate trustees or custodians that were willing and able to open HSAs at that time. The IRS provided transitional relief, which expired on April 15, 2005. [I.R.S. Notice 2004-25, 2004-15 I.R.B. 727, modifying I.R.S. Notice 2004-2, Q&A 26, 2004-2 I.R.B. 269]

Transitional relief. For calendar year 2004, qualified medical expenses incurred on or after the later of January 1, 2004, or the first day of the month the individual became eligible for an HSA (i.e., covered under the HDHP) may be reimbursed from the HSA on a tax-free basis, as long as the HSA is established on or before April 15, 2005. In all other cases, qualified medical expenses may be paid or reimbursed by an HSA only if incurred after the HSA has been established (see Q 6:16).

Q 6:18   Are distributions from an HSA for expenses that were already reimbursed by another health plan excludable from gross income?

No. Distributions from an HSA made for expenses reimbursed by another health plan are not excludable from gross income, whether or not the other health plan is an HDHP. [I.R.S. Notice 2004-50, Q&A 36, 2004-33 I.R.B. 196; See also I.R.S. Notice 2004-2, Q&A 26, 2002-2 I.R.B. 269]

Q 6:19   In cases where both spouses have an HSA and one spouse (i.e., the account owner) uses distributions from his or her HSA to pay or reimburse the qualified medical expenses of the other spouse, are the distributions excluded from the account owner's gross income?

Yes. In the case of married account beneficiaries, each spouse owns his or her own HSA (no joint HSA between a married couple is possible), and qualified medical expenses of either spouse may be paid from either HSA. However, both HSAs may not reimburse the same expenses. [I.R.S. Notice 2004-50, Q&A 38, 2004-50, 2004-33 I.R.B. 196]

Q 6:20   What is the time limit for taking a distribution from an HSA to pay for a qualified medical expense incurred during the current year?

There is no time limit for taking a distribution from an HSA to pay for a qualified medical expense incurred during any year subsequent to the date the HSA is established. In other words, a qualified medical expense incurred in year one could provide the basis for a tax-free HSA distribution in year 10. However, the account owner must keep sufficient documentation to later show that amounts distributed were used for qualified medical expenses and were not previously paid or reimbursed from another source or claimed as an itemized deduction in a prior year. [I.R.S. Notice 2004-50, Q&A 39, 2004-33 I.R.B. 196]

Q 6:21   Do the Code Section 105(h) discrimination rules, which apply to self-insured plans, apply to a distribution from an HSA?

No. A self-insured medical reimbursement plan must satisfy the requirements of Code Section 105(h). That section is not satisfied if the plan discriminates in favor of highly compensated individuals (generally, the top-paid 25 percent of the workforce) as to eligibility to participate or to receive benefits. Because the exclusion from gross income for amounts distributed from an HSA is not determined by Code Section 105(b) but by Code Section 223(b), Section 105(h) does not apply to HSAs. [I.R.C. §§ 105(h), 223(b); I.R.S. Notice 2004-50, Q&A 83, 2004-33 I.R.B. 196]

Medical Care Paid from an HSA

Q 6:22   Who must incur the expense in order to qualify for tax-free distributions from the HSA?

Medical expenses incurred by the account owner, the account owner's spouse, or dependents (as defined in Code Section 152; see Q 2:33) qualify for tax-free distributions from the HSA, but only to the extent that such amounts are not compensated for by insurance or otherwise. [I.R.C. § 223(d)(2)(A)]

Q 6:23   What are qualified medical expenses for purposes of an HSA under Code Section 223?

Qualified medical expenses for purposes of an HSA are those expenses—incurred by the account owner, his or her spouse, and dependents—that would generally qualify for the medical and dental expenses deduction under Code Section 213(a) (except for premiums for health coverage). (See IRS Publication 969, *Health Savings Accounts and Other Tax-Favored Plans*, p. 6 (2005); IRS Publication 502, *Medical and Dental Expenses*.) Examples include amounts paid for doctors' fees, prescription medicines, and necessary hospital services not paid for by insurance. In addition, nonprescription medicines are also qualified medical expenses (notwithstanding that such amounts are not deductible). [See I.R.S. Notice 2004-2, Q&A 26, 2004-2 I.R.B. 269] Qualified medical expenses and deduction for medical expenses are more fully discussed below.

Q 6:24   What types of expenses are deductible under Code Section 213(a) as medical expenses?

Code Section 213(a) allows a deduction for uncompensated expenses for medical care of an individual, the individual's spouse, or a dependent, to the extent that the expenses exceed 7.5 percent of adjusted gross income. *Medical care* means amounts paid for the diagnosis, cure, mitigation, treatment, or prevention of disease, or for the purpose of affecting any structure or function of the body, and includes related transportation, lodging, and premium expenses. [I.R.C. § 213(a), 213(d), 213(d)(1)]

Practice Pointer. If an expense is not deductible under Code Section 213(a) because the 7.5 percent threshold is not satisfied, that expense may still be considered a qualified medical expense for HSA purposes.

Caution. Even though premiums for health coverage are deductible under Code Section 213, such amounts are generally not qualified medical expenses for HSA purposes (except for limited exceptions, see Q 6:33).

Q 6:25   Are HSA distributions coordinated with the medical expense deduction?

Yes. Any distribution for qualified medical expenses from an HSA that is not includible in the account owner's income will not be permitted to be used for purposes of determining whether the taxpayer has a deduction for medical expenses in excess of 7.5 percent of adjusted gross income (AGI) under Code Section 212 (see Q 6:24). Thus, "double dipping" is not permitted.

Q 6:26   May a payment or distribution from an HSA for a qualified medical expense also be deducted as an expense for medical care under Code Section 213(a)?

No. For purposes of determining the amount of the deduction for medical expenses under Code Section 213, any payment or distribution from an HSA for qualified medical expenses is not treated as an expense paid for medical care. [I.R.C. § 223(f)(6)]

Q 6:27   What requirements must medical care expenses satisfy to be deductible?

The deduction for medical care expenses will be confined strictly to expenses incurred primarily for the prevention or alleviation of a physical or mental defect or illness. Whether an expenditure is "primarily for" medical care is a question of fact. An expense that is merely beneficial to the general health of an individual is not an expense for medical care. [Treas. Reg. § 1.213-1(e)(1)(ii)]

Note. Code Section 262 provides that, except as otherwise expressly provided by the Code, no deduction is allowed for personal, living, or family expenses.

Medical care that is deductible and can therefore be paid from an HSA includes:

- Amounts paid for the diagnosis, cure, mitigation, treatment, or prevention of disease, or for the purpose of affecting any structure or function of the body (see Q 6:24) [I.R.C. § 213(d)(1)(A)]
- Expenses for transportation primarily for and essential to medical care referred to above (see Q 6:28)
- Amounts paid for certain lodging while away from home primarily for and essential to medical care (see Q 6:29)

(See Q 6:30, example 2.)

Q 6:28   Are transportation expenses related to medical care deductible?

Maybe. The term *medical care* also includes transportation that is "primarily for and essential to" medical care referred to in Code Section 213.

Example 1. Mandy, for purely personal reasons, travels to another locality to obtain an operation and other medical care prescribed by a doctor. Since the travel expenses were not "primarily for and essential to" medical care, Mandy may not deduct the costs of transportation as a medical expense. [I.R.C. § 213(d)(1); Treas. Reg. § 1.213-1(e)(1)(iv)]

Example 2. Sybil lives away from home at a psychiatric center. Her parents incur transportation costs to visit Sybil at regular intervals on the advice of the child's doctors and as an essential part of the child's therapy. The transportation costs are primarily for and essential to medical care and are deductible. (See Q 6:30 example 2.) [I.R.C. § 213; Rev. Rul. 58-533, 1958-2 C.B. 108]

Q 6:29   Are lodging expenses related to medical care deductible?

Possibly. The cost of lodging (up to $50 per night) while away from home that is primarily for and essential to medical care is an amount paid for medical care if:

1. The medical care is provided by a physician in a licensed hospital or a related or equivalent facility, and

2. There is no significant element of personal pleasure, recreation, or vacation in the travel away from home.

(See Q 6:30 example 2.) [I.R.C. § 213(d), 213(d)(1)(A)]

Q 6:30   Are meal expenses related to medical care deductible?

Meal expenses are deductible as expenses for medical care if they are provided at a hospital or similar institution at which the taxpayer, the taxpayer's spouse, or dependent is receiving medical care. [Treas. Reg. § 1.213-1(e)(1)(iv); Treas. Reg. § 1.213-1(e)(1)(v)]

Example 1. Upon the recommendation of a physician, Fluffy takes a cruise to relax. She incurs transportation expenses to get to the cruise and pays for the cost of the cruise. On the cruise, doctors provide both instructional seminars relating to nutrition, exercise, and adequate sleep, and certain medical services such as counseling. The seminars are for the preservation of Fluffy's general health only, and the medical services are available in Fluffy's hometown. Therefore, the transportation costs and costs of the cruise are not primarily for and essential to medical care;, thus they are not deductible. [Rev. Rul. 76-79, 1976-1 C.B. 70]

The following example illustrates Qs 6:27 through 6:29.

Example 2. Earl, a taxpayer, resides in City Q and is the parent of Dorothy, who is Earl's dependent. Dorothy suffers from a chronic disease and is being treated by physician C. At C's recommendation and for the purpose of obtaining medical information that may be useful in making decisions concerning Dorothy's treatment or in providing care to Dorothy, Earl travels to City W to attend a conference sponsored by an association that supports research and education concerning the disease. The conference is attended by medical practitioners and by individuals with the disease and their families. Earl spends the majority of his time at the conference attending sessions that disseminate medical information concerning Dorothy's disease. Other sessions at the conference involve presentations or discussions of legal issues, family finances, and other matters commonly arising in families in which a member has the disease. While in City W, Earl's social and recreational activities outside of the conference are secondary to Earl's attendance at the conference.

Earl pays the following expenses in connection with the conference:

- Transportation to City W
- Local transportation to the conference site
- A registration fee
- Meals while attending the conference
- Lodging at a hotel while attending the conference

Under these facts, the registration fee paid by Earl to attend the conference is primarily for medical care, and Earl's travel is primarily for and essential to medical care. Accordingly, Earl may deduct the registration fee and transportation expenses under Code Section 213 (subject to the limitations of that section). Earl may not deduct the cost of meals and lodging while attending the conference because neither Earl, Earl's spouse, nor a dependent is receiving medical care from a physician at a licensed hospital or similar institution. [I.R.C. § 213(d)(2); Treas. Reg. § 1.213-1(e)(1)(iv)] The result would be the same if Earl, and not Earl's dependent, was the individual with the disease. Thus, amounts paid by an individual for expenses of admission and transportation to a medical conference relating to the chronic disease of the individual's dependent are deductible as medical expenses under Code Section 213 (subject to the limitations of that section) if the costs are primarily for and essential to the medical care of the dependent. The costs of meals and lodging while attending the conference are not deductible as medical expenses under Code Section 213. [Rev. Rul. 2000-24, 2000-1 C.B. 963; Rev. Rul. 76-79, 1976-1 C.B. 70 is distinguished]

Q 6:31   Is cosmetic surgery deductible?

Generally, no. The term *medical care* generally does not include cosmetic surgery unless the surgery is necessary to ameliorate a deformity arising from, or directly related to, a congenital abnormality, a personal injury resulting from an accident or trauma, or a disfiguring disease.

In Letter Ruling 200344010, the IRS ruled that the costs of an individual's repeated cosmetic surgeries, performed to reduce a facial deformity arising out of earlier surgeries to treat several congenital abnormalities, are deductible medical expenses. [I.R.C. § 213(a), 213(d)(1)(A), 213(d)(9)(A), 213(d)(9)(B); Ltr. Rul. 200344010 (Mar. 27, 2003)]

Q 6:32   Are nonprescription drugs a qualified medical expense for purposes of an HSA?

Yes, qualified medical expenses include nonprescription drugs as described in Revenue Ruling 2003-102, as long as such drugs are used to alleviate an injury or medical condition, and not merely to improve general health. Such expenses are only qualified medical expenses to the extent that the expenses are not covered by insurance or otherwise (see Q 6:23). [I.R.S. Notice 2004-2, Q&A 26, 2004-2 I.R.B. 269; Rev. Rul. 2003-102, 2003-38 I.R.B. 559]

The term *qualified medical expenses* includes nonprescription drug expenses for medical care (see Q 6:23) paid by the account owner, or his or her spouse or dependents (as defined in Code Section 152). [I.R.S. Notice 2004-2, Q&A 26, 2004-2 I.R.B. 269]

Example. Gretta established an HSA. She buys a nonprescription antacid, allergy medicine, pain reliever, and cold medicine from a pharmacy. The items are either for personal use or use by Gretta's spouse or dependents to alleviate or treat personal injuries or sickness. Gretta also buys dietary supplements—vitamins—without a prescription to maintain general health.

Gretta is not compensated for the expenses by insurance or other sources. The employee's expenses for everything but the vitamins were for medical care and are qualified medical expenses. The vitamins were merely beneficial to the employee's general health and not an expense for medical care (see Q 6:42). [Rev. Rul. 2003-102, 2003-38 I.R.B. 559; see also Rev. Rul. 2003-58, 2003-22 I.R.B. 959, regarding expenses for certain nonprescription equipment, supplies, or diagnostic devices]

Q 6:33   Are health insurance premiums qualified medical expenses for purposes of an HSA?

Generally, no. Amounts in the HSA may generally not be used to pay health insurance premiums on a tax-free basis. The account owner would be subject to income tax and a 10 percent penalty for doing so. The four exceptions to this rule are as follows (see Q 2:27):

1. For HSA account owners who are age 65 and over;
2. For COBRA beneficiaries;
3. For individuals receiving unemployment compensation; and
4. For long-term care premiums (see Q 6:47).

[I.R.C. § 223(d)(2)(B); 223(d)(2)(C)]

Q 6:34   Are Medicare premiums that are deducted from a retiree Medicare beneficiary's Social Security benefits considered qualified medical expenses for purposes of an HSA?

Yes. HSA distributions used to reimburse a retiree Medicare beneficiary for premiums deducted from his or her Social Security benefits are qualified medical expenses. [I.R.S. Notice 2004-50, Q&A 45, 2004-33 I.R.B. 196]

Q 6:35   Can medical expenses paid or reimbursed by distributions from an HSA be treated as expenses paid for medical care for purposes of taking an itemized deduction under Code Section 213(a)?

No. For purposes of determining the itemized deduction for medical expenses, medical expenses paid or reimbursed by distributions from an HSA are not treated as expenses paid for medical care under Code Section 213. [I.R.S. Notice 2004-2, Q&A 26, 2004-2 I.R.B. 269]

Q 6:36   What are Medigap policies?

Medigap policies are Medicare supplement insurance policies sold by private insurance companies to fill "gaps" in Original Medicare Plan coverage. Except in Massachusetts, Minnesota, and Wisconsin, there are ten standardized plans, labeled Plan A through Plan J. Medigap policies work only with the Original

Medicare Plan. [www.medicare.gov/glossary/search.asp (search Medigap Policy)]

Q 6:37   Are premiums for Medigap policies treated as qualified medical expenses?

No. Premiums for Medigap policies are not qualified medical expenses. [I.R.S. Notice 2004-2, Q&A 27, 2004-2 I.R.B. 269]

Q 6:38   Can accident or disability premiums be paid out of an HSA?

No. Accident or disability premiums generally cannot be paid out of an HSA (see Q 3:39). An HSA (e.g., for age 65 or older) limits tax-free reimbursement of insurance to insurance that covers "medical care" as defined in Code Section 213(d)(1)(D) (i.e., insurance premiums that can be deducted). The regulations under Code Section 213 make clear that a policy providing an indemnity for loss of income (i.e., disability) or for loss of life, limb, or sight (i.e., accident) shall not be treated as covering expenses for medical care, unless such insurance contains a separate medical care component that is separately stated in the contract or furnished to the policyholder in a separate statement. [Treas. Reg. § 1.213-1(e)(4)]

Q 6:39   Are distributions from an HSA for long-term care services considered qualified medical expenses that are excluded from the account holder's income?

Yes. Code Section 213(d) provides that amounts paid for qualified long-term care services are medical care, and these amounts are, therefore, *qualified medical expenses* for purposes of an HSA. Amounts paid or distributed from an HSA and used to pay for qualified medical expenses are not includible in gross income. [I.R.C. §§ 213(d)(1)(C), 223(f)(1); I.R.S. Notice 2004-2, Q&A 27, 2004-2 I.R.B. 2; I.R.S. Notice 2004-50, Q&A 42, 2004-33 I.R.B. 196]

Note. Employer-provided coverage for long-term care services provided through a flexible spending or similar arrangement is included in an employee's gross income under Code Section 106. [I.R.C. § 106(c)] Although that section applies to benefits provided by a flexible spending or similar arrangement, it does not apply to distributions from an HSA (which is a personal health care savings vehicle used to pay for qualified medical expenses through a trust or custodial account) whether or not the HSA is funded by salary-reduction contributions through a Section 125 cafeteria plan. [I.R.C. § 223(f)(1)]

Q 6:40   May a retiree who is age 65 or older receive tax-free distributions from an HSA to pay the retiree's contribution to an employer's self-insured retiree health coverage?

Yes. Although the purchase of health insurance is generally not a qualified medical expense that can be paid or reimbursed by an HSA, there is an exception for coverage for health insurance once an account owner has attained age 65. [I.R.C. § 223(d)(2)(B), 223(d)(2)(C)(iv); see I.R.S. Notice 2004-2, Q&A 27, 2004-2 I.R.B. 269] The exception applies to both insured and self-insured plans, but not to Medigap coverage (see Qs 6:35, Q 6:36). [I.R.S. Notice 2004-50, Q&A 43, 2004-33 I.R.B. 196]. In addition, even if an account owner is not age 65, he or she (or his or her spouse and/or dependents) can receive tax-free HSA distributions for health insurance premiums if he or she is a COBRA beneficiary or an individual receiving unemployment compensation (see Q 6:33). Further, long-term care premiums may be purchased with HSA funds on a tax-free basis at any time, to the extent that they constitute deductible medical expense (see Q 6:47).

Q 6:41   May an individual who is under age 65 and has end stage renal disease or is disabled receive tax-free distributions from an HSA to pay for health insurance premiums?

Maybe. An HSA may not be used to pay for health insurance premiums on a tax-free basis unless the account owner has attained the age specified in Section 1811 of the Social Security Act (i.e., age 65), is a COBRA beneficiary, or is an individual receiving unemployment compensation). [I.R.C. § 223(d)(2)(B), 223(d)(2)(C)(iv); I.R.S. Notice 2004-50, Q&A 44, 2004-33 I.R.B. 196]

Q 6:42   Are amounts paid by an individual for equipment, supplies, and diagnostic devices that may be purchased without a prescription from a physician qualified medical expenses for purposes of an HSA?

Yes, they are.

Example. Larry, who is a diabetic with an injured leg, uses crutches and bandages and takes aspirin on the recommendation of his doctor. Code Section 213(b) allows deductions only for prescribed drugs and insulin. That section, however, applies only to medicines and drugs; other expenses, such as crutches, are deductible if they otherwise meet the definition of medical care (see Qs 2:26, Q 6:24). In addition, *medical care* includes amounts paid for the diagnosis, cure, mitigation, treatment, or prevention of disease or for the purpose of affecting any structure or function of the body. [I.R.C. §§ 213(d)(1), 213(d)(1)]

Because aspirin is a drug and does not require a physician's prescription, its cost is not deductible as a medical expense, even if a physician recommends its use to a patient. However, the cost of the aspirin may be paid from the HSA on a tax-free basis (see Q 6:45). In this case, the crutches and bandages mitigate the effect of Larry's injured leg, and the blood sugar test kit monitors and assists in treating Larry's diabetes. Therefore, the costs of these items are amounts paid for medical care and are deductible (subject to the limitations of Code Section 213). [Rev. Rul. 2003-58, 2003-22 I.R.B. 959, distinguished by Rev. Rul. 2003-102; 2003-38 I.R.B. 559]

Medicine and Drugs

Q 6:43   What does the term *medicine and drugs* include?

The term *medicine and drugs* includes only items that are legally procured and generally accepted as falling within the category of medicine and drugs. Toiletries (e.g., toothpaste), cosmetics (e.g., face creams), and sundry items are not medicines and drugs, and amounts expended for these items are not expenditures for medical care. [Treas. Reg. § 1.213-1(e)(2)]

Q 6:44   Can an HSA reimburse the cost of prescription drugs imported from Canada (or other countries)?

Generally, no. Medicines and drugs qualify as medical care under Code Section 213(d) only if they are "legally procured" and meet other IRS restrictions. Beginning with the 2004 version of IRS Publication 502—*Medical and Dental Expenses*, the IRS added the following item entitled "Medicines and Drugs from Other Countries":

> In general, you cannot include in your medical expenses the cost of a prescribed drug brought in (or ordered shipped) from another country, because you can only include the cost of a drug that was imported legally.

Exceptions. IRS Publication 502 contains two exceptions from the general prohibition; they are:

1. Prescribed drugs that the Food and Drug Administration (FDA) announces can be legally imported by individuals; and
2. Prescribed drugs purchased and consumed in another country, if the drugs are legal in both the United States and the other country. Consequently, whether an HSA can reimburse claims for prescription drugs imported from Canada generally will depend upon whether the FDA has declared importation of that particular drug to be legal.
   [Pub. 502 (for 2005), p. 15]

The FDA takes the position that "virtually all shipments of prescription drugs imported from a Canadian pharmacy will run afoul of the [Federal Food, Drug, and Cosmetic] Act." [See FDA Position on Foreign Drug Imports available at www.fda.gov/ora/import/] The Secretary of the Department of Health and Human Services and the Secretary of the Department of Commerce indicate that there are very significant safety and economic issues that must be addressed before importation of prescription drugs is permitted. [See *HHS Report on Prescription Drug Importation*, available at www/hhs.gov/importtaskforce/]

Q 6:45   Are amounts paid by an individual for medicines that may be purchased without a prescription of a physician qualified medical expenses for purposes of an HSA?

Yes; amounts paid by an individual for medicines that may be purchased without a prescription of a physician are qualified medical expenses for HSA purposes as long as the medicine or drug is for medical care (e.g., pain reliever, antacid, allergy medicine, aspirin, or cold medicine) and not merely to improve general health (e.g., vitamins). [Rev. Rul. 2003-102, 2003-38 I.R.B. 559; I.R.S. Notice 2004-2, Q&A 26, 2004-2 I.R.B. 269]

Q 6:46   What is meant by the term *prescribed drug*?

A *prescribed drug* is a drug or biological that requires a prescription from a physician for its use by an individual.

Distributions Used for Long-Term Care Premiums

Q 6:47   May an account owner pay qualified long-term care insurance premiums with a tax-free distribution from an HSA?

Yes, within limits. For HSA purposes, the payment for coverage under a qualified long-term care insurance contract by any HSA account owner, spouse, or dependent is a qualified medical expense. [I.R.C. § 223(d)(2)(C)(ii)] However, the amount that is permitted to be distributed from an HSA on a tax-free basis is subject to an age-based limit set forth in Code Section 213(d)(10) (see Q 6:49) [I.R.C. § 213(d)(10); I.R.S. Notice 2004-50, Q&A 40 and 41, 2004-33 I.R.B. 196]

The term *qualified long-term care insurance contract* is defined in Code Section 7702B(2).

Q 6:48   May an account owner pay qualified long-term care insurance premiums with tax-free distributions from an HSA if contributions to the HSA are made by salary reduction though a Code Section 125 cafeteria plan?

Yes. Section 125(f) provides that the term *qualified benefit* under a Code Section 125 cafeteria plan does not include any product that is advertised, marketed, or offered as long-term care insurance. However, for HSA purposes, the payment for coverage under a qualified long-term care insurance contract is a qualified medical expense (see Q 6:47). [I.R.S. Notice 2004-50, Q&A 40, 2004-33 I.R.B. 196]

> **Note.** Where an HSA that is offered under a cafeteria plan pays or reimburses individuals for qualified long-term care insurance premiums, the cafeteria plan rules are not applicable, because it is the HSA, not the long-term care insurance, that is offered under the cafeteria plan.

Q 6:49   Are tax-free distributions from an HSA for long-term care premiums limited in amount?

Yes. Code Section 213(d)(10) limits the deduction for *eligible long-term care premiums;* thus, the amount of distributions for qualified medical expenses that may be excluded from an account owner's income under an HSA may be less than the actual premium paid (see example below). [I.R.C. § 213(d)(10); I.R.S. Notice 2004-50, Q&A 41, 2004-33 I.R.B. 196]

> **Note.** Although eligible long-term care premiums are deductible medical expenses under Code Section 213, the deduction is limited to the annually adjusted amounts in Code Section 213(d)(10), which are based on age. Thus, HSA distributions to pay or reimburse qualified long-term care insurance premiums are qualified medical expenses, but the exclusion from gross income (tax-free return) is limited to the adjusted amounts. The limitations under Code Section 213(d)(10) regarding eligible long-term care premiums includible in the term *medical care* for 2006 and 2005 are shown in Table 6-1.

Any excess premium reimbursements are includible in gross income and may also be subject to the 10 percent additional tax (see Q 6:60).

Table 6-1. Eligible Long-Term Care Premiums

Attained Age on Last Day of Taxable Year	Limitation on Premiums	
	2006	*2005*
40 or below	$ 280	$ 270
41–50	$ 530	$ 510
51–60	$1,060	$1,020
61–70	$2,830	$2,720
71 and above	$3,530	$3,400

[Rev. Proc. 2005-70, § 3.19, 2005-47 I.R.B. 979; Rev. Proc. 2004-71, § 3.19, 2004-50 I.R.B. 1]

> **Example.** In 2006, Candace, age 41, pays premiums of $730 for a qualified long-term care insurance contract. The Code Section 213(d)(10) limit in calendar year 2006 for deductions for persons ages 41 through 50 is $530. Candace's HSA may reimburse Candace up to $530 on a tax-free basis for the long-term care premiums. The remaining $200 ($730 − $530), if reimbursed from the HSA, is not for qualified medical expenses and is includible in gross income. It may also be subject to an additional 10 percent tax (see Q 6:60).

Deemed Distribution Due to Prohibited Transactions

Q 6:50 Are account beneficiaries prohibited from engaging in any transactions involving an HSA?

Yes. The account owner (and his or her HSA account beneficiary) may not enter into activities that are termed *prohibited transactions* involving an HSA (see Q 6:53). [I.R.C. §§ 223(e)(2), 408(e)(2)]

Q 6:51 What are the results if an individual engages in a prohibited transaction?

If an account owner (or his or her account beneficiary) engages in a prohibited transaction during a taxable year involving the HSA, the HSA account ceases to be an HSA as of the first day of the taxable year and is deemed distributed at that time. The deemed distribution will be treated as not being used for qualified medical expenses. Therefore, the taxpayer will be subject to income taxes and to the 10 percent additional tax on HSA distributions that are not used for qualified medical expenses (see Q 6:60). [I.R.C. § 223(f)(2); I.R.S. Notice 2004-2, Q&A 25, 2004-2 I.R.B. 269]

The prohibited transaction penalty tax does not apply (see Q 6:55).

Q 6:52 May an account owner pledge his or her HSA as security for a loan?

No. If an account owner pledges any portion of an HSA as security for a loan, the portion so pledged is treated as a deemed distribution as of the first day of the taxable year and is subject to income tax and the 10 percent additional tax on HSA distributions that are not used for qualified medical expenses. [I.R.C. §§ 223(e)(2), 408(e)(4)] The prohibited transaction penalty tax does not apply (see Q 6:55).

Note. Any amount treated as distributed as the result of the pledging of an HSA account will not be treated as used to pay for qualified medical expenses. The account owner must, therefore, include the distribution in gross income and generally will be subject to the additional 10 percent tax on distributions not made for qualified medical expenses. [I.R.C. § 223(f)(2); I.R.S. Notice 2004-2, Q&A 25, 2004-2 I.R.B. 269]

Q 6:53 Is an HSA subject to the prohibited transaction provisions of the Code?

Yes. Notwithstanding whether an HSA is a plan within the meaning of Title I of ERISA (see Qs 8:1, 8:2), the prohibited transaction provisions of Code Section 4975 apply to an HSA. [I.R.C. §§ 223(e)(2), 408(e), 4975(e)(1)] However, if the account ceases be an HSA as of the first day of the year because the account owner engages in a prohibited transaction, the 15 percent prohibited transaction penalty tax does not apply. Neither will the tax apply if the account is treated as distributing all of its assets as of the first day of the year because the account owner pledged the account or a portion of the account as security for a loan. [I.R.C. § 4975(c)(6)]

Q 6:54 What is a prohibited transaction?

A prohibited transaction includes any direct or indirect:

- Sale, exchange, or lease of any property between a plan and a disqualified person (see Q 6:57);

- Loan of money or other extension of credit between a plan and a disqualified person;

- Provision of goods, services, or facilities between a plan and a disqualified person;

- Transfer to, or use by or for the benefit of, a disqualified person of the income or assets of a plan;

- Act by a disqualified person who is a fiduciary whereby he or she deals with the income or assets of a plan in his or her own interest or for his or her own account; or

- Receipt of any consideration for his or her own personal account by any disqualified person who is a fiduciary from any party dealing with the plan in connection with a transaction involving the income or assets of the plan.

[I.R.C. § 4975(c); ERISA § 406; see DOL Interp. Bull. 94-3, 59 Fed. Reg. 66735 (1994) (in-kind contributions to satisfy statutory or contractual funding obligations); Marshall v. Snyder, 430 F. Supp. 1224 (E.D.N.Y. 1977), *aff'd in part and remanded in part*, 572 F.2d 894 (2d Cir. 1978) (furnishing of goods, services, or facilities); Leigh v. Engle, 727 F.2d 113 (7th Cir. 1984) (self-dealing); New York State Teamsters Council Health & Hosp. Fund v. Estate of De Perno, 816 F. Supp. 138 (N.D.N.Y. 1993), *aff'd in part and remanded*, 18 F.3d 179 (2d Cir. 1994) (self-dealing, financial loss to trust fund not necessary); see also DOL Adv. Ops. 86-01A, 88-03A, 89-089A, 93-06A (direct expenses of salary and related cost of employees that work on plans)]

Personalized Investment Advice

The Pension Protection Act of 2006 (PPA) (H.R. 4) adds a new category of prohibited transaction exemption under ERISA and the Code in connection with the provision of investment advice through an "eligible investment advice arrangement" to beneficiaries of an HSA plan who direct the investment of their accounts under the plan. If the requirements of the exemption are met, the following are exempt from prohibited transaction treatment:

1. The provision of investment advice;

2. An investment transaction (i.e., a sale, acquisition, or holding of a security or other property) pursuant to the advice;

3. The direct or indirect receipt of fees or other compensation in connection with the provision of the advice or an investment transaction pursuant to the advice.

Note 1. The prohibited transaction exemptions provided under the provision does not in any manner alter existing individual or class exemptions provided by statute or administrative action.

Note 2. The PPA also directs the Secretary of Labor, in consultation with the Secretary of the Treasury, to determine, based on certain information to be solicited by the Secretary of Labor, whether there is any computer model investment advice program that meets the requirements of the provision and may be used by an HSA (or IRA). [See DOL Advisory Opinion 2001-09A (Dec, 14, 2001) available at *http://www.dol.gov/ebsa/programs/ori/advisory2001/2001-09A.htm*]

The determination is to be made by December 31, 2007. If the Secretary of Labor determines there is such a program, the exemption described above applies in connection with the use of the program with respect to HSA beneficiaries. If the Secretary of Labor determines that there is not such a program, such Secretary is directed to grant a class exemption from prohibited transaction treatment (as discussed below) for the provision of investment advice, investment transactions pursuant to such advice, and related fees to beneficiaries of such arrangements.

Eligible investment advice arrangements. The exemption applies in connection with the provision of investment advice by a fiduciary adviser under an "eligible investment advice arrangement." An *eligible investment advice arrangement* is an arrangement

1. That meets certain requirements (discussed below), and
2. Which either
   a. Provides that any fees (including any commission or compensation) received by the fiduciary adviser for investment advice or with respect to an investment transaction with respect to plan assets do not vary depending on the basis of any investment option selected, or
   b. Uses a computer model under an investment advice program as described below in connection with the provision of investment advice to a participant or beneficiary.

In the case of an eligible investment advice arrangement, the arrangement must be expressly authorized by a plan fiduciary other than the person offering the investment advice program, or any person providing investment options under the plan, and including an affiliate of either person.

Investment advice program using computer model. In general, if an eligible investment advice arrangement provides investment advice pursuant to a computer model, the model must satisfy all of the following requirements:

1. Applies generally accepted investment theories that takes into account the historic returns of different asset classes over defined periods of time;
2. Uses relevant information about the participant or beneficiary;
3. Uses prescribed objective criteria to provide asset allocation portfolios comprised of investment options under the plan;
4. Operates in a manner that is not biased in favor of any investment options offered by the fiduciary adviser or related person; and
5. Takes into account all the investment options under the plan in specifying how a participant's or beneficiary's account should be invested without inappropriate weighting of any investment option.

An eligible investment expert must certify, before the model is used and in accordance with rules prescribed by the Secretary, that the model meets these requirements. The certification must be renewed if there are material changes to the model as determined under regulations. For this purpose, an eligible investment expert is a person who meets requirements prescribed by the Secretary and who does not bear any material affiliation or contractual relationship with any investment adviser or related person.

In addition, if a computer model is used, the only investment advice that may be provided under the arrangement is the advice generated by the computer model, and any investment transaction pursuant the advice must occur solely at the direction of the participant or beneficiary. This requirement does not preclude the participant or beneficiary from requesting other investment advice, but only if the request has not been solicited by any person connected with carrying out the investment advice arrangement.

Audit requirements. In the case of an eligible investment advice arrangement with respect to an IRA an based plan, an audit is required at such times and in such manner as prescribed by the Secretary of Labor.

Notice requirements. Before the initial provision of investment advice, the fiduciary adviser must provide written notice (which may be in electronic form) containing various information to the recipient of the advice, including information relating to:

1. The role of any related party in the development of the investment advice program or the selection of investment options under the plan;
2. Past performance and rates of return for each investment option offered under the plan;
3. Any fees or other compensation to be received by the fiduciary adviser or affiliate;
4. Any material affiliation or contractual relationship of the fiduciary adviser or affiliates in the security or other property involved in the investment transaction;
5. The manner and under what circumstances any participant or beneficiary information will be used or disclosed;
6. The types of services provided by the fiduciary adviser in connection with the provision of investment advice;
7. The adviser's status as a fiduciary of the plan in connection with the provision of the advice; and
8. The ability of the recipient of the advice separately to arrange for the provision of advice by another adviser that could have no material affiliation with and receive no fees or other compensation in connection with the security or other property.

This information must be maintained in accurate form and must be provided to the recipient of the investment advice, without charge, on an annual basis, on request, or in the case of any material change.

Any notification must be written in a clear and conspicuous manner, calculated to be understood by the average plan participant, and sufficiently accurate and comprehensive so as to reasonably apprise participants and beneficiaries of the required information. The Treasury Department is directed to issue a model form for the disclosure of fees and other compensation as required by the provision. The fiduciary adviser must maintain for at least six years any records necessary for determining whether the requirements for the prohibited transaction exemption were met. A prohibited transaction will not be considered to have occurred solely because records were lost or destroyed before the end of six years due to circumstances beyond the adviser's control.

*Additional requirements.*In order for the exemption to apply, the following additional requirements must be satisfied:

1. The fiduciary adviser must provide disclosures applicable under securities laws;

2. An investment transaction must occur solely at the direction of the recipient of the advice;

3. Compensation received by the fiduciary adviser or affiliates in connection with an investment transaction must be reasonable; and

4. The terms of the investment transaction must be at least as favorable to the plan as an arm's length transaction would be.

Fiduciary adviser. For purposes of the exemption, a "fiduciary adviser" is defined as a person who is a fiduciary of the plan by reason of the provision of investment advice to a participant or beneficiary and who is also: (1) registered as an investment adviser under the Investment Advisers Act of 1940 or under state laws; (2) a bank, a similar financial institution supervised by the United states or a state, or a savings association (as defined under the Federal Deposit Insurance Act), but only if the advice is provided through a trust department that is subject to periodic examination and review by federal or state banking authorities; (3) an insurance company qualified to do business under state law; (4) registered as a broker or dealer under the Securities Exchange Act of 1934; (5) an affiliate of any of the preceding; or (6) an employee, agent or registered representative of any of the preceding who satisfies the requirements of applicable insurance, banking, and securities laws relating to the provision of advice. A person who develops the computer model or markets the investment advice program or computer model is treated as a person who is a plan fiduciary by reason of the provision of investment advice and is treated as a fiduciary adviser, except that the Secretary may prescribe rules under which only one fiduciary adviser may elect treatment as a plan fiduciary. "Affiliate" means an affiliated person as defined under Section 2(a)(3) of the Investment Company Act of 1940. "Registered representative" means a person described in Section 3(a)(18) of the Securities Exchange Act of 1934 or a person described in Section 202(a)(17) of the Investment Advisers Act of 1940.

Fiduciary rules. Subject to certain requirements, an employer or other person who is a plan fiduciary, other than a fiduciary adviser, is not treated as failing to meet the fiduciary requirements of ERISA, solely by reason of the provision of investment advice as permitted under the provision or of contracting for or otherwise arranging for the provision of the advice. This rule applies if (1) the advice is provided under an arrangement between the employer or plan fiduciary and the fiduciary adviser for the provision of investment advice by the fiduciary adviser as permitted under the provision; (2) the terms of the arrangement require compliance by the fiduciary adviser with the requirements of the provision; and (3) the terms of the arrangement include a written acknowledgement by the fiduciary adviser that the fiduciary adviser is a plan fiduciary with respect to the provision of the advice.

Practice Pointer. The employer or a plan fiduciary retains responsibility under ERISA for the prudent selection and periodic review of a fiduciary adviser with whom the employer or plan fiduciary has arranged for the provision of investment advice. However, the employer or plan fiduciary does not have the duty to monitor the specific investment advice given by a fiduciary adviser. The provision also provides that nothing in the fiduciary responsibility provisions of ERISA is to be construed to preclude the use of plan assets to pay for reasonable expenses in providing investment advice.

Special HSA/IRA determination. Under the provision, the Secretary of Labor must determine, in consultation with the Secretary of the Treasury, whether there is any computer model investment advice program that can be used by IRAs and HSAs and that meets the requirements of the provision. Thus, the exemptions provided under the provision with respect to an eligible investment advice arrangement involving a computer model do not apply to IRAs and HSAs. If the Secretary of Labor determines that there is a computer model investment advice program that can be used by IRAs and HSAs, the exemptions provided under the provision with respect to an eligible investment advice arrangement involving a computer model can apply to IRAs and HSAs.

Any person may request the Secretary of Labor to make a determination with respect to any computer model investment advice program as to whether it can be used by IRAs and HSAs, and the Secretary must make such determination within 90 days of the request.

Effective date. The investment advisor provisions are effective with respect to investment advice provided on or after January 1, 2007. The provision relating to the study by the Secretary of Labor is effective on the date of enactment. [ERISA §§ 408(b)(14), 408(g), 4975(d)(17), 4975(f)(8), as amended by PPA § 601]

Transactions with Service Providers

The PPA offers relief in that a transaction between a plan and a party in interest, who is not a fiduciary, is not a prohibited transaction (i.e., sale, exchange, lease, loan, or use of plan assets) under ERISA section 406 as long as the plan receives no less than adequate consideration, or pays no more than adequate consideration for the transaction. [IRC § 4975(d)(20); ERISA 406(a)(1)(A), (B) and (D); 408(b)(17) See PPA § 611].

Other Prohibited Transaction Exemptions

Prohibited transaction exemptions include:

- *Block trades.* Additional relief is provided for "block trades" (any trade of at least 10,000 shares or a fair market value of at least $200,000), which will be allocated among two or more client accounts of a fiduciary. [PPA § 611]
- *Electronic communication networks.* An exemption is provided for certain transactions on electronic communication networks. [PPA § 611(c)]
- *Foreign exchange transactions.* An exemption is provided for certain foreign exchange transactions. [PPA § 611(e)]

- *Cross-trading.* An exemption for certain cross-trading transactions is provided. [PPA § 611(g)]

- *Special correction period.* A prohibited transaction involving securities or commodities would be exempt if the correction is completed within 14 days after the fiduciary discovers (or should have discovered) that the transaction was prohibited. This prohibited transaction exemption does not apply to transactions involving employer securities. It also does not apply if, at the time of the transaction, the fiduciary or other party-in-interest (or any person knowingly participating in the transaction) knew (or should have known) that the transaction was prohibited. [PPA § 612]

Effective date. The new exemptions would be effective for transactions occurring after the PPA's enactment date, August , 2006. The correction period exemption applies to prohibited transactions that the fiduciary discovers (or should have discovered) after the date of enactment.

Q 6:55   What is the prohibited transaction penalty tax rate?

The penalty for initial violations is 15 percent of the amount involved for prohibited transactions occurring after August 5, 1997. If the transaction is not corrected, there is a second-tier excise tax of 100 percent of the amount involved. [I.R.C. § 4975(a); SBJA § 1453(a); TRA'97 § 1074(a)] The penalty tax does not apply, however, if the account ceased to be an HSA as of the first day of the year because the account owner engaged in a prohibited transaction or pledged the HSA as security for a loan. [I.R.C. § 4975(c)(6)] Excise taxes are not deductible.

Q 6:56   May the prohibited transaction rules be waived?

Yes. The Secretary of the Treasury has established a procedure under which a conditional or unconditional exemption from all or part of the prohibited transaction rules may be granted to any disqualified person or transaction or to any class of disqualified persons or transactions. [C.F.R. § 2570.30–2570.52] The Secretary of Labor generally may not grant an exemption unless he or she finds that such an exemption is

1. Administratively feasible;

2. In the interests of the plan and its participants and beneficiaries; and

3. Protective of the rights of participants and beneficiaries of the plan.

[I.R.C. § 4975(c)(2); Reorganization Plan No. 4 of 1978, 43 Fed. Reg. 47713 (Oct. 17, 1978) (transferring the authority of the Secretary of the Treasury to issue rulings under Code Section 4975 to the Secretary of Labor)] The Secretary of the Treasury has delegated this authority, along with most other responsibilities under ERISA, to the Assistant Secretary for the EBSA. [Sec'y of Labor's Order 1-87, 52 Fed. Reg. 13139 (Apr. 28, 1987)]

Q 6:57   What is meant by a disqualified person under the Code and by a party in interest under ERISA?

For purposes of the Code, the term *disqualified person* refers to any of the following:

1. A fiduciary (see Q 6:58);

2. A person providing services to a plan;

3. An employer, any of whose employees are covered by a plan;

4. An employee organization, any of whose members are covered by a plan;

5. An owner, direct or indirect, of 50 percent or more of the combined voting power of all classes of stock entitled to vote or the total value of shares of all classes of stock of a corporation, the capital interest or the profits interest of a partnership, or the beneficial interest of a trust or unincorporated enterprise that is an employer or an employee organization described in item 3 or 4;

6. A member of the family (spouse, ancestor, lineal descendant, or any spouse of a lineal descendant) of a person described in item 1, 2, 3, or 5;

7. A corporation, partnership, or trust or estate of which (or in which) 50 percent or more of the combined voting power of all classes of stock entitled to vote or the total value of shares of all classes of stock of such corporation, the capital interest or profits interest of such partnership, or the beneficial interest of such trust or estate is owned directly or indirectly or held by a person described in item 1, 2, 3, 4, or 5;

8. An officer or director (or an individual having powers or responsibilities similar to those of an officer or a director), a 10 percent or more shareholder, or a highly compensated employee (earning 10 percent or more of the yearly wages of an employer) of a person described in item 3, 4, 5, or 7; or

9. A 10 percent or more (in capital or profits) partner or joint venturer of a person described in item 3, 4, 5, or 7.

Note. ERISA prohibits certain transactions between a plan and a party in interest. Under the Code, the term *disqualified person* is used instead of *party in interest,* and it is defined slightly differently.

[I.R.C. § 4975(e)(2)]

For purposes of ERISA, the term *party in interest* refers to the following:

1. Any fiduciary (including, but not limited to, any administrator, officer, trustee, or custodian), counsel, or employee of an employee benefit plan;

2. A person providing services to a plan; [See Harris Trust and Savings Bank v. Solomon Smith Barney, 530 U.S. 238 (2000) (broker-dealer providing nondiscretionary equity trades to plan automatically classified as party in interest)]

3. An employer, any of whose employees are covered by a plan;

4. An employee organization, any of whose members are covered by a plan;

5. An owner, direct or indirect, of 50 percent or more of the combined voting power of all classes of stock entitled to vote or the total value of shares of all classes of stock of a corporation, the capital interest or the profits interest of a partnership, or the beneficial interest of a trust or unincorporated enterprise that is an employer or an employee organization described in item 3 or 4;

6. A relative (spouse, ancestor, lineal descendant, or any spouse of a lineal descendant) of any person described in item 1, 2, 3, or 5;

7. A corporation, partnership, or trust or estate of which (or in which) 50 percent or more of the combined voting power of all classes of stock entitled to vote or the total value of shares of all classes of stock of such corporation, the capital interest or profits interest of such partnership, or the beneficial interest of such trust or estate is owned directly or indirectly or held by persons described in item 1, 2, 3, 4, or 5;

8. An employee, an officer or director (or an individual having powers or responsibilities similar to those of an officer or a director), a 10 percent or more shareholder, or a highly compensated employee (earning 10 percent or more of the yearly wages of an employer) of a person described in item 2, 3, 4, or 5; or

9. A 10 percent or more (in capital or profits) partner or joint venturer of a person described in item 2, 3, 4, 5, or 7.

[E.R.I.S.A § 3(14)]

Q 6:58 What is meant by the term *fiduciary* for purposes of ERISA?

The term *fiduciary* refers to any person who:

1. Exercises any discretionary authority or discretionary control respecting management of a plan or exercises any authority or control respecting management or disposition of its assets;

2. Renders investment advice for a fee or other compensation, direct or indirect, with respect to any monies or other property of a plan, or has any authority or responsibility to do so; or

3. Has any discretionary authority or discretionary responsibility in the administration of a plan. Because the administration of a plan is the responsibility of the plan administrator, under ERISA the plan administrator is a fiduciary and thus is subject to the fiduciary duties imposed by ERISA.

Note. A person designated by a named fiduciary to carry out fiduciary responsibilities (other than trustee responsibilities under the plan) is treated as a fiduciary.

Accountants, attorneys, actuaries, insurance agents, and consultants who provide services to a plan are not considered fiduciaries unless they exercise discretionary authority or control over the management or administration of the plan or the assets of the plan, even if such activities are unauthorized. [ERISA § 3(21)(A); PWBA Interpretive Bulletin 75-5, Q&A D-1; C.F.R. § 2509.75-5, Q&A D-1; John Hancock Mut. Life Ins. Co. v. Harris Trust & Sav. Bank, 510 U.S. 86 (1993); Kaniewski v. Equitable Life Assurance Soc'y, No. 88-01296, 1993 W.L. 88200 (6th Cir. Mar. 26, 1993) (unpublished opinion); Kyle Rys Inc. v. Pacific Admin. Servs. Inc., 990 F.2d 513 (9th Cir. 1993) (third-party administrator); Nieto v. Ecker, 845 F.2d 868 (9th Cir. 1988) (attorneys); Olson v. EF Hutton & Co., 957 F.2d 622 (8th Cir. 1992); Procacci v. Drexel Burnham Lambert, No. 89-0555 (E.D. Pa. 1989); Painters of Phila. Dist. Council No. 21 Welfare Fund v. Price Waterhouse, 879 F.2d 1146 (3d Cir. 1989)(accountants); Pappas v. Buck Consultants Inc., 923 F.2d 531 (7th Cir. 1991) (actuaries); Schloegel v. Boswell, 994 F.2d 266 (5th Cir. 1993) (insurance agent)]. Fiduciary status is more fully discussed in chapter 23 of *The Pension Answer Book* (2005 edition).

Note. Since an HSA account owner likely exercises discretionary authority or discretionary control with respect to management or disposition of its assets, the account owner will likely be a fiduciary. In addition, although accountants, attorneys, actuaries, insurance agents, and consultants may not be considered fiduciaries, such individuals may be liable to a plan under traditional theories of malpractice.

Q 6:59   May an insurer offer a cash incentive to establish an HSA and an HDHP without violating the prohibited transaction rules?

Yes. The Department of Labor approved an insurer's program that awarded a $100 bonus payment to anyone who signed up for an HSA and an HDHP with the insurer. The DOL also approved a similar situation involving a bank that had a contractual relationship with an insurer. In that instance, the bank offered a $100 cash bonus if an individual established an HSA with the bank and an HDHP with the insurer. In both cases, (1) the individual was not required to make a contribution to receive the $100 bonus payment; (2) the payment, which could not be diverted, was made directly into the individual's HSA; and (3) neither the HDHP premiums nor the HSA account charges would vary (increase or decrease) as a result of the cash bonus payment. Thus, in those situations, the $100 cash bonus payment program was not a prohibited transaction. [I.R.C. § 4975(c)(2), 4975(e)(1)(E); DOL Adv. Op. 2004-09A (Dec. 22, 2004)] See appendix C.

If the cash bonus payment were to be made to the individual (or other disqualified person), rather than to the HSA, the payment would have constituted a prohibited transaction. Similarly, if the cash bonus payment were conditioned on the investment in products of the bank or insurer, the cash bonus program would likely have constituted a prohibited transaction. The controlled group rules under Code Section 414(b), (c), and (m) would also have to be considered in some situations in determining the identity of all disqualified persons (see Q 6:55). [DOL Adv. Op. 2004-09A (Dec. 22, 2004) footnotes 2 and 4]

The 10 Percent Additional Tax

Q 6:60   When is a distribution from an HSA subject to the 10 percent additional tax?

Unless an exception applies all HSA distributions that are not used exclusively to pay or reimburse qualified medical expenses of the account owner, his or her spouse, or a dependent are subject to a 10 percent additional tax. [I.R.C. § 223(f)(4)(A); I.R.S. Notice 2004-2, Q&A 25, 2004-2 I.R.B. 269]

Q 6:61   May a distribution that does not violate the contribution limit be treated as a distribution of an excess amount?

No. An individual may not elect to treat a distribution as a correction of an excess contribution unless the contribution exceeds the contribution limits discussed in chapter 4. [I.R.S. Notice 2004-50, Q&A 35, 2004-33 I.R.B. 196] Any distribution from the account that is not a correction of a true excess is subject to the additional 10 percent tax to the extent it is not used for qualified medical expenses, unless another exception applies.

Q 6:62   What are the exceptions to the 10 percent additional tax on distribution not used exclusively to pay or reimburse qualified medical expenses of the account owner, his or her spouse, or a dependent?

The four general exceptions to the 10 percent additional tax are as follows:

1. *Disability*. Distributions made after the account owner becomes disabled [I.R.C. § 223(f)(4)(B)];
2. *Death*. Distributions made to the designated beneficiary (or beneficiaries) upon the death of the account owner [I.R.C. § 223(f)(4)(B)];
3. *Age (currently 65)*. Distributions made to an account owner after he or she becomes eligible for Medicare (i.e., the age specified in Section 1811 of the Social Security Act, currently age 65) [I.R.C. § 223(f)(4)(C)];
4. *Rollovers and transfers*. Distributions from an HSA that are rolled over to another HSA within 60 days after the day of receipt of the distribution or transferred directly from one HSA to another HSA (see chapter 5).

Note. If an account owner withdraws earnings from an HSA due to having excess contributions (see Q 4:74) and such amounts are not used for one of the exceptions above, the 10 percent additional tax does not appear to apply (see Q 7:71). [See I.R.S. Notice 2004-50, Q&A 34, 2004-33 I.R.B. 196 (no suggestion of 10 percent additional tax)]

There are several additional exceptions that avoid the 10 percent additional tax, including the following:

- A distribution made by a mistake of fact due to reasonable cause that is timely repaid into an HSA (see Q 6:66)

- An eligible rollover distribution that is deposited into another HSA within 60 days of the receipt of the distribution (see Q 5:1) [I.R.C. §§ 223(f)(2), 223(f)(5)]
- A direct transfer (trustee-to-trustee) of an HSA account from one spouse to another spouse, or former spouse, under a divorce or separation instrument (see Q 5:36) [I.R.C. § 223(f)(7)]

Rollovers and transfers are more fully discussed in chapter 5.

Q 6:63   When is an individual disabled?

An individual is disabled if all three of the following conditions are satisfied:

1. The individual is unable to engage in any substantial gainful activity due to a medically determinable physical or mental impairment;
2. The disability is expected to result in death or to be of a long-continued and indefinite duration; and
3. The individual furnishes proof of the disability in the form and manner required by IRS.

[I.R.C. § 72(m)(7)]

Whether or not the impairment in a particular case constitutes a disability will be determined with reference to all the facts in the case. The following are examples of impairments that would ordinarily be considered as preventing substantial gainful activity:

- Cancer that is inoperable or progressive;
- Loss of use of two limbs;
- Certain progressive diseases that have resulted in the physical loss or atrophy of a limb (e.g., diabetes, multiple sclerosis, or Buerger's disease);
- Diseases of the heart, lungs, or blood vessels that have resulted in major loss of heart or lung reserve as evidenced by X-ray, electrocardiogram, or other objective findings, so that, despite medical treatment, breathlessness, pain, or fatigue is produced on slight exertion (e.g., walking several blocks, using public transportation, or doing small chores);
- Damage to the brain or a brain abnormality that has resulted in severe loss of judgment, intellect, orientation, or memory;
- Mental diseases (e.g., psychosis or severe psychoneurosis) requiring continued institutionalization or constant supervision of the individual;
- Loss or diminution of vision to the extent that the affected individual has a central visual acuity of no better than 20/200 in the better eye after best correction, or has a limitation in the fields of vision such that the widest diameter of the visual fields subtends an angle no greater than 20 degrees;
- Permanent and total loss of speech; and
- Total deafness uncorrectable by a hearing aid.

It should be noted that the existence of one or more of the impairments described above (or of an impairment of greater severity) will not, in and of itself, always permit a finding that an individual is disabled. Any impairment, whether of lesser or greater severity, must be evaluated in terms of whether it does, in fact, prevent the individual from engaging in the individual's customary or any comparable substantial gainful activity. [Treas. Reg. § 1.72-17A(f)(2)]

Q 6:64 What is a substantial gainful activity for purposes of the disability exception?

The term *substantial gainful activity* means an activity or any comparable activity in which an individual customarily engaged prior to the advent of the disability. [Treas. Reg. § 1.72-17A(f)(1)]

In determining whether an individual's impairment renders the individual unable to engage in any substantial gainful activity, primary consideration is given to the nature and severity of the impairment. Consideration is also given to other factors (e.g., the individual's education, training, and work experience). Substantial gainful activity is the activity, or a comparable activity, in which the individual customarily engaged prior to the advent of the disability or prior to retirement if the individual was retired at the time the disability arose. [Treas. Reg. § 1.72-17A(f)(1)]

An impairment that is remediable does not constitute a disability. An individual will not be deemed disabled if, with reasonable effort and safety, the impairment can be diminished to the extent that the individual will not be prevented by the impairment from engaging in the customary or any comparable substantial gainful activity. [Treas. Reg. § 1.72-17A(f)(4)]

Q 6:65 What is an indefinite duration for purposes of the disability exception?

The term *indefinite duration* means that the individual is unable to reasonably anticipate that the disability will, in the foreseeable future, be so diminished as no longer to prevent any substantial gainful activity. For example, an individual who suffers a broken bone that prevents him or her from working cannot be considered disabled if his or her recovery can be expected in the foreseeable future. [Treas. Reg. § 1.72-17A(f)(3)]

The term *indefinite* is used in the sense that it cannot reasonably be anticipated that the impairment will, in the foreseeable future, be so diminished as no longer to prevent substantial gainful activity. For example, an individual who suffers a bone fracture that prevents the individual from working for an extended period of time will not be considered disabled, if recovery can be expected in the foreseeable future; however, if the fracture persistently fails to knit, the individual would ordinarily be considered disabled. [Treas. Reg. § 1.72-17A(f)(3); Williams v. Comm., T.C. Summ. Op. 2004-57 (May 13, 2004); Meyer v. Comm., T.C. Memo 2003-12 (Jan. 13, 2003)

Returning Distributions Mistakenly Made

Q 6:66   May a distribution made erroneously be redeposited into an HSA?

Possibly. If there is clear and convincing evidence that amounts were distributed from an HSA because of a mistake of fact due to reasonable cause, the account owner can repay the mistaken distribution no later than April 15 following the first year the account owner knew or should have known that the distribution was a mistake (provided the trustee allows this; see Q 6:66). [I.R.S. Notice 2004-50, Q&A 37, 2004-33 I.R.B. 196]

Q 6:67   What is reasonable cause that would permit a mistake-of-fact distribution from an HSA to be redeposited into an HSA?

In general, reasonable cause exists when there is "clear and convincing evidence" that the account owner reasonably, but mistakenly, believed that an expense was a qualified medical expense and was reimbursed for that expense from the HSA. [I.R.S. Notice 2004-50, Q&A 37, 2004-33 I.R.B. 196]

Q 6:68   Are trustees and custodians required to accept the return of mistaken distributions?

No. A trustee or custodian is not obligated to accept a return of a mistaken distribution. If the trustee agrees to accept a return due to a mistake of fact, the trustee may rely upon the account owner's representation that the contribution is a repayment of a mistake-of-fact distribution and not subject to the contribution limit. [I.R.S. Notice 2004-50, Q&A 76, 2004-33 I.R.B. 196]

Q 6:69   What is the tax treatment of a mistake-of-fact HSA distribution that is properly and timely repaid into an HSA?

A mistake-of-fact HSA distribution that is properly and timely redeposited into an HSA is treated as follows:

1. The distribution is not included in gross income.
2. The distribution is not subject to the 10 percent additional tax (see Q 6:60).
3. The repayment is not subject to the 6 percent excise tax on excess contributions (see Q 4:74).

[I.R.S. Notice 2004-50, Q&A 37, 2004-33 I.R.B. 196] (See also Q 7:32.)

Death Distributions to Designated Beneficiaries

Q 6:70　What happens to an HSA upon the death of the account owner?

The answer depends upon who is designated—the spouse or another beneficiary—as the account owner. A beneficiary may be selected when the HSA account is selected.

Q 6:71　What are the federal income tax consequences of the HSA account owner's death?

General rules upon death of the HSA owner (account owner) depend upon the identity of the designated beneficiary, as follows:

1. *Spouse beneficiary.* If the taxpayer designated his or her spouse as the designated beneficiary, the surviving spouse is automatically treated as the account owner of the HSA after the taxpayer's death. Thus, if the surviving spouse is the designated beneficiary when the HSA owner dies, then the HSA is assumed automatically by the surviving spouse. [I.R.C. § 223(f)(8)(A)]

2. *Non-spouse beneficiary.* If a non-spouse beneficiary (other than the estate) is the designated beneficiary, the HSA ceases to be an HSA on the date of death and the fair-market value of the HSA account on the date of death is treated as taxable to the non-spouse beneficiary in the tax year that included the date of death. [I.R.C. § 223(f)(8)(B)(i)(I), 223(f)(8)(B)(i)(II); I.R.S. Notice 2004-2, Q&A 31, 2004-2 I.R.B. 269]

Practice Pointer. A non-spouse designated beneficiary is entitled to the Income in Respect to a Decedent deduction under Code Section 691. [I.R.C. §§ 223(f)(8)(B)(i), 691(c)]

Note. In the case of a non-spouse beneficiary, any earnings on the account after the date of death (box 1 minus box 4 of Form 1099-SA) are taxable. In the case of an HSA, the amount included on the federal income tax return (other than an estate) is first reduced by any payments from the HSA made for the decedent's qualified medical expenses incurred before the decedent's death and paid within one year after the date of death. (See Q 7:57.)

3. *Estate beneficiary.* If the taxpayer's estate is the designated beneficiary, the fair market value of the HSA on the date of death is includible on the decedent's final return.

Distributions made to a designated beneficiary are not taxable to the extent that the decedent incurred qualified medical expenses prior to death and the designated beneficiary pays such amounts within one year of the date of death. [I.R.C. § 223(f)(8)(B)(ii)(I)]

If the designated beneficiary is the estate, and the decedent's gross income for the last taxable year is increased by the amount of the distribution, then the estate taxes are reduced by that amount. [I.R.C. § 223(f)(8)(B)(ii)(II)]

Q 6:72 Is a surviving spouse who assumes ownership of an HSA upon the death of his or her spouse (and former HSA account owner) subject to income tax upon transfer of the HSA?

No; the surviving spouse who assumes ownership of an HSA is subject to income taxes only to the extent that HSA distributions are not used to pay for qualified medical expenses. [I.R.S. Notice 2004-2, Q&A 31, 2004-2 I.R.B. 269]

Q 6:73 How is an HSA treated for federal estate tax purposes?

Generally, there is no specific exclusion for HSAs under the federal estate tax rules. Therefore, in the event of death, the HSA balance will be includible in the account owner's gross estate for federal estate tax purposes. However, if the surviving spouse is the beneficiary of the HSA, the amount in the HSA may qualify for the marital deduction available under Code Section 2056.

Q 6:74 How is an HSA treated for federal gift tax purposes?

The amount that a beneficiary receives from an HSA plan is not treated as a transfer of property for federal gift tax purposes. [I.R.C. § 2503(e)(1), 2503(e)(2)(A)]

Income Tax Withholding on HSA Distributions

Q 6:75 Is a distribution from an HSA subject to federal income tax withholding?

No. Code Section 3405 does not apply, because an HSA would not be considered a pension plan. Since distributions used to pay for qualified medical expenses are not subject to income tax, no withholding of federal income tax would apply. However, in cases where the HSA distribution is not used for medical expenses, or the HSA account owner dies and the designated beneficiary is either a non-spouse or the account owner's estate, the value of the distribution would become taxable.

Q 6:76 Are payors required to withhold on distributions that are not used for qualified medical expenses?

No. Although certain distributions may be taxable, the payer of the HSA distribution is not required to withhold income taxes from the HSA distribution. The account owner is responsible for determining the taxability or nontaxability of any distribution from an HSA (see Q 6:8).

Chapter 7

Administration and Compliance

This chapter examines the administrative and compliance issues relating to trustees and custodians with respect to IRS reporting and participant information reporting. The sponsor's use of model documents for establishing Health Savings Accounts (HSAs) is also discussed in this chapter, as well as restrictions on investments and distributions. Finally, the specific requirements for filing IRS forms are addressed in this chapter. See appendix I for administrative forms.

HSA Documents

Q 7:1   Must an HSA be offered in the form of a trust?

No. HSAs may be offered in the form of a trust or a custodial account. [I.R.C. § 223(d)(1), 223(d)(4)(E)]

Q 7:2   What is the difference between an HSA custodian and an HSA trustee?

The differences between a *custodian* and a *trustee* are minor. A trust is a legal entity under which assets are actually owned and held on behalf of a beneficiary.

As the legal owner, a trustee has some level of discretionary fiduciary authority over the assets of the fund. The trustee must exercise that authority in the best interests of the beneficial owner (i.e., the account owner).

A custodial arrangement is similar to a trust, but the custodian simply holds the assets on behalf of the owner of the assets. Other than holding the assets and doing as the owner orders, the custodian has no fiduciary obligations to the owner.

Q 7:3   Does federal or state law determine whether an arrangement is a trust or custodial account?

Whether an arrangement constitutes a trust or custodial arrangement is determined under state law.

Q 7:4   Has the IRS issued documents through which an individual may establish an HSA?

Yes. Model forms that trustees and custodians can use to allow individuals to establish an HSA (Model Form 5305-B—*Health Savings Trust Account* (rev. Aug. 2004) and Form 305-C—*Health Savings Custodial Account* (rev. Aug. 2004)) were issued in August 2004. [I.R.S. Notice 2004-50, Q&A 62, 2004-33 I.R.B. 196] Draft versions of HSA model forms became available June 25, 2004 (see Q 7:5).

Q 7:5   May an HSA be established using the draft version of Forms 5305-B or 5305-C?

No. The purpose of issuing draft forms was to allow HSA trustees and custodians to use some or all of the language from the draft forms in their own trust or custodial agreements. The draft forms are not intended to be used as stand-alone trust or custodial agreements. They may be used as such only when they became finalized. [Treasury Press Release, Office of Public Affairs, June 25, 2004 (JS-1748)]

Q 7:6   How do the model HSA Forms 5305-B and 5305-C differ from the draft versions of those forms?

The final versions of Forms 5305-B and 5305-C differ from the draft versions of those forms in only a few respects. The changes mainly clarify that:

1. An individual is no longer eligible to contribute to an HSA after he or she is *enrolled* in Medicare (as opposed to when an individual "is eligible for Medicare" or "reaches age 65"). Thus, an otherwise eligible individual who is not actually enrolled in Medicare Part A or Part B may contribute to an HSA until the month in which he or she actually enrolls in Medicare.

2. Eligibility and contribution limits are determined monthly.

3. An insurance company (not only a life insurance company) can be the trustee or custodian of an HSA.

4. If the beneficiary is the account owner's estate, the fair market value (FMV) of the account as of the date of the account owner's death is taxable

on the account owner's final return. For other beneficiaries, the FMV of the account is taxable to that person in the tax year that includes the date of the account owner's death.

Q 7:7　Should Form 5305-B or 5305-C be filed with the IRS?

No. The model forms are pre-approved by the IRS (see Q 7:10]. The model forms are not to be filed with the IRS and should be kept with the account owner's permanent tax records.

Q 7:8　May a sponsor of a model HSA Form 5305-B or Form 5305-C add additional provisions to the model forms?

Yes. Provisions may be added to or incorporated into Article XI (in both model forms) and any that follow it, as long as they are agreed to by the account owner and trustee/custodian.

Q 7:9　What type of additional provisions can be added to model Form 5305-B and 5305-C?

The model forms contain specific instructions that list numerous examples of provisions that may be added or incorporated into the HSA model forms. The sponsor may attach additional pages if necessary. Among the additional provisions that may be included are: definitions; restrictions on rollover contributions from HSAs or Archer MSAs (e.g., requiring a rollover not later than 60 days after receipt of a distribution and limited to one rollover during a one-year period); investment powers; voting rights; exculpatory provisions; amendment and termination; removal of trustee/custodian; trustee/custodian's fees; state law requirements; treatment of excess contributions; distribution procedures (e.g., frequency or minimum dollar amount); use of debit, credit, or stored-value cards; return of mistaken distributions; and descriptions of prohibited transactions.

Q 7:10　What is the result if the provisions added by a trustee or custodian are inconsistent with Code Section 223 or published IRS guidance?

The model forms treat any provision that is added or incorporated as being void if it is inconsistent with Code Section 223 or IRS published guidance. [Form 5305-B, Art. IX; Form 5305-C, Art. IX]

Q 7:11　When are the model HSA forms deemed established?

Model Forms 5305-B and 5305-C are considered established when the form is fully executed by both the account owner and the trustee or custodian. The form can be completed at any time during the tax year. However, an HSA account cannot be effective before the effective date of the eligible individual's HDHP coverage (see Q 2:6).

Q 7:12   Must the HSA be created in the United States?

Yes. An HSA trust or custodial account must be created in the United States for the exclusive benefit of the account owner.

Q 7:13   What is the taxpayer's "identifying number" for use in establishing an HSA using model Form 5305-B or Form 5305-C?

The model HSA trust or custodial account requires the use of the account owner's Social Security number as the identifying number.

Q 7:14   What documents should a trustee or custodian provide to the account owner when an HSA is established?

The plan sponsor should provide a trust document or custodial agreement, a disclosure statement, and an adoption agreement for the account owner to complete and sign. Organizations that offer an HSA may also use certain administrative forms to facilitate such items as beneficiary designations, contributions, and distribution requests.

Q 7:15   May a sponsor design an IRS-approved prototype HSA?

Yes. However, the IRS has not announced a procedure for a sponsor to obtain IRS approval on a prototype HSA trust or custodial account. Nonetheless, the IRS issued draft forms in June 2004 "to allow HSA trustees and custodians to use some or all of the language from the draft forms in their own trust or custodial agreements." A master and prototype (M&P) program for HSA accounts will likely be announced shortly.

Note. The draft forms were not intended to be used as stand-alone trust or custodial agreements until they became finalized. [Treasury Press Release, Office of Public Affairs, June 25, 2004 (JS-1748)]

Permissible Investments

Q 7:16   How may HSA assets be invested?

HSA funds may be invested in any investments approved for IRAs (e.g., bank accounts, annuities, certificates of deposit, stocks, mutual funds, or bonds). [I.R.S. Notice 2004-50, Q&A 65, 2004-33 I.R.B. 196] HSAs may not invest in life insurance contracts or in collectibles (e.g., any work of art, antique, metal, gem, stamp, coin, alcoholic beverage, or other tangible personal property specified in IRS guidance under Code Section 408(m)(3)). HSAs may invest in certain types of bullion or coins, as described in Code Section 408(m)(3).

Q 7:17   May an HSA trust or custodial agreement restrict investments to certain types of permissible investments?

The HSA trust or custodial agreement may restrict investments to certain types of permissible investments (e.g., particular investment funds). [I.R.S. Notice 2004-50, Q&A 65, 2004-33 I.R.B. 196]

Q 7:18   May HSA funds be commingled in a common trust fund or common investment fund?

Yes. Code Section 223(d)(1)(D) states that the HSA trust assets may not be commingled except in a common trust fund or common investment fund. Thus, individual accounts maintained on behalf of individual HSA account beneficiaries may be held in a common trust fund or common investment fund. [I.R.C. § 223(d)(1)(D)] A common trust fund is defined in Treasury Regulations Section 1.408-2(b)(5)(ii). A common investment fund is defined in Code Section 584(a)(1).

Note. An employer identification number (EIN) is required for a common trust fund created for HSAs.

Q 7:19   Are HSA trustees and custodians also subject to the rules against prohibited transactions?

Yes. The same rules that apply to account beneficiaries apply to trustees and custodians. [I.R.S. Notice 2004-50, Q&A 68, 2004-33 I.R.B. 196]

Account Fees

Q 7:20   If administration and account maintenance fees are withdrawn from the HSA, are the withdrawn amounts treated as taxable distributions to the account owner?

No. Amounts withdrawn from an HSA for administration and account maintenance fees (e.g., flat administrative fees) will not be treated as a taxable distribution and will not be included in the account owner's gross income. [I.R.S. Notice 2004-50, Q&A 69, 2004-33 I.R.B. 196]

Q 7:21   If administration and account maintenance fees are withdrawn from the HSA, does the withdrawn amount increase the maximum annual HSA contribution limit?

No. For example, if the maximum annual contribution limit is $2,700, and a $25 administration fee is withdrawn from the HSA, the annual contribution limit is still $2,700, not $2,725. [I.R.S. Notice 2004-50, Q&A 70, 2004-33 I.R.B. 196]

**Q 7:22   If administration and account maintenance fees are paid
by the account owner or employer directly to the
trustee or custodian, do these payments count toward the
annual maximum contribution limit for the HSA?**

No. Administration and account maintenance fees paid directly by the
account owner or employer will not be considered contributions to the HSA.

> **Example.** An individual, Eric, contributes the maximum annual amount of
> $2,700 to his HSA. Eric pays an annual administration fee of $25 directly to
> the trustee. Eric's maximum annual contribution limit is not affected by the
> payment of the administration fee. [I.R.S. Notice 2004-50, Q&A 71, 2004-33
> I.R.B. 196]

Trustees and Custodians

**Q 7:23   Is any insurance company a qualified HSA trustee or
custodian?**

Yes. Any insurance company or any bank (including a similar financial
institution as defined in Code Section 408(n)) can be an HSA trustee or custodian. Insured banks and credit unions are automatically qualified to handle
HSAs. Any bank, credit union, or any other entity that currently meets the IRS
standards for being a trustee or custodian for an IRA or Archer Medical Savings
Account (MSA) can be an HSA trustee or custodian.

In addition, any other person already approved by the IRS to be a trustee or
custodian of an IRA or Archer MSA is automatically approved to be an HSA
trustee or custodian. Other persons may request approval to be a trustee or
custodian in accordance with the procedures set forth in Treasury Regulations
Section 1.408-2(e) (relating to IRA nonbank trustees). [I.R.S. Notice 2004-50,
Q&A 72, 2004-33 I.R.B. 196]

**Q 7:24   Would an individual qualify to be an HSA trustee or
custodian?**

No. An individual would not qualify to be an HSA trustee or custodian (see Q
7:23). An individual would not satisfy many of the requirements to be a nonbank
trustee or custodian (e.g., continuity of existence).

**Q 7:25   Is there a limit on the annual HSA contribution which the
trustee or custodian may accept?**

Yes. Except in the case of rollover contributions or trustee-to-trustee transfer
(see Q 5:37), the trustee or custodian may not accept annual contributions to any
HSA that exceed the annual contribution limit (see Q 4:19) and catch-up contribution amount (see Q 4:28). [I.R.S. Notice 2004-50, Q&A 73, 2004-33 I.R.B. 196]

Q 7:26   May contributions of property be accepted by a trustee or custodian?

All contributions must be in cash, other than rollover contributions or trustee-to-trustee transfers. [I.R.C. § 223(d)(1)(A); I.R.S. Notice 2004-50, Q&A 73, 2004-33 I.R.B. 196]

Q 7:27   Who is responsible for determining whether contributions to an HSA exceed the maximum annual contribution for a particular account owner?

The account owner is responsible for determining whether contributions to an HSA exceed the maximum annual contribution for that particular account owner. [I.R.S. Notice 2004-50, Q&A 74, 2004-33 I.R.B. 196]

Q 7:28   Who is responsible for notifying the trustee or custodian of any excess contribution and requesting a withdrawal of the excess contribution?

The account owner is responsible for notifying the trustee or custodian of any excess contribution and requesting a withdrawal of the excess contribution together with any net income attributable to the excess contribution. [I.R.S. Notice 2004-50, Q&A 74, 2004-33 I.R.B. 196]

Q 7:29   Is the trustee or custodian responsible for accepting cash contributions?

Yes. The HSA trustee or custodian is responsible for accepting cash contributions within the limits up to the maximum annual contribution limit.

Q 7:30   Is the trustee or custodian responsible for filing required information returns with the IRS?

Yes. The trustee or custodian is responsible for filing required information returns with the IRS (Form 5498-SA and Form 1099-SA). [I.R.C. § 223(h); I.R.S. Notice 2004-50, Q&A 74, 2004-33 I.R.B. 196]

Q 7:31   Is the trustee or custodian responsible for tracking the account owner's age?

Yes. However, the trustee or custodian may rely on the account owner's representation as to his or her date of birth. [I.R.S. Notice 2004-50, Q&A 75, 2004-33 I.R.B. 196]

Q 7:32   Must the trustee or custodian allow account beneficiaries to return mistaken distributions to the HSA?

No. The trustee or custodian is not required to permit account beneficiaries to return mistaken distributions to the HSA. However, if the HSA trust or custodial agreement allows the return of mistaken distributions (see Q 6:66), the trustee or custodian may rely on the account owner's representation that the distribution was, in fact, a mistake. [I.R.S. Notice 2004-50, Q&A 76, 2004-33 I.R.B. 196] The trustee or custodian is required to correct with the IRS and account beneficiary any filed Form 1099-SA that reflected the mistaken distributions. This must be done because such repayments are not included in gross income or subject to the 10 percent additional tax, and the payment is not subject to the excise tax on excess contributions. It should also be noted that the repayment is not treated as a contribution on Form 5498-SA.

Q 7:33 May an HSA trust or custodial agreement restrict the account owner's ability to roll over amounts from that HSA?

No (see Q 5:19). [I.R.S. Notice 2004-50, Q&A 77, 2004-33 I.R.B. 196]

Q 7:34 Are HSA trustees or custodians required to accept rollover contributions or trustee-to-trustee transfers?

No. Rollover contributions or trustee-to-trustee transfers from other HSAs or from Archer MSAs are allowed, but trustees or custodians are not required to accept them. [I.R.S. Notice 2004-50, Q&A 78, 2004-33 I.R.B. 196; I.R.S. Notice 2004-2, Q&A 23, 2004-2 I.R.B. 269]

Q 7:35 May an HSA trust or custodial agreement restrict HSA distributions to pay or reimburse only the account owner's qualified medical expenses?

No. The HSA trust or custodial agreement may not contain a provision that restricts HSA distributions to pay or reimburse only the account owner's qualified medical expenses (see Q 6:10). [I.R.S. Notice 2004-50, Q&A 79, 2004-33 I.R.B. 196]

Q 7:36 May a trustee or custodian restrict the frequency or minimum amount of distributions from an HSA?

Yes. Trustees or custodians may place reasonable restrictions on both the frequency and the minimum amount of distributions from an HSA (see Q 6:9). [I.R.S. Notice 2004-50, Q&A 80, 2004-33 I.R.B. 196]

Q 7:37 May a trustee or custodian that does not sponsor the HDHP require proof or certification that the account owner is an eligible individual?

Where a trustee or custodian does not sponsor the HDHP, the trustee or custodian may require proof or certification that the account owner is an eligible individual. [I.R.S. Notice 2004-2, Q&A 10, 2004-2 I.R.B. 269]

Q 7:38 May a trustee or custodian that does not sponsor the HDHP require proof or certification that the account owner is covered by an HDHP?

Where a trustee or custodian does not sponsor the HDHP, the trustee or custodian may require proof or certification that the account owner is covered by a health plan that meets all of the requirements of an HDHP. [I.R.S. Notice 2004-2, Q&A 10, 2004-2 I.R.B. 269]

Reports

Q 7:39 What reports may be required by the IRS in connection with an HSA?

There are two types of reports that may be required in connection with an HSA. (See Qs 7:43, 7:50, 7:58) [I.R.C. § 223(h)] The Secretary of the Treasury may require:

1. The trustee of a health savings account to make such reports regarding such account to the Secretary and to the account owner with respect to contributions, distributions, the return of excess contributions, and such other matters as the Secretary determines to be appropriate. [I.R.C. § 223(h)(1)]
2. Any person who provides an individual with a HDHP to make such reports to the Secretary and to the account owner with respect to such plan as the Secretary determines to be appropriate. [I.R.C. § 223(h)(2)]

Q 7:40 When must reports regarding HSA accounts be provided?

The reports required by the Secretary of the Treasury are to be filed at such time and in such manner and furnished to such individuals at such time and in such manner as may be required by the Secretary (see Qs 7:46, 7:47, 7:54, 7:61, 7:64). [I.R.C. § 223(f)]

Q 7:41 What is the penalty if a trustee or employer fails to provide a required report?

Generally, if a trustee or an employer fails to file a required report (other than an information return or a payee statement), there is a penalty of $50 for each failure unless it is shown that such failure is due to reasonable cause. [I.R.C. §§ 223(h), 6693(a)(1), 6693(a)(2)(c), 6724(d)(1)(C)(i) (concerning information returns), 6724(d)(2)(W) (concerning payee statements)]

Form Filing Requirements

Q 7:42 Is an SPD required to be provided by an employer?

No, unless it is an ERISA-covered plan (see chapter 8).

Reporting HSA Contributions on Form 5498-SA

Q 7:43 What is the purpose of Form 5498-SA—*HSA, Archer MSA, or Medicare Advantage MSA Information*?

Form 5498-SA is used to report contributions to HSA, Archer MSA, or Medicare Advantage MSAs (MA-MSA). A separate Form 5498-SA must be filed for each type of account.

Q 7:44 For whom is Form 5498-SA required to be filed?

The trustee or custodian must file Form 5498-SA—*HSA, Archer MSA, or Medicare Advantage MSA Information*, with the IRS and for each person for whom it maintained an HSA (or Archer MSA, or MA-MSA) during 2006.

Rollovers. The receipt of a rollover from an Archer MSA or an HSA to an HSA (and receipt of a rollover from one Archer MSA to another Archer MSA) are reported in Box 4.

Transfers. A trustee-to-trustee transfer from an Archer MSA to an HSA, or from one HSA to another HSA (or one Archer MSA or MA-MSA to another Archer MSA or MA-MSA) are not required to be reported. For reporting purposes, contributions and rollovers do not include these transfers.

Q 7:45 Is Form 5498-SA required if no contributions were made and there was a total distribution made from the HSA?

Generally, if a total distribution was made from an HSA during the year and no contributions were made for that year, Form 5498-SA is not required to be filed, nor must a statement be furnished the participant to reflect that the fair-market value (FMV) on December 31 was zero.

Q 7:46 When must Form 5498-SA be filed with the IRS?

If required to be filed, the 2006 version of Form 5498-SA must be filed with the IRS by May 31, 2007.

Q 7:47 When must Form 5498-SA be provided to the recipient?

If Form 5498-SA is required to be filed with the IRS, a statement must be provided to the recipient (generally Copy B) by May 31, 2007. The participant may be, but is not required to be, provided with a statement of the December 31, 2006, FMV of the participant's account by January 31, 2007. [See part H in the 2006 *General Instructions for Forms 1099, 1098, 5498, and W-2G.*]

Q 7:48   Must Form 5498-SA be filed if the owner of an HSA dies?

In the year during which an HSA owner dies, Form 5498-SA is generally required to be filed and a statement of the December 31, 2006 account value provided for the decedent.

Note. If the beneficiary is the spouse, the spouse becomes the owner of the HSA and the spouse (if an eligible individual) may make contributions into the HSA. If the beneficiary is not the spouse or there is no named beneficiary, the account ceases to be an HSA, Archer MSA, or MA-MSA (see Q 6:71).

Q 7:49   How are the boxes on Form 5498-SA completed for an HSA?

For 2006, the HSA distribution reporting codes for purposes of Form 5498-SA for 2006 are as follows:

Box 1: This box is used to report Archer MSA contributions. Do not report HSA contributions in this box.

Box 2: *Total Contributions Made in 2006.* Enter total HSA (or Archer MSA) contributions made in 2006, including contributions made in 2006 and desig nated for 2005.

Note. For contributions made between January 1 and April 15, 2007, the trustee or custodian should obtain the participant's designation of the year for which the contributions are made.

Box 3: *Total HSA (or Archer MSA contributions) made in 2007 for 2006.* Enter total HSA contributions made in 2007 for 2006. Do not include repayments of mistaken distributions. The trustee or custodian may have to file a corrected Form 1099-SA (see Q 7:32).

Box 4: *Rollover Contributions.* Enter any rollover contribution to an HSA (or Archer MSA) received during 2006. Do not report any direct trustee-to-trustee transfers.

A *rollover* means that the account holder takes a distribution from one account and redeposits (rollover) the distribution into another account within a 60-day period.

Box 5: *Fair Market Value.* Enter the FMV of the HSA (or MSA) on December 31, 2006.

Box 6: *Checkbox.* Check the "HSA" box.

Reporting HSA Distributions on Form 1099-SA

Q 7:50   What is the purpose of Form 1099-SA?

Form 1099-SA—*Distributions from an HSA, Archer MSA, or Medicare Advantage MSA* is used to report distributions made from an HSA, Archer MSA, or MA-MSA. A separate return must be filed for each plan type. Form 1099-SA is not required to be filed if no distributions have been made from the account for a year.

Q 7:51   In what year are distributions from an HSA required to be reported?

All distributions from an HSA are required to be reported in the year during which a distribution takes place.

Q 7:52   Must Form 1099-SA be provided to the account owner and/or account beneficiaries?

If Form 1099-SA is required to be filed with the IRS, the payor must also furnish a statement to recipients containing the information furnished to the IRS.

Q 7:53   When is Form 1099-SA required to be provided to the recipient?

If required to be filed, Copy B of Form 1099-SA or a substitute statement must be provided to the recipient by January 31 following the year of the distribution.

Q 7:54   When is Form 1099-SA required to be filed with the IRS?

If required to be filed, the 2006 version of Form 1099-SA must be filed with the IRS by February 28, 2007, or by March 31, 2007, if filed electronically.

Q 7:55   What is a substitute statement for Form 1099-SA?

Generally, a substitute is any statement other than Copy B (and C in some cases) of the official form. Substitute statements may be developed or purchased from a private printer. However, the substitutes must comply with the format and content requirements specified in IRS Publication 1179, *General Rules and Specifications for Substitute Forms 1096, 1098, 1099, 5498, and W-2G (and 1042-S).*

Q 7:56   How are transfers between trustees and/or custodians treated for purposes of Form 1099-SA?

For reporting purposes, contributions and rollovers do not include direct transfers from an Archer MSA to an HSA or from one HSA to another HSA.

Q 7:57   How is Form 1099-SA completed for an HSA?

The rules and coding for Form 1099-SA depend upon when the distribution is made (i.e., in the year of death or in the year after the year of death). If the HSA account holder dies and the beneficiary is the spouse, the spouse becomes the account holder. If the named beneficiary is anyone other than the spouse, the HSA ceases to be an HSA on the date of the account holder's death. If there is no named beneficiary, or the beneficiary becomes the person's estate, the FMV of the HSA as of the date of death is required to be reported in Box 4 of Form 1099-SA.

Note. It is the responsibility of the account beneficiary to determine whether a distribution is used for qualified medical expenses and to determine any taxes or penalties due (see chapter 6).

For 2006, the numbered Boxes on Form 1099-SA (2006) are completed as follows:

Box 1: Gross Distribution. Box 1 shows the amount distributed from the HSA for the year. Enter the gross amount of the distribution, including any earnings on excess contributions reported in Box 2. The payer is not responsible for determining the taxable amount of a distribution. The distribution may have been paid directly to a medical service provider or the account holder. If the payment was made directly to a medical service provider, show the account holder as the recipient.

Death. The gross distribution is also reported when a final distribution is made to the beneficiary in the year of the account holder's death or in a year after the year of death.

Box 2: Earnings on Excess Contributions. Enter only the earnings attributable to an excess contribution made to an HSA or Archer MSA that was returned to the account holder by the due date of the account holder's tax return. This amount is also included in Box 1. However, earnings on other distributions are reported only in Box 1.

Note. In the case of a non-spouse beneficiary, any earnings on the account after the date of death (Box 1 minus Box 4 of Form 1099-SA) are taxable. In the case of an HSA, the amount included on the federal income tax return (other than an estate) is first reduced by any payments from the HSA made for the decedent's qualified medical expenses incurred before the decedent's death and paid within one year after the date of death.

Box 3: Distribution Code. Enter one of the following distribution codes. (If more than one code applies to multiple distributions from the same account, separate Forms 1099-SA must be filed showing the proper code for that distribution):

Code 1: *Normal Distributions.* Use Code 1 for normal distributions to the account holder and any direct payments to a medical service provider. Use this code if no other code applies.

Death. If final distribution is made to a surviving spouse beneficiary after the year of death, use Code 1.

Pledge of Account. To the extent that assets in an HSA are pledged as security for a loan and treated as distributed, use Code 5. [I.R.C. § 223(e)(2)]

Code 2: *Excess Contributions.* Use Code 2 for distributions of excess HSA contributions.

Code 3: *Disability.* Use Code 3 if distributions are made after the account holder was disabled (see Q 6:65).

Code 4: *Death Distribution (Other Than Code 6).* Use Code 4 for payments to a decedent's estate in the year of death. Also use Code 4 for payments to an estate after the year of death.

Note. If the beneficiary is the estate, enter the estate's name and taxpayer identification number (TIN) in place of the recipient's on the form.

Code 5: *Prohibited Transaction.* Use Code 5 for amounts treated as distributed if the HSA account loses its exemption from taxation when the owner or owner's beneficiary engages in a prohibited transaction. [I.R.C. § 223(e)(2)]

Code 6: *Death Distribution After Year of Death to a Non-spouse Beneficiary.* Use Code 6 for payments to a non-spouse beneficiary, other than an estate, after the year of death. (See Codes 1 and 4.)

Box 4: FMV on Date of Death. Enter the FMV of the account on the account holder's date of death in Box 4.

Note. If an HSA is inherited by a non-spouse beneficiary, the FMV on the date of death is reported on the beneficiary's tax return for the year the account owner dies even if the distribution is received in a later year.

Box 5: Checkbox. Box 5 shows the type of account that is being reported. Check the appropriate box (e.g., HSA, Archer MSA, or MA-MSA).

Form 5329: Reporting Additional Taxes on Excess HSA Contributions

Q 7:58   What is the purpose of Form 5329?

Form 5329—*Additional Taxes on Qualified Plans (Including IRAs) and Other Tax-Favored Accounts* is used by individuals to report additional taxes on many different types of retirement, education, and health arrangements. Part VII of Form 5329 addresses the tax on excess contributions to an HSA under Code Section 4973 (see Q 7:28).

Q 7:59   Under what circumstances must Form 5329 be filed with respect to an HSA?

An individual must file Form 5329 for 2006 only if contributions in respect to 2006 exceed the maximum contribution limit.

Note. Form 5329 is also required if there was a tax due from an excess contribution on line 17 (regarding traditional IRAs), 25 (regarding Roth IRAs), 33 (regarding Coverdell Education Savings Accounts (ESAs)), or 41 (regarding Archer MSAs) of the prior year's (2005) Form 5329. However, excess contributions to an HSA for the prior year are addressed on Form 8889 (discussed in Qs 7:66–7:71).

Q 7:60   Can spouses use one form 5329 if applicable?

No. In the case of a joint return, if both spouses are required to file Form 5329, a separate form must be completed for each spouse. The combined tax is reported on Form 1040 (line 59: based on the 2005 version of the form).

Amended return. If filing an amended 2006 Form 5329, check the box at the top of page 1 of the form. Do not use the 2006 Form 5329 to amend a return for any other year (see Q 7:61).

Q 7:61   When is Form 5329 required to be filed?

Form 5329 is to be filed as an attachment to Form 1040 by the due date, including extensions, of Form 1040. If Form 1040 is not required to be filed, complete and file Form 5329 by itself at the time and place Form 1040 would be required to be filed.

Note. Be sure to include address information and signature. Enclose, but do not attach, a check or money order payable to "United States Treasury" for any taxes due. Write the SSN and "2006 Form 5329" on the check.

Prior tax years. If filing Form 5329 for a prior year, use that year's version of the form. Unless there are other changes, the form can be filed by itself; otherwise, file Form 5329 for that year with Form 1040X—*Amended U.S. Individual Income Tax Return.*

Q 7:62   How is Part VII of Form 5329 completed for an HSA?

If the contributions to an individual's HSA exceed the contribution limit and were not timely removed (see Qs 4:19, 4:79), line 42 must be completed, as follows:

Line 42: Enter the contributions made for 2006 unless withdrawn (see below) that exceed the contribution limit. The instructions for Form 8889 (see Qs 7:66–7:71) explain how to figure excess contributions. Some or all of the excess contributions for 2006 may be withdrawn, and they will not be treated as having been contributed if:

• The withdrawal is made by the due date, including extensions, of the 2006 return

• No exclusion from income is claimed for the amount of the withdrawn contributions, and

• Any earnings on the withdrawn contributions are also withdrawn and included in gross income

Line 43: Calculate and report the 6 percent tax (or FMV of account, if less) on Line 43. Also enter the amount of tax on Form 1040 (line 60; based on the 2005 version of form).

Extension for timely filers. If the tax return was timely filed without withdrawing the excess contributions, the withdrawal can be made no later than six months after the due date of the tax return, excluding extensions. If applicable, file an amended return with "Filed pursuant to Section 301.9100-2" written at the top. Report any related earnings for 2006 on the amended return and include an explanation of the withdrawal. Make any other necessary changes on the amended return (e.g., if the contributions were reported as excess contributions on the original return, include an amended Form 5329 reflecting that the withdrawn contributions are no longer treated as having been contributed).

Reporting Excise Tax on Prohibited Transactions

Q 7:63   What is the purpose of Form 5330?

Form 5330—*Return on Excise Taxes Related to Employee Benefit Plans* is used to report any tax on a prohibited transaction (see Q 6:54). Code Section 4975 generally imposes an excise tax on a disqualified person that engages in a prohibited transaction with an HSA (as well as other types of health, education, and retirement plans).

Note. If the account owner engages in a prohibited transaction with respect to an HSA, the account ceases to be an HSA (see Q 6:51) and the prohibited transaction tax does *not* apply. Other individuals that are disqualified individuals (e.g., the employer), however, may have participated in the prohibited transaction and are required to file Form 5330.

Caution. Regardless of whether an HSA is an ERISA plan (see Qs 1:6, 6:51), an HSA remains subject to the excise tax on prohibited transactions under Code Section 4975.

[I.R.C. § 4975. See also I.R.C. §§ 4975(d), 4975(f)(6)(B)(ii), and 4975(f)(6)(B)(iii) for specific exemptions to prohibited transactions. Also see I.R.C. § 4975(c)(2) for certain other transactions or classes of transactions that may be exempt.]

Q 7:64   When is Form 5330 required to be filed?

If a prohibited transaction is subject to the prohibited transaction excise tax, Form 5330 is required to be filed by the last day of the seventh month after the end of the tax year of the employer or other person who must file the return.

Q 7:65   How is Form 5330 completed when a disqualified person participates in a prohibited transaction involving an HSA?

When a disqualified person participates in a prohibited transaction involving an HSA (other than his or her own HSA; see Q 6:51) the disqualified person must complete Part IV, *Tax on Prohibited Transactions*, and Part V, *Schedule of Other Participating Disqualified Persons and Description of Correction*, of Form 5330. If not all prohibited transactions have been corrected by the end of the tax year, an explanation must be attached indicating when the correction has been or will be made. Then enter the tax determined in Part IV (line 25c) on line 6a of the form on page 1. Show the total tax due on line 13c. "Form 5330, Section(s) 4975, ____ {enter applicable Code Sections}____ " should be shown on the payment along with the taxpayer's name and tax identifying number.

Form 8889: Health Savings Accounts (HSAs)

Q 7:66   What is the purpose of Form 8889?

The purpose of Form 8889—*Health Savings Accounts (HSAs)* is to:

- Report HSA contributions (including those made on the HSA owner's behalf and employer contributions)
- Figure the HSA deduction, and
- Report distributions from HSAs

Q 7:67   Who must file Form 8889?

The HSA owner must file Form 8889 with the IRS as an attachment to Form 1040 by the HSA owner if any of the following apply:

- Contributions were made to the HSA, including contributions made on the owner's behalf and by the owner's employer, in 2006
- The owner received distributions from his or her HSA in 2006

In addition, Form 8889 must be filed if a beneficiary (including an estate) acquired an interest in an HSA because of the death of the account owner.

Note. Forms 1040EZ or 1040A are designed to be filed without attachments, so a taxpayer (who is otherwise qualified to use either form) would be unable to report contributions and distributions if filing Form 1040EZ or 1040A. Form 8889 must be attached to Form 1040.

Q 7:68   How is Form 8889 completed upon the death of the owner?

If the account beneficiary's surviving spouse is the designated beneficiary, the HSA is treated as if the surviving spouse were the account beneficiary. The surviving spouse completes Form 8889 as though the HSA belonged to him or her.

If the designated beneficiary is not the account beneficiary's surviving spouse, or there is no designated beneficiary, the account ceases to be an HSA as of the date of the account owner's death. The beneficiary completes Form 8889 as follows:

1. Enter "Death of HSA account beneficiary" across the top of Form 8889.
2. Enter the name(s) and the SSN shown on the beneficiary's tax return in the spaces provided at the top of the form and skip Part I, regarding contributions and deductions.
3. On line 12a, enter the fair market value of the HSA as of the date of death.
4. On line 13, for a beneficiary other than the estate, enter qualified medical expenses incurred by the account beneficiary before the date of death that are paid within one year after the date of death.
5. Complete the rest of Part II.

If the account beneficiary's estate is the beneficiary, the value of the HSA as of the date of death is included on the account beneficiary's final income tax return. Complete Form 8889 as described above, except that Part I should be completed if applicable.

> **Note.** The distribution is not subject to the additional 10 percent tax. Report any earnings on the account after the date of death as income on the beneficiary's tax return.

Q 7:69   How are contributions, excess contributions, and deductions reported on Form 8889?

Part I of Form 8889 is used to figure the HSA deduction, any excess contributions made (including those made on the owner's behalf), and any excess contributions made by an employer. The amount that may be deducted for HSA contributions is limited by the applicable portion of the HDHP's annual deductible (line 3), reduced by any contributions to the taxpayer's Archer MSAs (line 4) and any employer contributions (line 9).

If the taxpayer is age 55 or older at the end of 2006, the contribution limit can be increased by up to $700 (the 2006 limit; line 3 or line 7, depending on the type of coverage and marital status). An individual can make deductible contributions to an HSA even if his or her employer made contributions.

Complete lines 1 through 11 as instructed on the form. However, if spouses are filing jointly, and each spouse has a separate HSA and an HDHP with family coverage, complete a separate Form 8889 for each spouse using the rules stated in Q 4:20. Combine the amounts on line 11 of both Forms 8889 and enter this amount on Form 1040, line 25. Be sure to attach both Forms 8889 to the tax return. See also Table 4-4.

If an individual does not have the same coverage on the first day of every month during 2006, or was age 55 or older at the end of 2006, go through the chart at Q 4:31 (also in the instructions for Form 8889) for each month of 2006. Enter the result on the worksheet next to the corresponding month. If eligibility and coverage did not change from one month to the next, enter the same number that was entered for the previous month.

Employer contributions include any amount an employer contributes to an HSA. These contributions should be shown in Box 12 of Form W-2 with Code W. If an employer made excess contributions, the excess may have to be reported as income. The excess employer contributions are the excess, if any, of the employer's contribution over the taxpayer's limitation shown on line 8 of Form 8889. If the excess was not included in income on Form W-2, it is to be reported as "Other income" on Form 1040 (unless corrected, see Q 4:73). The allowable HSA deduction (taking into account employer contributions that were excluded from income) is shown on line 11 of Form 8889.

> **Practice Pointer.** If line 2 (actual contributions) is more than line 11 (deductible contributions), the individual made an excess contribution. See prior

discussion of Form 5329 for methods of correction to avoid the 6 percent tax on excess contributions.

Reporting Deemed Distributions

Q 7:70   How are deemed distributions from an HSA reported on Form 8889?

The following situations, resulting in deemed distributions from an HSA, are reported on Form 8889 in the following manner:

1. *The owner participated in a prohibited transaction with respect to an HSA, at any time in 2006.* The account ceases be an HSA as of January 1, 2006, and the FMV of all assets in the account of January 1, 2006, must be included on line 12a.

2. *Any portion of an HSA was used as security for a loan at any time in 2006.* The FMV of the assets used as security for the loan must be included as income on Form 1040, line 21. On the dotted line next to line 21, enter "HSA" and the amount.

Q 7:71   How is Form 8889 completed if a distribution is made from the account?

If a distribution is made from an HSA, Part II, *HSA Distributions*, of Form 8889 must be completed. Complete Part II as follows.

Line 12a: Enter the total distributions received in 2006 from all HSAs. Show these amounts in Box 1 of Form 1099-SA.

Line 12b: Include on line 12b any distributions received in 2006 that qualified as a rollover contribution to another HSA. Also include any excess contributions (and the earnings on those excess contributions) included on line 12a that were withdrawn by the due date, including extensions, of the return.

Line 13: In general, include on line 13 distributions from all HSAs in 2006 that were used for the qualified medical expenses of the account beneficiary and his or her spouse or dependents that were incurred on or after the first day of the first month during which the HSA owner became an eligible individual.

Caution. No deduction may be claimed on Schedule A (Form 1040) for any amount included on line 13.

Lines 15a and 15b Additional 10% Tax: HSA distributions included in income (line 14) are subject to an additional 10 percent tax unless an exception applies (see Q 6:62). The additional 10 percent tax does not apply to distributions made after the account beneficiary dies, becomes disabled, or turns age 65. If any of these exceptions apply to any of the distributions included on line 14, check the box on line 15a. Enter on line 15b only 10 percent (.10) of any amount included on line 14 that does not meet any of the exceptions.

Note. It appears that the 10 percent additional tax does not apply to earnings that must be distributed in connection with the correction of an excess contribution. The earnings are reported in Box 2 of Form 1099-SA. Although included in gross income, the earnings are not reported on Form 8889 and are not, therefore, included in the amount subject to the 10 percent additional tax shown on line 14.

Reporting Employer Contributions on Form W-2

Q 7:72 How is Form W-2, *Wage and Tax Statement* completed if an employer makes contributions to an HSA?

Employer contributions to an HSA are reported in Box 12 of Form W-2, using Code W. Generally employer contributions to an employee's HSA are not subject to income, Social Security/Medicare, or Railroad Retirement taxes and will not affect amounts otherwise reported in Boxes 1, 3, and 5 of Form W-2. The amount shown as an HSA contribution in Box 12 of Form W-2 is to be entered on line 9 of Form 8889 (see Q 7:69).

Q 7:73 How should pretax contributions made to an HSA through an employer's cafeteria plan be reported?

Pretax contributions of employees made through a cafeteria plan should be reported by the employer on Form W-2 in Box 12 (but not in boxes 1, 3, and 5). Pretax salary reduction contributions are treated as employer contributions for purposes of the Tax Code (see Q 7:72). It makes sense to report these contributions on Form W-2, because when an employee is completing Form 8889—*Health Savings Accounts (HSAs)*, these contributions will be designated as amounts that are not deductible. This applies regardless of whether the contributions are (1) made from employee contributions deducted pursuant to a cafeteria plan election or (2) made by the employer outside of Code Section 125 under the comparability requirements. The amount is entered by the HSA owner on Form 8889.

Chapter 8

Federal and State Laws Affecting HSAs

Although most of the requirements of HSAs are set forth in the Internal Revenue Code and IRS guidance, another federal law that could affect HSAs is the Employee Retirement Income Security Act of 1974 (ERISA). In addition, certain state laws may affect HSA administration or influence whether an HDHP can be offered in a particular state. Finally, because an HSA is an investment vehicle, federal laws that regulate securities may also apply. This chapter begins by examining both the Department of Labor (DOL) guidance that sets the parameters regarding ERISA plan status and the consequences of such status. The effect that state law may have on HSAs and their accompanying HDHPs is also discussed in this chapter. Finally, the chapter discusses the potential effect of other federal laws, including the securities laws on HSAs.

ERISA

Q 8:1   What guidance did the DOL issue regarding HSAs and ERISA?

In April 2004, DOL issued guidance that should allow most HSAs to be outside the scope of ERISA, as long as specific requirements are satisfied. The guidance was issued in the form of a Field Assistance Bulletin (FAB 2004-01) and provides that, although an HDHP sponsored by an employer will be considered an ERISA plan, the HSA itself will generally not be considered an ERISA plan—even if the employer makes contributions to the HSA and selects only one HSA provider to which it forwards employer and employee contributions—as long as certain conditions are satisfied. See appendix C.

Q 8:2   What conditions must be satisfied in order for an HSA to be exempt from ERISA?

There are six conditions that the employer must satisfy in order for an HSA to be exempt from ERISA. In order to be exempt, the employer may *not* do any of the following:

1. Require employees to establish an HSA (i.e., an employee's establishment of an HSA must be completely voluntary);
2. Limit the ability of participants to roll funds over to another HSA, if such rollovers are allowed by the Code;
3. Impose conditions on the use of HSA funds (e.g., state that HSA distributions may be used only for medical expenses);
4. Make or influence the employee's investment decisions with respect to funds contributed to an HSA;
5. Represent that the HSAs are an employee welfare benefit plan established and maintained by the employer; and
6. Receive any payment or compensation in connection with an HSA.

Q 8:3   How does this guidance differ from earlier DOL guidance with respect to other arrangements?

This guidance represents a major departure from existing safe harbor guidance that allows group or group-type insurance programs (see Q 8:4) and individual retirement arrangements to be exempt from ERISA. [29 C.F.R. § 2510.3-1(j); 29 C.F.R. § 2510.3-2(d)] In order to be covered by those safe harbors, an employer may not make any contributions to those plans. In this guidance, DOL highlights differences between HSAs and group insurance arrangements and concludes that, even if an employer contributes to an HSA, the HSA is still not subject to ERISA as long as the factors described above are satisfied.

Q 8:4   What are the safe harbor rules that apply to determine whether Title I coverage under ERISA applies to a group or group-type insurance program offered to employees by an employer?

Under the safe harbor rules, Title I of ERISA, relating to the protection of employee benefit rights, does not apply to a group or group-type insurance program offered by an insurer to employees or to members of an employee organization, under which:

1. No contributions are made by an employer or employee organization (but see Qs 8:1 and 8:3, describing that an employer may contribute to an HSA);

2. Participation the program is completely voluntary for employees or members;

3. The sole functions of the employer or employee organization with respect to the program are, without endorsing the program (see Q 8:), to permit the insurer to publicize the program to employees or members, to collect premiums through payroll deductions or dues check-offs, and to remit them to the insurer; and

4. The employer or employee organization receives no consideration in the form of cash or otherwise in connection with the program, other than reasonable compensation, excluding any profit, for administrative services actually rendered in connection with payroll deductions or dues checkoffs.

29 C.F.R. Reg. § 2510.3-1(j); see also 29 C.F.R. Reg. §§ 2509-99-1 and 2510.3-2 for similar rules relating to payroll deduction IRAs]

Q 8:5   What weight would a court give to a Field Assistance Bulletin?

A Field Assistance Bulletin (FAB) is guidance that the DOL issues to its enforcement staff to follow in conducting an audit. Although the guidance is not directly binding on employers, as is a legislative rule [see *Chevron U.S.A., Inc. v. Natural Resources Defense Council*, 467 U.S. 837 (1984)], a court would likely defer to the position taken by DOL in a FAB since FABs are considered views of the agency responsible for interpreting and issuing guidance with respect to ERISA. [See *In re WorldCom, Inc.*, 2005 WL 221263 (S.D.N.Y. Feb. 1, 2005) (Court relied heavily on a DOL Field Assistance Bulletin in ruling that Merrill Lynch had no liability as a directed trustee in connection with losses suffered by the WorldCom 401(k) plan resulting from its holdings in WorldCom stock.)]

Q 8:6   What types of employer actions could be viewed by DOL as "representing that an HSA is an employee welfare plan established and maintained by the employer," thus causing the HSA to be subject to ERISA?

There is some DOL guidance and case law involving the group insurance safe harbor under 29 C.F.R. § 2510.3-1(j) that illustrates what types of actions could lead to a determination that the employer has established and maintained a group insurance arrangement, causing the arrangement to be outside the safe harbor and subject to ERISA. This guidance is helpful in determining what actions may potentially cause the HSA to be subject to ERISA. These actions include the following:

1. Use of the employer's name on HSA communication and promotional materials without a disclaimer indicating that the employer is not the sponsor of the HSA and does not endorse it;

2. A statement by the employer on HSA documents indicating that ERISA applies;

3. Listing the employer as plan administrator of the HSA and agent for legal service of process in the summary plan description (SPD); or

4. Giving the employer sole authority to cancel the HSA arrangement.

[DOL Adv. Op. 94-26A (July 11, 1994); DOL Adv. Op. 80-21A (Apr. 17, 1980); DOL Adv. Op. 75-06 (Nov. 3, 1975); Nicholas v. Standard Ins. Co., 29 EBC 1570 (6th Cir. 2002); Adams v. Unum Life Ins. Co. of Am., 200 F. Supp. 2d 796 (N.D. Ohio 2002)]

As noted in Q 8:1, the employer is permitted to contribute to an HSA and select one HSA provider to which it will forward salary reduction contributions without causing the HSA to be subject to ERISA. Thus, the employer is permitted more latitude in the HSA context than in the group insurance context. Nevertheless, in order to avoid ERISA plan status for an HSA, actions such as those described above should be avoided.

Example 1. Employer A wishes to make HSAs available to employees who participate in the HDHP that Employer A sponsors. Employer A contacts potential HSA trustees and selects one HSA trustee to provide trust services to its employees. Employer A signs a contract with the HSA trustee that identifies the specific services that the HSA trustee will provide to Employer A's employees, including accepting pretax salary reduction contributions from Employer A's payroll system. Employer A also signs a trust agreement with the HSA trustee on behalf of all employees (employees do not execute their own individual trust agreements with the HSA trustee). Employer A distributes enrollment materials bearing only the Employer's logo to employees with instructions that employees may establish an HSA by completing and returning such materials to Employer A during the open enrollment period. Employer A distributes an HSA SPD bearing only Employer A's logo to each employee who enrolls in the HSA option. The SPD indicates that Employer A is the plan administrator of the HSA, and that all questions about the HSA should be directed to Employer A. Under this fact pattern, it would appear that the employer has represented that it is establishing and maintaining the HSA. Thus, the HSA would likely be subject to ERISA.

Example 2. Same facts as above, except that Employer B:

1. Does not sign a trust agreement with the HSA trustee. Rather, Employer B specifies in the contract with the HSA trustee that the trustee must execute separate trust agreements with each of Employer B's employees who decide to enroll in the HSA.

2. Distributes enrollment materials that clearly identify the HSA trustee and indicate that the employer is merely facilitating enrollment in the HSA but is not the sponsor of the HSA. The enrollment materials advise employees to direct questions about the operation of the HSA directly to the HSA trustee. A contact name and phone number of the HSA trustee are provided.

3. Distributes an SPD that briefly describes the HSA but also clearly identifies the HSA trustee, states that Employer B is not the plan administrator of the HSA, and states that the HSA is not intended to be subject to ERISA.

Under this fact pattern, it would not appear that Employer B has represented that it is establishing and maintaining the HSA. Thus, in the absence of other circumstances prohibited in the DOL FAB, the HSA would likely not be subject to ERISA.

Q 8:7 If an employer offering an HSA to employees asks the HSA provider for specific investment options, will the HSA be subject to ERISA?

Probably. If an employer requests that specific investment options be offered in connection with an HSA, there is a risk that DOL will consider the HSA to be subject to ERISA. Under Field Assistance Bulletin 2004-01, an employer is permitted to contribute to an HSA and select one HSA trustee to which it will forward salary reduction contributions without causing the HSA to be subject to ERISA. (See Q 8:1, appendix C.) [FAB 2004-01 (April 7, 2004)] However, for the HSA to be outside the scope of ERISA, the employer must, among other things, limit its involvement in the design of the HSA and refrain from making or influencing investment decisions with respect to funds contributed to an HSA. (See Q 8:2.) Thus, if the employer requests that the HSA trustee/custodian modify one of its standard offerings to accommodate the employer's unique preferences for its workforce, such as a particular investment option, such action could be viewed as violating both of these prohibitions, making the HSA subject to ERISA.

Q 8:8 Can an employer select a single HSA trustee that offers a limited range of investment options to provide HSA services to its employees without violating the FAB prohibition against making or selecting investment options?

Yes. The DOL FAB expressly provides that an employer is permitted to select a single HSA provider to which it will forward employer and employee contributions. By choosing one HSA provider over another, an employer is, to a certain extent, limiting an employee's HSA investment options. However, as long as the employer does not request that the HSA provider change its standard offerings the mere act of selecting a single HSA trustee, even one with limited investment options, should not be viewed by DOL as a violation of the prohibition against making or selecting investment options.

Practice Pointer. No matter which HSA provider the employer selects, the employee may establish a second HSA with any trustee or custodian and transfer or roll over amounts from the employer HSA into the second HSA (see Qs 5:1, 5:36).

Caution. Qs 8:9 through 8:14, relating to the safe harbor exception from ERISA coverage are based on the authors' knowledge of the payroll deduction

IRA exceptions from ERISA's *pension plan* definition contained in the DOL Interpretive Bulletin on payroll-deduction IRAs and the "group" or group-type insurance exception from ERISA. [See 29 C.F.R. §§ 2530-3.1(j), 2509.99-1, 2510-3.2] It is the authors' opinion that similar rules are likely to apply to an employer's HSA contribution programs, although it is possible that DOL could disagree.

Q 8:9   When is an employer considered to "endorse" an HSA program?

In the authors' opinion, an employer is considered to endorse an HSA contribution program when the employer does not maintain "neutrality" with respect to the sponsor it selects. If an employer maintains neutrality with respect to the sponsor in its communications with its employees, the employer should not be considered to "endorse" an HSA program. [29 C.F.R. § 2510-3.1(j)(3); using the phrase "sole involvement of the employer or employee organization is without endorsement . . . ."; 2510-3.2(d)(iii), using the term "sole function of the employer or employee organization is without endorsement . . . ."; see also 29 C.F.R. § 2509.99-1(c)(1), relating to payroll deduction IRAs] (see above, Caution).

Q 8:10   May an employer encourage participation in the HSA program?

To a certain extent an employer may encourage participation by employees by providing general information on the HSA program and other educational materials that explain the prudence of savings for medical expenses, including the advantages of contributing to an HSA, without thereby converting the program to an ERISA-covered plan.

Caution. The employer must make it clear that its involvement in the program is limited to forwarding the participants' contributions and remitting them promptly to the sponsor and that it does not provide any additional benefit or promise any particular investment return on the employees' savings.

[See 29 C.F.R. § 2509.99-1(c)(1) relating to payroll-deduction IRAs] (see above, Caution)

Q 8:11   How may an employer demonstrate its neutrality with respect to a sponsor?

An employer may demonstrate its neutrality with respect to a sponsor in a variety of ways, including (but not limited to) ensuring that materials distributed to employees in connection with the HSA program clearly and prominently state, in language reasonably calculated to be understood by the average employee, that:

1. The HSA contribution program is completely voluntary;
2. The employer does not endorse or recommend either the sponsor or the funding media;
3. Other HSA funding media are available to employees outside of the payroll deduction program;

4. An HSA may not be appropriate for all individuals; and

5. The tax consequences of contributing to an HSA through the contribution reduction program (with the exception of the FICA tax savings) are generally the same as the consequences of contributing to an HSA outside of the program (where FICA will generally have been paid) and taking an income tax deduction.

Note. The employer would not be considered neutral to the extent that the materials distributed to the employees identify the funding medium as having as one of its purposes investing in securities of the employer or its affiliates or the funding medium has significant investments in such securities.

Note. If the program resulted from an agreement between the employer and an employee organization, then informational materials that identified the funding medium as having as one of its purposes investing in an investment vehicle that is designed to benefit an employee organization by providing more jobs for its members, or loans to its members, or similar direct benefits (or the funding medium's actual investments in any such investment vehicles) would indicate that the employee organization's involvement in the program is less than neutral. [See 29 C.F.R. Reg. § 2509.99-1(c)(1), footnote 2, relating to payroll deduction IRAs] (see above, Note)

Q 8:12   What is considered *reasonable compensation* that an employer can receive without causing the HSA to be subject to ERISA?

Reasonable compensation does not include any profit to the employer. Payments that an employer receives from an HSA provider for the employer's cost of operating the HSA program do constitute reasonable compensation to the extent that they constitute compensation for the actual costs of the program to the employer.

Example. The HSA provider agrees to make or to permit particular investments of HSA contributions in consideration for the employer's agreement to make an HSA contribution program available to its employees. Such an arrangement would exceed "reasonable compensation"for the services actually rendered by the employer in connection with the program.

[See 29 C.F.R § 2509.99-1(f) relating to payroll deduction IRAs] (see above, Note)

Q 8:13   What actions may an employer take without converting the HSA contribution program into an ERISA covered plan?

Specifically, without converting the HSA contribution program into an ERISA covered plan, an employer may:

1. Answer employees' specific inquiries about the mechanics of the HSA contribution program and refer other inquiries to the appropriate HSA provider;

2. Provide to employees informational materials written by the HSA provider describing the sponsor's HSA programs or addressing topics of general interest regarding investments and savings for medical expenses, provided that the material does not itself suggest that the employer is other than neutral with respect to the HSA provider and its products;

3. Request that the HSA provider prepare such informational materials and review such materials for appropriateness and completeness.

[See 29 C.F.R § 2509.99-1(c)(2) relating to payroll deduction IRAs] (see above, Note)

Q 8:14 May an employer that makes an HSA program available to employees pay the fees imposed by the HSA provider without causing the HSA to be subject to ERISA, or without generating adverse tax consequences for employees?

Yes. The employer should be permitted to pay any fee the HSA provider imposes on HSA account owners for services the HSA provider performs in connection with the establishment and maintenance of the contribution deduction process itself without causing the HSA to be subject to ERISA. Although the DOL has not specifically stated this, FAB 2004-1 provides that an employer is permitted to make contributions to an HSA without causing the HSA to be subject to ERISA (see Q 8:1). It follows that payment of administrative fees should also not cause the HSA to be subject to ERISA. Similarly, the employer should also be permitted to assume the internal costs (e.g., for overhead, bookkeeping, and so on) of implementing and maintaining the contribution deduction program without causing the HSA to be subject to ERISA. [See 29 C.F.R. § 2509.99-1(c)(2) relating to payroll deduction IRAs] (see above, Note)

In addition, these fees should be excludable from the employees' gross income and not counted as wages for FICA and FUTA purposes. Although there is no authority directly on point, this is generally how administrative fees are treated with respect to IRAs and employer-sponsored group health arrangements, and the tax treatment of HSA administrative fees should be analagous. In the IRA context, the IRS has ruled that expenses charged by an insurance company under an annuity contract, including a flat annual charge per participant account, could be paid directly by the employer and still be excludable from the employees' income and wages for FICA and FUTA purposes. [See, e.g., Priv. Ltr. Ruls. 7948017, 7951122] Similarly, for health plans that are subject to Code Section 106(a), it is generally accepted that the employer's payment of administrative fees associated with such coverage should be excludable from the employee's income (even though not technically a "health benefit"). For example, fees that an employer pays to a health insurer as part of the insurance premium are not required to be segregated from the premium and imputed as taxable income.

Q 8:15   If an employer makes arrangements with an HSA trustee to offer an HSA with a debit card to employees, can the employer specify that the debit card be used only for medical expenses without violating the FAB prohibition against imposing conditions on the use of HSA funds?

Probably. Although there is no direct guidance from DOL on this point, as long as an HSA account holder has the ability to make withdrawals from the HSA in some reasonable manner (e.g., a checkbook or withdrawal request form), it would appear that a debit card accompanying the HSA could be limited to use for medical expenses without violating the prohibition in the FAB against imposing conditions on the use of HSA funds. In addition, this should not violate the IRS requirement that the use of the HSA not be limited to medical expenses. [See I.R.S. Notice 2004-50, Q&A 79, 2004-33 I.R.B. 196] (See Q 8:2.)

Q 8:16   If an employer is in the business of providing HSAs, can it offer HSAs to its employees on the same terms as offered to the public without causing the HSA to be subject to ERISA?

Probably. The DOL has not, in the HSA context, addressed whether an employer who is in the business of providing HSA services can offer those services to employees without creating an ERISA plan. However, the DOL has addressed this issue for IRA providers, which seems analogous, since HSAs and ERISA are both "plans" under Code Section 4975. In the IRA guidance, the DOL has indicated that a financial institution may select itself to be the exclusive provider for payroll deduction IRAs offered to its own employees without creating an ERISA-covered IRA. [29 C.F.R. § 2509.99-1(g)] In that case, the DOL indicated that the financial institution was not considered an "employer" in relation to the IRA and therefore an ERISA plan was not maintained. [See, e.g., DOL Adv. Op. 2000-15A (Nov. 15, 2000)] Importantly, the DOL regulations require the IRA provider to offer the IRA on the same terms as it does to the general public.

> **Practice Pointer.** Because an employer is permitted to make contributions to the HSAs of employees (see Q 8:3), it would seem that an employer who is in the business of providing HSAs could waive administrative fees normally charged to the public for its own employees without causing the HSA to be subject to ERISA. However, there is no DOL guidance on this issue.

Q 8:17   Can an employer offer the HDHP and HSA as a single option without making the HSA subject to ERISA?

Probably. As long as an employee is not required to make salary reduction contributions to the HSA, this arrangement should not be viewed by DOL as violating the rule that HSA participation must be voluntary. If the other requirements of DOL's FAB 2004-01 are satisfied, the HDHP/HSA options should not be viewed as subject to ERISA. [FAB 2004-1 (Apr. 7, 2004)] (See appendix C.)

Q 8:18   Can an employer limit an employee's HSA contributions without causing the HSA to be subject to ERISA?

Probably not. If the employer imposes restrictions on the amount that an employee is permitted to contribute to the HSA linked to the employer's HDHP, such contribution cap could be viewed as impermissible employer involvement under DOL's FAB 2004-01, causing the HSA to be subject to ERISA. The statute itself [I.R.C. § 223] already contains contribution limits, and the DOL could easily take the position that an employer that restricts an employee from fully funding a particular HSA up to this limit has imposed restrictions that cause the HSA to be an ERISA plan.

Q 8:19   What are the consequences if an HSA is not subject to ERISA?

If the HSA is not subject to ERISA, there is no obligation to file a Form 5500 [ERISA § 103], provide an SPD [ERISA § 102], adopt a claims procedure [ERISA § 503], offer COBRA coverage [ERISA Part 6], or comply with portability or nondiscrimination rules under the Health Insurance Portability and Accountability Act (HIPAA) [ERISA Part 7] with respect to the HSA. In addition, the fiduciary responsibility requirements of ERISA Part 4 will not apply. Similarly, ERISA Section 502 and the legal actions available under Part 5 of ERISA will not apply. If an employer or insurer is sued in connection with an HSA, state law, rather than ERISA, will control, since ERISA preemption [ERISA § 514] would not apply. Note that the prohibited transaction rules in Code Section 4975 will continue to apply, (see Qs 6:51, 8:17).

Q 8:20   What are the employer's legal obligations and consequences if the HSA is subject to ERISA?

Although there is no DOL guidance on this point, if the HSA is subject to ERISA, presumably the employer is required to treat the HSA as it would any other group health plan that is subject to ERISA. This would include complying with applicable Form 5500 filing requirements, maintaining a plan document, and providing an SPD to participants. In addition, as described below (see Qs 8:21–8:23), the employer will have to determine how, if at all, to comply with the federal mandates that apply to group health plans, including COBRA rules, HIPAA portability/nondiscrimination rules, and claims procedure requirements for group health plans, notwithstanding that, from a practical standpoint, these rules may not make sense in the HSA context. Finally, the ERISA fiduciary rules will apply (see Q 8:25), and, if an employer or insurer is sued in connection with an HSA, ERISA, rather than state law, will generally control because of ERISA preemption.

Q 8:21   If an HSA is subject to ERISA, would an employer be required to distribute a COBRA General Notice?

Probably not. IRS Notice 2004-2, Q&A 35 [2004-2 I.R.B. 269] provides that HSAs are not subject to COBRA continuation coverage under Code Section

4980B. However, IRS left open the question of whether HSAs are subject to COBRA continuation coverage under ERISA Part 6. DOL has not addressed this issue, and it is possible that if DOL considers an HSA sponsored by an employer to be a *group health plan* under ERISA Part 6, an employer would have to satisfy all applicable COBRA notice and disclosure requirements, including providing a COBRA General Notice within 90 days of enrollment in the HSA.

However, IRS and DOL jointly administer COBRA, with the IRS responsible for interpreting the substantive rules and DOL responsible for interpreting the notice and disclosure rules. [Treas. Reg. § 54.4980B-1-10; 29 C.F.R. § 2590.606] It is, therefore, unlikely that DOL would unilaterally enforce a COBRA obligation where IRS has stated in guidance that COBRA does not apply for purposes of the Code. Further, because the HSA account must be nonforfeitable to satisfy requirements under Code Section 223 (see Qs 2:1, 6:2), an HSA account owner should never lose HSA coverage. Thus, there would generally not be a qualifying event with respect to an HSA for purposes of COBRA. [ERISA § 603]

Q 8:22   If an HSA is subject to ERISA, is an employer required to distribute a HIPAA certificate of creditable coverage and comply with the HIPAA nondiscrimination rules?

Possibly. DOL has not addressed this issue, but if DOL considers an HSA sponsored by an employer to be a *group health plan* for purposes of ERISA Part 7, an employer would technically be required to comply with the HIPAA portability and nondiscrimination rules, including providing a HIPAA certificate of creditable coverage upon request and not discriminating between HSA participants on the basis of a health factor (but see note below regarding preexisting conditions and special enrollment). ERISA Section 733(a) provides that the term *group health plan* means an employee welfare benefit plan that provides medical care to employees or their dependents (as defined under the terms of the plan) directly or through insurance, reimbursement, or otherwise. The term *medical care* for this purpose means amounts paid for:

1. The diagnosis, cure, mitigation, treatment, or prevention of disease, or amounts paid for the purpose of affecting any structure or function of the body;
2. Amounts paid for transportation primarily for and essential to medical care referred to in item 1;
3. Amounts paid for insurance covering medical care referred to in items 1 and 2.

Because an HSA is primarily designed to provide funds for medical care, the HIPAA portability and nondiscrimination rules will technically apply to an HSA, requiring an employer with two or more active employees [ERISA § 732(a)] enrolled in an HSA to comply with the HIPAA portability and nondiscrimination requirements of ERISA Part 7. These rules would, among other things, require an employer to issue a certificate of creditable coverage with respect to the HSA upon request of the HSA account owner in order to comply with ERISA § 701(e)(1)(A) and 29 C.F.R. § 2590.701-5(a)(2)(iii). Although a certificate of coverage is also required upon loss of coverage, an HSA account owner generally will not lose HSA coverage (as noted in Q 8:21). In addition, the HIPAA nondiscrimination rules (described in ERISA § 702 and 29 C.F.R. § 2590.702) prohibit an employer that sponsors a group health plan from discriminating on the basis of any health factor. These rules could be relevant in the HSA context if, for example, the employer wished to contribute an additional amount to the HSAs of employees who were willing to participate in a wellness program, for which DOL sets forth specific requirements. [ERISA § 702(b)(2)(B); 29 C.F.R. § 2590.702(c)(3)]

> **Note.** The final HIPAA portability regulations note in the preamble that, as a practical matter, the rules pertaining to preexisting conditions and special enrollment will generally not apply to HSAs. [69 Fed. Reg. 78720, 78734 (Dec. 30, 2004); (29 C.F.R. Part 2590; 26 C.F.R Parts 54 and 602; 45 C.F.R. Parts 144 and 146)]

Q 8:23 If an HSA is subject to ERISA, is an employer required to comply with the DOL claims procedure rules that apply to group health plans?

Possibly. DOL has not addressed this issue, but if DOL should consider an HSA sponsored by an employer to be a welfare plan for purposes of ERISA generally, an employer would be required to implement a claims procedure that satisfies certain requirements. [ERISA § 503; 29 C.F.R. § 2560.503-1] Presumably, that claims procedure would have to comply with the requirements applicable to group health plans. An ERISA welfare benefit plan is defined in ERISA Section 3(1) as any plan, fund, or program established or maintained by an employer or by an employee organization, or by both, for the purpose of providing benefits for its participants or their beneficiaries that include medical, surgical, or hospital care or benefits, or benefits in the event of sickness. Because an HSA is primarily designed to provide funds for medical care, in the absence of further DOL guidance, it appears that the claims procedure rules would apply. These rules would, for example, require an employer to provide a notice of adverse determination and appeal rights within a certain time frame when an employee requests a withdrawal from an HSA that contains insufficient funds.

However, the claims procedures, if required by DOL, will have limited applicability. IRS Notice 2004-2, Q&A 29 and 30 [2004-2 I.R.B. 269] provides that an HSA account owner is not required to submit receipts for medical expenses to trustees, custodians, or employers. Rather, a self-substantiation rule is in place (i.e., an HSA account owner is responsible for determining on his or her own whether an item is a medical expense). Thus, there will be few circumstances in which the employee makes a "claim" with the employer for HSA funds. However, as noted above, if an employee attempts to withdraw amounts from an HSA with insufficient funds, the employer would presumably be required to provide a notice of adverse determination and appeal rights. In addition, for urgent care claims and pre-service claims, the DOL claims procedures require that claimants be apprised of the plan's benefit determination, whether the determination is adverse or a complete grant, in accordance with the time frames generally applicable to urgent care and pre-service claims. [See 29 C.F.R. § 2560.503-1(f)(2)(i) and (iii)] Such notices must contain sufficient information to fully apprise the claimant of the plan's decision to approve the requested benefits. Accordingly, it appears that there may be situations in which an employer is technically required to provide a notice of approval when an employee withdraws an amount from his or her HSA. However, this rule will be difficult to administer in practice, given the fact that the employer may not know the reason that an employee requests an HSA distribution.

Q 8:24   If an HSA is subject to ERISA, could its funds be held in a custodial account rather than a trust?

Probably not. Although there is an IRA exception to the ERISA Section 403 trust requirement in ERISA Section 403(b)(3)(B) that permits plan assets for ERISA-covered IRAs to be held in custodial accounts, this rule does not, on its face, extend to HSAs.

Practice Pointer. If an HSA is subject to ERISA, but an entity that would normally act as trustee (e.g., a bank) wishes to limit liability, the employer could be the trustee and the bank could continue in a custodial role. Alternatively, the bank could be a directed trustee, which would limit its liability more than if it were a regular trustee (but the liability would be greater than if the bank were a custodian).

Q 8:25   If an HSA is subject to ERISA, what fiduciary standards would apply to the HSA trustee or custodian?

If an HSA is subject to ERISA, the following fiduciary standards, set forth in ERISA Part 4, would have to be satisfied:

1. *Written plan document.* The HSA written plan document would have to describe the funding policy, procedure for allocation of responsibilities under plan, procedure for amending the plan, and basis on which payments are made to and from the plan. A fiduciary must follow the written plan document. [ERISA § 402]

2. *Trust/custodial account.* HSA plan assets would be required to be held in a trust or custodial account. [ERISA § 403] This is also a requirement for purposes of Code Section 223 (see Q 7:1).

3. *Prudent man standard.* The "prudent man" standard of care requires a fiduciary to discharge its duties with the care, skill, prudence, and diligence under the circumstances then prevailing that a prudent man acting in a like capacity and familiar with such matters would use in the conduct of an enterprise of like character and with like aims. [ERISA

§ 404(a)(1)(B)] The fiduciary of an HSA would have to comply with this standard. Although ERISA Section 404(c) is available to protect fiduciaries who oversee participant-directed pension plans, this section would not apply to HSAs. Thus, the fiduciary could be exposed to liability for loss on participant-directed investments in an HSA.

4. *Diversification.* The duty to diversify plan investments would require an HSA fiduciary to diversify the investments of the HSA so as to minimize the risk of large losses, unless under the circumstances it is clearly prudent not to do so. [ERISA § 404(a)(1)(C)]

5. *Exclusive benefit rule.* The exclusive benefit rule requires that plan money must be spent only on benefits or expenses of plan administration. [ERISA § 404(a)(1)(A)] The exclusive benefit rule would prohibit a fiduciary from using HSA assets for any purpose other than to benefit the HSA account owner or to pay HSA plan expenses.

Q 8:26   Does an entity incur additional risk and responsibilities as an HSA trustee as compared to an HSA custodian?

Yes. A trustee has fiduciary responsibilities and potential liabilities that a custodian does not have. A custodian simply holds the assets on behalf of the owner of the assets. Other than holding the assets and doing as the owner orders, the custodian has no fiduciary obligations to the owner. A trustee may also have custody of the assets, but, in addition, a trustee is also a fiduciary under ERISA (and common law as well). This means that a trustee's duties to take care of the assets may extend beyond what the trustee has agreed to do under contract. The trustee's duties include following the terms of the written plan document, adhering to a "prudent man" standard of care in discharging fiduciary duties, diversifying plan investments to minimize the risk of large losses if prudent to do so, and limiting the use of plan assets for any purpose other than to benefit the beneficiary or to pay plan expenses. In addition, the trustee could be found to have a duty to disclose certain relevant information to beneficiaries under principles of common law. This duty would generally not apply to the custodian. The trustee is subject to liability for failure to satisfy any of these duties.

Q 8:27   Is it possible to designate one entity as the trustee of an HSA and another entity as the custodian of an HSA?

Yes. The custodian and trustee do not have to be the same entity. So, for example, if an HSA is subject to ERISA (e.g., because of a high level of employer involvement), it would be possible to designate the bank as custodian of the HSA and some other party, such as the employer, as trustee of the HSA. Alternatively, a trustee can contract to be a "directed trustee." In this regard, ERISA Section 403(a) specifically recognizes that, where a plan expressly provides that the trustee is subject to the direction of a named fiduciary who is not a trustee (e.g., an HSA account holder), such trustee will have limited authority or discretion. This limited authority or discretion, in turn, limits a trustee's fiduciary liabilities (although a directed trustee would still have more fiduciary liability than a custodian). [DOL/FAB 2004-03 (Dec. 17, 2004]

Q 8:28 What are the potential consequences when a fiduciary violates ERISA?

The potential consequences of a fiduciary violation of ERISA are as follows:

1. The fiduciary is personally liable to make good any losses suffered by the plan on account of the fiduciary's violation and to restore to the plan any profits that the fiduciary made by use of plan assets in violation of its fiduciary duties. [ERISA §§ 409, 502(a)(2)]

2. DOL, plan participants and beneficiaries, and other fiduciaries can sue and, if they win, can be awarded attorneys fees and court costs in addition to the cost of making up losses and restoring any improper profits. [ERISA § 502(g)(3)]

3. In any action or settlement involving DOL, DOL must assess a penalty of 20 percent of the "applicable recovery amount" in a case of a breach of fiduciary duty or co-fiduciary liability. DOL may waive or reduce the penalty only if it concludes that (1) the fiduciary acted reasonably and in good faith or (2) the fiduciary could not be expected to make the plan whole without severe hardship unless a waiver is granted. [ERISA § 502(l)]

4. A court can order the fiduciary removed from its position as a fiduciary, can enjoin further breaches by the fiduciary or other party in interest, and can order other equitable relief. [ERISA § 501(a)(5),(8)]

5. In the case of a criminal, willful violation of the reporting and disclosure rules of ERISA Part 1, an individual may be subject to fines of up to $100,000 and imprisonment for up to ten years, and a corporation may be subject to fines of up to $500,000. [ERISA § 501]

6. In the case of a prohibited transaction by a party in interest (which is the same as a "disqualified person" (see Q 6:57)) IRS may assess a penalty of 15 percent of the "amount involved" (defined under Code Section 4975(f)(4)) in each transaction for each year or part thereof during which the prohibited transaction continues. If the transaction is not corrected within the taxable period, such penalty may be in an amount not more than 100 percent of the amount involved. [I.R.C. § 4975]

Q 8:29 If an HSA is not subject to ERISA, what fiduciary standards would apply to the HSA trustee or custodian?

If an HSA is not subject to ERISA, state law fiduciary trust requirements (which may be similar to the ERISA requirements described in Q 8:28), will apply. The following is an illustration of such requirements under Minnesota and Connecticut law:

Trust document. A trustee is required to administer the trust in accordance with the terms of its underlying trust documents. This is particularly relevant with regard to investment strategy and the allocation of receipts to and disbursements from the trust. To the extent the trust documents are silent, state law may impose different duties on the trustee. [*e.g.*, Minn. Trust Companies § 48A.07 (where no written instruction, bank or trust company must use best judgment in selection of authorized securities and is responsible for the validity, regularity, quality and value of them at the time made, and for their safekeeping); Conn. Principal and Income Act § 45a–542b; § 45a–542c (if unable to comply with written terms of trust, a trustee shall consider all factors relevant to the trust and its beneficiaries, including the needs for liquidity, regularity of income and preservation and appreciation of capital)]

Best judgment/prudent investor rules. A trustee must invest the trust assets with reasonable care and must diversify the trust assets unless contrary to the purposes of the trust. [Minn. Trust Companies § 48A.07; Conn. Uniform Prudent Investor Act § 45a–541b]

Loyalty. A trustee must administer the trust solely in the interest of the trust's beneficiaries. [Minn. Uniform Custodial Trust Act § 529.06; Conn. Uniform Prudent Investor Act § 45–541e]

Records. The trustee must maintain adequate records supporting all transactions with the trust and the records must be made reasonably available to the trust beneficiaries. The trustee must also separately account for each beneficiary under the trust. [Minn. Uniform Custodial Trust Act § 529.05, 529.06]

Q 8:30   Has DOL issued any guidance other than FAB 2004-01 relating to HSAs?

Yes. DOL issued Advisory Opinion 2004-09A (Dec. 22, 2004), which held that an incentive payment deposited by an HSA trustee to an account holder's HSA would not violate the prohibited transaction rules of Code Section 4975 or ERISA Section 406. (See Q 6:54 for further discussion; see appendix C.)

Q 8:31   Do the prohibited transaction rules apply if an HSA is not subject to ERISA?

Yes. The prohibited transaction rules are located in both the Internal Revenue Code [I.R.C. § 4975] and ERISA [ERISA § 406]. Even if an HSA is not subject to ERISA, the prohibited transaction rules of Code Section 4975 will apply. [I.R.C. § 4975(e)(1)(E)]

HIPAA Privacy

Q 8:32   Is an HSA subject to the HIPAA privacy regulations?

Possibly. The Centers for Medicare and Medicaid Services (CMS) has not yet issued any guidance concerning whether an HSA is subject to the HIPAA privacy regulations. However, the regulations apply to health plans, which are broadly defined to include "any other individual or group plan or combination of individual, or group plans, that provides or pays for the cost of medical care." [45 C.F.R. § 160.103] It would seem that this definition would be broad enough to encompass an HSA arrangement, whether provided by the employer or individually, since it is an arrangement primarily intended to pay for medical care. Whether an HSA is subject to ERISA is not relevant to this determination. As a practical matter, health information may not actually be used or disclosed, since HSA account holders are not required to submit receipts for medical care in order to obtain reimbursement. Accordingly, there may be little need for safeguards. Nevertheless, the privacy notice and business associate requirements may technically apply.

> **Practice Pointer.** The fact that someone is a participant in a plan can be considered protected health information. Accordingly, the HSA (e.g., trustee/administrator) must not disclose a list of participants for purposes other than administering the plan (e.g., it is not permitted to sell or provide a list of participants for marketing purposes). The trustee or administrator should consider providing a privacy notice when an employee enrolls in the HSA, including language explaining that HSA funds used for medical expenses are self-substantiated, and so, generally, the HSA has no access to health information. However, to the extent it does, the notice would apply. If the employer is involved in assisting employees with establishing an HSA with a particular trustee or custodian, the employer should enter into a business associate contract with the administrator or trustee or custodian.

Q 8:33   Would the HIPAA Electronic Standards Regulations apply to HSAs?

They may, depending on how payments from the HSA are structured. The HIPAA Electronic Standards Regulations require that a *covered entity* that conducts certain transactions electronically with another covered entity must conduct those transactions under the standards set by the Secretary of the Department of Health and Human Services (HHS). [45 C.F.R. § 162.923(a)] In addition, if any party requests that a health plan conduct one of the listed transactions as a standard transaction, the health plan must do so. [45 C.F.R. § 162.925(a)]

A *covered entity* is defined as a health plan, provider, or clearinghouse. For example, if a provider submits a claim to a health plan electronically, the claim must be submitted and received using the standard transactions. When the health plan sends a payment to the provider electronically, this transmission also must be conducted in accordance with the standard transactions. The regulations do not apply to a transmission involving a noncovered entity, including an individual. So, if an individual submits a claim to a plan and the plan sends payment to the individual, these transmissions would fall outside the regulations because they would not be between two covered entities.

If the HSA is considered a *health plan* for HIPAA purposes (see Q 8:32), the HIPAA Electronic Standard Regulations may apply. Note that CMS has not issued guidance on this question. However, if this is the case and if the party submitting the request for payment and receiving the payment is the individual, the transmission would not involve two covered entities and would fall outside the regulations. CMS addressed a similar fact pattern as in Q 8:15, discussing the use of a debit card under an FSA or HRA, and stated that this transmission would be between an individual and a plan, and so would fall outside of the regulations. [See www.questions.cms.hhs.gov, Answer ID 2352 (search on "FSA")]

However, if the HSA is considered a *health plan* for HIPAA purposes and the HSA is structured so that a provider can directly submit claims to, and receive payment from, the HSA, and these transmissions are conducted electronically, CMS may consider these transmissions to be covered under the Electronic Standards Regulations. Note that the regulations also state that any party may request a health plan to conduct a transaction as a standard transaction. So, if an individual or other party did request an HSA to receive claims or make payments using the standard transactions, the HSA would have to do so. However, this seems very unlikely.

Medicare Part D

Q 8:34   Is an HSA a plan for which an employer must issue a certificate of creditable coverage for purposes of Medicare Part D?

No. The Centers for Medicare and Medicaid Services (CMS) issued final regulations [42 C.F.R. § 423] implementing the new Voluntary Medicare Part D prescription drug benefit that took effect in January 2006 pursuant to the Medicare Prescription Drug Improvement and Modernization Act of 2003. Under the CMS final regulations [42 C.F.R. § 423.56], all group health plan sponsors that offer prescription drug coverage are required to provide a notice to all Medicare-eligible participants that states whether prescription drug coverage under its plan is "creditable" when compared to the prescription drug coverage under Medicare Part D. CMS believes that this information will help participants decide whether to enroll in Part D. In addition, a participant who has a certificate of creditable coverage has the ability to stay in the employer-sponsored health plan and enroll in Medicare Part D at a later date without incurring a late enrollment penalty. Coverage is considered "creditable" if its actuarial value equals or exceeds the value of Medicare Part D coverage. With respect to HSAs, however, CMS subsequently issued guidance on account-based plans which indicates that HSAs are not retiree plans for purposes of the creditable coverage rules due to the fact that no contributions can be made to HSAs once the retiree becomes entitled to Medicare. The guidance is available at: www.cms.hhs.gov/EmployerRetireeDrugSubsid/downloads/AccountbasedPlansGuidanceRev1.pdf.

> **Practice Pointer.** Even though an employer is not required to provide a notice of creditable coverage with respect to the HSA, such notice will still be required for Medicare-eligible individuals participating in the HDHP.

Q 8:35   Is an HSA a plan for which an employer may apply for the employer subsidy under Medicare Part D?

No. Beginning in 2006, employer and union sponsors of qualified retiree prescription drug plans have the ability to receive tax-free retiree drug subsidy payments for a portion of their plan's prescription drug costs. For each qualifying covered retiree, the sponsor is eligible to receive payments of 28 percent of the allowable drug costs attributable to gross prescription drug costs between the cost theshold ($250 in 2006) and the cost limit ($5,000 in 2006). [42 C.F.R. § 423] With respect to HSAs, however, CMS issued guidance on account-based plans which indicates that HSAs are not retiree plans for purposes of the employer subsidy because no contributions can be made to HSAs once the retiree becomes entitled to Medicare. Accordingly, employers and unions cannot receive retiree drug subsidy payments with respect to HSAs. The guidance is available at: www.cms.hhs.gov/EmployerRetireeDrugSubsid/downloads/AccountbasedPlans-GuidanceRev1.pdf.

State Benefit Mandates

Q 8:36   What state laws could affect the HDHP that accompanies the HSA?

A state could have laws that regulate insured HDHPs. These laws may, for example, require certain benefits to be covered under an HDHP without regard to whether the deductible is satisfied. Unless a state's mandated benefits satisfy the definition of preventive care for federal purposes, this would cause the HDHP to fail to satisfy the federal requirements under Code Section 223. Thus, an individual in a state with those laws could not contribute to an HSA. Other state laws may require an insurer or HMO to comply with limits on deductibles, which could also conflict with federal requirements. See appendix E for a list of states with mandates that could cause an HDHP to fail to satisfy applicable requirements.

Q 8:37   What transition relief has IRS issued with respect to HDHPs that are subject to state mandates?

IRS addressed the fact that, in certain states, it is not possible to issue an HDHP that satifies both state and federal requirements by issuing transition relief for months prior to January 1, 2006, with respect to state requirements in effect on January 1, 2004 (see Q 3:20). [I.R.S. Notice 2004-43, 2004-27 I.R.B. 10] This guidance states that, during this time, an HDHP will not be considered to violate federal requirements if the sole reason it does not comply with federal requirements is that it is complying with state benefit mandates. However, after January 1, 2006, individuals who are covered by calendar-year insured HDHPs or HMOs subject to state laws that conflict with Code Section 223 requirements will not be considered *eligible individuals* who are permitted to contribute to HSAs.

In Notice 2005-83 [I.R.S. Notice 2005-83, 2005-49 I.R.B. 1075), IRS extended the expiration date of the transition guidance provided in Notice 2004-43 for noncalendar-year HDHPs to the earlier of (1) the health plan's next renewal date or (2) December 31, 2006 (see Q 3:21). The reason for this extension is that, generally, a health plan may not reduce existing benefits before the plan's renewal date. Thus, even though a state may amend its laws before January 1, 2006, to authorize HDHPs that comply with Code Section 223(c)(2), non-calendar-year plans may still fail to qualify as HDHPs after January 1, 2006, because existing benefits cannot be changed until the next renewal date. Accordingly, the IRS concluded in Notice 2005-83 that additional transitional relief is appropriate for noncalendar-year health plans. Under this additional transition relief, for any coverage period of 12 months or less beginning before January 1, 2006, a health plan that otherwise qualifies as an HDHP as defined in Code Section 223(c)(2), except that it complied on its most recent renewal date before January 1, 2006, with state-mandated requirements (in effect on January 1, 2004) to provide certain benefits without regard to a deductible or with a deductible below the minimum annual deductible specified in Code Section 223(c)(2), will be treated as an HDHP.

Example. A state amends its laws to authorize HDHPs, effective November 1, 2005. A health plan with a renewal date of July 1, 2005, is required to retain the state-mandated low-deductible coverage for the plan year July 1, 2005, through June 30, 2006, because under state law, the benefits can only be modified on the renewal date. Under the transition relief provided in Notice 2005-83 [2005-49 I.R.B. 1075], the health plan man be treated as an HDHP until the renewal date of the policy, when it can be amended to comply with federal requirements (i.e., for the months of January through June 2006).

Q 8:38   Can an employer make the same HDHP/HSA available to its employees in Hawaii as is available in other states?

Generally, no. The state of Hawaii has a unique exception from the preemption provision of ERISA that allows it to regulate directly the terms of ERISA health plans, including self-funded plans. [ERISA § 514(b)(5)] Hawaii's Prepaid Health Care Act (PHCA) requires employers to provide health benefits to Hawaii-based employees who are employed at least 20 hours per week for four consecutive weeks. [Haw. Rev. Stat. §§ 393-3(8), 393-4, 393-11] In addition, the PHCA also sets forth various requirements concerning plan benefits and cost-sharing. [Haw. Rev. Stat. § 393] Accordingly, an HDHP offered by an employer in Hawaii, whether self-insured or insured, must satisfy the requirements of the PHCA.

An employer in Hawaii essentially has three options in deciding how to satisfy the PHCA's benefit requirements:

1. The employer may buy health insurance coverage that has been preapproved by Hawaii Department of Labor and Industrial Relations (DLIR);
2. The employer may seek DLIR approval for a health insurance policy not yet approved by DLIR; or
3. The employer may seek DLIR approval for self-funded plan coverage.

There are not yet any preapproved HDHP/HSA products available on the Hawaii insurance market. If an employer offers a plan that has not been preapproved by the DLIR, it must submit an application to the state and request approval. It appears, based on informal comments from the DLIR, that in order to view the HDHP as satisfying the requirements of the PHCA, the DLIR may require significant employer HSA contributions to ensure that most of the high deductible is covered by the employer, not the employee.

Q 8.39 Is it possible to have an HDHP in New Jersey that satisfies federal requirements?

Yes. New Jersey's recently enacted A4543, P.L. 2005 Chpt. 248 (Dec. 21, 2005) makes it possible to offer HDHPs that satisfy federal requirements in that state. New Jersey imposes requirements upon insurers and HMOs for groups with greater than 50 persons requiring that insurers and HMOs provide coverage below the deductible to children to pay for lead poisoning screening, medical evaluation, and necessary medical follow up and treatment for lead poisoned children. This caused a problem for HDHPs, because the rule under Code Section 223 is that the only benefits that can be provided below the deductible are those that satisfy the definition of "preventive care." (See Q 3:45.) Since New Jersey requires treatment, which would not be preventive care, it would not have been possible to offer an insured HDHP in New Jersey without statutory change. (IRS did have limited transition guidance in place under Notice 2004-43 [2004-27 I.R.B. 10], but that only covered months before January 1, 2006, for calendar year plans.) This law creates an exception to this rule for HDHPs that are intended to be used with an HSA. Under the exception, a deductible for lead poisoning benefits can be imposed under the HDHP, unless such services satisfy the definition of preventive care under federal law.

State Tax Consequences

Q 8:40 If an HSA satisfies applicable federal requirements, will a participant have the same favorable tax consequences under state law as under federal law?

Not necessarily. Although most states follow the federal tax law with respect to determination of taxable income, some states do not provide tax benefits for HSA participation. There are currently six states in which the state tax consequences of HSA participation differ from the federal tax consequences (e.g., where HSA employer contributions that are excludable for federal tax purposes are required to be included in income, where interest earned on the HSA is taxed, or where deduction for state tax purposes is not available). These are Alabama, California, New Jersey, and Wisconsin. See appendix E for a complete list of states and tax consequences.

Q 8:41   What impact did California's Assembly Bill 115 have upon HSAs?

California's Assembly Bill 115 [(Stat. 2005, Ch. 691(Oct. 17, 2005)] conforms California income tax law to federal tax law law as of April 15, 2005, but specifically excepts HSAs. Under A.B. 115, HSA contributions may not be made on a pretax basis, no deduction is available for after-tax contributions, and earnings are taxed.

Q 8:42   What impact did The Health Savings Account Act in Pennsylvania have on HSAs?

The Health Savings Account Act, H.B. 107, Pub. L. No. 278, No. 48 (July 14, 2005), which applies to taxable years beginning after December 31, 2004, makes interest income earned by an HSA and withdrawals used to pay for eligible medical or dental expenses exempt from Pennsylvania state personal income tax. However, HSA contributions made by an employer or made through an employer's cafeteria plan will still be includible in the individual's income for purposes of Pennsylvania's tax law. In addition, after-tax contributions made by an individual may not be deducted. An earlier version of the bill would have allowed these tax benefits, but these provisions were removed from the final bill. Finally, as under federal law, distributions from HSAs that are not used for qualified medical expenses of the beneficiary, or any excess contributions, are taxable.

Davis-Bacon Act

Q 8:43   Do employer contributions to an HSA count as fringe benefits under the Davis-Bacon Act?

Probably. The Davis-Bacon Act requires contractors and subcontractors working on federally funded construction projects in excess of $2,000 to pay their laborers and mechanics a wage that is not less than the prevailing wage for similarly situated employees in the locality. [40 U.S.C. §§ 3141–3144, 3146, 3147] Included in the *prevailing wage* are two components: (1) basic hourly wages and (2) fringe benefits. Although the basic hourly wages must be paid in cash, fringe benefit obligations may be satisfied by paying fringe benefits in cash as additional wages, contributing payments to a bona fide plan, or both. [See 40 U.S.C. § 1341; 29 C.F.R. § 5.31]

Employer contributions to HSAs are likely to count as fringe benefits under the Act because HSAs are designed to pay for medical expenses, which are a benefit listed under the Act. In addition, HSAs are funded, and non-forfeitable and, therefore, appear to satisfy the requirements for funded plans under 29 C.F.R. § 5.26. Although the funds in an HSA could be used for nonmedical purposes if a participant is willing to incur income tax and a 10 percent additional tax, a contractor is permitted to substitute cash for the fringe benefits. Accordingly, it is likely that DOL would consider employer contributions to an HSA to satisfy the requirements for fringe benefits under the Act.

USA Patriot Act

Q 8:44   Do the Customer Identification Procedures of the USA Patriot Act apply to HSAs for which a bank is trustee or custodian?

Yes. The USA Patriot Act, Title III, "International Money Laundering Abatement and Anti-terrorist Financing Act of 2001," adds several new provisions to the Bank Secrecy Act (BSA) (31 U.S.C. § 5311 et seq.) that are designed to facilitate the prevention, detection, and prosecution of international money laundering and the financing of terrorism. [USA Patriot Act (Pub. L. No. 107-56)]

Section 326 of the Act adds a new subsection (1) to 31 U.S.C. 5318 of the BSA, which directs the Secretary of the Treasury to draft regulations establishing minimum standards that apply in connection with the opening of an account at a financial institution regarding the identity of the customer. The regulation under 31 C.F.R. § 103.121 entitled "Customer Identification Programs for banks, savings associations, credit unions, and certain non-federally regulated banks" (CIP regulation) sets forth minimum information that a bank must obtain from a customer before opening an account.

These rules generally require that a bank implement a written Customer Identification Program appropriate for its size and type of business that includes obtaining the name, date of birth, address, and taxpayer identification number of a customer prior to opening an account. After obtaining this information, the bank must verify the identity of the customer within a reasonable time after the account is opened (e.g., by reviewing a customer's unexpired government-issued identification, such as a driver's license or passport). If the bank cannot form a reasonable belief that it knows the true identity of a customer, the bank must follow procedures that it has describing (1) when the bank should not open an account, (2) when a customer may use an account while the bank attempts to verify the customer's identity, (3) when the bank should close an account (after attempts to verify a customer's identity have failed), and (4) when the bank should file a Suspicious Activity Report in accordance with applicable law and regulation. The CIP regulation also requires that the bank keep records of identifying information about a customer, including any document that was relied on to verify the identity of the customer. These records must be retained for five years after the date the account is closed. Finally, the bank must adopt procedures for determining whether the customer appears on any list of known or suspected terrorists or terrorist organizations issued by any federal government agency. Bank customers must also be given notice that the bank is requesting information to verify their identities. A sample notice is provided in the regulation for this purpose.

Securities Law

Q 8:45   Is an HSA subject to regulation by the Securities and Exchange Commission?

Possibly, although the Securities and Exchange Commission (SEC) has not issued any guidance on this issue. The threshold question is whether HSAs are *securities*. If HSAs are securities, then persons in the business of selling HSAs would have to register as brokers or dealers. In addition, if HSAs are securities, it is likely that interests in HSAs would have to be registered as securities under the Securities Act of 1933 and that the issuer of the HSA may have to register as an investment company under the Investment Company Act of 1940.

Q 8:46   Under what circumstances would an HSA be considered a security for purposes of the federal securities laws?

The federal securities laws define the term *security* as including an *investment contract* (e.g., Securities Exchange Act of 1934 Section 3(10)). Therefore, an HSA will be a security if it qualifies as an investment contract. An investment contract involves a contract, transaction, or scheme whereby (1) a person invests his or her money (2) in a common enterprise, (3) with an expectation of profit, (4) solely from the efforts of a promoter or other third party. [SEC v. W.J. Howey Co., 328 U.S. 293 (1946)]

Q 8:47   Is guidance relating to IRAs relevant for purposes of determining whether an HSA is a security?

Possibly. Because HSAs have many of the same features as IRAs, and because Code Section 223 refers to IRA rules with respect to certain issues (e.g., identity of trustee), SEC guidance regarding IRAs may be helpful in determining the status of HSAs under federal securities laws.

Q 8:48   What is the SEC's position regarding IRAs?

The SEC has taken the position that most IRAs are investment contracts. [SEC Release 33-6188, 1980 WL 2942, at *13 (Feb. 1, 1980) (Rel. No. 6188)] However, the SEC has also opined that certain types of IRAs do not constitute securities separate from the underlying investment by the IRA. Thus, IRAs invested in the following manner generally need not be registered under federal securities laws:

- IRAs involving direct investment by an individual in an exempt security (e.g., government-issued securities or certain securities issued by a bank),
- IRAs involving direct investment by an individual in an underlying investment that is not a security (e.g., a traditional fixed annuity), and
- IRAs funded solely by mutual fund shares registered under the Securities Act of 1933.

If the SEC were to take a similar position with respect to HSAs, HSAs invested in the same manner would not be required to be registered.

Use of Electronic Media

Q 8:49   To what extent can an employer use electronic technologies for providing employee benefit notices and transmitting employee benefit elections and consents?

The Treasury Department and IRS recently issued proposed regulations regarding the use of electronic media to provide notices to employee benefit plan participants and beneficiaries and to transmit elections or consents from participants and beneficiaries to employee benefit plans. The standards set forth in these proposed regulations would apply to any "notice, election, or similar communication" made to or by a participant or beneficiary under an HSA. [Prop. Treas. Reg. § 35.3404-1 (70 Fed. Reg. 40675 (July 14, 2005)]

Appendix A

Extracts from Relevant Code Sections

Appendix A reflects all changes made to the Internal Revenue Code through December 31, 2005, including additions, amendments, and technical corrections made by the Katrina Emergency Tax Act of 2005 (KETA) (Pub. L. No. 109-73) and the Gulf Opportunity Zone Act of 2005 (GOZA) (Pub. L. No. 109-135).

A Code section can be divided into several parts. The Ï symbol is frequently used to abbreviate the word *section*. For example, the parts to the citation Ï 223(d)(1)(A)(i)(I) are as follows:

Ï 223 (d) (1) (A) (i) (I)
   223 Section
    (d) Subsection
     (1) Paragraph
      (A) Subparagraph
       (i) Clause
        (I) Subclause

Code Section 62—Adjusted Gross Income Defined

(a) GENERAL RULE.—For purposes of this subtitle, the term "adjusted gross income" means, in the case of an individual, gross income minus the following deductions:

* * *

(16) ARCHER MSAs.—The deduction allowed by section 220.

(17) INTEREST ON EDUCATION LOANS.—The deduction allowed by section 221.

* * *

Code Section 106—Contributions by Employer to Accident and Health Plans

(a) GENERAL RULE.—Except as otherwise provided in this section, gross income of an employee does not include employer-provided coverage under an accident or health plan.

* * *

(d) CONTRIBUTIONS TO HEALTH SAVINGS ACCOUNTS.

(1) IN GENERAL.—In the case of an employee who is an eligible individual (as defined in section 223(c)(1)), amounts contributed by such employee's employer to any health savings account (as defined in section 223(d)) of such employee shall be treated as employer-provided coverage for medical expenses under an accident or health plan to the extent such amounts do not exceed the limitation under section 223(b) (determined without regard to this subsection) which is applicable to such employee for such taxable year.

(2) SPECIAL RULES.—Rules similar to the rules of paragraphs (2), (3), (4), and (5) of subsection (b) shall apply for purposes of this subsection.

(3) CROSS REFERENCE.—For penalty on failure by employer to make comparable contributions to the health savings accounts of comparable employees, see section 4980G.

Code Section 152—Dependent Defined (Effective 01/01/05)

(a) IN GENERAL.—For purposes of this subtitle, the term "dependent" means—

(1) a qualifying child, or

(2) a qualifying relative.

(b) EXCEPTIONS.—For purposes of this section—

(1) DEPENDENTS INELIGIBLE.—If an individual is a dependent of a tax-payer for any taxable year of such taxpayer beginning in a calendar year, such individual shall be treated as having no dependents for any taxable year of such individual beginning in such calendar year.

Note. For HSA purposes, the term *qualified medical expenses* is determined without regard to subsection (1) above or subsection (2) below for tax years beginning after 2004. [See I.R.C. § 223(d)(2)(A)]

(2) MARRIED DEPENDENTS.—An individual shall not be treated as a dependent of a taxpayer under subsection (a) if such individual has made a joint return with the individual's spouse under section 6013 for the taxable year beginning in the calendar year in which the taxable year of the taxpayer begins.

(3) CITIZENS OR NATIONALS OF OTHER COUNTRIES—

(A) IN GENERAL.—The term "dependent" does not include an individual who is not a citizen or national of the United States unless such individual is a resident of the United States or a country contiguous to the United States.

(B) EXCEPTION FOR ADOPTED CHILD.—Subparagraph (A) shall not exclude any child of a taxpayer (within the meaning of subsection (f) (1)(B)) from the definition of "dependent" if—

(i) for the taxable year of the taxpayer, the child has the same principal place of abode as the taxpayer and is a member of the taxpayer's household, and

(ii) the taxpayer is a citizen or national of the United States.

(c) QUALIFYING CHILD.—For purposes of this section—

(1) IN GENERAL.—The term "qualifying child" means, with respect to any taxpayer for any taxable year, an individual—

(A) who bears a relationship to the taxpayer described in paragraph (2),

(B) who has the same principal place of abode as the taxpayer for more than one-half of such taxable year,

(C) who meets the age requirements of paragraph (3), and

(D) who has not provided over one-half of such individual's own support for the calendar year in which the taxable year of the taxpayer begins.

(2) RELATIONSHIP.—For purposes of paragraph (1)(A), an individual bears a relationship to the taxpayer described in this paragraph if such individual is—

(A) a child of the taxpayer or a descendant of such a child, or

(B) a brother, sister, stepbrother, or stepsister of the taxpayer or a descendant of any such relative.

(3) AGE REQUIREMENTS.—

    (A) IN GENERAL.—For purposes of paragraph (1)(C), an individual meets the requirements of this paragraph if such individual—

        (i) has not attained the age of 19 as of the close of the calendar year in which the taxable year of the taxpayer begins, or

        (ii) is a student who has not attained the age of 24 as of the close of such calendar year.

    (B) SPECIAL RULE FOR DISABLED.—In the case of an individual who is permanently and totally disabled (as defined in section 22(e)(3)) at any time during such calendar year, the requirements of subparagraph (A) shall be treated as met with respect to such individual.

(4) SPECIAL RULE RELATING TO 2 OR MORE CLAIMING QUALIFYING CHILD. * * *

(d) QUALIFYING RELATIVE.—For purposes of this section—

(1) IN GENERAL.—The term "qualifying relative" means, with respect to any taxpayer for any taxable year, an individual—

    (A) who bears a relationship to the taxpayer described in paragraph (2),

Note. For HSA purposes, the term *"qualified medical expenses"* is determined without regard to subparagraph (B) below for tax years beginning after 2004. [See I.R.C. § 223(d)(2)(A)]

    (B) whose gross income for the calendar year in which such taxable year begins is less than the exemption amount (as defined in section 151(d)),

Note. For 2006, the exemption amount is $3,300 ($3,200 for 2005).

    (C) with respect to whom the taxpayer provides over one-half of the individual's support for the calendar year in which such taxable year begins, and

    (D) who is not a qualifying child of such taxpayer or of any other taxpayer for any taxable year beginning in the calendar year in which such taxable year begins.

(2) RELATIONSHIP.—For purposes of paragraph (1)(A), an individual bears a relationship to the taxpayer described in this paragraph if the individual is any of the following with respect to the taxpayer:

    (A) A child or a descendant of a child.

    (B) A brother, sister, stepbrother, or stepsister.

    (C) The father or mother, or an ancestor of either.

    (D) A stepfather or stepmother.

    (E) A son or daughter of a brother or sister of the taxpayer.

    (F) A brother or sister of the father or mother of the taxpayer.

    (G) A son-in-law, daughter-in-law, father-in-law, mother-in-law, brother-in-law, or sister-in-law.

(H) An individual (other than an individual who at any time during the taxable year was the spouse, determined without regard to section 7703, of the taxpayer) who, for the taxable year of the taxpayer, has the same principal place of abode as the taxpayer and is a member of the taxpayer's household.

(3) SPECIAL RULE RELATING TO MULTIPLE SUPPORT AGREEMENTS. * * *

(4) SPECIAL RULE RELATING TO INCOME OF HANDICAPPED DEPENDENTS.* * *

(e) SPECIAL RULE FOR DIVORCED PARENTS, ETC.—

(1) IN GENERAL.—Notwithstanding subsection (c)(1)(B), (c)(4), or (d)(1) (C), if—

(A) a child receives over one-half of the child's support during the calendar year from the child's parents—

(i) who are divorced or legally separated under a decree of divorce or separate maintenance,

(ii) who are separated under a written separation agreement, or

(iii) who live apart at all times during the last 6 months of the calendar year, and

Caution: Code Section 152(e)(1)(B), below, as amended by the Gulf Opportunity Zone Act of 2005 (H.R. 4440 § 404(a)) conforms the definition of dependent for HSAs to that which is applicable to other health plans and MSAs. The amendment is effective for taxable years beginning after 2004.

(B) such child is in the custody of 1 or both of the child's parents for more than one-half of the calendar year, such child shall be treated as being the qualifying child or qualifying relative of the noncustodial parent for a calendar year if the requirements described in paragraph (2) or (3) are met.

(2) REQUIREMENTS. * * *

(3) CUSTODIAL PARENT AND NONCUSTODIAL PARENT. * * *

(4) EXCEPTION FOR MULTIPLE-SUPPORT AGREEMENTS. * * *

(f) OTHER DEFINITIONS AND RULES.—For purposes of this section—

(1) CHILD DEFINED.—

(A) IN GENERAL.—The term "child" means an individual who is—

(i) a son, daughter, stepson, or stepdaughter of the taxpayer, or

(ii) an eligible foster child of the taxpayer.

(B) ADOPTED CHILD.—In determining whether any of the relationships specified in subparagraph (A)(i) or paragraph (4) exists, a legally adopted individual of the taxpayer, or an individual who is lawfully placed with the taxpayer for legal adoption by the taxpayer, shall be treated as a child of such individual by blood.

(C) ELIGIBLE FOSTER CHILD.—For purposes of subparagraph (A)(ii), the term "eligible foster child" means an individual who is placed with the taxpayer by an authorized placement agency or by judgment, decree, or other order of any court of competent jurisdiction.

(2) STUDENT DEFINED.—The term "student" means an individual who during each of 5 calendar months during the calendar year in which the taxable year of the taxpayer begins—

(A) is a full-time student at an educational organization described in section 170(b)(1)(A)(ii), or

(B) is pursuing a full-time course of institutional on-farm training under the supervision of an accredited agent of an educational organization described in section 170(b)(1)(A)(ii) or of a State or political subdivision of a State.

(3) DETERMINATION OF HOUSEHOLD STATUS.—An individual shall not be treated as a member of the taxpayer's household if at any time during the taxable year of the taxpayer the relationship between such individual and the taxpayer is in violation of local law.

(4) BROTHER AND SISTER.—The terms "brother" and "sister" include a brother or sister by the half blood.

(5) SPECIAL SUPPORT TEST IN CASE OF STUDENTS.—For purposes of subsections (c)(1)(D) and (d)(1)(C), in the case of an individual who is—

(A) a child of the taxpayer, and

(B) a student,

amounts received as scholarships for study at an educational organization described in section 170(b)(1)(A)(ii) shall not be taken into account.

(6) TREATMENT OF MISSING CHILDREN. * * *

(7) CROSS REFERENCES.—For provision treating child as dependent of both parents for purposes of certain provisions, see sections 105(b) and 213(d)(5).

Code Section 213—Medical, Dental, Etc., Expenses

(a) ALLOWANCE OF DEDUCTION.—There shall be allowed as a deduction the expenses paid during the taxable year, not compensated for by insurance or otherwise, for medical care of the taxpayer, his spouse, or a dependent (as defined in section 152, determined without regard to subsections (b)(1), (b)(2), and (d)(1)(B) thereof), to the extent that such expenses exceed 7.5 percent of adjusted gross income.

Caution: Code section 213(a), above, as amended by the Working Families Tax Relief Act of 2004 (P.L. 108–311), added ", determined without regard to subsections (b)(1), (b)(2), and (d)(1)(B) thereof" after "section 152", for tax years beginning after December 31, 2004.

(b) LIMITATION WITH RESPECT TO MEDICINE AND DRUGS.—An amount paid during the taxable year for medicine or a drug shall be taken into account under subsection (a) only if such medicine or drug is a prescribed drug or is insulin.

(c) SPECIAL RULE FOR DECEDENTS.—

(1) TREATMENT OF EXPENSES PAID AFTER DEATH.—For purposes of subsection (a), expenses for the medical care of the taxpayer which are paid out of his estate during the 1-year period beginning with the day after the date of his death shall be treated as paid by the taxpayer at the time incurred.

(2) LIMITATION.—Paragraph (1) shall not apply if the amount paid is allowable under section 2053 as a deduction in computing the taxable estate of the decedent, but this paragraph shall not apply if (within the time and in the manner and form prescribed by the Secretary) there is filed—

(A) a statement that such amount has not been allowed as a deduction under section 2053, and

(B) a waiver of the right to have such amount allowed at any time as a deduction under section 2053.

(d) DEFINITIONS.—For purposes of this section—

(1) THE TERM "MEDICAL CARE" MEANS AMOUNTS PAID—

(A) for the diagnosis, cure, mitigation, treatment, or prevention of disease, or for the purpose of affecting any structure or function of the body,

(B) for transportation primarily for and essential to medical care referred to in subparagraph (A),

(C) for qualified long-term care services (as defined in section 7702B(c)), or

(D) for insurance (including amounts paid as premiums under part B of title XVIII of the Social Security Act, relating to supplementary medical insurance for the aged) covering medical care referred to in subparagraphs (A) and (B) or for any qualified long-term care insurance contract (as defined in section 7702B(b)).

In the case of a qualified long-term care insurance contract (as defined in section 7702B(b)), only eligible long-term care premiums (as defined in paragraph (10)) shall be taken into account under subparagraph (D).

(2) AMOUNTS PAID FOR CERTAIN LODGING AWAY FROM HOME TREATED AS PAID FOR MEDICAL CARE.—Amounts paid for lodging (not lavish or extravagant under the circumstances) while away from home primarily for and essential to medical care referred to in paragraph (1)(A) shall be treated as amounts paid for medical care if—

(A) the medical care referred to in paragraph (1)(A) is provided by a physician in a licensed hospital (or in a medical care facility which is related to, or the equivalent of, a licensed hospital), and

(B) there is no significant element of personal pleasure, recreation, or vacation in the travel away from home.

The amount taken into account under the preceding sentence shall not exceed $50 for each night for each individual.

(3) PRESCRIBED DRUG.—The term "prescribed drug" means a drug or biological which requires a prescription of a physician for its use by an individual.

(4) PHYSICIAN.—The term "physician" has the meaning given to such term by section 1861(r) of the Social Security Act (42 U.S.C. 1395x(r)).

(5) SPECIAL RULE IN THE CASE OF CHILD OF DIVORCED PARENTS, ETC.—Any child to whom section 152(e) applies shall be treated as a dependent of both parents for purposes of this section.

(6) In the case of an insurance contract under which amounts are payable for other than medical care referred to in subparagraphs (A), (B) and (C) of paragraph (1)—

(A) no amount shall be treated as paid for insurance to which paragraph (1)(D) applies unless the charge for such insurance is either separately stated in the contract, or furnished to the policyholder by the insurance company in a separate statement,

(B) the amount taken into account as the amount paid for such insurance shall not exceed such charge, and

(C) no amount shall be treated as paid for such insurance if the amount specified in the contract (or furnished to the policyholder by the insurance company in a separate statement) as the charge for such insurance is unreasonably large in relation to the total charges under the contract.

(7) Subject to the limitations of paragraph (6), premiums paid during the taxable year by a taxpayer before he attains the age of 65 for insurance covering medical care (within the meaning of subparagraphs (A), (B), and (C) of paragraph (1)) for the taxpayer, his spouse, or a dependent after the taxpayer attains the age of 65 shall be treated as expenses paid during the taxable year for insurance which constitutes medical care if premiums for such insurance are payable (on a level payment basis) under the contract for a period of 10 years or more or until the year in which the taxpayer attains the age of 65 (but in no case for a period of less than 5 years).

(8) The determination of whether an individual is married at any time during the taxable year shall be made in accordance with the provisions of section 6013(d) (relating to determination of status as husband and wife).

(9) COSMETIC SURGERY.—

(A) IN GENERAL.—The term "medical care" does not include cosmetic surgery or other similar procedures, unless the surgery or procedure is necessary to ameliorate a deformity arising from, or directly related to, a congenital abnormality, a personal injury resulting from an accident or trauma, or disfiguring disease.

(B) COSMETIC SURGERY DEFINED.—For purposes of this paragraph, the term "cosmetic surgery" means any procedure which is directed at improving the patient's appearance and does not meaningfully promote the proper function of the body or prevent or treat illness or disease.

(10) ELIGIBLE LONG-TERM CARE PREMIUMS.—

(A) IN GENERAL.—For purposes of this section, the term "eligible long-term care premiums" means the amount paid during a taxable year for any qualified long-term care insurance contract (as defined in section 7702B(b)) covering an individual, to the extent such amount does not exceed the limitation determined under the following table:

In the case of an individual with an attained age before the close of the taxable of:

	The limitation is:
40 or less	$ 200
More than 40 but not more than 50	375
More than 50 but not more than 60	750
More than 60 but not more than 70	2,000
More than 70	2,500

Note. For taxable years beginning in 2005 and 2006, the limitations under Code Section 213(d)(10) (regarding eligible long-term care premiums includible in the term *medical care*) have been indexed as follows: [See Rev. Proc. 2004-71, § 3.19, 2004-50 I.R.B. 970; Rev. Proc. 2005-70, § 3.19, 2005-47 I.R.B. 979]

Attained Age Before the Close of the Taxable Year	Limitation on Premiums	
	2005	2006
40 or less	$ 270	$ 280
More than 40 but not more than 50	$ 510	$ 530
More than 50 but not more than 60	$1,020	$1,060
More than 60 but not more than 70	$2,720	$2,830
More than 70	$3,400	$3,530

(B) INDEXING.—

(i) IN GENERAL.—In the case of any taxable year beginning in a calendar year after 1997, each dollar amount contained in subparagraph (A) shall be increased by the medical care cost adjustment of such amount for such calendar year. If any increase determined under the preceding sentence is not a multiple of $10, such increase shall be rounded to the nearest multiple of $10.

(ii) MEDICAL CARE COST ADJUSTMENT.—For purposes of clause (i), the medical care cost adjustment for any calendar year is the percentage (if any) by which—

(I) the medical care component of the Consumer Price Index (as defined in section 1(f)(5) for August of the preceding calendar year, exceeds

(II) such component for August of 1996.

The Secretary shall, in consultation with the Secretary of Health and Human Services, prescribe an adjustment which the Secretary determines is more appropriate for purposes of this paragraph than the adjustment described in the preceding sentence, and the adjustment so prescribed shall apply in lieu of the adjustment described in the preceding sentence.

(11) CERTAIN PAYMENTS TO RELATIVES TREATED AS NOT PAID FOR MEDICAL CARE.—An amount paid for a qualified long-term care service (as defined in section 7702B(c)) provided to an individual shall be treated as not paid for medical care if such service is provided—

(A) by the spouse of the individual or by a relative (directly or through a partnership, corporation, or other entity) unless the service is provided by a licensed professional with respect to such service, or

(B) by a corporation or partnership which is related (within the meaning of section 267(b) or 707(b)) to the individual.

For purposes of this paragraph, the term "relative" means an individual bearing a relationship to the individual which is described in any of subparagraphs (A) through (G) of section 152(d)(2). This paragraph shall not apply for purposes of section 105(b) with respect to reimbursements through insurance.

Caution:. Code section 213(d)(11), above, as amended by the Working Families Tax Relief Act of 2004 (P.L. 108-311), inserted "subparagraphs (A) through (G) of section 152(d)(2)" and removed "paragraphs (1) through (8) of section 152(a)" from the second sentence, for tax years beginning after December 31, 2004.

(e) EXCLUSION OF AMOUNTS ALLOWED FOR CARE OF CERTAIN DEPEN-DENTS.—Any expense allowed as a credit under section 21 shall not be treated as an expense paid for medical care.

Code Section 219—Retirement Savings

(a) ALLOWANCE OF DEDUCTION. * * *

    * * *

(d) OTHER LIMITATIONS AND RESTRICTIONS.—

(2) RECONTRIBUTED AMOUNTS.—No deduction shall be allowed under this section with respect to a rollover contribution described in section 402 (c), 403(a)(4), 403(b)(8), 408(d)(3), or 457(e)(16).

    * * *

(f) OTHER DEFINITIONS AND SPECIAL RULES

* * *

(3) TIME WHEN CONTRIBUTIONS DEEMED MADE.—For purposes of this section, a taxpayer shall be deemed to have made a contribution to an individual retirement plan on the last day of the preceding taxable year if the contribution is made on account of such taxable year and is made not later than the time prescribed by law for filing the return for such taxable year (not including extensions thereof).

* * *

(5) EMPLOYER PAYMENTS.—For purposes of this title, any amount paid by an employer to an individual retirement plan shall be treated as payment of compensation to the employee (other than a self-employed individual who is an employee within the meaning of section 401(c)(1)) includible in his gross income in the taxable year for which the amount was contributed, whether or not a deduction for such payment is allowable under this section to the employee.

* * *

Code Section 220—Archer MSAs

(a) DEDUCTION ALLOWED.—* * *

* * *

(f) TAX TREATMENT OF DISTRIBUTIONS.—

(5) ROLLOVER CONTRIBUTION.—An amount is described in this paragraph as a rollover contribution if it meets the requirements of subparagraphs (A) and (B).

(A) IN GENERAL.—Paragraph (2) shall not apply to any amount paid or distributed from an Archer MSA to the account holder to the extent the amount received is paid into an Archer MSA or a health savings account (as defined in section 223(d)) for the benefit of such holder not later than the 60th day after the day on which the holder receives the payment or distribution.

(B) LIMITATION.—This paragraph shall not apply to any amount described in subparagraph (A) received by an individual from an Archer MSA if, at any time during the 1-year period ending on the day of such receipt, such individual received any other amount described in subparagraph (A) from an Archer MSA which was not includible in the individual's gross income because of the application of this paragraph.

(6) COORDINATION WITH MEDICAL EXPENSE DEDUCTION.—For purposes of determining the amount of the deduction under section 213, any

payment or distribution out of an Archer MSA for qualified medical expenses shall not be treated as an expense paid for medical care.

Code Section 223—Health Savings Accounts

(a) DEDUCTION ALLOWED.—In the case of an individual who is an eligible individual for any month during the taxable year, there shall be allowed as a deduction for the taxable year an amount equal to the aggregate amount paid in cash during such taxable year by or on behalf of such individual to a health savings account of such individual.

(b) LIMITATIONS.—

(1) IN GENERAL.—The amount allowable as a deduction under subsection (a) to an individual for the taxable year shall not exceed the sum of the monthly limitations for months during such taxable year that the individual is an eligible individual.

(2) MONTHLY LIMITATION.—The monthly limitation for any month is 1/12 of—

(A) in the case of an eligible individual who has self-only coverage under a high deductible health plan as of the first day of such month, the lesser of—

(i) the annual deductible under such coverage, or

(ii) $2,250, or

Note. For calendar year 2006, the monthly limitation on deductions under Code Section 223(b)(2)(A) for an individual with self-only coverage under a high deductible plan as of the first day of such month is 1/12 of the lesser of (1) the annual deductible, or (2) $2,700 (see Q 4:10). See appendix D.

(B) in the case of an eligible individual who has family coverage under a high deductible health plan as of the first day of such month, the lesser of—

(i) the annual deductible under such coverage, or

(ii) $4,500.

Note. For calendar year 2006, the monthly limitation on deductions under Code Section 223(b)(2)(B) for an individual with family coverage under a high deductible plan as of the first day of such month is 1/12 of the lesser of (1) the annual deductible, or (2) $5,250 (see Q 4:10). See appendix D.

(3) ADDITIONAL CONTRIBUTIONS FOR INDIVIDUALS 55 OR OLDER.—

(A) IN GENERAL.—In the case of an individual who has attained age 55 before the close of the taxable year, the applicable limitation under subparagraphs (A) and (B) of paragraph (2) shall be increased by the additional contribution amount.

(B) ADDITIONAL CONTRIBUTION AMOUNT.—For purposes of this section, the additional contribution amount is the amount determined in accordance with the following table:

For taxable years beginning in:	The additional contribution amount is:
2004	$ 500
2005	$ 600
2006	$ 700
2007	$ 800
2008	$ 900
2009 and thereafter	$1,000

(4) COORDINATION WITH OTHER CONTRIBUTIONS.—The limitation which would (but for this paragraph) apply under this subsection to an individual for any taxable year shall be reduced (but not below zero) by the sum of—

(A) the aggregate amount paid for such taxable year to Archer MSAs of such individual, and

(B) the aggregate amount contributed to health savings accounts of such individual which is excludable from the taxpayer's gross income for such taxable year under section 106(d) (and such amount shall not be allowed as a deduction under subsection (a)).

Subparagraph (A) shall not apply with respect to any individual to whom paragraph (5) applies.

(5) SPECIAL RULE FOR MARRIED INDIVIDUALS.—In the case of individuals who are married to each other, if either spouse has family coverage—

(A) both spouses shall be treated as having only such family coverage (and if such spouses each have family coverage under different plans, as having the family coverage with the lowest annual deductible), and

(B) the limitation under paragraph (1) (after the application of subparagraph (A) and without regard to any additional contribution amount under paragraph (3))—

(i) shall be reduced by the aggregate amount paid to Archer MSAs of such spouses for the taxable year, and

(ii) after such reduction, shall be divided equally between them unless they agree on a different division.

(6) DENIAL OF DEDUCTION TO DEPENDENTS.—No deduction shall be allowed under this section to any individual with respect to whom a deduction under section 151 is allowable to another taxpayer for a taxable year beginning in the calendar year in which such individual's taxable year begins.

(7) MEDICARE ELIGIBLE INDIVIDUALS.—The limitation under this subsection for any month with respect to an individual shall be zero for the first month such individual is entitled to benefits under title XVIII of the Social Security Act and for each month thereafter.

(c) DEFINITIONS AND SPECIAL RULES.—For purposes of this section—

    (1) ELIGIBLE INDIVIDUAL.—

      (A) IN GENERAL.—The term "eligible individual" means, with respect to any month, any individual if—

        (i) such individual is covered under a high deductible health plan as of the 1st day of such month, and

        (ii) such individual is not, while covered under a high deductible health plan, covered under any health plan—

          (I) which is not a high deductible health plan, and

          (II) which provides coverage for any benefit which is covered under the high deductible health plan.

      (B) CERTAIN COVERAGE DISREGARDED.—Subparagraph (A)(ii) shall be applied without regard to—

        (i) coverage for any benefit provided by permitted insurance, and

        (ii) coverage (whether through insurance or otherwise) for accidents, disability, dental care, vision care, or long-term care.

    (2) HIGH DEDUCTIBLE HEALTH PLAN.—

      (A) IN GENERAL.—The term "high deductible health plan" means a health plan—

        (i) which has an annual deductible which is not less than—

          (I) $1,000 for self-only coverage, and

          (II) twice the dollar amount in subclause (I) for family coverage, and

        (ii) the sum of the annual deductible and the other annual out-of-pocket expenses required to be paid under the plan (other than for premiums) for covered benefits does not exceed—

          (I) $5,000 for self-only coverage, and

          (II) twice the dollar amount in subclause (I) for family coverage.

Note. For calendar year 2006, a high deductible health plan is defined under Code Section 223(c)(2)(A) as a health plan with an annual deductible that is not less than $1,050 for self-only coverage or $2,100 for family coverage, and the annual out-of-pocket expenses (deductibles, co-payments, and other amounts, but not premiums) do not exceed $5,250 for self-only coverage or $10,500 for family coverage (see Q 3:1). See appendix D for dollar limitation for other years.

      (B) EXCLUSION OF CERTAIN PLANS.—Such term does not include a health plan if substantially all of its coverage is coverage described in paragraph (1)(B).

      (C) SAFE HARBOR FOR ABSENCE OF PREVENTIVE CARE DEDUCTIBLE.—A plan shall not fail to be treated as a high deductible health plan by reason of failing to have a deductible for preventive care (within the meaning of section 1871 of the Social Security Act, except as otherwise provided by the Secretary).

(D) SPECIAL RULES FOR NETWORK PLANS.—In the case of a plan using a network of providers—

(i) ANNUAL OUT-OF-POCKET LIMITATION.—Such plan shall not fail to be treated as a high deductible health plan by reason of having an out-of-pocket limitation for services provided outside of such network which exceeds the applicable limitation under subparagraph (A)(ii).

(ii) ANNUAL DEDUCTIBLE.—Such plan's annual deductible for services provided outside of such network shall not be taken into account for purposes of subsection (b)(2).

(3) PERMITTED INSURANCE.—The term "permitted insurance" means—
(A) insurance if substantially all of the coverage provided under such insurance relates to—
(i) liabilities incurred under workers' compensation laws,
(ii) tort liabilities,
(iii) liabilities relating to ownership or use of property, or
(iv) such other similar liabilities as the Secretary may specify by regulations,
(B) insurance for a specified disease or illness, and
(C) insurance paying a fixed amount per day (or other period) of hospitalization.

(4) FAMILY COVERAGE.—The term "family coverage" means any coverage other than self-only coverage.

(5) ARCHER MSA.—The term "Archer MSA" has the meaning given such term in section 220(d).

(d) HEALTH SAVINGS ACCOUNT.—For purposes of this section—

(1) IN GENERAL.—The term "health savings account" means a trust created or organized in the United States as a health savings account exclusively for the purpose of paying the qualified medical expenses of the account beneficiary, but only if the written governing instrument creating the trust meets the following requirements:

(A) Except in the case of a rollover contribution described in subsection (f)(5) or section 220(f)(5), no contribution will be accepted—

(i) unless it is in cash, or

(ii) to the extent such contribution, when added to previous contributions to the trust for the calendar year, exceeds the sum of—

(I) the dollar amount in effect under subsection (b)(2)(B)(ii), and

(II) the dollar amount in effect under subsection (b)(3)(B).

(B) The trustee is a bank (as defined in section 408(n)), an insurance company (as defined in section 816), or another person who demonstrates to the satisfaction of the Secretary that the manner in which such person will administer the trust will be consistent with the requirements of this section.

(C) No part of the trust assets will be invested in life insurance contracts.

(D) The assets of the trust will not be commingled with other property except in a common trust fund or common investment fund.

(E) The interest of an individual in the balance in his account is non-forfeitable.

(2) QUALIFIED MEDICAL EXPENSES.—

Caution. Code Section 223(d)(2)(A), below, as amended by the Gulf Opportunity Zone Act of 2005 (H.R. 4440, § 404(c)) conforms the definition of dependent for HSAs to that which is applicable to other health plans and MSAs. The amendment is effective for taxable years beginning after 2004 (H.R. 4440, § 404(d)).

(A) IN GENERAL.—The term "qualified medical expenses" means, with respect to an account beneficiary, amounts paid by such beneficiary for medical care (as defined in section 213(d) for such individual, the spouse of such individual, and any dependent (as defined in section 152, determined without regard to subsections (b)(1), (b)(2), and (d)(1)(B) thereof) of such individual, but only to the extent such amounts are not compensated for by insurance or otherwise.

(B) HEALTH INSURANCE MAY NOT BE PURCHASED FROM ACCOUNT.—Subparagraph (A) shall not apply to any payment for insurance.

(C) EXCEPTIONS.—Subparagraph (B) shall not apply to any expense for coverage under—

(i) a health plan during any period of continuation coverage required under any Federal law,

(ii) a qualified long-term care insurance contract (as defined in section 7702B(b)),

(iii) a health plan during a period in which the individual is receiving unemployment compensation under any Federal or State law, or

(iv) in the case of an account beneficiary who has attained the age specified in section 1811 of the Social Security Act, any health insurance other than a medicare supplemental policy (as defined in section 1882 of the Social Security Act).

(3) ACCOUNT BENEFICIARY.—The term "account beneficiary" means the individual on whose behalf the health savings account was established.

(4) CERTAIN RULES TO APPLY.—Rules similar to the following rules shall apply for purposes of this section:

(A) Section 219(d)(2) (relating to no deduction for rollovers).

(B) Section 219(f)(3) (relating to time when contributions deemed made).

(C) Except as provided in section 106(d), section 219(f)(5) (relating to employer payments).

(D) Section 408(g) (relating to community property laws).

(E) Section 408(h) (relating to custodial accounts).

(e) TAX TREATMENT OF ACCOUNTS.—

(1) IN GENERAL.—A health savings account is exempt from taxation under this subtitle unless such account has ceased to be a health savings account. Notwithstanding the preceding sentence, any such account is subject to the taxes imposed by section 511 (relating to imposition of tax on unrelated business income of charitable, etc. organizations).

(2) ACCOUNT TERMINATIONS.—Rules similar to the rules of paragraphs (2) and (4) of section 408(e) shall apply to health savings accounts, and any amount treated as distributed under such rules shall be treated as not used to pay qualified medical expenses.

(f) TAX TREATMENT OF DISTRIBUTIONS.—

(1) AMOUNTS USED FOR QUALIFIED MEDICAL EXPENSES.—Any amount paid or distributed out of a health savings account which is used exclusively to pay qualified medical expenses of any account beneficiary shall not be includible in gross income.

(2) INCLUSION OF AMOUNTS NOT USED FOR QUALIFIED MEDICAL EXPENSES.—Any amount paid or distributed out of a health savings account which is not used exclusively to pay the qualified medical expenses of the account beneficiary shall be included in the gross income of such beneficiary.

(3) EXCESS CONTRIBUTIONS RETURNED BEFORE DUE DATE OF RETURN.—

(A) IN GENERAL.—If any excess contribution is contributed for a taxable year to any health savings account of an individual, paragraph (2) shall not apply to distributions from the health savings accounts of such individual (to the extent such distributions do not exceed the aggregate excess contributions to all such accounts of such individual for such year) if—

(i) such distribution is received by the individual on or before the last day prescribed by law (including extensions of time) for filing such individual's return for such taxable year, and

(ii) such distribution is accompanied by the amount of net income attributable to such excess contribution.

Any net income described in clause (ii) shall be included in the gross income of the individual for the taxable year in which it is received.

(B) EXCESS CONTRIBUTION.—For purposes of subparagraph (A), the term "excess contribution" means any contribution (other than a rollover contribution described in paragraph (5) or section 220(f)(5)) which is neither excludable from gross income under section 106(d) nor deductible under this section.

(4) ADDITIONAL TAX ON DISTRIBUTIONS NOT USED FOR QUALIFIED MEDICAL EXPENSES.—

(A) IN GENERAL.—The tax imposed by this chapter on the account beneficiary for any taxable year in which there is a payment or distribution from a health savings account of such beneficiary which is includible in gross income under paragraph (2) shall be increased by 10 percent of the amount which is so includible.

(B) EXCEPTION FOR DISABILITY OR DEATH.—Subparagraph (A) shall not apply if the payment or distribution is made after the account beneficiary becomes disabled within the meaning of section 72(m)(7) or dies.

(C) EXCEPTION FOR DISTRIBUTIONS AFTER MEDICARE ELIGIBILITY.—Subparagraph (A) shall not apply to any payment or distribution after the date on which the account beneficiary attains the age specified in section 1811 of the Social Security Act.

(5) ROLLOVER CONTRIBUTION.—An amount is described in this paragraph as a rollover contribution if it meets the requirements of subparagraphs (A) and (B).

(A) IN GENERAL.—Paragraph (2) shall not apply to any amount paid or distributed from a health savings account to the account beneficiary to the extent the amount received is paid into a health savings account for the benefit of such beneficiary not later than the 60th day after the day on which the beneficiary receives the payment or distribution.

(B) LIMITATION.—This paragraph shall not apply to any amount described in subparagraph (A) received by an individual from a health savings account if, at any time during the 1-year period ending on the day of such receipt, such individual received any other amount described in subparagraph (A) from a health savings account which was not includible in the individual's gross income because of the application of this paragraph.

(6) COORDINATION WITH MEDICAL EXPENSE DEDUCTION.—For purposes of determining the amount of the deduction under section 213, any payment or distribution out of a health savings account for qualified medical expenses shall not be treated as an expense paid for medical care.

(7) TRANSFER OF ACCOUNT INCIDENT TO DIVORCE.—The transfer of an individual's interest in a health savings account to an individual's spouse or former spouse under a divorce or separation instrument described in subparagraph (A) of section 71(b)(2) shall not be considered a taxable transfer made by such individual notwithstanding any other provision of this |subtitle, and such interest shall, after such transfer, be treated as a health savings account with respect to which such spouse is the account beneficiary.

(8) TREATMENT AFTER DEATH OF ACCOUNT BENEFICIARY.—

(A) TREATMENT IF DESIGNATED BENEFICIARY IS SPOUSE.—If the account beneficiary's surviving spouse acquires such beneficiary's interest in a health savings account by reason of being the designated beneficiary of such account at the death of the account beneficiary, such health savings account shall be treated as if the spouse were the account beneficiary.

(B) OTHER CASES.—

(i) IN GENERAL.—If, by reason of the death of the account beneficiary, any person acquires the account beneficiary's interest in a health savings account in a case to which subparagraph (A) does not apply—

(I) such account shall cease to be a health savings account as of the date of death, and

(II) an amount equal to the fair market value of the assets in such account on such date shall be includible if such person is not the estate of such beneficiary, in such person's gross income for the taxable year which includes such date, or if such person is the estate of such beneficiary, in such beneficiary's gross income for the last taxable year of such beneficiary.

(ii) SPECIAL RULES.—

(I) REDUCTION OF INCLUSION FOR PREDEATH EXPENSES.— The amount includible in gross income under clause (i) by any person (other than the estate) shall be reduced by the amount of qualified medical expenses which were incurred by the decedent before the date of the decedent's death and paid by such person within 1 year after such date.

(II) DEDUCTION FOR ESTATE TAXES.—An appropriate deduction shall be allowed under section 691(c) to any person (other than the decedent or the decedent's spouse) with respect to amounts included in gross income under clause (i) by such person.

(g) COST-OF-LIVING ADJUSTMENT.—

(1) IN GENERAL.—Each dollar amount in subsections (b)(2) and (c)(2)(A) shall be increased by an amount equal to—

(A) such dollar amount, multiplied by

(B) the cost-of-living adjustment determined under section 1(f)(3) for the calendar year in which such taxable year begins determined by substituting for "calendar year 1992" in subparagraph (B) thereof—

(i) except as provided in clause (ii), "calendar year 1997", and

(ii) in the case of each dollar amount in subsection (c)(2)(A), "calendar year 2003".

(2) ROUNDING.—If any increase under paragraph (1) is not a multiple of $50, such increase shall be rounded to the nearest multiple of $50.

(h) REPORTS.—The Secretary may require—

(1) the trustee of a health savings account to make such reports regarding such account to the Secretary and to the account beneficiary with respect to contributions, distributions, the return of excess contributions, and such other matters as the Secretary determines appropriate, and

(2) any person who provides an individual with a high deductible health plan to make such reports to the Secretary and to the account beneficiary with respect to such plan as the Secretary determines appropriate.

The reports required by this subsection shall be filed at such time and in such manner and furnished to such individuals at such time and in such manner as may be required by the Secretary.

Code Section 408—Individual Retirement Accounts

(a) INDIVIDUAL RETIREMENT ACCOUNT.—* * *

* * *

(g) COMMUNITY PROPERTY LAWS.—This section shall be applied without regard to any community property laws.

(h) CUSTODIAL ACCOUNTS.—For purposes of this section, a custodial account shall be treated as a trust if the assets of such account are held by a bank (as defined in subsection (n)) or another person who demonstrates, to the satisfaction of the Secretary, that the manner in which he will administer the account will be consistent with the requirements of this section, and if the custodial account would, except for the fact that it is not a trust, constitute an individual retirement account described in subsection (a). For purposes of this title, in the case of a custodial account treated as a trust by reason of the preceding sentence, the custodian of such account shall be treated as the trustee thereof.

* * *

Code Section 4973—Tax on Excess Contributions to Certain Tax-Favored Accounts and Annuities

(a) TAX IMPOSED.—In the case of—

(1) an individual retirement account (within the meaning of section 408(a)),

(2) an Archer MSA (within the meaning of section 220(d)),

(3) an individual retirement annuity (within the meaning of section 408(b)), a custodial account treated as an annuity contract under section 403(b)(7)(A) (relating to custodial accounts for regulated investment company stock),

(4) a Coverdell education savings account (as defined in section 530, or

(5) a health savings account (within the meaning of section 223(d)),

there is imposed for each taxable year a tax in an amount equal to 6 percent of the amount of the excess contributions to such individual's accounts or annuities (determined as of the close of the taxable year). The amount of such tax for any taxable year shall not exceed 6 percent of the value of the account or annuity (determined as of the close of the taxable year). In the case of an endowment contract described in section 408(b), the tax imposed by this section does not apply to any amount allocable to life, health, accident, or other insurance under such contract. The tax imposed by this subsection shall be paid by such individual.

(b) EXCESS CONTRIBUTIONS.—For purposes of this section, in the case of individual retirement accounts or individual retirement annuities, the term "excess contributions" means the sum of—

    (1) the excess (if any) of—

        (A) the amount contributed for the taxable year to the accounts or for the annuities (other than a contribution to a Roth IRA or a rollover contribution described in section 402(c), 403(a)(4), 403(b)(8), 408(d)(3), or 457(e)(16)), over

        (B) the amount allowable as a deduction under section 219 for such contributions, and

    (2) the amount determined under this subsection for the preceding taxable year reduced by the sum of—

        (A) the distributions out of the account for the taxable year which were included in the gross income of the payee under section 408(d)(1),

        (B) the distributions out of the account for the taxable year to which section 408(d)(5) applies, and

        (C) the excess (if any) of the maximum amount allowable as a deduction under section 219 for the taxable year over the amount contributed (determined without regard to section 219(f)(6)) to the accounts or for the annuities (including the amount contributed to a Roth IRA) for the taxable year.

For purposes of this subsection, any contribution which is distributed from the individual retirement account or the individual retirement annuity in a distribution to which section 408(d)(4) applies shall be treated as an amount not contributed. For purposes of paragraphs (1)(B) and (2)(C), the amount allowable as a deduction under section 219 shall be computed without regard to section 219(g).

* * *

(g) EXCESS CONTRIBUTIONS TO HEALTH SAVINGS ACCOUNTS.—For purposes of this section, in the case of health savings accounts (within the meaning of section 223(d)), the term "excess contributions" means the sum of—

    (1) the aggregate amount contributed for the taxable year to the accounts (other than a rollover contribution described in section 220(f)(5) or 223(f)(5)) which is neither excludable from gross income under section 106(d) nor allowable as a deduction under section 223 for such year, and

(2) the amount determined under this subsection for the preceding taxable year, reduced by the sum of—

(A) the distributions out of the accounts which were included in gross income under section 223(f)(2), and

(B) the excess (if any) of—

(i) the maximum amount allowable as a deduction under section 223(b) (determined without regard to section 106(d)) for the taxable year, over

(ii) the amount contributed to the accounts for the taxable year.

For purposes of this subsection, any contribution which is distributed out of the health savings account in a distribution to which section 223(f)(3) applies shall be treated as an amount not contributed.

Code Section 4975—Tax on Prohibited Transactions

(a) INITIAL TAXES ON DISQUALIFIED PERSON.—There is hereby imposed a tax on each prohibited transaction. The rate of tax shall be equal to 15 percent of the amount involved with respect to the prohibited transaction for each year (or part thereof) in the taxable period. The tax imposed by this subsection shall be paid by any disqualified person who participates in the prohibited transaction (other than a fiduciary acting only as such).

(b) ADDITIONAL TAXES ON DISQUALIFIED PERSON.—In any case in which an initial tax is imposed by subsection (a) on a prohibited transaction and the transaction is not corrected within the taxable period, there is hereby imposed a tax equal to 100 percent of the amount involved. The tax imposed by this subsection shall be paid by any disqualified person who participated in the prohibited transaction (other than a fiduciary acting only as such).

(c) PROHIBITED TRANSACTION.—

(1) GENERAL RULE.—For purposes of this section, the term "prohibited transaction" means any direct or indirect—

(A) sale or exchange, or leasing, of any property between a plan and a disqualified person;

(B) lending of money or other extension of credit between a plan and a disqualified person;

(C) furnishing of goods, services, or facilities between a plan and a disqualified person;

(D) transfer to, or use by or for the benefit of, a disqualified person of the income or assets of a plan;

(E) act by a disqualified person who is a fiduciary whereby he deals with the income or assets of a plan in his own interest or for his own account; or

(F) receipt of any consideration for his own personal account by any disqualified person who is a fiduciary from any party dealing with the plan in connection with a transaction involving the income or assets of the plan.

(2) SPECIAL EXEMPTION.—The Secretary shall establish an exemption procedure for purposes of this subsection. Pursuant to such procedure, he may grant a conditional or unconditional exemption of any disqualified person or transaction, or class of disqualified persons or transactions, from all or part of the restrictions imposed by paragraph (1) of this subsection. Action under this subparagraph may be taken only after consultation and coordination with the Secretary of Labor. The Secretary may not grant an exemption under this paragraph unless he finds that such exemption is—

(A) administratively feasible,

(B) in the interests of the plan and of its participants and beneficiaries, and

(C) protective of the rights of participants and beneficiaries of the plan.

Before granting an exemption under this paragraph, the Secretary shall require adequate notice to be given to interested persons and shall publish notice in the Federal Register of the pendency of such exemption and shall afford interested persons an opportunity to present views. No exemption may be granted under this paragraph with respect to a transaction described in subparagraph (E) or (F) of paragraph (1) unless the Secretary affords an opportunity for a hearing and makes a determination on the record with respect to the findings required under subparagraphs (A), (B), and (C) of this paragraph, except that in lieu of such hearing the Secretary may accept any record made by the Secretary of Labor with respect to an application for exemption under section 408(a) of title I of the Employee Retirement Income Security Act of 1974.

(3) SPECIAL RULE FOR INDIVIDUAL RETIREMENT ACCOUNTS. * * *

(4) SPECIAL RULE FOR ARCHER MSAs. * * *

(5) SPECIAL RULE FOR COVERDELL EDUCATION SAVINGS ACCOUNTS.
    * * *

(6) SPECIAL RULE FOR HEALTH SAVINGS ACCOUNTS.—An individual for whose benefit a health savings account (within the meaning of section 223 (d)) is established shall be exempt from the tax imposed by this section with respect to any transaction concerning such account (which would otherwise be taxable under this section) if, with respect to such transaction, the account ceases to be a health savings account by reason of the application of section 223(e)(2) to such account.

(d) EXEMPTIONS.—Except as provided in subsection (f)(6), the prohibitions provided in subsection (c) shall not apply to—

(1) any loan made by the plan to a disqualified person who is a participant or beneficiary of the plan if such loan—

(A) is available to all such participants or beneficiaries on a reasonably equivalent basis,

(B) is not made available to highly compensated employees (within the meaning of section 414(q)) in an amount greater than the amount made available to other employees,

(C) is made in accordance with specific provisions regarding such loans set forth in the plan,

(D) bears a reasonable rate of interest, and

(E) is adequately secured;

(2) any contract, or reasonable arrangement, made with a disqualified person for office space, or legal, accounting, or other services necessary for the establishment or operation of the plan, if no more than reasonable compensation is paid therefor;

(3) any loan to a leveraged employee stock ownership plan (as defined in subsection (e)(7)), if—

(A) such loan is primarily for the benefit of participants and beneficiaries of the plan, and

(B) such loan is at a reasonable rate of interest, and any collateral which is given to a disqualified person by the plan consists only of qualifying employer securities (as defined in subsection (e)(8));

(4) the investment of all or part of a plan's assets in deposits which bear a reasonable interest rate in a bank or similar financial institution supervised by the United States or a State, if such bank or other institution is a fiduciary of such plan and if—

(A) the plan covers only employees of such bank or other institution and employees of affiliates of such bank or other institution, or

(B) such investment is expressly authorized by a provision of the plan or by a fiduciary (other than such bank or institution or affiliates thereof) who is expressly empowered by the plan to so instruct the trustee with respect to such investment;

(5) any contract for life insurance, health insurance, or annuities with one or more insurers which are qualified to do business in a State if the plan pays no more than adequate consideration, and if each such insurer or insurers is—

(A) the employer maintaining the plan, or

(B) a disqualified person which is wholly owned (directly or indirectly) by the employer establishing the plan, or by any person which is a disqualified person with respect to the plan, but only if the total premiums and annuity considerations written by such insurers for life insurance, health insurance, or annuities for all plans (and their employers) with respect to which such insurers are disqualified persons (not including premiums or annuity considerations written by the employer maintaining the plan) do not exceed 5 percent of the total premiums and annuity considerations written for all lines of insurance in that year by such insurers (not including premiums or annuity considerations written by the employer maintaining the plan);

(6) the provision of any ancillary service by a bank or similar financial institution supervised by the United States or a State, if such service is provided at not more than reasonable compensation, if such bank or other institution is a fiduciary of such plan, and if—

    (A) such bank or similar financial institution has adopted adequate internal safeguards which assure that the provision of such ancillary service is consistent with sound banking and financial practice, as determined by Federal or State supervisory authority, and

    (B) the extent to which such ancillary service is provided is subject to specific guidelines issued by such bank or similar financial institution (as determined by the Secretary after consultation with Federal and State supervisory authority), and under such guidelines the bank or similar financial institution does not provide such ancillary service—

        (i) in an excessive or unreasonable manner, and

        (ii) in a manner that would be inconsistent with the best interests of participants and beneficiaries of employee benefit plans;

(7) the exercise of a privilege to convert securities, to the extent provided in regulations of the Secretary but only if the plan receives no less than adequate consideration pursuant to such conversion;

(8) any transaction between a plan and a common or collective trust fund or pooled investment fund maintained by a disqualified person which is a bank or trust company supervised by a State or Federal agency or between a plan and a pooled investment fund of an insurance company qualified to do business in a State if—

    (A) the transaction is a sale or purchase of an interest in the fund,

    (B) the bank, trust company, or insurance company receives not more than reasonable compensation, and

    (C) such transaction is expressly permitted by the instrument under which the plan is maintained, or by a fiduciary (other than the bank, trust company, or insurance company, or an affiliate thereof) who has authority to manage and control the assets of the plan;

(9) receipt by a disqualified person of any benefit to which he may be entitled as a participant or beneficiary in the plan, so long as the benefit is computed and paid on a basis which is consistent with the terms of the plan as applied to all other participants and beneficiaries;

(10) receipt by a disqualified person of any reasonable compensation for services rendered, or for the reimbursement of expenses properly and actually incurred, in the performance of his duties with the plan, but no person so serving who already receives full-time pay from an employer or an association of employers, whose employees are participants in the plan or from an employee organization whose members are participants in such plan shall receive compensation from such fund, except for reimbursement of expenses properly and actually incurred;

(11) service by a disqualified person as a fiduciary in addition to being an officer, employee, agent, or other representative of a disqualified person;

(12) the making by a fiduciary of a distribution of the assets of the trust in accordance with the terms of the plan if such assets are distributed in the same manner as provided under section 4044 of title IV of the Employee Retirement Income Security Act of 1974 (relating to allocation of assets);

(13) any transaction which is exempt from section 406 of such Act by reason of section 408(e) of such Act (or which would be so exempt if such section 406 applied to such transaction) or which is exempt from section 406 of such Act by reason of section 408(b)(12) of such Act;

(14) any transaction required or permitted under part 1 of subtitle E of title IV or section 4223 of the Employee Retirement Income Security Act of 1974, but this paragraph shall not apply with respect to the application of subsection (c)(1) (E) or (F);

(15) a merger of multiemployer plans, or the transfer of assets or liabilities between multiemployer plans, determined by the Pension Benefit Guaranty Corporation to meet the requirements of section 4231 of such Act, but this paragraph shall not apply with respect to the application of subsection (c)(1) (E) or (F); or

Caution: Code Section 4975(d)(16), as added by American Jobs Creation Act of 2004 (P.L. 108-357), is effective October 22, 2004.

(16) a sale of stock held by a trust which constitutes an individual retirement account under section 408(a) to the individual for whose benefit such account is established if—

(A) such stock is in a bank (as defined in section 581),

(B) such stock is held by such trust as of the date of the enactment of this paragraph,

(C) such sale is pursuant to an election under section 1362(a) by such bank,

(D) such sale is for fair market value at the time of sale (as established by an independent appraiser) and the terms of the sale are otherwise at least as favorable to such trust as the terms that would apply on a sale to an unrelated party,

(E) such trust does not pay any commissions, costs, or other expenses in connection with the sale, and

(F) the stock is sold in a single transaction for cash not later than 120 days after the S corporation election is made.

(e) DEFINITIONS.—

(1) PLAN.—For purposes of this section, the term "plan" means—

(A) a trust described in section 401(a) which forms a part of a plan, or a plan described in section 403(a), which trust or plan is exempt from tax under section 501(a),

(B) an individual retirement account described in section 408(a),

(C) an individual retirement annuity described in section 408(b),

(D) an Archer MSA described in section 220(d),

(E) a health savings account described in section 223(d),

(F) a Coverdell education savings account described in section 530, or

(G) a trust, plan, account, or annuity which, at any time, has been determined by the Secretary to be described in any preceding subparagraph of this paragraph.

(2) DISQUALIFIED PERSON.—For purposes of this section, the term "disqualified person" means a person who is—

(A) a fiduciary;

(B) a person providing services to the plan;

(C) an employer any of whose employees are covered by the plan;

(D) an employee organization any of whose members are covered by the plan;

(E) an owner, direct or indirect, of 50 percent or more of—

    (i) the combined voting power of all classes of stock entitled to vote or the total value of shares of all classes of stock of a corporation,

    (ii) the capital interest or the profits interest of a partnership, or

    (iii) the beneficial interest of a trust or unincorporated enterprise,

which is an employer or an employee organization described in subparagraph (C) or (D);

(F) a member of the family (as defined in paragraph (6)) of any individual described in subparagraph (A), (B), (C), or (E);

(G) a corporation, partnership, or trust or estate of which (or in which) 50 percent or more of—

    (i) the combined voting power of all classes of stock entitled to vote or the total value of shares of all classes of stock of such corporation,

    (ii) the capital interest or profits interest of such partnership, or

    (iii) the beneficial interest of such trust or estate,

is owned directly or indirectly, or held by persons described in subparagraph (A), (B), (C), (D), or (E);

(H) an officer, director (or an individual having powers or responsibilities similar to those of officers or directors), a 10 percent or more shareholder, or a highly compensated employee (earning 10 percent or more of the yearly wages of an employer) of a person described in subparagraph (C), (D), (E), or (G); or

(I) a 10 percent or more (in capital or profits) partner or joint venturer of a person described in subparagraph (C), (D), (E), or (G).

The Secretary, after consultation and coordination with the Secretary of Labor or his delegate, may by regulation prescribe a percentage lower than 50 percent for subparagraphs (E) and (G) and lower than 10 percent for subparagraphs (H) and (I).

(3) FIDUCIARY.—For purposes of this section, the term "fiduciary" means any person who—

(A) exercises any discretionary authority or discretionary control respecting management of such plan or exercises any authority or control respecting management or disposition of its assets,

(B) renders investment advice for a fee or other compensation, direct or indirect, with respect to any moneys or other property of such plan, or has any authority or responsibility to do so, or

(C) has any discretionary authority or discretionary responsibility in the administration of such plan.

Such term includes any person designated under section 405(c)(1)(B) of the Employee Retirement Income Security Act of 1974.

(4) STOCKHOLDINGS.—For purposes of paragraphs (2)(E)(i) and (G)(i) there shall be taken into account indirect stockholdings which would be taken into account under section 267(c), except that, for purposes of this paragraph, section 267(c)(4) shall be treated as providing that the members of the family of an individual are the members within the meaning of paragraph (6).

(5) PARTNERSHIPS; TRUSTS.—For purposes of paragraphs (2)(E)(ii) and (iii), (G)(ii) and (iii), and (I) the ownership of profits or beneficial interests shall be determined in accordance with the rules for constructive ownership of stock provided in section 267(c) (other than paragraph (3) thereof), except that section 267(c)(4) shall be treated as providing that the members of the family of an individual are the members within the meaning of paragraph (6).

(6) MEMBER OF FAMILY.—For purposes of paragraph (2)(F), the family of any individual shall include his spouse, ancestor, lineal descendant, and any spouse of a lineal descendant.

(7) EMPLOYEE STOCK OWNERSHIP PLAN.—The term "employee stock ownership plan" means a defined contribution plan—

(A) which is a stock bonus plan which is qualified, or a stock bonus and a money purchase plan both of which are qualified under section 401(a), and which are designed to invest primarily in qualifying employer securities; and

(B) which is otherwise defined in regulations prescribed by the Secretary.

Caution: Code Section 4975(e)(7), closing paragraph, below, as amended by Economic Growth & Tax Relief Reconciliation Act of 2001 (P.L. 107-16), generally applies to plan years beginning after December 31, 2004.

A plan shall not be treated as an employee stock ownership plan unless it meets the requirements of section 409(h), section 409(o), and, if applicable, section 409(n), 409(p), and section 664(g) and, if the employer has a registration-type class of securities (as defined in section 409(e)(4)), it meets the requirements of section 409(e).

(8) QUALIFYING EMPLOYER SECURITY.—The term "qualifying employer security" means any employer security within the meaning of section 409(l). If any moneys or other property of a plan are invested in shares of an investment company registered under the Investment Company Act of 1940, the investment shall not cause that investment company or that investment company's investment adviser or principal underwriter to be treated as a fiduciary or a disqualified person for purposes of this section, except when an investment company or its investment adviser or principal underwriter acts in connection with a plan covering employees of the investment company, its investment adviser, or its principal underwriter.

(9) SECTION MADE APPLICABLE TO WITHDRAWAL LIABILITY PAYMENT FUNDS.—For purposes of this section—

(A) IN GENERAL.—The term "plan" includes a trust described in section 501(c)(22). * * *

(B) DISQUALIFIED PERSON.—* * *

(f) OTHER DEFINITIONS AND SPECIAL RULES.—For purposes of this section—

(1) JOINT AND SEVERAL LIABILITY.—If more than one person is liable under subsection (a) or (b) with respect to any one prohibited transaction, all such persons shall be jointly and severally liable under such subsection with respect to such transaction.

(2) TAXABLE PERIOD.—The term "taxable period" means, with respect to any prohibited transaction, the period beginning with the date on which the prohibited transaction occurs and ending on the earliest of—

(A) the date of mailing a notice of deficiency with respect to the tax imposed by subsection (a) under section 6212,

(B) the date on which the tax imposed by subsection (a) is assessed, or

(C) the date on which correction of the prohibited transaction is completed.

(3) SALE OR EXCHANGE; ENCUMBERED PROPERTY.—A transfer of real or personal property by a disqualified person to a plan shall be treated as a sale or exchange if the property is subject to a mortgage or similar lien which the plan assumes or if it is subject to a mortgage or similar lien which a disqualified person placed on the property within the 10-year period ending on the date of the transfer.

(4) AMOUNT INVOLVED.—The term "amount involved" means, with respect to a prohibited transaction, the greater of the amount of money and the fair market value of the other property given or the amount of money and the fair market value of the other property received; except that, in the case of services described in paragraphs (2) and (10) of subsection (d) the amount

involved shall be only the excess compensation. For purposes of the preceding sentence, the fair market value—

(A) in the case of the tax imposed by subsection (a), shall be determined as of the date on which the prohibited transaction occurs; and

(B) in the case of the tax imposed by subsection (b), shall be the highest fair market value during the taxable period.

(5) CORRECTION.—The terms "correction" and "correct" mean, with respect to a prohibited transaction, undoing the transaction to the extent possible, but in any case placing the plan in a financial position not worse than that in which it would be if the disqualified person were acting under the highest fiduciary standards.

(6) EXEMPTIONS NOT TO APPLY TO CERTAIN TRANSACTIONS.—

(A) IN GENERAL.—In the case of a trust described in section 401(a) which is part of a plan providing contributions or benefits for employees some or all of whom are owner-employees (as defined in section 401(c)(3), the exemptions provided by subsection (d) (other than paragraphs (9) and (12)) shall not apply to a transaction in which the plan directly or indirectly—* * *

(7) S CORPORATION REPAYMENT OF LOANS FOR QUALIFYING EMPLOYER SECURITIES. * * *

(g) APPLICATION OF SECTION.—This section shall not apply—

(1) in the case of a plan to which a guaranteed benefit policy (as defined in section 401(b)(2)(B) of the Employee Retirement Income Security Act of 1974) is issued, to any assets of the insurance company, insurance service, or insurance organization merely because of its issuance of such policy;

(2) to a governmental plan (within the meaning of section 414(d)); or

(3) to a church plan (within the meaning of section 414(e)) with respect to which the election provided by section 410(d) has not been made.

In the case of a plan which invests in any security issued by an investment company registered under the Investment Company Act of 1940, the assets of such plan shall be deemed to include such security but shall not, by reason of such investment, be deemed to include any assets of such company.

(h) NOTIFICATION OF SECRETARY OF LABOR.—Before sending a notice of deficiency with respect to the tax imposed by subsection (a) or (b), the Secretary shall notify the Secretary of Labor and provide him a reasonable opportunity to obtain a correction of the prohibited transaction or to comment on the imposition of such tax.

(i) CROSS REFERENCE.—For provisions concerning coordination procedures between Secretary of Labor and Secretary of the Treasury with respect to application of tax imposed by this section and for authority to waive imposition of the tax imposed by subsection (b), see section 3003 of the Employee Retirement Income Security Act of 1974.

Code Section 6693—Failure to Provide Reports on Certain Tax-Favored Accounts or Annuities; Penalties Relating to Designated Nondeductible Contributions

(a) REPORTS.—

(1) IN GENERAL.—If a person required to file a report under a provision referred to in paragraph (2) fails to file such report at the time and in the manner required by such provision, such person shall pay a penalty of $50 for each failure unless it is shown that such failure is due to reasonable cause.

(2) PROVISIONS.—The provisions referred to in this paragraph are—

(A) subsections (i) and (l) of section 408 (relating to individual retirement plans),

(B) section 220(h) (relating to Archer MSAs),

(C) section 223(h) (relating to health savings accounts),

(D) section 529(d) (relating to qualified tuition programs), and

(E) section 530(h) (relating to Coverdell education savings accounts).

This subsection shall not apply to any report which is an information return described in section 6724(d)(1)(C)(i) or a payee statement described in section 6724(d)(2)(W). This subsection shall not apply to any report which is an information return described in section 6724(d)(1)(C)(i) or a payee statement described in section 6724(d)(2)(X).

* * *

Code Section 7702B—Treatment of Qualified Long-Term Care Insurance

(a) IN GENERAL.—For purposes of this title—

(1) a qualified long-term care insurance contract shall be treated as an accident and health insurance contract,

* * *

(b) QUALIFIED LONG-TERM CARE INSURANCE CONTRACT.—For purposes of this title—

(1) IN GENERAL.—The term "qualified long-term care insurance contract" means any insurance contract if—

(A) the only insurance protection provided under such contract is coverage of qualified long-term care services,

(B) such contract does not pay or reimburse expenses incurred for services or items to the extent that such expenses are reimbursable under title

XVIII of the Social Security Act or would be so reimbursable but for the application of a deductible or coinsurance amount,

(C) such contract is guaranteed renewable,

(D) such contract does not provide for a cash surrender value or other money that can be—

    (i) paid, assigned, or pledged as collateral for a loan, or

    (ii) borrowed,
      other than as provided in subparagraph (E) or paragraph (2)(C),

(E) all refunds of premiums, and all policyholder dividends or similar amounts, under such contract are to be applied as a reduction in future premiums or to increase future benefits, and

(F) such contract meets the requirements of subsection (g).

SPECIAL RULES.—

(A) PER DIEM, ETC. PAYMENTS PERMITTED.—A contract shall not fail to be described in subparagraph (A) or (B) of paragraph (1) by reason of payments being made on a per diem or other periodic basis without regard to the expenses incurred during the period to which the payments relate.

(B) SPECIAL RULES RELATING TO MEDICARE.—(i) Paragraph (1)(B) shall not apply to expenses which are reimbursable under title XVIII of the Social Security Act only as a secondary payor.

    (i) No provision of law shall be construed or applied so as to prohibit the offering of a qualified long-term care insurance contract on the basis that the contract coordinates its benefits with those provided under such title.

(C) REFUNDS OF PREMIUMS.—Paragraph (1)(E) shall not apply to any refund on the death of the insured, or on a complete surrender or cancellation of the contract, which cannot exceed the aggregate premiums paid under the contract. Any refund on a complete surrender or cancellation of the contract shall be includible in gross income to the extent that any deduction or exclusion was allowable with respect to the premiums.

* * *

Appendix B

IRS Notices and Announcements

Notices

Notice 2005-86 (2005-49 I.R.B. 1075)

[**Summary:** The IRS provides guidance on an individual's eligibility to contribute to an HSA during a cafeteria plan grace period and how an employer may amend the cafeteria plan document to enable a health FSA participant to become HSA eligible during the grace period.]

PURPOSE

This notice provides guidance on eligibility to contribute to a Health Savings Account (HSA) during a cafeteria plan grace period as described in Notice 2005-42, 2005-23 I.R.B. 1204. As discussed below, an individual participating in a health flexible spending arrangement (health FSA) who is covered by the grace period is generally not eligible to contribute to an HSA until the first day of the first month following the end of the grace period, even if the participant's health FSA has no unused benefits at the end of the prior cafeteria plan year. This notice, however, provides guidance on how an employer may amend the cafeteria plan document to enable a health FSA participant to become HSA eligible during the grace period.

BACKGROUND

Cafeteria Plans

Section 125(a) states that, in general, no amount is included in the gross income of a participant in a cafeteria plan solely because, under the plan, the participant may choose among the benefits of the plan. Section 125(d) defines a cafeteria plan as a written plan under which all participants are employees, and the participants may choose among two or more benefits consisting of cash and qualified benefits. "Qualified benefits" mean any benefit which, with the application of §125(a), is not includible in the gross income of the employee by reason of an express provision of Chapter 1 of the Internal Revenue Code, including employer-provided accident and health coverage under §§106 and 105(b). A high deductible health plan (HDHP) as defined in §223(c)(2)(A) can be employer-provided accident and health coverage. A health FSA, which pays or reimburses certain §213(d) medical expenses (other than health insurance or long-term care services or insurance), is also employer-provided accident and health coverage. The term "qualified medical expenses" as used in this Notice, means expenses which may be paid or reimbursed under a health FSA.

Cafeteria Plan Grace Period

Notice 2005-42, 2005-23 I.R.B. 1204, modifies the application of the rule prohibiting deferred compensation under a cafeteria plan (i.e., the "use-it-or-lose-it" rule). The notice permits a cafeteria plan to be amended, at the employer's option, to provide a grace period immediately following the end of each plan year, during which an individual who incurs expenses for a qualified benefit during the grace period, may be paid or reimbursed for those expenses from the unused benefits or contributions relating to that benefit. A plan providing a grace period is required to provide the grace period to all participants who are covered on the last day of the plan year (including participants whose coverage is extended to the last day of the plan year through COBRA continuation coverage). The grace period remains in effect for the entire period even though the participant may terminate employment on or before the last day of the grace period. But an employer may limit the availability of the grace period to only certain cafeteria plan benefits and not others. For example, a cafeteria plan offering both a health FSA and a dependent care FSA may limit the grace period to the health FSA. The grace period must not extend beyond the fifteenth day of the third calendar month after the end of the immediately preceding plan year to which it relates, but may be adopted for a shorter period.

Interaction Between HSAs and Health FSAs

Section 223(a) allows a deduction for contributions to an HSA for an "eligible individual" for any month during the taxable year. An "eligible individual" is defined in §223(c)(1)(A) and means, in general, with respect to any month, any individual who is covered under an HDHP on the first day of such month and is not, while covered under an HDHP, "covered under any health plan which is not a high-deductible health plan, and which provides coverage for any benefit which is covered under the high-deductible health plan."

In addition to coverage under an HDHP, §223(c)(1)(B) provides that an eligible individual may have disregarded coverage, including "permitted insurance" and "permitted coverage." Section 223(c)(2)(C) also provides a safe harbor for the absence of a preventive care deductible. See Notice 2004-23, 2004-1 C.B. 725. Therefore, under §223, an individual who is eligible to contribute to an HSA must be covered by a health plan that is an HDHP, and may also have permitted insurance, permitted coverage and preventive care, but no other coverage. A health FSA that reimburses all qualified §213(d) medical expenses without other restrictions is a health plan that constitutes other coverage. Consequently, an individual who is covered by a health FSA that pays or reimburses all qualified medical expenses is not an eligible individual for purposes of making contributions to an HSA. This result is the same even if the individual is covered by a health FSA sponsored by a spouse's employer.

However, as described in Rev. Rul. 2004-45, 2004-1 C.B. 971, an individual who is otherwise eligible for an HSA may be covered under specific types of health FSAs and remain eligible to contribute to an HSA. One arrangement is a limited-purpose health FSA, which pays or reimburses expenses only for preventive care and "permitted coverage" (e.g., dental care and vision care). Another HSA-compatible arrangement is a post-deductible health FSA, which pays or reimburses preventive care and for other qualified medical expenses only if incurred after the minimum annual deductible for the HDHP under §223(c)(2)(A) is satisfied. This means that qualified medical expenses incurred before the HDHP deductible is satisfied may not be reimbursed by a post-deductible HDHP even after the HDHP deductible had been satisfied. [Editors Note: The term "post-deductible HDHP" would appear to be incorrect. A "post-deductible FSA" or "post-deductible health FSA" is probably meant.] To summarize, an otherwise HSA eligible individual will remain eligible if covered under a limited-purpose health FSA or a post-deductible FSA, or a combination of both.

OPTIONS AVAILABLE TO AN EMPLOYER

An employer may adopt either of the following two options, which will affect participants' HSA eligibility during the cafeteria plan grace period:

(1) General Purpose Health FSA During Grace Period

Employer amends the cafeteria plan document to provide a grace period but takes no other action with respect to the general purpose health FSA. Because a health FSA that pays or reimburses all qualified medical expenses constitutes impermissible "other coverage" for HSA eligibility purposes, an individual who participated in the health FSA (or a spouse whose medical expenses are eligible for reimbursement under the health FSA) for the immediately preceding cafeteria plan year and who is covered by the grace period, is not eligible to contribute to an HSA until the first day of the first month following the end of the grace period. For example, if the health FSA grace period ends March 15, 2006, an individual who did not elect coverage by a general health FSA or other disqualifying coverage for 2006 is HSA eligible on April 1, 2006, and may contribute 9/12ths of the 2006 HSA contribution limit. The result is the same even if a participant's health FSA has no unused contributions remaining at the end of the immediately preceding cafeteria plan year.

(2) Mandatory Conversion from Health FSA to HSA-compatible Health FSA for All Participants

Employer amends the cafeteria plan document to provide for both a grace period and a mandatory conversion of the general purpose health FSA to a limited-purpose or post-deductible FSA (or combined limited-purpose and post-deductible health FSA) during the grace period. The amendments do not permit an individual participant to elect between an HSA-compatible FSA or an FSA that is not HSA-compatible. The amendments apply to the entire grace period and to all participants in the health FSA who are covered by the grace period. The amendments must satisfy all other requirements of Notice 2005-42. Coverage of these participants by the HSA-compatible FSA during the grace period does not disqualify participants who are otherwise eligible individuals from contributing to an HSA during the grace period.

TRANSITION RELIEF

For cafeteria plan years ending before June 5, 2006, an individual participating in a general purpose health FSA that provides coverage during a grace period will be eligible to contribute to an HSA during the grace period if the following requirements are met: (1) If not for the coverage under a general purpose health FSA described in clause (2), the individual would be an "eligible individual" as defined in §223(c)(1)(A) during the grace period (in general, is covered under an HDHP and is not, while covered under an HDHP, covered under any impermissible other health coverage); and (3) Either (A) the individual's (and the individual's spouse's) general purpose health FSA has no unused contributions or benefits remaining at the end of the immediately preceding cafeteria plan year, or (B) in the case of an individual who is not covered during the grace period under a general purpose health FSA maintained by the employer of the individual's spouse, the individual's employer amends its cafeteria plan document to provide that the grace period does not provide coverage to an individual who elects HDHP coverage.

EFFECT ON OTHER DOCUMENTS

Notice 2005-42 and Rev. Rul. 2004-45 are amplified.

DRAFTING INFORMATION * * *

Notice 2005-83 (2005-49 I.R.B. 1075)

[**Summary:** The IRS provides additional transitional relief for certain health plans with non-calendar year renewal dates, that otherwise qualify as a HDHP, except that the plans provide state-mandated benefits without regard to a deductible or with a deductible below the minimum annual deductible specified in Code Section 223(c)(2).]

PURPOSE

This notice provides relief for certain health plans with non-calendar year renewal dates that otherwise qualify as high-deductible health plans (HDHPs), except that the plans provide state-mandated benefits without regard to a deductible or with a deductible below the minimum annual deductible specified in §223(c)(2) of the Internal Revenue Code.

BACKGROUND AND APPLICATION

Some states require that health plans provide certain benefits without regard to a deductible or with a deductible below the minimum annual deductible specified in §223(c)(2) (e.g., first-dollar coverage or coverage with a low deductible). These health plans are not HDHPs under §223(c)(2) and individuals covered under these health plans are generally not eligible to contribute to Health Savings Accounts (HSAs). Notice 2004-43, 2004-2 C.B. 10, provides transition relief that treats health plans as meeting the requirement of §223(c)(2) when the sole reason the plans are not HDHPs is because of certain state-mandated benefits. For months before January 1, 2006, otherwise eligible individuals covered under these health plans will be treated as eligible individuals for purposes of §223(c)(1) and may contribute to an HSA. The transition period provided in Notice 2004-43 covers months before January 1, 2006, for state-mandated requirements in effect on January 1, 2004.

Generally, a health plan may not reduce existing benefits before the plan's renewal date. Thus, even though a state may amend its laws before January 1, 2006, to authorize HDHPs that comply with §223(c)(2), non-calendar year plans may still fail to qualify as HDHPs after January 1, 2006 because existing benefits cannot be changed until the next renewal date. For example, a state amends its laws to authorize HDHPs, effective November 1, 2005. A health plan with a renewal date of July 1, 2005 is required to retain the state-mandated low-deductible coverage for the plan year July 1, 2005 through June 30, 2006 because the benefits can only be modified on the renewal date. As a result, although the state has amended its statute, the health plan will fail to be an HDHP for months after January 1, 2006 (i.e., for the months of January through June, 2006).

Therefore, additional transitional relief is appropriate for non-calendar year health plans. Accordingly, the transition relief in Notice 2004-43 is amplified to provide that for any coverage period of twelve months or less beginning before January 1, 2006, a health plan that otherwise qualifies as an HDHP as defined in §223(c)(2), except that it complied on its most recent renewal date before January 1, 2006 with state-mandated requirements (in effect on January 1, 2004) to provide certain benefits without regard to a deductible or with a deductible below the minimum annual deductible specified in §223(c)(2), will be treated as an HDHP. In no event will the additional transitional relief provided in this Notice extend beyond the earlier of the health plan's next renewal date or December 31, 2006.

EFFECT ON OTHER DOCUMENTS

Notice 2004-43, 2004-2 C.B. 10, is amplified.

DRAFTING INFORMATION * * *

Notice 2005-8 (2005-4 I.R.B.1)

[**Summary:** The IRS has provided additional guidance on a partnership's contributions to a partner's health savings account and an S corporation's contributions to a 2 percent shareholder-employee's HSA.]

PURPOSE

This notice provides guidance on a partnership's contributions to a partner's Health Savings Account (HSA) and an S corporation's contributions to a 2 percent shareholder-employee's HSA.

BACKGROUND

Section 1201 of the Medicare Prescription Drug, Improvement, and Modernization Act of 2003, Pub. L. No. 108-173, added section 223 to the Internal Revenue Code to permit eligible individuals to establish Health Savings Accounts (HSAs) for taxable years beginning after December 31, 2003. Generally, contributions made to an HSA, within permissible limits, by or on behalf of a taxpayer who is an eligible individual are deductible by a taxpayer under section 223(a). The deduction is an adjustment to gross income (i.e., an above the line deduction) under section 62(a)(19). If an employer makes a contribution, within permissible limits, to the HSA on behalf of an employee who is an eligible individual, the contribution is excluded from the employee's gross income and wages. *See* section 106(d). A partnership may also contribute to a partner's HSA and an S corporation may contribute to the HSA of a 2 percent shareholder-employee (as defined below). The Questions and Answers below discuss the tax treatment of HSA contributions made on behalf of such partners and 2 percent shareholder-employees who are eligible individuals.

QUESTIONS AND ANSWERS

Q-1. **What is the tax treatment of a partnership's contributions to a partner's HSA that are treated as distributions to the partner under section 731?**

A-1. Contributions by a partnership to a bona fide partner's HSA are not contributions by an employer to the HSA of an employee. *See* Rev. Rul. 69-184, 1969-1.C.B. 256. Contributions by a partnership to a partner's HSA that are treated as distributions to the partner under section 731 are not deductible by the partnership and do not affect the distributive shares of partnership income and deductions. *See* Rev. Rul. 91-26, 1991-1 C.B. 184 (analysis of situation 1, last paragraph). The contributions are reported as distributions of money on Schedule K-1 (Form 1065). These distributions are not included in the partner's net earnings from self-employment under section 1402(a) because the distributions under section 731 do not affect a partner's distributive share of partnership income or loss under section 702(a)(8). The partner, if an eligible individual as defined in section 223(c)(1), is entitled under sections 223(a) and 62(a)(19) to deduct the amount of the contributions made to the partner's HSA during the taxable year as an adjustment to gross income on his or her federal income tax return.

Q-2. What is the tax treatment of a partnership's contributions to a partner's HSA that are treated as guaranteed payments under section 707(c), are derived from the partnership's trade or business, and are for services rendered to the partnership?

A-2. Contributions by a partnership to a bona fide partner's HSA are not contributions by an employer to the HSA of an employee. *See* Rev. Rul. 69-184. Contributions by a partnership to a partner's HSA for services rendered to the partnership that are treated as guaranteed payments under section 707(c) are deductible by the partnership under section 162 (if the requirements of that section are satisfied (taking into account the rules of section 263)) and are includible in the partner's gross income. The contributions are not excludible from the partner's gross income under section 106(d) because the contributions are treated as a distributive share of partnership income under Treas. Reg. §1.707-1(c) for purposes of all Code sections other than sections 61(a) and 162(a). *See* Rev. Rul. 91-26. Contributions by a partnership to a partner's HSA that are treated as guaranteed payments under section 707(c), are reported as guaranteed payments on Schedule K-1 (Form 1065). Because the contributions are guaranteed payments that are derived from the partnership's trade or business, and are for services rendered to the partnership, the contributions are included in the partner's net earnings from self-employment under section 1402(a) on the partner's Schedule SE (Form 1040). The partner, if an eligible individual as defined in section 223(c)(1), is entitled under sections 223(a) and 62(a)(19) to deduct the amount of the contributions made to the partner's HSA during the taxable year as an adjustment to gross income on his or her federal income tax return.

The following example illustrates the answers in A-1 and A-2.

Example. Partnership is a limited partnership with three equal individual partners, A (a general partner), B (a limited partner), and C (a limited partner). C is to be paid $500 annually for services rendered to Partnership in his capacity as a partner and without regard to Partnership income (a section 707 (c) guaranteed payment). The $500 payment to C is derived from Partnership's trade or business. Partnership has no employees. A, B, and C are eligible individuals as defined in section 223(c)(1) and each has an HSA. During Partnership's Year 1 taxable year, Partnership makes the following contributions: a $300 contribution to each of A's and B's HSAs which are treated by Partnership as section 731 distributions to A and B; and a $500 contribution to C's HSA in lieu of paying C the guaranteed payment directly.

Partnership's contributions to A's and B's HSAs are not deductible by Partnership and, therefore, do not affect Partnership's calculation of its taxable income or loss. *See* Rev. Rul. 91-26. A and B are entitled to an above the line deduction, under sections 223(a) and 62(a)(19), for the amount of the contributions made to their individual HSAs. The section 731 distributions to A's and B's individual HSAs are reported as cash distributions to A and B on A's and B's Schedule K-1 (Form 1065). The distributions to A's and B's HSAs are not includible in A's and B's net earnings from self employment under section 1402(a), because distributions under section 731 do not affect a partner's distributive share of the partnership's income or loss under section 702(a)(8).

Partnership's contribution to C's HSA that is treated as a guaranteed payment under section 707(c) for services rendered to the partnership is deductible by Partnership under section 162 (if the requirements of that section are satisfied (taking into account the rules of section 263)) and is includible in C's gross income. The contribution is not excludible from C's gross income under section 106(d) because the contribution is treated as a distributive share of partnership income for purposes of all Code sections other than sections 61(a) and 162(a), and a guaranteed payment to a partner is not treated as compensation to an employee. See Rev. Rul. 91-26. The payment to C's HSA should be reported as a guaranteed payment on Schedule K-1 (Form 1065). Because the contribution is a guaranteed payment that is derived from the partnership's trade or business and is for services rendered to the partnership, the contribution constitutes net earnings from self-employment to C under section 1402(a) which should be reported on Schedule SE (Form 1040). C is entitled under sections 223(a) and 62 (a)(19) to deduct as an adjustment to gross income the amount of the contribution made to C's HSA.

Q-3. **What is the tax treatment of an S corporation's contributions to the HSA of a 2 percent shareholder (as defined in section 1372(b)) who is also an employee (2 percent shareholder-employee) in consideration for services rendered to the S corporation?**

A-3. Under section 1372, for purposes of applying the provisions of Subtitle A that relate to fringe benefits, an S corporation is treated as a partnership, and any 2 percent shareholder of the S corporation is treated as a partner of such partnership. Therefore, contributions by an S corporation to an HSA of a 2 percent shareholder-employee in consideration for services rendered are treated as guaranteed payments under section 707(c). Accordingly, the contributions are deductible by the S corporation under section 162 (if the requirements of that section are satisfied (taking into account the rules of section 263)) and are includible in the 2 percent shareholder-employee's gross income. In addition, the 2 percent shareholder-employee is not entitled to exclude the contribution from gross income under section 106(d). See Rev. Rul. 91-26.

For employment tax purposes, when contributions are made by an S corporation to an HSA of a 2 percent shareholder-employee, the 2 percent shareholder-employee is treated as an employee subject to Federal Insurance Contributions Act (FICA) tax and not as an individual subject to Self-Employment Contributions Act (SECA) tax. (See Announcement 92-16, 1992-5 I.R.B. 53, clarifying the FICA (Social Security and Medicare) tax treatment of accident and health premiums paid by an S corporation on behalf of a 2 percent shareholder-employee.) However, if the requirements for the exclusion under section 3121(a)(2)(B) are satisfied, the S corporation's contributions to an HSA of a 2 percent shareholder-employee are not wages subject to FICA tax, even though the amounts must be included in wages for income tax withholding purposes on the 2 percent shareholder-employee's Form W-2, Wage and Tax Statement. The 2 percent shareholder-employee, if an eligible individual as defined in section 223(c)(1), is entitled under sections 223(a) and 62(a)(19) to deduct the amount of the contributions made to the 2 percent shareholder-employee's HSA during the taxable year as an adjustment to gross income on his or her federal income tax return. *See* Notice 2004-2, Q&A 19, 2004-2 I.R.B. 269, for employment tax rules for employer contributions to HSAs of employees other than 2 percent shareholder-employees.

DRAFTING INFORMATION * * *

Notice 2004-79 (2004-49 I.R.B. 898)

[**Summary:** The IRS has provided guidance on the effect of the Working Families Tax Relief Act of 2004 on the definition of dependent under Code Section 106. For tax years beginning January 1, 2005, the term "dependent" for section 106 purposes will have the same meaning as in Code Section 105(b), the IRS said.]

I. PURPOSE

This notice provides guidance regarding the effect of the Working Families Tax Relief Act of 2004 (WFTRA), Pub. L. No. 108-311, 118 Stat. 1166, on the exclusion from the gross income of an employee under §106 of the Internal Revenue Code (Code) of employer-provided coverage under an accident or health plan.

II. BACKGROUND

Section 201 of WFTRA amended the definition of dependent in §152, effective for taxable years beginning after December 31, 2004. Pursuant to §152, as amended, an individual must be either a "qualifying child" or a "qualifying relative" to be a dependent. Section 152(c), as amended, provides that an individual must meet relationship, residency, and age requirements to be a qualifying child. In addition, an individual is not a qualifying child if the individual provided over one-half of his or her own support for the calendar year. Section 152(c)(3)(A) provides that an individual meets the age requirement if the individual has not attained age 19 as of the close of the calendar year or if the individual is a student who has not attained age 24 as of the close of the calendar year. Under §152(c)(3)(B), an individual is treated as meeting the age requirement if the individual is permanently and totally disabled (as defined in §22(e)(3)) at any time during the calendar year.

Section 152(d)(1), as amended, provides, in general, that a qualifying relative is an individual who bears a relationship to the taxpayer described in §152(d)(2), whose gross income is less than the exemption amount (as defined in §151(d)), who receives over one-half of his or her support from the taxpayer, and who is not a qualifying child of the taxpayer or any other taxpayer.

Section 207 of WFTRA contains several technical and conforming amendments to Code sections that refer to the §152 definition of dependent, including an amendment to §105(b). Section 105(b) generally excludes from an employee's gross income employer-provided medical care reimbursements paid directly or indirectly to the employee for the medical care of the employee and the employee's spouse and dependents, as defined in §152. Under the WFTRA amendment to §105(b), an individual's status as a dependent for purposes of §105(b) will be determined without regard to new §152(b)(1) and (b)(2), which contain certain exceptions to the definition of dependent, and without regard to new §152(d)(1)(B), which contains the gross income limitation for a qualifying relative. It appears that the intent of Congress in making these conforming amendments was to maintain the current law definition of dependent for purposes of employer-provided medical care reimbursements.

Section 106(a) provides that the gross income of an employee does not include employer-provided coverage under an accident or health plan. Thus, premiums and other amounts that an employer pays on behalf of an employee to an accident or health plan are not included in gross income. Treas. Reg. §1.106-1 provides that the exclusion from gross income extends to contributions which the employer makes to an accident or health plan on behalf of the employee and the employee's spouse or dependents, as defined in §152. Because the reference to "dependents" under §106 appears only in the regulations under that section and not in the statute itself, Congress made no conforming amendments to §106 in WFTRA.

Under current law, the exclusion under §106(a) for employer-provided coverage under an accident or health plan parallels the exclusion under §105(b) for employer-provided reimbursements of medical care expenses incurred by the employee and the employee's spouse and dependents, as defined in §152. However, as a result of the changes made by WFTRA, the definition of dependent in §105(b) differs from the definition in the regulations under §106(a). Accordingly, if the regulations under §106(a) continued to be applied as currently written after the effective date of section 201 of WFTRA, the value of employer-provided coverage for an individual who is not a qualifying child and who does not meet the gross income limitation for a qualifying relative would have to be included in the employee's gross income. Because the intent of Congress was not to change the definition of dependent for purposes of employer-provided health plans, regulations under §106 should be revised to provide that the same definition of dependent applies to §106 as applies to amended §105(b).

III. APPLICATION

The IRS intends to revise the regulations at 26 C.F.R. 1.106-1 to provide that the term "dependent" for purposes of §106 shall have the same meaning as in §105(b). The revised regulations will be effective for taxable years beginning after December 31, 2004.

Taxpayers may rely on this Notice pending the issuance of the revised regulations. Accordingly, an employee may exclude from gross income the value of employer-provided coverage for an individual who meets the definition of a qualifying relative except that the individual's gross income equals or exceeds the exemption amount.

DRAFTING INFORMATION * * *

Notice 2004-50 (2004-33 (I.R.B. 196)

[**Summary:** Additional guidance on the requirements for HDHPs and HSAs address questions the IRS received after December 2003. This guidance clarifies that for those age 65 or older, Medicare eligibility does make an individual ineligible to contribute to an HSA provided the individual is not actually enrolled in Medicare. The IRS has also provided that employee assistance programs (EAP) that provide short-term counseling regarding such problems as substance abuse, emotional disorders, or financial difficulties, or that provide evidence-based information and case monitoring of care provided by a health plan, or that provide such services as fitness and sports activities are not health plans because they do not provide significant benefits in the nature of medical care or treatment. Therefore, coverage under such an EAP does not render an individual ineligible to contribute to an HSA.]

PURPOSE

This notice provides guidance on Health Savings Accounts.

BACKGROUND

Section 1201 of the Medicare Prescription Drug, Improvement, and Modernization Act of 2003, Pub. L. No. 108-173, added section 223 to the Internal Revenue Code to permit eligible individuals to establish Health Savings Accounts (HSAs) for taxable years beginning after December 31, 2003. Notice 2004-2, 2004-2 I.R.B. 269, provides certain basic information on HSAs in question and answer format. This notice addresses additional questions relating to HSAs.[1]

OUTLINE TABLE OF CONTENTS

The following is an outline of the questions and answers covered in this notice:

I. Eligible Individuals

Q&A 1. Choice between low-deductible health plan and HDHP

Q&A 2. Eligible for Medicare and contributions to HSA

Q&A 3. Eligible for Medicare and catch-up contributions

Q&A 4. Government retiree and enrollment in Medicare Part B

Q&A 5. Eligible for medical benefits from VA

Q&A 6. Coverage under TRICARE

Q&A 86. HDHP and cost-of-living adjustments

Q&A 87. HSAs and bona-fide residents of Commonwealth of Puerto Rico, American Samoa, the U.S. Virgin Islands, Guam, the Commonwealth of the Northern Mariana Islands

Q&A 88. C corporation contributions to HSAs of shareholders

QUESTIONS AND ANSWERS

I. Eligible individuals

Q-1. If an employer offers an employee a choice between a low-deductible health plan and a high-deductible health plan (HDHP), and the employee selects coverage only under the HDHP, is the employee an eligible individual under section 223(c)(1)?

A-1. Yes, if the employee is otherwise an eligible individual. To determine if an individual is an eligible individual, the actual health coverage selected by the individual is controlling. Thus, it does not matter that the individual could have chosen, but did not choose, a low-deductible health plan or other coverage that would have disqualified the individual from contributing to an HSA.

Q-2. May an otherwise eligible individual who is eligible for Medicare, but not enrolled in Medicare Part A or Part B, contribute to an HSA?

A-2. Yes. Section 223(b)(7) states that an individual ceases to be an eligible individual starting with the month he or she is entitled to benefits under Medicare. Under this provision, mere eligibility for Medicare does not make an individual ineligible to contribute to an HSA. Rather, the term "entitled to benefits under" Medicare means both eligibility and enrollment in Medicare. Thus, an otherwise eligible individual under section 223(c)(1) who is not actually enrolled in Medicare Part A or Part B may contribute to an HSA until the month that individual is enrolled in Medicare.

> **Example (1).** Y, age 66, is covered under her employer's HDHP. Although Y is eligible for Medicare, Y is not actually entitled to Medicare because she did not apply for benefits under Medicare (i.e., enroll in Medicare Part A or Part B). If Y is otherwise an eligible individual under section 223(c)(1), she may contribute to an HSA.

> **Example (2).** In August 2004, X attains age 65 and applies for and begins receiving Social Security benefits. X is automatically enrolled in Medicare. As of August 1, 2004, X is no longer an eligible individual and may not contribute to an HSA.

Q-3. May an otherwise eligible individual under section 223(c)(1) who is age 65 or older and thus eligible for Medicare, but is not enrolled in Medicare Part A or Part B, make the additional catch-up contribution under section 223(b)(3) for persons age 55 or older?

A-3. Yes. See Notice 2004-2, Q&A 14, on catch-up contributions.

Q-4. Is a government retiree who is enrolled in Medicare Part B (but not Part A) an eligible individual under section 223(c)(1)?

A-4. No. Under section 223(b)(7), an individual who is enrolled in Medicare may not contribute to an HSA.

Q-5. If an otherwise eligible individual under section 223(c)(1) is eligible for medical benefits through the Department of Veterans Affairs (VA), may he or she contribute to an HSA?

A-5. An otherwise eligible individual who is eligible to receive VA medical benefits, but who has not actually received such benefits during the preceding three months, is an eligible individual under section 223(c)(1). An individual is not eligible to make HSA contributions for any month, however, if the individual has received medical benefits from the VA at any time during the previous three months.

Q-6. May an otherwise eligible individual who is covered by an HDHP and also receives health benefits under TRICARE (the health care program for active duty and retired members of the uniformed services, their families and survivors) contribute to an HSA?

A-6. No. Coverage options under TRICARE do not meet the minimum annual deductible requirements for an HDHP under section 223(c)(2). Thus, an individual covered under TRICARE is not an eligible individual and may not contribute to an HSA.

Q-7. May an otherwise eligible individual who is covered by both an HDHP and also by insurance contracts for one or more specific diseases or illnesses, such as cancer, diabetes, asthma or congestive heart failure, contribute to an HSA if the insurance provides benefits before the deductible of the HDHP is satisfied?

A-7. Yes. Section 223(c)(1)(B)(i) provides that an eligible individual covered under an HDHP may also be covered "for any benefit provided by permitted insurance." Section 223(c)(3)(B) provides that the term "permitted insurance" includes "insurance for a specified disease or illness." Therefore, an eligible individual may be covered by an HDHP and also by permitted insurance for one or more specific diseases, such as cancer, diabetes, asthma or congestive heart failure, as long as the principal health coverage is provided by the HDHP.

Q-8. Must coverage for "permitted insurance" described in section 223(c)(3) (liabilities incurred under workers' compensation laws, tort liabilities, liabilities relating to ownership or use of property, insurance for a specified disease or illness, and insurance paying a fixed amount per day (or other period) of hospitalization), be provided under insurance contracts?

A-8. Yes. Benefits for "permitted insurance" under section 223(c)(3) must generally be provided through insurance contracts and not on a self-insured basis. However, where benefits (such as workers' compensation benefits) are provided in satisfaction of a statutory requirement and any resulting benefits for medical care are secondary or incidental to other benefits, the benefits will qualify as "permitted insurance" even if self-insured.

Q-9. May an individual who is covered by an HDHP and also has a discount card that enables the user to obtain discounts for health care services or products, contribute to an HSA?

A-9. Yes. Discount cards that entitle holders to obtain discounts for health care services or products at managed care market rates will not disqualify an individual from being an eligible individual for HSA purposes if the individual is required to pay the costs of the health care (taking into account the discount) until the deductible of the HDHP is satisfied.

> **Example.** An employer provides its employees with a pharmacy discount card. For a fixed annual fee (paid by the employer), each employee receives a card that entitles the holder to choose any participating pharmacy. During the one-year life of the card, the card holder receives discounts of 15 percent to 50 percent off the usual and customary fees charged by the providers, with no dollar cap on the amount of discounts received during the year. The cardholder is responsible for paying the costs of any drugs (taking into account the discount) until the deductible of any other health plan covering the individual is satisfied. An employee who is otherwise eligible for an HSA will not become ineligible solely as a result of having this benefit.

Q-10. Does coverage under an Employee Assistance Program (EAP), disease management program, or wellness program make an individual ineligible to contribute to an HSA?

A-10. An individual will not fail to be an eligible individual under section 223(c)(1)(A) solely because the individual is covered under an EAP, disease management program or wellness program if the program does not provide significant benefits in the nature of medical care or treatment, and therefore, is not considered a "health plan" for purposes of section 223(c)(1). To determine whether a program provides significant benefits in the nature of medical care or treatment, screening and other preventive care services as described in Notice 2004-23 will be disregarded. See also Q&A 48 on incentives for employees who participate in these programs.

> **Example (1).** An employer offers a program that provides employees with benefits under an EAP, regardless of enrollment in a health plan. The EAP is specifically designed to assist the employer in improving productivity by helping employees identify and resolve personal and work concerns that affect job performance and the work environment. The benefits consist primarily of free or low-cost confidential short-term counseling to identify an employee's problem that may affect job performance and, when appropriate, referrals to an outside organization, facility or program to assist the employee in resolving the problem. The issues addressed during the short-term counseling include, but are not limited to, substance abuse, alcoholism, mental health or emotional disorders, financial or legal difficulties, and dependent care needs. This EAP is not a "health plan" under section 223(c)(1) because it does not provide significant benefits in the nature of medical care or treatment.

> **Example (2).** An employer maintains a disease management program that identifies employees and their family members who have, or are at risk for, certain chronic conditions. The disease management program provides evidence-based information, disease specific support, case monitoring and

coordination of the care and treatment provided by a health plan. Typical interventions include monitoring laboratory or other test results, telephone contacts or web-based reminders of health care schedules, and providing information to minimize health risks. This disease management program is not a "health plan" under section 223(c)(1) because it does not provide significant benefits in the nature of medical care or treatment.

Example (3). An employer offers a wellness program for all employees regardless of participation in a health plan. The wellness program provides a wide-range of education and fitness services designed to improve the over-all health of the employees and prevent illness. Typical services include education, fitness, sports, and recreation activities, stress management and health screenings. Any costs charged to the individual for participating in the services are separate from the individual's coverage under the health plan. This wellness program is not a "health plan" under section 223(c)(1) because it does not provide significant benefits in the nature of medical care or treatment.

Q-11. If an employee begins HDHP coverage mid-month, when does the employee become an eligible individual? (For example, coverage under the HDHP begins on the first day of a biweekly payroll period.)

A-11. Under section 223(b)(2), an eligible individual must have HDHP coverage as of the first day of the month. An individual with employer-provided HDHP coverage on a payroll-by-payroll basis becomes an eligible individual on the first day of the month on or following the first day of the pay period when HDHP coverage begins.

Example. An employee begins HDHP coverage on the first day of a pay period, which is August 16, 2004, and continues to be covered by the HDHP throughout 2004. For purposes of contributing to an HSA, the employee becomes an eligible individual on September 1, 2004.

II. High Deductible Health Plans (HDHPs)

Q-12. What is family HDHP coverage under section 223?

A-12. Under section 223(c)(4), the term "family coverage" means any coverage other than self-only coverage. Self-only coverage is a health plan covering only one individual; self-only HDHP coverage is an HDHP covering only one individual if that individual is an eligible individual. Family HDHP coverage is a health plan covering one eligible individual and at least one other individual (whether or not the other individual is an eligible individual).

Example. An individual, who is an eligible individual, and his dependent child are covered under an "employee plus one" HDHP offered by the individual's employer. The coverage is family HDHP coverage under section 223 (c)(4).

Q-13. Can a state high-risk health insurance plan (high-risk pool) qualify as an HDHP?

A-13. Yes. If the state's high-risk pool does not pay benefits below the minimum annual deductible of an HDHP as set forth in section 223(c)(2)(A), the plan can qualify as an HDHP.

Q-14. May an HDHP impose a lifetime limit on benefits?

A-14. Yes. An HDHP may impose a reasonable lifetime limit on benefits provided under the plan. In such cases, amounts paid by the covered individual above the lifetime limit will not be treated as out-of-pocket expenses in determining the annual out-of-pocket maximum. However, a lifetime limit on benefits designed to circumvent the maximum annual out-of-pocket amount in section 223(c)(2)(A) is not reasonable.

> **Example.** A health plan has an annual deductible that satisfies the minimum annual deductible under section 223(c)(2)(A)(i) for self-only coverage and for family coverage. After satisfying the deductible, the plan pays 100 percent of covered expenses, up to a lifetime limit of $1 million. The lifetime limit of $1 million is reasonable and the health plan is not disqualified from being an HDHP because of the lifetime limit on benefits.

Q-15. If a plan imposes an annual or lifetime limit on specific benefits, are amounts paid by covered individuals after satisfying the deductible treated as out-of-pocket expenses under section 223?

A-15. The out-of-pocket maximum in section 223(c)(2)(A) applies only to covered benefits. Plans may be designed with reasonable benefit restrictions limiting the plan's covered benefits. A restriction or exclusion on benefits is reasonable only if significant other benefits remain available under the plan in addition to the benefits subject to the restriction or exclusion.

> **Example (1).** In 2004, a self-only health plan with a $1,000 deductible includes a $1 million lifetime limit on covered benefits. The plan provides no benefits for experimental treatments, mental health, or chiropractic care visits. Although the plan provides benefits for substance abuse treatment, it limits payments to 26 treatments per year, after the deductible is satisfied. Although the plan provides benefits for fertility treatments, it limits lifetime reimbursements to $10,000, after the deductible is satisfied. Other than these limits on covered benefits, the plan pays 80 percent of major medical expenses incurred after satisfying the deductible. When the 20 percent coinsurance paid by the covered individuals reaches $4,000, the plan pays 100 percent. Under these facts, the plan is an HDHP and no expenses incurred by a covered individual other than the deductible and the 20 percent coinsurance are treated as out-of-pocket expenses under section 223(c)(2)(A).

> **Example (2).** In 2004, a self-only health plan with a $1,000 deductible imposes a lifetime limit on reimbursements for covered benefits of $1 million. While the plan pays 100 percent of expenses incurred for covered benefits after satisfying the deductible, the plan imposes a $10,000 annual limit on benefits for any single condition. The $10,000 annual limit under these facts is not reasonable because significant other benefits do not remain available under the plan. Under these facts, any expenses incurred by a

covered individual after satisfying the deductible are treated as out-of-pocket expenses under section 223(c)(2)(A).

Q-16. If a plan limits benefits to usual, customary and reasonable (UCR) amounts, are amounts paid by covered individuals in excess of UCR included in determining the maximum out-of-pocket expenses paid?

A-16. Restricting benefits to UCR is a reasonable restriction on benefits. Thus, amounts paid by covered individuals in excess of UCR that are not paid by an HDHP are not included in determining maximum out-of-pocket expenses.

Q-17. Can a plan with no express limit on out-of-pocket expenses qualify as an HDHP?

A-17. A health plan without an express limit on out-of-pocket expenses is generally not an HDHP unless such limit is not necessary to prevent exceeding the out-of-pocket maximum.

> **Example (1).** A plan provides self-only coverage with a $2,000 deductible and pays 100 percent of covered benefits above the deductible. Because the plan pays 100 percent of covered benefits after the deductible is satisfied, the maximum out-of-pocket expenses paid by a covered individual would never exceed the deductible. Thus, the plan does not require a specific limit on out-of-pocket expenses to insure that the covered individual will not be subject to out-of-pocket expenses in excess of the maximum set forth in section 223(c)(2)(A).

> **Example (2).** A plan provides self-only coverage with a $2,000 deductible. The plan imposes a lifetime limit on reimbursements for covered benefits of $1 million. For expenses for covered benefits incurred above the deductible, the plan reimburses 80 percent of the UCR costs. The plan includes no express limit on out-of-pocket expenses. This plan does not qualify as a HDHP because it does not have a limit on out-of-pocket expenses.

> **Example (3).** The same facts as Example 2, except that after the 20 percent coinsurance paid by the covered individual reaches $3,000, the plan pays 100 percent of the UCR costs until the $1 million limit is reached. For the purpose of determining the individual's out-of-pocket expenses, the plan only takes into account the 20 percent of UCR paid by the individual. This plan satisfies the out-of-pocket limit.

Q-18. A health plan which otherwise qualifies as an HDHP imposes a flat dollar penalty on a participant who fails to obtain pre-certification for a specific provider or for certain medical procedures. Is the penalty paid by the covered individual included in determining the maximum out-of-pocket expenses paid?

A-18. No. The penalty is not an out-of-pocket expense and, therefore, does not count toward the expense limits in section 223(c)(2)(A).

Q-19. A health plan which otherwise qualifies as an HDHP generally requires a 10 percent coinsurance payment after a covered individual satisfies the deductible. However, if an individual fails to get pre-certification for a specific provider, the plan requires a 20 percent coinsurance payment. Is the increased coinsurance amount included in determining the maximum out-of-pocket expenses paid?

A-19. No. Under the facts set forth, only the generally applicable 10 percent coinsurance payment is included in computing the maximum out-of-pocket expenses paid. The result is the same if the plan imposes a higher coinsurance amount for an out-of-network provider. See also Notice 2004-2, Q&A 4.

Q-20. Are cumulative embedded deductibles under family coverage subject to the out-of-pocket maximum?

A-20. Yes. An HDHP generally must limit the out-of-pocket expenses paid by the covered individuals, either by design or by its express terms.

> **Example (1).** In 2004, a plan which otherwise qualifies as an HDHP provides family coverage with a $2,000 deductible for each family member. The plan pays 100 percent of covered benefits for each family member after that family member satisfies the $2,000 deductible. The plan contains no express limit on out-of-pocket expenses. Section 223(c)(2)(A)(ii)(II) limits the maximum out-of-pocket expenses to $10,000 for family coverage. The plan is an HDHP for any family with two to five covered individuals ($2,000 × 5 = $10,000). However, the plan is not an HDHP for a family with six or more covered individuals.

> **Example (2).** The same facts as Example 1, except that the plan includes an umbrella deductible of $10,000. The plan reimburses 100 percent of covered benefits if the family satisfies the $10,000 in the aggregate, even if no single family member satisfies the $2,000 embedded deductible. This plan qualifies as an HDHP for the family, regardless of the number of covered individuals.

Q-21. Are amounts incurred by an individual for medical care before a health plan's deductible is satisfied included in computing the plan's out-of-pocket expenses under section 223(c)(2)(A)?

A-21. A health plan's out-of-pocket limit includes the deductible, co-payments, and other amounts, but not premiums. Notice 2004-2, Q&A 3. Amounts incurred for noncovered benefits (including amounts in excess of UCR and financial penalties) also are not counted toward the deductible or the out-of-pocket limit. If a plan does not take copayments into account in determining if the deductible is satisfied, the copayments must still be taken into account in determining if the out-of-pocket maximum is exceeded.

> **Example.** In 2004, a health plan has a $1,000 deductible for self-only coverage. After the deductible is satisfied, the plan pays 100 percent of UCR for covered benefits. In addition, the plan pays 100 percent for preventive care, minus a $20 copayment per screening. The plan does not take into account copayments in determining if the $1,000 deductible has been satisfied. The copayments must be included in determining if the plan meets the out-of-pocket maximum. Unless the plan includes an express limit on out-of-pocket expenses taking into account the copayments, or limits the copayments to $4,000, the plan is not an HDHP.

Q-22. If an employer changes health plans mid-year, does the new health plan fail to satisfy section 223(c)(2)(A) merely because it provides a credit towards the deductible for expenses incurred during the previous health plan's short plan year and not reimbursed?

A-22. No. If the period during which expenses are incurred for purposes of satisfying the deductible is 12 months or less and the plan satisfies the requirements for an HDHP, the new plan's taking into account expenses incurred during the prior plan's short plan year (whether or not the prior plan is an HDHP) and not reimbursed, does not violate the requirements of section 223(c)(2)(A).

> **Example.** An employer with a calendar year health plan switches from a non-HDHP plan to a new plan with the first day of coverage under the new plan of July 1. The annual deductible under the new plan satisfies the minimum annual deductible for an HDHP under section 223(c)(2)(A)(i) and counts expenses incurred under the prior plan during the first six months of the year in determining if the new plan's annual deductible is satisfied. The new plan satisfies the HDHP deductible limit under section 223(c)(2)(A).

Q-23. If an eligible individual changes coverage during the plan year from self-only HDHP coverage to family HDHP coverage, does the individual (or any other person covered under the family coverage) fail to be covered by an HDHP merely because the family HDHP coverage takes into account expenses incurred while the individual had self-only coverage?

A-23. No.

> **Example.** An eligible individual has self-only coverage from January 1 through March 31, marries in March and from April 1 through December 31, has family coverage under a plan otherwise qualifying as an HDHP. The family coverage plan applies expenses incurred by the individual from January through March toward satisfying the family deductible. The individual does not fail to be covered by an HDHP. The family coverage satisfies the deductible limit in section 223(c)(2)(A)(i)(II). The individual's contribution to an HSA is based on three months of the self-only coverage (i.e., 3/12 of the deductible for the self-only coverage) and nine months of family coverage (9/12 of the deductible for family coverage).

Q-24. How are the minimum deductible in section 223(c)(2)(A) for an HDHP and the maximum contribution to an HSA in section 223(b) calculated when the period for satisfying a health plan's deductible is longer than 12 months?

A-24. The deductible limits in section 223(c)(2)(A) are based on 12 months. If a plan's deductible may be satisfied over a period longer than 12 months, the minimum annual deductible under section 223(c)(2)(A) must be increased to take into account the longer period in determining if the plan satisfies the HDHP deductible requirements. The adjustment will be done as follows:

(1) Multiply the minimum annual deductible in section 223(c)(2)(A)(i) (as adjusted under section 223(g)) by the number of months allowed to satisfy the deductible.

(2) Divide the amount in (1) above by 12. This is the adjusted deductible for the longer period that is used to test for compliance with section 223(c)(2)(A).

(3) Compare the amount in (2) to the plan's deductible. If the plan's deductible equals or exceeds the amount in (2), the plan satisfies the requirements for the minimum deductible in section 223(c)(2)(A). (Note that the deductible for an HDHP may not exceed the out-of-pocket maximum under section 223(c)(2)(A)(ii).)

If the plan qualifies as an HDHP, an eligible individual's maximum annual HSA contribution will be the lesser of the amounts in (1) or (2) below:

(1) Divide the plan's deductible by the number of months allowed to satisfy the deductible, and multiply this amount by 12;

(2) The statutory amount in section 223(b)(2)(A)(ii) for self-only coverage ($2,600 in 2004) or section 223(b)(2)(B)(ii) for family coverage ($5,150 in 2004), as applicable.

> **Example.** For 2004, a health plan takes into account medical expenses incurred in the last three months of 2003 to satisfy its deductible for calendar year 2004. The plan's deductible for self-only coverage is $1,500 and covers 15 months (the last three months of 2003 and 12 months of 2004). To determine if the plan's deductible satisfies section 223(c)(2)(A) the following calculations are performed: (1) multiply $1,000, the minimum annual deductible in section 223(c)(2)(A)(i), by 15, the number of months in which expenses incurred are taken into account to satisfy the deductible, = $15,000; (2) divide $15,000 by 12 = $1,250; (3) The HDHP minimum deductible for self-only coverage for 15 months must be at least $1,250. Because the plan's deductible, $1,500, exceeds $1,250, the plan's self-only coverage satisfies the deductible rule in section 223(c)(2)(A). The maximum annual HSA contribution in 2004 for an eligible individual with self-only coverage under these facts is $1,200, the lesser of (1) ($1,500/15) × 12 = $1,200; or (2) $2,600.

Q-25. A health plan which otherwise meets the definition of an HDHP negotiates discounted prices for health care services from providers. Covered individuals receive benefits at the discounted prices, regardless of whether they have satisfied the plan's deductible. Do the discounted prices prevent the health plan from being an HDHP as defined in section 223(c)(2)?

A-25. No.

III. Preventive care

Q-26. Does a preventive care service or screening that also includes the treatment of a related condition during that procedure come within the safe harbor for preventive care in Notice 2004-23?

A-26. Yes. Although Notice 2004-23 states that preventive care generally does not include any service or benefit intended to treat an existing illness, injury, or condition, in situations where it would be unreasonable or impracticable to perform another procedure to treat the condition, any treatment that is incidental or ancillary to a preventive care service or screening as described in Notice 2004-23 also falls within the safe-harbor for preventive care. For example, removal of polyps during a diagnostic colonoscopy is preventive care that can be provided before the deductible in an HDHP has been satisfied.

Q-27. To what extent do drugs or medications come within the safe-harbor for preventive care services under section 223(c)(2)(C)?

A-27. Notice 2004-23 sets out a preventive care deductible safe harbor for HDHPs under section 223(c)(2)(C). Solely for this purpose, drugs or medications are preventive care when taken by a person who has developed risk factors for a disease that has not yet manifested itself or not yet become clinically apparent (i.e., asymptomatic), or to prevent the reoccurrence of a disease from which a person has recovered. For example, the treatment of high cholesterol with cholesterol-lowering medications (e.g., statins) to prevent heart disease or the treatment of recovered heart attack or stroke victims with Angiotensin-converting Enzyme (ACE) inhibitors to prevent a reoccurrence, constitute preventive care. In addition, drugs or medications used as part of procedures providing preventive care services specified in Notice 2004-23, including obesity weight-loss and tobacco cessation programs, are also preventive care. However, the preventive care safe harbor under section 223(c)(2)(C) does not include any service or benefit intended to treat an existing illness, injury, or condition, including drugs or medications used to treat an existing illness, injury or condition.

IV. Contributions

Q-28. Who may make contributions on behalf of an eligible individual?

A-28. Although Q&A 11 of Notice 2004-2 only refers to contributions by employers or family members, any person (an employer, a family member or any other person) may make contributions to an HSA on behalf of an eligible individual.

Q-29. May a state government make an HSA contribution on behalf of eligible individuals insured under the state's comprehensive health insurance programs for high-risk individuals (state high-risk pool)?

A-29. Yes. See also Q&A 13.

Q-30. How is the maximum annual HSA contribution limit in section 223(b)(2) determined for an eligible individual with family coverage under an HDHP that includes embedded individual deductibles and an umbrella deductible?

A-30. Generally, under section 223(b)(2)(B), the maximum annual HSA contribution limit for an eligible individual with family coverage under an HDHP (without regard to catch-up contributions) is the lesser of: (1) the annual deductible under the HDHP, or (2) the statutory limit on family coverage contributions as indexed by section 223(g). An HDHP often has a stated maximum amount of expenses the family could incur before receiving benefits (i.e., the umbrella deductible), but also provides payments for covered medical expenses if any individual member of the family incurs medical expenses in excess of the minimum annual deductible in section 223(c)(2)(A)(i)(II) (the embedded individual deductible). The maximum annual HSA contribution limit for an eligible individual who has family coverage under an HDHP with embedded individual deductibles and an umbrella deductible as described above, is the least of the following amounts:

(1) The maximum annual contribution limit for family coverage specified in section 223(b)(2)(B)(ii) ($5,150 for calendar year 2004);

(2) The umbrella deductible; or

(3) The embedded individual deductible multiplied by the number of family members covered by the plan.

See Notice 2004-2, Q&A 3, which requires that the embedded individual deductible satisfy the minimum annual deductible for an HDHP.

Example (1). In 2004, H and W, a married couple, have HDHP coverage for themselves and their two dependent children. The HDHP will pay benefits for any family member whose covered expenses exceed $2,000 (the embedded individual deductible), and will pay benefits for all family members after their covered expenses exceed $5,000 (the umbrella deductible). The maximum annual contribution limit under section 223(b)(2)(B)(ii) is $5,150. The embedded deductible multiplied by the number of family members covered is $8,000 (4 × $2,000). The maximum annual contribution which H and W can make to their HSAs is $5,000 (the least of $5,000, $5,150 or $8,000). The $5,000 limit is divided equally between H and W, unless they agree to a different division. See Q&A 32 and Notice 2004-2, Q&A 15.

Example (2). The same facts as Example 1, except the HDHP provides coverage only for H and W. The maximum annual contribution limit under section 223(b)(2)(B)(ii) is $5,150. The umbrella deductible is $5,000. The embedded individual deductible multiplied by the number of family members covered is $4,000 (2 × $2,000). The maximum annual contribution which H and W can make to their HSAs for 2004 is $4,000 (the least of $5,000, $5,150 or $4,000).

Q-31. How do the maximum annual HSA contribution limits apply to family HDHP coverage that may include an ineligible individual?

A-31. The maximum annual HSA contribution for a married couple with family HDHP coverage is the lesser of: (1) the lowest HDHP family deductible applicable to the family (minimum $2,000) or (2) the section 223(b)(2)(B) statutory maximum ($5,150 in 2004). Although the special rule for married individuals in section 223(b)(5) generally allows a married couple to divide the maximum HSA contribution between spouses, if only one spouse is an eligible individual, only that spouse may contribute to an HSA (notwithstanding the treatment under section 223(b)(5)(A) of both spouses as having only family coverage). For an HDHP with embedded individual deductibles see Q&A 30.

Example (1). In 2004, H and W are a married couple and neither qualifies for catch-up contributions under section 223(b)(3). H and W have family HDHP coverage with a $5,000 deductible. H is an eligible individual and has no other coverage. W also has self-only coverage with a $200 deductible. W, who has coverage under a low-deductible plan, is not an eligible individual. H may contribute $5,000 (the lesser of $5,000 or $5,150) to an HSA while W may not contribute to an HSA.

Example (2). The same facts as Example 1, except that, in addition to the family HDHP with a $5,000 deductible, W has self-only HDHP coverage with a $2,000 deductible rather than self-only coverage with a $200 deductible. Both H and W are eligible individuals. H and W are treated as having only family coverage under section 223(b)(5). The maximum combined HSA contribution by H and W is $5,000, to be divided between them by agreement.

Example (3). The same facts as Example 1, except that, in addition to the family HDHP with a $5,000 deductible, W has family HDHP coverage with a $3,000 deductible rather than self-only coverage with a $200 deductible. Both H and W are eligible individuals. H and W are treated as having family HDHP coverage with the lowest annual deductible under section 223(b)(5)(A). The maximum combined HSA contribution by H and W is $3,000, to be divided between them by agreement.

Example (4). The same facts as Example 1, except that, in addition to family coverage under the HDHP with a $5,000 deductible, W has family coverage with a $500 deductible rather than self-only coverage with a $200 deductible. H and W are treated as having family coverage with the lowest annual deductible under section 223(b)(5)(A). Neither H nor W is an eligible individual and neither may contribute to an HSA.

Example (5). The same facts as Example 1, except that, in addition to the family HDHP with a $5,000 deductible, W is enrolled in Medicare rather than having self-only coverage with a $200 deductible. W is not an eligible individual. H may contribute $5,000 to an HSA while W may not contribute to an HSA.

Example (6). Individual X is a single individual who does not qualify for catch-up contributions. X is an eligible individual and has a dependent. X and his dependent have family HDHP coverage with a $5,000 deductible. The dependent also has self-only coverage with a $200 deductible. X may contribute $5,000 to an HSA while the dependent may not contribute to an HSA.

Q-32. How may spouses agree to divide the annual HSA contribution limit between themselves?

A-32. Section 223(b)(5) provides special rules for married individuals and states that HSA contributions (without regard to the catch-up contribution) "shall be divided equally between them unless they agree on a different division." Thus, spouses can divide the annual HSA contribution in any way they want, including allocating nothing to one spouse. See also Notice 2004-2, Q&A 15.

Example. In 2004, X, an eligible individual, has self-only HDHP coverage with a $1,200 deductible from January 1 through March 31. In March, X and Y marry. Neither X nor Y qualifies for the catch-up contribution. From April 1 through December 31, 2004 X and Y have HDHP family coverage with a $2,400 deductible. Y is an eligible individual from April 1 through December 31, 2004. X and Y's contribution limit for the nine months of family coverage is $1,800 (nine months of the deductible for family coverage (9/12 × $2,400)). X and Y divide the $1,800 between them. X's contribution limit to his HSA for the three months of single coverage is $300 (three months of the deductible for self-only coverage (3/12 × $1,200)). The $300 limit is not divided between X and Y. See also Q&A 23.

Q-33. What is the contribution limit for an eligible individual covered by an HDHP and also by a post-deductible health reimbursement arrangement (HRA)?

A-33. Rev. Rul. 2004-45, Situation 4, describes a post-deductible HRA that does not pay or reimburse any medical expense incurred before the minimum annual deductible under section 223(c)(2)(A)(i) is satisfied. The ruling states that the deductible for the HRA need not be the same as the deductible for the HDHP, but in no event may the HDHP or other coverage provide benefits before the minimum annual deductible under section 223(c)(2)(A)(i) is satisfied. Where the HDHP and the other coverage do not have identical deductibles, contributions to the HSA are limited to the lower of the deductibles. In addition, although the deductibles of the HDHP and the other coverage may be satisfied independently by separate expenses, no benefits may be paid by the HDHP or the other coverage before the minimum annual deductible under section 223(c)(2)(A)(i) has been satisfied.

Example. In 2004, an individual has self-only coverage under an HDHP with a deductible of $2,500. The individual is also covered under a post-deductible HRA (as described in Rev. Rul. 2004-45) which pays or reimburses qualified medical expenses only after $2,000 of the HDHP's deductible has been satisfied (i.e., if the individual incurs covered medical expenses of $2,250, the HRA will pay $250). Because the HRA's deductible of $2,000 is less than the HDHP's deductible of $2,500, the individual's HSA contribution limit is $2,000.

Q-34. An account beneficiary wants to withdraw an excess contribution from an HSA before the due date of his or her federal income tax return (including extensions), to avoid the 6 percent excise tax under section 4973(a)(5). How is the net income attributable to the excess contribution computed?

A-34. Section 223(f)(3)(A)(ii) provides that any distribution of excess contribution to an HSA must be "accompanied by the amount of net income attributable to such excess contribution." Any net income is included in the individual's gross income. The rules for computing attributable net income for excess IRA contributions apply to HSAs. See Treas. Reg. §1.408-11 and Notice 2004-2, Q&A 22.

Q-35. May an individual who has not made excess HSA contributions treat a distribution from an HSA other than for qualified medical expenses as the withdrawal of excess HSA contributions?

A-35. No. This withdrawal is deemed a withdrawal for non-qualified medical expenses and includable in the individual's gross income under section 223(f)

(2). (The additional tax under section 223(f)(4) also applies, unless otherwise excepted).

V. Distributions

Q-36. If an account beneficiary's spouse or dependents are covered under a non-HDHP, are distributions from an HSA to pay their qualified medical expenses excluded from the account beneficiary's gross income?

A-36. Yes. Distributions from an HSA are excluded from income if made for any qualified medical expense of the account beneficiary, the account beneficiary's spouse and dependents (without regard to their status as eligible individuals). However, distributions made for expenses reimbursed by another health plan are not excludable from gross income, whether or not the other health plan is an HDHP. See Notice 2004-2, Q&A 26.

Q-37. An account beneficiary receives an HSA distribution as the result of a mistake of fact due to reasonable cause (e.g., the account beneficiary reasonably, but mistakenly, believed that an expense was a qualified medical expense and was reimbursed for that expense from the HSA). The account beneficiary then repays the mistaken distribution to the HSA. Is the mistaken distribution included in gross income under section 223(f)(2) and subject to the 10 percent additional tax under section 223(f)(4) or subject to the excise tax on excess contributions under section 4973(a)(5)?

A-37. If there is clear and convincing evidence that amounts were distributed from an HSA because of a mistake of fact due to reasonable cause, the account beneficiary may repay the mistaken distribution no later than April 15 following the first year the account beneficiary knew or should have known the distribution was a mistake. Under these circumstances, the distribution is not included in gross income under section 223(f)(2), or subject to the 10 percent additional tax under section 223(f)(4), and the repayment is not subject to the excise tax on excess contributions under section 4973(a)(5). But see Q&A 76 on the trustee's or custodian's obligation to accept a return of mistaken distributions.

Q-38. If both spouses have HSAs and one spouse uses distributions from his or her HSA to pay or reimburse the section 213(d) qualified medical expenses of the other spouse, are the distributions excluded from the account beneficiary's gross income under section 223(f)?

A-38. Yes. However, both HSAs may not reimburse the same expense amounts.

Q-39. When must a distribution from an HSA be taken to pay or reimburse, on a tax-free basis, qualified medical expenses incurred in the current year?

A-39. An account beneficiary may defer to later taxable years distributions from HSAs to pay or reimburse qualified medical expenses incurred in the current year as long as the expenses were incurred after the HSA was established. Similarly, a distribution from an HSA in the current year can be used to pay or reimburse expenses incurred in any prior year as long as the expenses were incurred after the HSA was established. Thus, there is no time limit on when the distribution must occur. However, to be excludable from the account beneficiary's gross income, he or she must keep records sufficient to later show that the distributions were exclusively to pay or reimburse qualified medical expenses, that the qualified medical expenses have not been previously paid or reimbursed from another source and that the medical expenses have not been taken as an itemized deduction in any prior taxable year. See Notice 2004-2, Q&A 31 and also Notice 2004-25, for transition relief in calendar year 2004 for reimbursement of medical expenses incurred before opening an HSA.

> **Example.** An eligible individual contributes $1,000 to an HSA in 2004. On December 1, 2004, the individual incurs a $1,500 qualified medical expense and has a balance in his HSA of $1,025. On January 3, 2005, the individual contributes another $1,000 to the HSA, bringing the balance in the HSA to $2,025. In June, 2005, the individual receives a distribution of $1,500 to reimburse him for the $1,500 medical expense incurred in 2004. The individual can show that the $1,500 HSA distribution in 2005 is a reimbursement for a qualified medical expense that has not been previously paid or otherwise reimbursed and has not been taken as an itemized deduction. The distribution is excludable from the account beneficiary's gross income.

Q-40. May an account beneficiary pay qualified long-term care insurance premiums with distributions from an HSA if contributions to the HSA are made by salary-reduction though a section 125 cafeteria plan?

A-40. Yes. Section 125(f) provides that the term "qualified benefit" under a section 125 cafeteria plan shall not include any product which is advertised, marketed, or offered as long-term care insurance. However, for HSA purposes, section 223(d)(2)(C)(ii) provides that the payment of any expense for coverage under a qualified long-term care insurance contract (as defined in section 7702B (b)) is a qualified medical expense. Where an HSA that is offered under a cafeteria plan pays or reimburses individuals for qualified long-term care insurance premiums, section 125(f) is not applicable because it is the HSA and not the long-term care insurance that is offered under the cafeteria plan.

Q-41. Do the section 213(d)(10) limits on the deduction for "eligible long-term care premiums" restrict the amount of distributions for qualified medical expenses that may be excluded from income under an HSA?

A-41. Yes. "Eligible long-term care premiums" are deductible medical expenses under section 213, but the deduction is limited to the annually adjusted amounts in section 213(d)(10) (based on age). See Rev. Proc. 2003-85 §3.18, 2003-49 I.R. B. 1184 for the 2004 limits. Thus, although HSA distributions to pay or reimburse qualified long-term care insurance premiums are qualified medical expenses, the exclusion from gross income is limited to the adjusted amounts under section 213(d)(10). Any excess premium reimbursements are includable in gross income and may also be subject to the 10 percent penalty under section 223 (f)(4).

> **Example.** In 2004, X, age 41, pays premiums of $1,290 for a qualified long-term care insurance contract. The section 213(d)(10) limit in calendar year 2004 for deductions for persons age 40, but not more than 50, is $490. X's HSA can reimburse X up to $490 on a tax-free basis for the long-term care

premiums. The remaining $800 ($1,290-$490), if reimbursed from the HSA, is not for qualified medical expenses and is includable in gross income.

Q-42. Are distributions from an HSA for long-term care services qualified medical expenses which are excluded from income?

A-42. Yes. Section 106(c) provides that employer-provided coverage for long-term care services provided through a flexible spending or similar arrangement are included in an employee's gross income. Section 213(d)(1)(C) provides that amounts paid for qualified long-term care services are medical care and section 223(f)(1) provides that amounts paid or distributed out of an HSA used to pay for qualified medical expenses are not includible in gross income. Qualified medical expenses are amounts paid for medical care (as defined in section 213(d)) for the account beneficiary, his or her spouse and dependents. Although section 106(c) applies to benefits provided by a flexible spending or similar arrangement, it does not apply to distributions from an HSA, which is a personal health care savings vehicle used to pay for qualified medical expenses through a trust or custodial account, whether or not the HSA is funded by salary-reduction contributions through a section 125 cafeteria plan.

Q-43. May a retiree who is age 65 or older receive tax-free distributions from an HSA to pay the retiree's contribution to an employer's self-insured retiree health coverage?

A-43. Yes. Pursuant to section 223(d)(2)(B), the purchase of health insurance is generally not a qualified medical expense that can be paid or reimbursed by an HSA. See Notice 2004-2, Q&A 27. However, section 223(d)(2)(C)(iv) provides an exception for coverage for health insurance once an account beneficiary has attained age 65. The exception applies to both insured and self-insured plans.

Q-44. May an individual who is under age 65 and has end stage renal disease (ESRD) or is disabled receive tax-free distributions from an HSA to pay for health insurance premiums?

A-44. No. Section 223(d)(2)(B) provides that health insurance may not be paid by an HSA. However, section 223(d)(2)(C)(iv) provides that payment of health insurance premiums are qualified medical expenses, but only in the case of an account beneficiary who has attained the age specified in section 1811 of the Social Security Act (i.e., age 65).

Q-45. If a retiree who is enrolled in Medicare receives a distribution from an HSA to reimburse the retiree's Medicare premiums, is the reimbursement a qualified medical expense under section 223(d)(2)?

A-45. Yes. Where premiums for Medicare are deducted from Social Security benefit payments, an HSA distribution to reimburse the Medicare beneficiary equal to the Medicare premium deduction is a qualified medical expense.

VI. Comparability

Q-46. Does an employer who offers to make available a contribution to the HSA of each employee who is an eligible individual in an amount equal to the employee's HSA contribution or a percentage of the employee's HSA contribution (i.e., "matching contributions") satisfy the requirement under section 4980G that all comparable participating employees receive comparable contributions?

A-46. If all employees who are eligible individuals do not contribute the same amount to their HSAs and, consequently, do not receive comparable contributions to their HSAs, the section 4980G comparability rules are not satisfied, notwithstanding that the employer offers to make available the same contribution amount to each employee who is an eligible individual. But see Q&A 47 on comparable contributions made through a cafeteria plan.

Q-47. If an employer makes contributions through a cafeteria plan to the HSA of each employee who is an eligible individual in an amount equal to the amount of the employee's HSA contribution or a percentage of the amount of the employee's HSA contribution (i.e., "matching contributions"), are the contributions subject to the section 4980G comparability rules?

A-47. No. The conference report for the Medicare Prescription Drug, Improvement, and Modernization Act of 2003 states that the comparability rules do not apply to contributions made through a cafeteria plan. Conf. Rep. No. 391, 108th Cong., 1st Sess. 840 (2003). Notice 2004-2, Q&A 32 similarly provides that the comparability rules do not apply to HSA contributions made through a cafeteria plan. Thus, where matching contributions are made by an employer through a cafeteria plan, the contributions are not subject to the comparability rules of section 4980G. However, contributions, including "matching contributions", to an HSA made under a cafeteria plan are subject to the section 125 nondiscrimination rules (eligibility rules, contributions and benefits tests and key employee concentration tests). See section 125(b), (c) and (g) and Prop. Treas. Reg. §1.125-1, Q&A 19.

Q-48. If an employer conditions contributions by the employer to an employee's HSA on an employee's participation in health assessments, disease management programs or wellness programs and makes the same contributions available to all employees who participate in the programs, do the contributions satisfy the section 4980G comparability rules?

A-48. If all eligible employees do not elect to participate in all the programs and consequently, all employees who are eligible individuals do not receive comparable contributions to their HSAs, the employer contributions fail to satisfy the section 4980G comparability rules. But see Q&A 49 on comparable contributions made through a cafeteria plan.

Q-49. If under the employer's cafeteria plan, employees who are eligible individuals and who participate in health assessments, disease management programs or wellness programs receive an employer contribution to an HSA, unless the employee elects cash, are the contributions subject to the section 4980G comparability rules?

A-49. No. The comparability rules under section 4980G do not apply to employer contributions to an HSA through a cafeteria plan.

Q-50. If an employer offers to make available additional HSA contributions to all employees who are eligible individuals and who have attained a specified age or who qualify for the additional contributions under section 223(b)(3) (catch-up contributions), do the contributions satisfy the section 4980G comparability rules?

A-50. No. If all employees who are eligible individuals do not meet the age requirement or do not qualify for the additional contributions under section 223 (b)(3), all employees who are eligible individuals do not receive comparable contributions to their HSAs and the employer contributions fail to satisfy the section 4980G comparability rules.

Q-51. How do the comparability rules in section 4980G apply to employer contributions to employees' HSAs if some employees work full-time during the entire calendar year, and other employees work full-time for less than the entire calendar year?

A-51. An employer contributing to HSAs of employees who work full-time for less than twelve months, satisfies the comparability rules if the contribution amount is comparable when determined on a month-to-month basis. For example, if the employer contributes $240 to the HSAs of each full-time employee who works the entire calendar year, the employer must contribute $60 to the HSA of a full-time employee who works three months of the year. See section 4980G(b) and section 4980E(d)(2)(B). See also Notice 2004-2, Q&A 32 on comparability rules for part-time employees (i.e., employees who are customarily employed for fewer than 30 hours per week).

Q-52. What is the testing period for making comparable contributions to employees' HSAs?

A-52. To satisfy the comparability rule in section 4980G, an employer must make comparable contributions for the calendar year to HSAs of employees who are eligible individuals. See section 4980G and section 4980E(d).

Q-53. Under section 4980G, must an employer make comparable contributions to all employees who are eligible individuals or only to those employees who are eligible individuals and are also covered by an HDHP provided by the employer?

A-53. If during a calendar year, an employer contributes to the HSA of any employee covered under an HDHP provided by the employer, the employer is required to make comparable contributions to all eligible individuals with coverage under any HDHP provided by the employer. An employer that contributes to the HSAs of employees with coverage under the HDHP provided by the employer is not required to make comparable contributions to HSAs of employees who are not covered under the HDHP provided by the employer. However, an employer that contributes to the HSA of any eligible individual with coverage under any HDHP, even if that coverage is not an HDHP of the employer, must make comparable contributions to all eligible individuals whether or not covered under an HDHP of the employer. See also Notice 2004-2, Q&A 32.

> **Example (1).** An employer offers an HDHP to its full-time employees. Most full-time employees are covered under the employer's HDHP and the

employer makes comparable contributions only to these employees' HSAs. Employee D, a full-time employee and an eligible individual (as defined in section 223(c)(1)), is covered under his spouse's HDHP and not under his employer's HDHP. The employer is not required to make comparable contributions to D's HSA.

Example (2). An employer does not offer an HDHP. Several full-time employees, who are eligible individuals (as defined in section 223(c)(1)), have HSAs. The employer contributes to these employees' HSAs. The employer must make comparable contributions to the HSAs of all full-time employees who are eligible individuals.

Example (3). An employer offers an HDHP to its full-time employees. Most full-time employees are covered under the employer's HDHP and the employer makes comparable contributions to these employees' HSAs and also to HSAs of full-time employees not covered under the employer's HDHP. Employee E, a full-time employee and an eligible individual (as defined in section 223(c)(1)), is covered under his spouse's HDHP and not under his employer's HDHP. The employer must make comparable contributions to E's HSA.

Q-54. If an employee requests that his or her employer deduct after-tax amounts from the employee's compensation and forward these amounts as employee contributions to the employee's HSA, do the section 4980G comparability rules apply to these amounts?

A-54. No. Section 106(d) provides that amounts contributed by an employer to an eligible employee's HSA shall be treated as employer-provided coverage for medical expenses and excludable from the employee's gross income up to the limit in section 223(b). After-tax employee contributions to the HSA are not subject to section 4980G because they are not employer contributions under section 106(d). See Notice 2004-2, Q&A 12 on aggregation of HSA contributions.

VII. Rollovers

Q-55. How frequently may an account beneficiary make rollover contributions to an HSA under section 223(f)(5)?

A-55. An account beneficiary may make only one rollover contribution to an HSA during a 1-year period. In addition, to qualify as a rollover, any amount paid or distributed from an HSA to an account beneficiary must be paid over to an HSA within 60 days after the date of receipt of the payment or distribution. But see Q&A 78 regarding trustee's or custodian's obligation to accept rollovers. See also Notice 2004-2, Q&A 23 for additional rules on rollovers.

Q-56. Are transfers of HSA amounts from one HSA trustee directly to another HSA trustee (trustee-to-trustee transfers), subject to the rollover restrictions?

A-56. No. The rules under section 223(f)(5) limiting the number of rollover contributions to one a year do not apply to trustee-to-trustee transfers. Thus, there is no limit on the number of trustee-to-trustee transfers allowed during a year.

VIII. Cafeteria Plans and HSAs

Q-57. Which requirements that apply to health flexible spending arrangements (FSAs) under a section 125 cafeteria plan do not apply to HSAs?

A-57. The following requirements for health FSAs under a section 125 cafeteria plan (which are generally imposed so that health FSAs operate in a manner similar to "insurance-type" accident or health plans under section 105) are not applicable to HSAs: (1) the prohibition against a benefit that defers compensation by permitting employees to carry over unused elective contributions or plan benefits from one plan year to another plan year (See section 125(d)(2)(D)); (2) the requirement that the maximum amount of reimbursement must be available at all times during the coverage period; and (3) the mandatory twelve-month period of coverage.

Q-58. Do the section 125 change in status rules apply to elections of HSA contributions through a cafeteria plan?

A-58. A cafeteria plan may permit an employee to revoke an election during a period of coverage with respect to a qualified benefit and make a new election for the remaining portion of the period only as provided in Treas. Reg. §1.125-4. Because the eligibility requirements and contribution limits for HSAs are determined on a month-by-month basis, rather than on an annual basis, an employee who elects to make HSA contributions under a cafeteria plan may start or stop the election or increase or decrease the election at any time as long as the change is effective prospectively (i.e., after the request for the change is received). If an employer places additional restrictions on the election of HSA contributions under a cafeteria plan, the same restrictions must apply to all employees.

Q-59. Can an employer permit employees to elect an HSA mid-year if offered as a new benefit under the employer's cafeteria plan?

A-59. Yes, if the election for the HSA is made on a prospective basis. However, the HSA election does not permit a change or revocation of any other coverage under the cafeteria plan unless the change is permitted by Treas. Reg. §1.125-4. Thus, while an HSA may be offered to and elected by an employee mid-year, the employee may have other coverage under the cafeteria plan that cannot be changed, (e.g., coverage under a health FSA), which may prevent the employee from being an eligible individual. See Rev. Rul. 2004-45.

Q-60. If an employee elects to make contributions to an HSA through the employer's cafeteria plan, may the employer contribute amounts to an employee's HSA to cover qualified medical expenses incurred by an employee that exceed the employee's current HSA balance?

A-60. Yes. Where an employee elects to make contributions to an HSA through a cafeteria plan, the employer may, but is not required to, contribute amounts to an employee's HSA up to the maximum amount elected by the employee. While any accelerated contribution made by the employer must be equally available to all participating employees throughout the plan year and must be provided to all participating employees on the same terms, the employee must repay the amount of the accelerated contribution by the end of the plan year. But see Q&A 82 on recoupment of HSA contributions by an employer.

Q-61. Can employers provide negative elections for HSAs if offered through a cafeteria plan?

A-61. Yes. See Rev. Rul. 2002-27, 2002-1 C.B. 925.

IX. Account Administration

Q-62. Are there model IRS forms for establishing HSAs?

A-62. Yes. See Form 5305-B "Health Savings Trust Account" and Form 5305-C "Health Savings Custodial Account."

Q-63. May a husband and wife have a joint HSA?

A-63. No. Each spouse who is an "eligible individual" as described in section 223 (c)(1) and wants to make contributions to an HSA must open a separate HSA. Thus, only one person may be the account beneficiary of an HSA. But see Q&A 32 concerning allocating contributions between spouses. See also Q&A 38 concerning reimbursements from spousal HSAs.

Q-64. May an eligible individual have more than one HSA?

A-64. Yes. An eligible individual may establish more than one HSA, and may contribute to more than one HSA. The same rules governing HSAs apply (e.g., maximum contribution limit), regardless of the number of HSAs established by an eligible individual. See also Notice 2004-2, Q&A 12.

> **Example.** For 2004, eligible individual A's maximum contribution to an HSA is $2,400. For 2004, A's employer contributes $1,000 to an HSA on behalf of A. A opens a second HSA and contributes $1,400. If additional contributions are made for 2004 to either of the HSAs, then there are excess contributions to A's HSAs.

Q-65. What are permissible investments for HSAs?

A-65. HSA funds may be invested in investments approved for IRAs (e.g., bank accounts, annuities, certificates of deposit, stocks, mutual funds, or bonds). HSAs may not invest in life insurance contracts, or in collectibles (e.g., any work of art, antique, metal, gem, stamp, coin, alcoholic beverage, or other tangible personal property specified in IRS guidance under section 408(m)). HSAs may, however, invest in certain types of bullion or coins, as described in section 408 (m)(3). The HSA trust or custodial agreement may restrict investments to certain types of permissible investments (e.g., particular investment funds).

Q-66. May HSA funds be commingled in a common trust fund or common investment fund?

A-66. Section 223(d)(1)(D) states that the HSA trust assets may not be commingled except in a common trust fund or common investment fund. Thus, individual accounts maintained on behalf of individual HSA account beneficiaries may be held in a common trust fund or common investment fund. A "common trust fund" is defined in Treas. Reg. §1.408-2(b)(5)(ii). A "common investment fund" is defined in section 584(a)(1).

Q-67. Are there any transactions which account beneficiaries are prohibited from entering into with an HSA?

A-67. Yes. Section 223(e)(2) provides that rules similar to the rules of section 408 (e)(2) and (4) shall apply to HSAs. Therefore, account beneficiaries may not enter into "prohibited transactions" with an HSA (e.g., the account beneficiary may not sell, exchange, or lease property, borrow or lend money, furnish goods, services or facilities, transfer to or use by or for the benefit of himself/herself any assets, pledge the HSA, etc.). Any amount treated as distributed as the result of a prohibited transaction will not be treated as used to pay for qualified medical expenses. The account beneficiary must, therefore, include the distribution in gross income and generally will be subject to the additional 10 percent tax on distributions not made for qualified medical expenses. See Notice 2004-2, Q&A 25.

Q-68. Are HSA trustees and custodians also subject to the rules against prohibited transactions?

A-68. Yes. The same rules that apply to account beneficiaries apply to trustees and custodians.

Q-69. If administration and account maintenance fees (e.g., flat administrative fees) are withdrawn from the HSA, are the withdrawn amounts treated as taxable distributions to the account beneficiary?

A-69. No. Amounts withdrawn from an HSA for administration and account maintenance fees will not be treated as a taxable distribution and will not be included in the account beneficiary's gross income.

Q-70. If administration and account maintenance fees are withdrawn from the HSA, does the withdrawn amount increase the maximum annual HSA contribution limit?

A-70. No. For example, if the maximum annual contribution limit is $2,000, and a $25 administration fee is withdrawn from the HSA, the annual contribution limit is still $2,000, not $2,025.

Q-71. If administration and account maintenance fees are paid by the account beneficiary or employer directly to the trustee or custodian, do these payments count toward the annual maximum contribution limit for the HSA?

A-71. No. Administration and account maintenance fees paid directly by the account beneficiary or employer will not be considered contributions to the HSA. For example, an individual contributes the maximum annual amount to his HSA of $2,000. The account beneficiary pays an annual administration fee of $25 directly to the trustee. The individual's maximum annual contribution limit is not affected by the payment of the administration fee.

X.   Trustees and Custodians

Q-72. Is any insurance company a qualified HSA trustee or custodian?

A-72. Yes. Any insurance company or any bank (including a similar financial institution as defined in section 408(n)) can be an HSA trustee or custodian. In addition, any other person already approved by the IRS to be a trustee or custodian of IRAs or Archer MSAs is automatically approved to be an HSA trustee or custodian. Other persons may request approval to be a trustee or custodian in accordance with the procedures set forth in Treas. Reg. §1.408-2(e) (relating to IRA nonbank trustees).

Q-73. Is there a limit on the annual HSA contribution which the trustee or custodian may accept?

A-73. Yes. Except in the case of rollover contributions described in section 223(f) (5) or trustee-to-trustee transfers, the trustee or custodian may not accept annual contributions to any HSA that exceed the sum of: (1) the dollar amount in effect under section 223(b)(2)(B)(ii) (i.e., the maximum family coverage deductible) plus (2) the dollar amount in effect under section 223(b)(3)(B) (i.e., the catch-up contribution amount). All contributions must be in cash, other than rollover contributions or trustee-to-trustee transfers. See section 223(d)(1)(A).

Q-74. Is the HSA trustee or custodian responsible for determining whether contributions to an HSA exceed the maximum annual contribution for a particular account beneficiary?

A-74. No. This is the responsibility of the account beneficiary, who is also responsible for notifying the trustee or custodian of any excess contribution and requesting a withdrawal of the excess contribution together with any net income attributable to the excess contribution. The HSA trustee or custodian is, however, responsible for accepting cash contributions within the limits in Q&A 73 and for filing required information returns with the IRS (Form 5498-SA and Form 1099-SA).

Q-75. Is the trustee or custodian responsible for tracking the account beneficiary's age?

A-75. Yes. However, the trustee or custodian may rely on the account beneficiary's representation as to his or her date of birth.

Q-76. Must the trustee or custodian allow account beneficiaries to return mistaken distributions to the HSA?

A-76. No, this is optional. If the HSA trust or custodial agreement allows the return of mistaken distributions as described in Q&A 37, the trustee or custodian may rely on the account beneficiary's representation that the distribution was, in fact, a mistake.

Q-77. May an HSA trust or custodial agreement restrict the account beneficiary's ability to rollover amounts from that HSA?

A-77. No. Section 223(f)(5) permits the rollover of amounts in an HSA to another HSA, and transfers from one trustee to another trustee.

Q-78. Are HSA trustees or custodians required to accept rollover contributions or trustee-to-trustee transfers?

A-78. No. Rollover contributions or trustee-to-trustee transfers from other HSAs or from Archer MSAs are allowed, but trustees or custodians are not required to accept them. See Notice 2004-2, Q&A 23.

Q-79. May an HSA trust or custodial agreement restrict HSA distributions to pay or reimburse only the account beneficiary's qualified medical expenses?

A-79. No. The HSA trust or custodial agreement may not contain a provision that restricts HSA distributions to pay or reimburse only the account beneficiary's qualified medical expenses. Thus, the account beneficiary is entitled to distributions for any purpose and distributions may be used to pay or reimburse qualified medical expenses or for other nonmedical expenditures. Only the account beneficiary may determine how the HSA distributions will be used. But see Notice 2004-2, Q&A 25 on the taxation of HSA distributions not used exclusively for qualified medical expenses. See also Q&A 80 on restrictions on the frequency or minimum amount of HSA distributions.

Q-80. May a trustee or custodian restrict the frequency or minimum amount of distributions from an HSA?

A-80. Yes. Trustees or custodians may place reasonable restrictions on both the frequency and the minimum amount of distributions from an HSA. For example, the trustee may prohibit distributions for amounts of less than $50 or only allow a certain number of distributions per month. Generally, the terms regarding the frequency or minimum amount of distributions from an HSA are matters of contract between the trustee and the account beneficiary.

XI.   Other Issues

Q-81. Are employers who contribute to an employee's HSA responsible for determining whether the employee is an eligible individual and the employee's maximum annual contribution limit?

A-81. Employers are only responsible for determining the following with respect to an employee's eligibility and maximum annual contribution limit on HSA contributions: (1) whether the employee is covered under an HDHP (and the deductible) or low deductible health plan or plans (including health FSAs and HRAs) sponsored by that employer; and (2) the employee's age (for catch-up contributions). The employer may rely on the employee's representation as to his or her date of birth.

Q-82. May the employer recoup from an employee's HSA any portion of the employer's contribution to the employee's HSA?

A-82. No. Under section 223(d)(1)(E), an account beneficiary's interest in an HSA is nonforfeitable. For example, on January 2, 2005, the employer makes the maximum annual contribution to employees' HSAs, in the expectation that the employees would work for the entire calendar year 2005. On February 1, 2005, one employee terminates employment. The employer may not recoup from that employee's HSA any portion of the contribution previously made to the employee's HSA.

Q-83. Is an HSA distribution subject to the nondiscrimination rules of section 105(h)?

A-83. No. For amounts reimbursed to a highly compensated individual by a self-insured medical reimbursement plan to be fully excludable from the individual's gross income under section 105(b), the self-insured medical reimbursement plan must satisfy the requirements of section 105(h). Section 105(h) is not satisfied if the plan discriminates in favor of highly compensated individuals as to eligibility to participate or benefits. Because the exclusion from gross income for amounts distributed from an HSA is not determined by section 105(b), but by section 223(b), section 105(h) does not apply to HSAs.

Q-84. Is a deduction under section 223(a) for contributions to a self-employed individual's own HSA taken into account in determining net earnings from self-employment under section 1402(a)?

A-84. No. The deduction is an adjustment to gross income under section 62(a)(19), and is reportable on the self-employed individual's Form 1040 as an adjustment to gross income. It is not a deduction attributable to the self-employed individual's trade or business so it is not taken as a deduction on Schedule C, Form 1040, nor is it taken into account in determining net earnings from self-employment on Schedule SE, Form 1040.

Q-85. Does an employer's contribution to an employee's HSA affect the computation of the earned income credit (EIC) under section 32?

A-85. No. An employer's contributions to an employee's HSAs are not treated as earned income for EIC purposes.

Q-86. May an HDHP apply any required cost-of-living adjustments under section 223(g) to the minimum annual deductible amounts or maximum annual out-of-pocket expense limits on the renewal date of the HDHP if that date is after January 1?

A-86. Yes. Generally, an HDHP is a health plan that satisfies certain requirements with respect to minimum annual deductibles and maximum annual out-of-pocket expense. These annual amounts are indexed for inflation using annual cost-of-living adjustments. Any required change to the deductibles and out-of-pocket expense limits may be applied as of the renewal date of the HDHP in cases where the renewal date is after the beginning of the calendar year, but in no event longer than a 12-month period ending on the renewal date. Thus, a fiscal year plan that satisfies the minimum annual deductible on the first day of the first month of its fiscal year may apply that deductible for the entire fiscal year, even if the minimum annual deductible increases on January 1 of the next calendar year.

Example. An individual obtains self-only coverage under an HDHP on June 1, 2004, the first day of the plan year, with an annual deductible of $1,000. Assume that the cost-of living adjustments require the minimum deductible amount to be increased for 2005. The plan's deductible is not increased to comply with the increased minimum deductible amount until the plan's renewal date of June 1, 2005. The plan satisfies the requirements for an HDHP with respect to deductibles through May 30, 2005.

Q-87. Are HSAs available to bona fide residents of the Commonwealth of Puerto Rico, American Samoa, the U.S. Virgin Islands, Guam, and the Commonwealth of the Northern Mariana Islands?

A-87. Bona fide residents of the U.S. Virgin Islands, Guam and the Commonwealth of the Northern Mariana Islands may establish HSAs. However, bona fide residents of Puerto Rico and American Samoa may establish HSAs only after statutory provisions similar to sections 223 and 106(d) are enacted.

Q-88. If a C corporation makes a contribution to the HSA of a shareholder who is not an employee of the C corporation, what are the tax consequences to the shareholder and to the C corporation?

A-88. If a C corporation makes a contribution to the HSA of a shareholder who is not an employee of the C corporation, the contribution will be treated as a distribution under section 301. The distribution is treated as a dividend to the extent the C corporation has earnings and profits. The portion of the distribution which is not a dividend is applied against and reduces the adjusted basis of the stock. To the extent the amount of the distribution exceeds the adjusted basis of the stock, the balance is treated as gain from a sale or exchange of property.

EFFECT ON OTHER DOCUMENTS

Notice 2004-2, 2004-2 I.R.B. 269 is changed as follows:

The second sentence of A-2 is changed to read: An "eligible individual" means . . . (3) is not enrolled in Medicare. . . ."

The last sentence of A-12 is changed to read: "In addition to the maximum contribution amount, catch-up contributions, as described in [Notice 2004-2] A-14, may be made by or on behalf of individuals age 55 and older, who are not enrolled in Medicare."

The first sentence of A-14 is changed to read: "For individuals (and their spouses covered under the HDHP) who have attained 55 and are also not enrolled in Medicare. . . ."

The first sentence of the Example in A-14 is changed to read: "An individual attains age 65 and becomes enrolled in Medicare. . . ."

TRANSITION RELIEF

For months before January 1, 2005, a health plan that would otherwise qualify as an HDHP but for the lack of an express maximum on payments above the deductible that complies with the out-of-pocket requirement, as set forth in Q&A 17 and 20 will be treated as an HDHP. Individuals covered under these health plans will continue to be eligible to contribute to HSAs before January 1, 2005.

For months before January 1, 2006, a health plan that would otherwise qualify as an HDHP but for an annual deductible that does not satisfy the rule in Q&A 24 (concerning deductibles for periods of more than 12 months) will be treated as an HDHP if the plan was in effect or submitted to approval to state insurance regulators as of the date of publication of this notice in the Internal Revenue Bulletin. Individuals covered under these health plans will continue to be eligible to contribute to HSAs before January 1, 2006.

DRAFTING INFORMATION * * *

[1] Specific issues on HSAs are also discussed in Rev. Rul. 2004-45, 2004-22 I.R.B. 971; Rev. Rul. 2004-38, 2004-15 I.R.B. 717; Rev. Proc. 2004-22, 2004-15 I.R.B. 727; Notice 2004-43, 2004-27 I.R.B. 10; Notice 2004-25, 2004-15 I.R.B. 727; Notice 2004-22, 2004-15 I.R.B. 725.

. . . .

Notice 2004-43 (2004-27 I.R.B. 10)

[**Summary**: The IRS provides transitional relief for individuals in states where high deductible health plans are not available as a result of state law. Amplified by Notice 2005-83, 2005-49 I.R.B. 1075.]

PURPOSE

This notice provides transition relief for individuals in states where high deductible health plans (HDHPs) as described in section 223(c)(2) are not available because state laws require health plans to provide certain benefits without regard to a deductible or below the minimum annual deductible of section 223(c)(2)(A)(i). The transition relief covers months before January 1, 2006, for state requirements in effect on January 1, 2004.

BACKGROUND

Section 1201 of the Medicare Prescription Drug, Improvement, and Modernization Act of 2003, Pub. L. 108-173, added section 223 to the Internal Revenue Code to permit eligible individuals to establish health savings accounts (HSAs) for taxable years beginning after December 31, 2003. An "eligible individual" under section 223(c)(1) must be covered by a "high deductible health plan" (HDHP). An HDHP under section 223(c)(2) must satisfy certain requirements with respect to minimum annual deductibles and maximum out-of-pocket expenses. However, section 223(c)(2)(C) permits a safe harbor for the absence of a preventive care deductible. An eligible individual may also have certain permitted insurance and permitted coverage under section 223(c)(1)(B).

Notice 2004-23, 2004-15 I.R.B. 725, describes a safe harbor for preventive care benefits that may be provided by an HDHP without a deductible or with a deductible below the minimum annual deductible for an HDHP. In addition, the notice indicates that whether health care required by state law without regard to a deductible is "preventive" will be based on the standards set forth in Notice

2004-23 and other guidance issued by the IRS, rather than on how the benefits are characterized by state law.

Several states currently require that health plans provide certain benefits without regard to a deductible or with a deductible below the minimum annual deductible requirements of section 223(c)(2) (e.g., first-dollar coverage or coverage with a low deductible). These health plans are not HDHPs under section 223(c)(2) and individuals covered under these health plans are not eligible to contribute to HSAs. Because of the short period between the enactment of HSAs and the effective date of section 223, these states have had insufficient time to modify their laws to conform to the standards of section 223. Thus, it is appropriate to provide transition relief that treats HDHPs as qualifying under section 223(c)(2) when the sole reason the plans are not HDHPs is because of state-mandated benefits. During the transition period, otherwise eligible individuals covered under these plans will be treated as eligible individuals for purposes of section 223(c)(1) and may contribute to an HSA.

APPLICATION

For months before January 1, 2006, a health plan which would otherwise qualify as an HDHP under section 223(c)(2), except that it complies with state law requirements that certain benefits be provided without a deductible or below the minimum annual deductible of section 223(c)(2)(A)(i), will be treated as an HDHP for purposes of section 223(c)(2), if the disqualifying benefits are required by state law in effect on January 1, 2004.

DRAFTING INFORMATION * * *

Notice 2004-25 (2004-15 I.R.B. 727)

[**Summary:** In general, a qualifying HSAs may pay for qualified medical expenses incurred on or after the later of January 1, 2004, or the first day of the month in which the individual became an eligible participant. The IRS has provided relief for individuals who establish health savings accounts (HSA) on or before April 15, 2005. In doing so, it modified prior guidance and provided 2004 calendar year transitional relief allowing qualified medical expenses to be paid or reimbursed by an HSA if even though the HSA account was not in effect at the time the expenses were incurred.]

PURPOSE

[1] This notice provides transition relief for calendar year 2004 for eligible individuals who establish an HSA on or before April 15, 2005 from the requirement that qualified medical expenses may only be paid or reimbursed by an HSA if incurred after the HSA has been established. This notice modifies prior guidance in Q&A 26 of Notice 2004-2, 2004-2 I.R.B. 269.

[2] Section 1201 of the Medicare Prescription Drug, Improvement, and Modernization Act of 2003, Pub. L. No. 108–173, added section 223 to the Internal Revenue Code to permit eligible individuals to establish Health Savings Accounts (HSAs) for taxable years beginning after December 31, 2003. Because

of the short period between the enactment of HSAs and the effective date of section 223, many taxpayers who otherwise would be eligible to establish and contribute to HSAs (i.e., generally, individuals covered by a high deductible health plan (HDHP)) have been unable to do so because they cannot locate trustees or custodians who are willing and able to open HSAs at this time.
BACKGROUND

[3] Contributions to an HSA may only be made by or on behalf of eligible individuals as defined in section 223(c)(1)(A). For any month, an eligible individual must, among other requirements, be covered on the first day of the month by a HDHP (as defined by section 223(c)(2)). Although the amount of the contribution to an HSA is based on the number of months an individual is an eligible individual (i.e., is covered by the HDHP), contributions up to the annual maximum limit generally may be made to the HSA as early as the first day of the taxable year and as late as April 15 of the year following the year for which contributions are made. Notice 2004-2, Q&A 21.

[4] On January 12, 2004, Notice 2004-2 was published, providing general guidance concerning HSAs under section 223. The notice provides that distributions from an HSA exclusively to pay or reimburse qualified medical expenses of the account beneficiary, his or her spouse, or dependents, are excluded from gross income. Answer 26 of the notice states that, "The qualified medical expenses must be incurred only after the HSA has been established." However, after an HSA is established, distributions from the HSA exclusively to pay or reimburse qualified medical expenses continue to be excluded from the account beneficiary's gross income whether or not the account beneficiary continues to be an eligible individual. Notice 2004-2, Q&A 28.

TRANSITION RELIEF FOR HSAs ESTABLISHED FOR CALENDAR YEAR 2004

[5] For calendar year 2004, an HSA established by an eligible individual on or before April 15, 2005, may pay or reimburse on a tax-free basis an otherwise qualified medical expense if the qualified medical expense was incurred on or after the later of: (1) January 1, 2004, or (2) the first day of the first month that the individual became an eligible individual under section 223.

EFFECT ON OTHER DOCUMENTS

[6] The rule in the second sentence of Notice 2004-2, Q&A 26, which states that, "The qualified medical expenses must be incurred only after the HSA has been established," is suspended and replaced by the transition relief in this notice. That rule continues to apply to HSAs established for calendar year 2005 and later years.

DRAFTING INFORMATION * * *

Notice 2004-23 (2004-15 I.R.B. 725)

[**Summary:** The IRS issued an HSA safe harbor for preventive care benefits provided under an HSA with a list of services and benefits which qualify as "preventive care" under Code Section 223(c)(2)(C). The IRS also indicated that "preventive care" will be characterized by reference to the notice and other IRS guidance, instead of state law.]

PURPOSE

[1] This notice provides a safe harbor for preventive care benefits allowed to be provided by a high deductible health plan (HDHP) without satisfying the minimum deductible under section 223(c)(2) of the Internal Revenue Code.

BACKGROUND

[2] Section 1201 of the Medicare Prescription Drug, Improvement, and Modernization Act of 2003, Pub. L. No. 108-173, added section 223 to the Internal Revenue Code to permit eligible individuals to establish Health Savings Accounts (HSAs) for taxable years beginning after December 31, 2003.

[3] Among the requirements for an individual to qualify as an eligible individual under section 223(c)(1) (and thus to be eligible to make tax-favored contributions to an HSA) is the requirement that the individual be covered under an HDHP. An HDHP is a health plan that satisfies certain requirements with respect to minimum deductibles and maximum out-of-pocket expenses. Generally, an HDHP may not provide benefits for any year until the deductible for that year is satisfied. However, section 223(c)(2)(C) provides a safe harbor for the absence of a preventive care deductible. That section states, "[a] plan shall not fail to be treated as a high deductible health plan by reason of failing to have a deductible for preventive care (within the meaning of section 1871 of the Social Security Act, except as otherwise provided by the Secretary)." An HDHP may therefore provide preventive care benefits without a deductible or with a deductible below the minimum annual deductible. On the other hand, there is no requirement in section 223 that an HDHP provide benefits for preventive care or provide preventive care with a deductible below the minimum annual deductible.

PREVENTIVE CARE SAFE HARBOR

[4] Preventive care for purposes of section 223(c)(2)(C) includes, but is not limited to, the following:

- Periodic health evaluations, including tests and diagnostic procedures ordered in connection with routine examinations, such as annual physicals.

- Routine prenatal and well-child care.

- Child and adult immunizations.

- Tobacco cessation programs.

- Obesity weight-loss programs.

- Screening services (see attached APPENDIX).

However, preventive care does not generally include any service or benefit intended to treat an existing illness, injury, or condition (See below for request for comments regarding drug treatments.)

INTERACTION WITH STATE LAW HEALTH CARE REQUIREMENTS

[5] Section 220(c)(2)(B)(ii) allows a high deductible health plan for purposes of an Archer Medical Savings Account to provide preventive care without a deductible if required by State law. However, section 220 does not define preventive care for this purpose. Section 223(c)(2)(C), for purposes of an HSA, does not condition the exception for preventive care on State law requirements. State insurance laws often require health plans to provide certain health care without regard to a deductible or on terms no less favorable than other care provided by the health plan. The determination of whether health care that is required by State law to be provided by an HDHP without regard to a deductible is "preventive" for purposes of the exception for preventive care under section 223(c)(2)(C) will be based on the standards set forth in this notice and other guidance issued by the IRS, rather than on how that care is characterized by State law.

COMMENTS REQUESTED * * *

DRAFTING INFORMATION * * *

APPENDIX

Safe Harbor Preventive Care Screening Services

Cancer Screening
Breast Cancer (e.g., Mammogram)
Cervical Cancer (e.g., Pap Smear)
Colorectal Cancer
Prostate Cancer (e.g., PSA Test)
Skin Cancer
Oral Cancer
Ovarian Cancer
Testicular Cancer
Thyroid Cancer
Heart and Vascular Diseases Screening
Abdominal Aortic Aneurysm
Carotid Artery Stenosis
Coronary Heart Disease
Hemoglobinopathies
Hypertension
Lipid Disorders
Infectious Diseases Screening
Bacteriuria
Chlamydial Infection

Gonorrhea

Hepatitis B Virus Infection

Hepatitis C

Human Immunodeficiency Virus (HIV) Infection

Syphilis

Tuberculosis Infection

Mental Health Conditions and Substance Abuse Screening

Dementia

Depression

Drug Abuse

Problem Drinking

Suicide Risk

Family Violence

Metabolic, Nutritional, and Endocrine Conditions Screening

Anemia, Iron Deficiency

Dental and Periodontal Disease

Diabetes Mellitus

Obesity in Adults

Thyroid Disease

Musculoskeletal Disorders Screening

Osteoporosis

Obstetric and Gynecologic Conditions Screening

Bacterial Vaginosis in Pregnancy

Gestational Diabetes Mellitus

Home Uterine Activity Monitoring

Neural Tube Defects

Preeclampsia

Rh Incompatibility

Rubella

Ultrasonography in Pregnancy

Pediatric Conditions Screening

Child Developmental Delay

Congenital Hypothyroidism

Lead Levels in Childhood and Pregnancy

Phenylketonuria

Scoliosis, Adolescent Idiopathic

Vision and Hearing Disorders Screening

Glaucoma

Hearing Impairment in Older Adults
Newborn Hearing

Notice 2004-2 (2004-2 I.R.B. 269)

[**Summary:** This guidance contains basic information about HSAs including information on establishing and contributing to HSAs, withdrawals from HSAs, and HSA portability. HSA funds are completely portable, and, similar to IRA funds, can accumulate interest. Unlike flexible spending account funds, unused HSA funds can be rolled over from year to year. The guidance details ways in which tax-advantaged HSA contributions and rollovers can be made and includes a request for comments. Note: Notice 2004-2 was modified by Notice 2004-25, Notice 2004-50, and Announcement 2004-67, reproduced in this appendix.]

PURPOSE

This notice provides guidance on Health Savings Accounts.

BACKGROUND

Section 1201 of the Medicare Prescription Drug, Improvement, and Modernization Act of 2003, Pub. L. No. 108-173, added section 223 to the Internal Revenue Code to permit eligible individuals to establish Health Savings Accounts (HSAs) for taxable years beginning after December 31, 2003. HSAs are established to receive tax-favored contributions by or on behalf of eligible individuals and amounts in an HSA may be accumulated over the years or distributed on a tax-free basis to pay or reimburse qualified medical expenses.

A number of the rules that apply to HSAs are similar to rules that apply to Individual Retirement Accounts (IRAs) under sections 219, 408 and 408A, and to Archer Medical Savings Accounts (Archer MSAs) under section 220. For example, like an Archer MSA, an HSA is established for the benefit of an individual, is owned by that individual, and is portable. Thus, if the individual is an employee who later changes employers or leaves the work force, the HSA does not stay behind with the former employer, but stays with the individual.

This notice provides certain basic information about HSAs in question and answer format, without attempting to enumerate all of the specific rules that apply under section 223.

The notice is divided into five parts. Part I of the notice explains what HSAs are and who can have them. Part II describes how HSAs can be established. Parts III and IV cover contributions to HSAs and distributions from HSAs. Part V discusses other matters relating to HSAs.

QUESTIONS AND ANSWERS

Set forth below are questions and answers concerning HSAs.

I. *What Are HSAs and Who Can Have Them?*

Q-1. What is an HSA?

A-1. An HSA is a tax-exempt trust or custodial account established exclusively for the purpose of paying qualified medical expenses of the account beneficiary who, for the months for which contributions are made to an HSA, is covered under a high-deductible health plan.

Q-2. Who is eligible to establish an HSA?

A-2. An "eligible individual" can establish an HSA. An "eligible individual" means, with respect to any month, any individual who: (1) is covered under a high-deductible health plan (HDHP) on the first day of such month; (2) is not also covered by any other health plan that is not an HDHP (with certain exceptions for plans providing certain limited types of coverage); (3) is not enrolled in Medicare (generally, has not yet reached age 65); and (4) may not be claimed as a dependent on another person's tax return.

Q-3. What is a "high-deductible health plan" (HDHP)?

A-3. Generally, an HDHP is a health plan that satisfies certain requirements with respect to deductibles and out-of-pocket expenses. Specifically, for self-only coverage, an HDHP has an annual deductible of at least $1,000 and annual out-of-pocket expenses required to be paid (deductibles, co-payments and other amounts, but not premiums) not exceeding $5,000. For family coverage, an HDHP has an annual deductible of at least $2,000 and annual out-of-pocket expenses required to be paid not exceeding $10,000. In the case of family coverage, a plan is an HDHP only if, under the terms of the plan and without regard to which family member or members incur expenses, no amounts are payable from the HDHP until the family has incurred annual covered medical expenses in excess of the minimum annual deductible. Amounts are indexed for inflation. A plan does not fail to qualify as an HDHP merely because it does not have a deductible (or has a small deductible) for preventive care (e.g., first dollar coverage for preventive care). However, except for preventive care, a plan may not provide benefits for any year until the deductible for that year is met. *See* A-4 and A-6 for special rules regarding network plans and plans providing certain types of coverage.

> **Example (1):** A Plan provides coverage for A and his family The Plan provides for the payment of covered medical expenses of any member of A's family if the member has incurred covered medical expenses during the year in excess of $1,000 even if the family has not incurred covered medical expenses in excess of $2,000. If A incurred covered medical expenses of

$1,500 in a year, the Plan would pay $500. Thus, benefits are potentially available under the Plan even if the family's covered medical expenses do not exceed $2,000. Because the Plan provides family coverage with an annual deductible of less than $2,000, the Plan is not an HDHP.

Example (2): Same facts as in example (1), except that the Plan has a $5,000 family deductible and provides payment for covered medical expenses if any member of A's family has incurred covered medical expenses during the year in excess of $2,000 The Plan satisfies the requirements for an HDHP with respect to the deductibles. *See* A-12 for HSA contribution limits.

Q-4. What are the special rules for determining whether a health plan that is a network plan meets the requirements of an HDHP?

A-4. A network plan is a plan that generally provides more favorable benefits for services provided by its network of providers than for services provided outside of the network. In the case of a plan using a network of providers, the plan does not fail to be an HDHP (if it would otherwise meet the requirements of an HDHP) solely because the out-of-pocket expense limits for services provided outside of the network exceeds the maximum annual out-of-pocket expense limits allowed for an HDHP. In addition, the plan's annual deductible for out-of-network services is not taken into account in determining the annual contribution limit. Rather, the annual contribution limit is determined by reference to the deductible for services within the network.

Q-5. What kind of other health coverage makes an individual ineligible for an HSA?

A-5. Generally, an individual is ineligible for an HSA if the individual, while covered under an HDHP, is also covered under a health plan (whether as an individual, spouse, or dependent) that is not an HDHP. *See also* A-6.

Q-6. What other kinds of health coverage may an individual maintain without losing eligibility for an HSA?

A-6. An individual does not fail to be eligible for an HSA merely because, in addition to an HDHP, the individual has coverage for any benefit provided by "permitted insurance." Permitted insurance is insurance under which substantially all of the coverage provided relates to liabilities incurred under workers' compensation laws, tort liabilities, liabilities relating to ownership or use of property (e.g., automobile insurance), insurance for a specified disease or illness, and insurance that pays a fixed amount per day (or other period) of hospitalization.

In addition to permitted insurance, an individual does not fail to be eligible for an HSA merely because, in addition to an HDHP, the individual has coverage (whether provided through insurance or otherwise) for accidents, disability, dental care, vision care, or long-term care. If a plan that is intended to be an HDHP is one in which substantially all of the coverage of the plan is through permitted insurance or other coverage as described in this answer, it is not an HDHP.

Q-7. Can a self-insured medical reimbursement plan sponsored by an employer be an HDHP?

A-7. Yes.

II. *How Can An HSA Be Established?*

Q-8. How does an eligible individual establish an HSA?

A-8. Beginning January 1, 2004, any eligible individual (as described in A-2) can establish an HSA with a qualified HSA trustee or custodian, in much the same way that individuals establish IRAs or Archer MSAs with qualified IRA or Archer MSA trustees or custodians. No permission or authorization from the Internal Revenue Service (IRS) is necessary to establish an HSA. An eligible individual who is an employee may establish an HSA with or without involvement of the employer.

Q-9. Who is a qualified HSA trustee or custodian?

A-9. Any insurance company or any bank (including a similar financial institution as defined in section 408(n)) can be an HSA trustee or custodian. In addition, any other person already approved by the IRS to be a trustee or custodian of IRAs or Archer MSAs is automatically approved to be an HSA trustee or custodian. Other persons may request approval to be a trustee or custodian in accordance with the procedures set forth in Treas. Reg. §1.408-2(e) (relating to IRA nonbank trustees). For additional information concerning non-bank trustees and custodians, *see* Announcement 2003-54, 2003-40 I.R.B. 761.

Q-10. Does the HSA have to be opened at the same institution that provides the HDHP?

A-10. No. The HSA can be established through a qualified trustee or custodian who is different from the HDHP provider. Where a trustee or custodian does not sponsor the HDHP, the trustee or custodian may require proof or certification that the account beneficiary is an eligible individual, including that the individual is covered by a health plan that meets all of the requirements of an HDHP.

III. *Contributions to HSAs.*

Q-11. Who may contribute to an HSA?

A-11. Any eligible individual may contribute to an HSA. For an HSA established by an employee, the employee, the employee's employer or both may contribute to the HSA of the employee in a given year. For an HSA established by a self-employed (or unemployed) individual, the individual may contribute to the HSA. Family members may also make contributions to an HSA on behalf of another family member as long as that other family member is an eligible individual.

Q-12. How much may be contributed to an HSA in calendar year 2004?

A-12. The maximum annual contribution to an HSA is the sum of the limits determined separately for each month, based on status, eligibility and health plan coverage as of the first day of the month. For calendar year 2004, the maximum monthly contribution for eligible individuals with self-only coverage under an HDHP is 1/12 of the lesser of 100% of the annual deductible under the HDHP (minimum of $1,000) but not more than $2,600. For eligible individuals with family coverage under an HDHP, the maximum monthly contribution is 1/12 of the lesser of 100% of the annual deductible under the HDHP (minimum of $2,000) but not more than $5,150. In addition to the maximum contribution amount, catch-up contributions, as described in A-14, may be made by or on behalf of individuals age 55 and older, who are not enrolled in Medicare.

All HSA contributions made by or on behalf of an eligible individual to an HSA are aggregated for purposes of applying the limit. The annual limit is decreased by the aggregate contributions to an Archer MSA. The same annual contribution limit applies whether the contributions are made by an employee, an employer, a self-employed person, or a family member. Unlike Archer MSAs, contributions may be made by or on behalf of eligible individuals even if the individuals have no compensation or if the contributions exceed their compensation. If an individual has more than one HSA, the aggregate annual contributions to all the HSAs are subject to the limit.

Q-13. How is the contribution limit computed for an individual who begins self-only coverage under an HDHP on June 1, 2004 and continues to be covered under the HDHP for the rest of the year?

A-13. The contribution limit is computed each month. If the annual deductible is $5,000 for the HDHP, then the lesser of the annual deductible and $2,600 is $2,600. The monthly contribution limit is $216.67 ($2,600/12). The annual contribution limit is $1,516.69 (7 × $216.67).

Q-14. What are the "catch-up contributions" for individuals age 55 or older?

A-14. For individuals (and their spouses covered under the HDHP) who have attained 55 and are also not enrolled in Medicare, the HSA contribution limit is increased by $500 in calendar year 2004. This catch-up amount will increase in $100 increments annually, until it reaches $1,000 in calendar year 2009. As with the annual contribution limit, the catch-up contribution is also computed on a monthly basis. After an individual has attained age 65 and becomes enrolled in Medicare benefits, contributions, including catch-up contributions, cannot be made to an individual's HSA.

> **Example:** An individual attains age 65 and becomes enrolled in Medicare in July, 2004 and had been participating in self-only coverage under an HDHP with an annual deductible of $1,000 The individual is no longer eligible to make HSA contributions (including catch-up contributions) after June, 2004. The monthly contribution limit is $125 ($1,000/12 + $500/12 for the catch-up

contribution). The individual may make contributions for January through June totaling $750 (6 × $125), but may not make any contributions for July through December, 2004.

Q-15. If one or both spouses have family coverage, how is the contribution limit computed?

A-15. In the case of individuals who are married to each other, if either spouse has family coverage, both are treated as having family coverage. If each spouse has family coverage under a separate health plan, both spouses are treated as covered under the plan with the lowest deductible. The contribution limit for the spouses is the lowest deductible amount, divided equally between the spouses unless they agree on a different division. The family coverage limit is reduced further by any contribution to an Archer MSA. However, both spouses may make the catch-up contributions for individuals age 55 or over without exceeding the family coverage limit.

Example (1): H and W are married H is 58 and W is 53. H and W both have family coverage under separate HDHPs. H has a $3,000 deductible under his HDHP and W has a $2,000 deductible under her HDHP. H and W are treated as covered under the plan with the $2,000 deductible. H can contribute $1,500 to an HSA (1/2 the deductible of $2,000 + $500 catch up contribution) and W can contribute $1,000 to an HSA (unless they agree to a different division).

Example (2): H and W are married H is 35 and W is 33. H and W each have a self-only HDHP. H has a $1,000 deductible under his HDHP and W has a $1,500 deductible under her HDHP. H can contribute $1,000 to an HSA and W can contribute $1,500 to an HSA.

Q-16. In what form must contributions be made to an HSA?

A-16. Contributions to an HSA must be made in cash. For example, contributions may not be made in the form of stock or other property. Payments for the HDHP and contributions to the HSA can be made through a cafeteria plan. *See* A-33.

Q-17. What is the tax treatment of an eligible individual's HSA contributions?

A-17. Contributions made by an eligible individual to an HSA (which are subject to the limits described in A-12) are deductible by the eligible individual in determining adjusted gross income (i.e., "above-the-line"). The contributions are deductible whether or not the eligible individual itemizes deductions. However, the individual cannot also deduct the contributions as medical expense deductions under section 213.

Q-18. What is the tax treatment of contributions made by a family member on behalf of an eligible individual?

A-18. Contributions made by a family member on behalf of an eligible individual to an HSA (which are subject to the limits described in A-12) are deductible by the eligible individual in computing adjusted gross income. The contributions are deductible whether or not the eligible individual itemizes deductions. An individual who may be claimed as a dependent on another person's tax return is not an eligible individual and may not deduct contributions to an HSA.

Q-19. What is the tax treatment of employer contributions to an employee's HSA?

A-19. In the case of an employee who is an eligible individual, employer contributions (provided they are within the limits described in A-12) to the employee's HSA are treated as employer-provided coverage for medical expenses under an accident or health plan and are excludable from the employee's gross income. The employer contributions are not subject to withholding from wages for income tax or subject to the Federal Insurance Contributions Act (FICA), the Federal Unemployment Tax Act (FUTA), or the Railroad Retirement Tax Act. Contributions to an employee's HSA through a cafeteria plan are treated as employer contributions. The employee cannot deduct employer contributions on his or her federal income tax return as HSA contributions or as medical expense deductions under section 213.

Q-20. What is the tax treatment of an HSA?

A-20. An HSA is generally exempt from tax (like an IRA or Archer MSA), unless it has ceased to be an HSA. Earnings on amounts in an HSA are not includable in gross income while held in the HSA (i.e., inside buildup is not taxable). *See* A-25 regarding the taxation of distributions to the account beneficiary.

Q-21. When may HSA contributions be made? Is there a deadline for contributions to an HSA for a taxable year?

A-21. Contributions for the taxable year can be made in one or more payments, at the convenience of the individual or the employer, at any time prior to the time prescribed by law (without extensions) for filing the eligible individual's federal income tax return for that year, but not before the beginning of that year. For calendar year taxpayers, the deadline for contributions to an HSA is generally April 15 following the year for which the contributions are made. Although the annual contribution is determined monthly, the maximum contribution may be made on the first day of the year. *See* A-22 regarding correcting excess contributions.

> **Example:** B has self-only coverage under an HDHP with a deductible of $1,500 and also has an HSA B's employer contributes $200 to B's HSA at the end of every quarter in 2004 and at the end of the first quarter in 2005 (March 31, 2005). B can exclude from income in 2004 all of the employer contributions (i.e., $1,000) because B's exclusion for all contributions does not exceed the maximum annual HSA contributions. *See* A-12.

Q-22. What happens when HSA contributions exceed the maximum amount that may be deducted or excluded from gross income in a taxable year?

A-22. Contributions by individuals to an HSA, or if made on behalf of an individual to an HSA, are not deductible to the extent they exceed the limits described in A-12. Contributions by an employer to an HSA for an employee are included in the gross income of the employee to the extent that they exceed the limits described in A-12 or if they are made on behalf of an employee who is not an eligible individual. In addition, an excise tax of 6% for each taxable year is imposed on the account beneficiary for excess individual and employer contributions.

However, if the excess contributions for a taxable year and the net income attributable to such excess contributions are paid to the account beneficiary before the last day prescribed by law (including extensions) for filing the account beneficiary's federal income tax return for the taxable year, then the net income attributable to the excess contributions is included in the account beneficiary's gross income for the taxable year in which the distribution is received but the excise tax is not imposed on the excess contribution and the distribution of the excess contributions is not taxed.

Q-23. Are rollover contributions to HSAs permitted?

A-23. Rollover contributions from Archer MSAs and other HSAs into an HSA are permitted. Rollover contributions need not be in cash. Rollovers are not subject to the annual contribution limits. Rollovers from an IRA, from a health reimbursement arrangement (HRA), or from a health flexible spending arrangement (FSA) to an HSA are not permitted.

IV. *Distributions from HSAs.*

Q-24. When is an individual permitted to receive distributions from an HSA?

A-24. An individual is permitted to receive distributions from an HSA at any time.

Q-25. How are distributions from an HSA taxed?

A-25. Distributions from an HSA used exclusively to pay for qualified medical expenses of the account beneficiary, his or her spouse, or dependents are excludable from gross income. In general, amounts in an HSA can be used for qualified medical expenses and will be excludable from gross income even if the individual is not currently eligible for contributions to the HSA.

However, any amount of the distribution not used exclusively to pay for qualified medical expenses of the account beneficiary, spouse or dependents is includable in gross income of the account beneficiary and is subject to an additional 10% tax on the amount includable, except in the case of distributions made after the account beneficiary's death, disability, or attaining age 65.

Q-26. What are the "qualified medical expenses" that are eligible for tax-free distributions?

A-26. The term "qualified medical expenses" are expenses paid by the account beneficiary, his or her spouse or dependents for medical care as defined in section 213(d) (including nonprescription drugs as described in Rev. Rul. 2003-102, 2003-38 I.R.B. 559), but only to the extent the expenses are not covered by insurance or otherwise. The qualified medical expenses must be incurred only after the HSA has been established. For purposes of determining the itemized deduction for medical expenses, medical expenses paid or reimbursed by distributions from an HSA are not treated as expenses paid for medical care under section 213.

Q-27. Are health insurance premiums qualified medical expenses?

A-27. Generally, health insurance premiums are not qualified medical expenses except for the following: qualified long-term care insurance, COBRA health care continuation coverage, and health care coverage while an individual is receiving unemployment compensation. In addition, for individuals over age 65, premiums for Medicare Part A or B, Medicare HMO, and the employee share of premiums for employer-sponsored health insurance, including premiums for employer-sponsored retiree health insurance can be paid from an HSA. Premiums for Medigap policies are not qualified medical expenses.

Q-28. How are distributions from an HSA taxed after the account beneficiary is no longer an eligible individual?

A-28. If the account beneficiary is no longer an eligible individual (e.g., the individual is over age 65 and entitled to Medicare benefits, or no longer has an HDHP), distributions used exclusively to pay for qualified medical expenses continue to be excludable from the account beneficiary's gross income.

Q-29. Must HSA trustees or custodians determine whether HSA distributions are used exclusively for qualified medical expenses?

A-29. No. HSA trustees or custodians are not required to determine whether HSA distributions are used for qualified medical expenses. Individuals who establish HSAs make that determination and should maintain records of their medical expenses sufficient to show that the distributions have been made exclusively for qualified medical expenses and are therefore excludable from gross income.

Q-30. Must employers who make contributions to an employee's HSA determine whether HSA distributions are used exclusively for qualified medical expenses?

A-30. No. The same rule that applies to trustees or custodians applies to employers. *See* A-29.

Q-31. What are the income tax consequences after the HSA account beneficiary's death?

A-31. Upon death, any balance remaining in the account beneficiary's HSA becomes the property of the individual named in the HSA instrument as the beneficiary of the account. If the account beneficiary's surviving spouse is the named beneficiary of the HSA, the HSA becomes the HSA of the surviving spouse. The surviving spouse is subject to income tax only to the extent distributions from the HSA are not used for qualified medical expenses.

If, by reason of the death of the account beneficiary, the HSA passes to a person other than the account beneficiary's surviving spouse, the HSA ceases to be an HSA as of the date of the account beneficiary's death, and the person is required to include in gross income the fair market value of the HSA assets as of the date of death. For such a person (except the decedent's estate), the includable amount is reduced by any payments from the HSA made for the decedent's qualified medical expenses, if paid within one year after death.

V. *Other Matters.*

Q-32. What discrimination rules apply to HSAs?

A-32. If an employer makes HSA contributions, the employer must make available comparable contributions on behalf of all "comparable participating employees" (i.e., eligible employees with comparable coverage) during the same period. Contributions are considered comparable if they are either the same amount or same percentage of the deductible under the HDHP.

The comparability rule is applied separately to part-time employees (i.e., employees who are customarily employed for fewer than 30 hours per week). The comparability rule does not apply to amounts rolled over from an employee's HSA or Archer MSA, or to contributions made through a cafeteria plan. If employer contributions do not satisfy the comparability rule during a period, the employer is subject to an excise tax equal to 35% of the aggregate amount contributed by the employer to HSAs for that period.

Example: Employer X offers its collectively bargained employees three health plans, including an HDHP with self-only coverage and a $2,000 deductible For each employee electing the HDHP self-only coverage, X contributes $1,000 per year on behalf of the employee to an HSA. X makes no HSA contributions for employees who do not elect the HDHP. X's plans and HSA contributions satisfy the comparability rule.

Q-33. Can an HSA be offered under a cafeteria plan?

A-33. Yes. Both an HSA and an HDHP may be offered as options under a cafeteria plan. Thus, an employee may elect to have amounts contributed as employer contributions to an HSA and an HDHP on a salary-reduction basis.

Q-34. What reporting is required for an HSA?

A-34. Employer contributions to an HSA must be reported on the employee's Form W-2. In addition, information reporting for HSAs will be similar to information reporting for Archer MSAs. The IRS will release forms and instructions, similar to those required for Archer MSAs, on how to report HSA contributions, deductions, and distributions.

Q-35. Are HSAs subject to COBRA continuation coverage under section 4980B?

A-35. No. Like Archer MSAs, HSAs are not subject to COBRA continuation coverage.

Q-36. How do the rules under section 419 affect contributions by an employer to an HSA?

A-36. Contributions by an employer to an HSA are not subject to the rules under section 419. An HSA is a trust that is exempt from tax under section 223. Thus, an HSA is not a "fund" under section 419(e)(3) and, therefore, is not a "welfare benefit fund" under section 419(e)(1).

Q-37. May eligible individuals use debit, credit or stored-value cards to receive distributions from an HSA for qualified medical expenses?

A-37. Yes.

Q-38. Are HSAs subject to other statutory rules and provisions?

A-38. Yes. HSAs are subject to other statutory rules and provisions not addressed in this notice. No inference should be drawn regarding issues not expressly addressed in this notice that may be suggested by a particular question or answer, or by the inclusion or exclusion of certain questions.

Announcements

Announcement 2004-67 (2004-36 I.R.B. 459)

[**Summary:** Clarified and corrected previously issued guidance to allow HSA contributions (including catch-up contributions) to be made after an individual has attained age 65 provided they are not enrolled in Medicare.]

PURPOSE

This document contains corrections to A-14 in Notice 2004-2, 2004-2 I.R.B. 269, relating to Health Savings Accounts. As published, A-14 of the notice contains errors that may prove to be misleading and are in need of clarification.

CORRECTIONS

The last sentence in A-14 of Notice 2004-2 which currently reads, "After an individual has attained age 65 (the Medicare eligibility age), contributions, including catch-up contributions, cannot be made to an individual's HSA", is corrected to read as follows: "After an individual has attained age 65 and becomes enrolled in Medicare benefits, contributions, including catch-up contributions, cannot be made to an individual's HSA." Additionally, the terms "becomes eligible for" in the first sentence of the Example in A-14 of Notice 2004-2 are replaced by "becomes enrolled in".

Announcement 2004-2 (2004-3 I.R.B. 322)

[**Summary:** The IRS announced that employer contributions to an employee's health savings account must now be reported on the 2004 W-2 Form in box 12 using Code W.]

PURPOSE

[1] The purpose of this announcement is to advise employers about an additional code for use on the 2004 Form W-2. This code will be used to identify the amount of an employer's contribution to an employee's Health Savings Account (HSA).

HEALTH SAVINGS ACCOUNTS (HSA)

[2] A new code (Code W—Employer's contribution to an employee's Health Savings Account (HSA)) for use in box 12 on the 2004 Form W-2 has been added to the 2004 Instructions for Forms W-2 and W-3.

[3] The Medicare Prescription Drug Improvement and Modernization Act of 2003 requires reporting of an employer's contributions to an employee's HSA on Form W-2. The amount that an employer contributes to an employee's HSA will be shown in box 12 of Form W-2, using Code W.

[4] Generally, employer contributions to an employee's MSA are not subject to income, social security/Medicare, or Railroad Retirement taxes and will not affect amounts otherwise reported in boxes 1, 3, and 5 of Form W-2.

Appendix C

Department of Labor Releases

Advisory Opinion 2004-09A

U.S. Department of Labor

Employee Benefits Security Administration

Office of Regulations and Interpretations

Advisory Opinion 2004-09A

December 22, 2004

Thomas G. Schendt, Esq.
Alston & Bird LLP
601 Pennsylvania Avenue, N.W.
North Building, 10th Floor
Washington, DC 20004-2601

Dear Mr. Schendt:

This is in response to your request for an advisory opinion from the U.S. Department of Labor (the Department) concerning the application of the prohibited transaction provisions under section 4975(c) of the Internal Revenue Code of 1986, as amended (the Code), to certain contributions to health savings accounts (HSAs), as described below.[1]

---

[1] Under Reorganization Plan No. 4 of 1978, 43 Fed. Reg. 47713 (Oct. 17, 1978), the authority of the Secretary of the Treasury to issue rulings under section 4975 of the Code has been transferred, with certain exceptions not here relevant, to the Secretary of Labor. See 5 USC App. at 214 (2000 ed.).

You represent that your client, an insurer (the Company) and its affiliates, offers various health benefit plans in the individual market, including high deductible health plans (HDHPs), as that term is defined in section 223(c)(2) of the Code. In addition, the Company either offers HSAs, as defined in section 223(d) of the Code, to individuals covered by HDHPs issued by the Company, or enters into a contractual arrangement with a specified bank that will offer HSAs to such individuals, as described below.

Your letter contains the following facts and representations.

Factual Scenario I

Under Factual Scenario I, only persons insured under HDHPs issued by the Company in the individual market are able to establish HSAs with the Company. However, a person does not have to establish an HSA with the Company to participate in an individual HDHP with the Company. If a person establishes an HSA with the Company, the Company will serve as both the trustee or custodian and the record-keeper of the HSA. The Company does not provide HSA custodial services in the employer group market.

To encourage participation in the Company's HSA program, the Company will offer an incentive to a person who establishes an HSA with the Company when he or she first enters into an individual HDHP with the Company. This incentive will be in the form of a $100 cash credit by the Company, as trustee or custodian, directly to the individual's HSA. This credit to the HSA will be automatic. The account holder will not be required to make any contribution to his or her HSA to receive the credit to his or her HSA. The credit is dependent on the establishment of an HSA with the Company. The account holder will not be able to divert the money to himself or herself before it is credited to the HSA.

If the person does not establish an HSA with the Company, he or she will not receive any incentive from the Company under this incentive program. Thus, for example, the individual will not receive any incentive from the Company in the form of a credit to an HSA not provided by the Company or in the form of money paid to him or her outside of the HSA. The credit to the account holder's HSA with the Company will be subject to the statutory requirements for HSAs set forth in section 223 of the Code, and the tax treatment of any distributions from the HSA attributable to this credit will be governed by the provisions of section 223(f) of the Code.

With respect to each HSA established with the Company pursuant to this incentive program, the Company represents that any arrangement for services by the Company to the HSA (e.g., as trustee or custodian and/or record-keeper of the HSA) will meet the requirements of section 4975(d)(2) of the Code and the Treasury's regulations at 26 CFR §54.4975-6.

The Company represents that the premiums payable under the HDHP will not vary based on the individual's choice of HSA custodian or trustee. Thus, the individual's insurance premiums will not be higher or lower as a result of his or her decision to establish an HSA either with the Company or with some other custodian or trustee. The Company also represents that any administrative fees the Company may charge the account holder with respect to his or her HSA will not change (i.e., will not increase or decrease) as a result of the credit to his or her HSA.

The Company states that although the duration of this incentive program has not been determined, it envisions that the incentive program could be used at various times for specified periods of time. The Company also anticipates that the amount of the incentive could change from time to time. However, for purposes of this request, the Company represents that the amount of the incentive will not exceed $100 per person.

Factual Scenario II

Under Factual Scenario II, the Company and its affiliates offer various health benefit plans in the group market, including HDHPs as defined under the Code.

The Company enters into a contractual relationship with a specified bank (the Bank) to provide HSAs for individuals covered by HDHPs issued by the Company. However, an individual does not have to establish an HSA with the Bank to participate in a group HDHP issued by the Company. The Bank serves as the trustee or custodian and the record-keeper of those HSAs and receives remuneration from the Company for its services in that regard. The Company also enters into a contractual relationship with a specified entity (the Vendor) to provide various services in relation to these HSAs, for which the Company compensates the Vendor. Neither the Bank nor the Vendor is a member of the Company's controlled group under sections 414(b), (c) and (m) of the Code.

To encourage the establishment of HSAs with the Bank in connection with group HDHPs issued by the Company, the Bank will offer an incentive to a person who establishes an HSA with the Bank when the Company first covers such person under a group HDHP. This incentive will be in the form of a $100 cash credit from the Bank directly to the individual's HSA. This credit to the HSA will be automatic. The account holder will not be required to make any contribution to his or her HSA to receive the credit to his or her HSA. The credit will be dependent on the establishment of an HSA with the Bank. The account holder will not be able to divert the money to himself or herself before it is credited to the HSA.

If the person does not establish an HSA with the Bank, he or she will not receive any incentive from the Bank under this incentive program. For example, the individual will not receive any incentive from the Company or the Bank in the form of a credit to an HSA not provided by the Bank or in the form of money paid to him or her outside of his or her HSA. The credit to the account holder's HSA with the Bank will be subject to the statutory requirements for HSAs set forth in section 223 of the Code, and the tax treatment of any distributions from the HSA attributable to this credit will be governed by the provisions of section 223(f) of the Code.

With respect to the HSAs established with the Bank pursuant to this incentive program, the Company, the Bank and the Vendor intend that any arrangements for services by the Bank or the Vendor to the HSA (e.g., as the trustee or custodian and/or record-keeper of the HSA) will meet the requirements of section 4975(d)(2) of the Code and the Treasury's regulations at 26 CFR §54.4975-6.[2]

The Company represents that the premiums charged for the individual's coverage under the group HDHP will not vary based on the individual's choice of HSA custodian or trustee. Thus, the premiums charged by the Company for the individual's coverage under the group HDHP will not be higher or lower as a result of his or her decision to establish an HSA either with the Bank or with some other custodian or trustee. In addition, any administrative fees the Bank or the Vendor may charge the account holder with respect to his or her HSA will not change (i.e., will not increase or decrease) as a result of this credit to his or her HSA.

The Company states that although the duration of this incentive program has not been determined, it envisions that the incentive program could be used at various times for specified periods of time. The Company also anticipates that the amount of the incentive could change from time to time. However, for purposes of this request, the Company represents that the amount of the incentive will not exceed $100 per person.

Advisory Opinions Requested

With respect to Factual Scenario I, you have requested an advisory opinion that the credit to an account holder's HSA will not constitute a prohibited transaction under section 4975(c) of the Code for either the account holder or the Company.

In addition, with respect to Factual Scenario II, you have requested an advisory opinion that the credit to an account holder's HSA will not constitute a prohibited transaction under section 4975(c) of the Code or section 406 of the Employee Retirement Income Security Act of 1974, as amended (ERISA).

Prohibited Transactions under the Internal Revenue Code

Section 4975(e)(1)(E) of the Code defines the term "plan" to include ". . . health savings account described in section 223(d)" of the Code.

A "prohibited transaction" under section 4975(c)(1) of the Code includes, among other things, any direct or indirect:

> (A) sale or exchange, or leasing, of any property between a plan and a disqualified person;
>
> (C) furnishing of goods, services, or facilities between a plan and a disqualified person;

---

[2] The Company is not requesting, and the Department is not providing, an opinion as to whether any arrangement for services by the Company, the Bank or the Vendor to an HSA will satisfy the requirements necessary for relief under section 4975(d)(2) of the Code and the regulations relating thereto. In this regard, the Department ordinarily does not issue advisory opinions on questions that are inherently factual in nature.

(D) transfer to, or use by or for the benefit of, a disqualified person of the income or assets of a plan;

(E) act by a disqualified person who is a fiduciary whereby he deals with the income or assets of a plan in his own interest or for his own account; or

(F) receipt of any consideration for his own personal account by any disqualified person who is a fiduciary from any party dealing with the plan in connection with a transaction involving the income or assets of the plan.

A "disqualified person" is defined under section 4975(e)(2) of the Code, in pertinent part, to include a person who is a fiduciary or a person providing services to the plan.

Analysis of Factual Scenarios I and II

Under Factual Scenario I, the Company will be a trustee or custodian of the HSA. As such, the Company would be a disqualified person with respect to the HSA.

Under Factual Scenario II, the Bank will be a trustee or custodian of the HSA. As such, the Bank is a disqualified person with respect to the HSA. However, as we understand the facts, the Company would not be a disqualified person with respect to the HSA. In both scenarios, the account holder is a fiduciary and disqualified person with respect to the HSA.

Under both Factual Scenarios, the $100 credit proposed by either the Company or the Bank, respectively, would be a cash contribution to the account holder's HSA. The Department notes that in accordance with IRS Notice 2004-50, Q&A 28, wherein it states that "any person . . . may make contributions to an HSA on behalf of an eligible individual," Code section 223 does not prohibit the Company or the Bank from making such contributions to its customers' HSAs. A cash contribution to a plan is not generally a sale or exchange of property prohibited by section 4975(c)(1)(A) of the Code. Additionally, the cash contribution would not be a transfer of an asset of a plan for the benefit of a disqualified person or an act of self-dealing by either the Company or the Bank under section 4975(c)(1)(D) or (E) of the Code involving the assets of a plan. Therefore, neither the Company's nor the Bank's contribution of a cash credit to the account holder's HSA, as described herein, would be a prohibited transaction under section 4975(c)(1) of the Code.[3]

Similarly, the HSA's receipt of the Company's or the Bank's contribution of a cash credit, under the facts described above, would not be an act of self-dealing on the part of the account holder nor a receipt by the account holder in his or her

---

[3] With respect to contributions or transfers of property to a plan that are considered to be an "exchange," see Adv. Op. 81-69A (July 28, 1981) and the Department's Interpretative Bulletin at 29 CFR 2509.94-3, relating to in-kind contributions to employee benefit plans.

individual capacity of any consideration from a party dealing with the HSA in connection with a transaction involving assets of the HSA. Even though the Company or the Bank, respectively, would make the contribution as an incentive to encourage the account holder's participation in the Company's or the Bank's HSA program, the contribution goes to the HSA and not to the account holder.[4] Therefore, the receipt by the HSA of such cash contributions would not be a prohibited transaction under section 4975(c)(1) of the Code.[5]

Since the Company is not a disqualified person with respect the HSA under Factual Scenario II, the Bank's contribution of the credit to the account holder's HSA would not be a prohibited transaction under section 4975(c) of the Code with respect to the Company.

Finally, with respect to the contribution of any cash credits by the Bank to an account holder's HSA under the facts described above, the same analysis and conclusions would apply, for purposes of the prohibited transaction provisions contained in section 406(a) and (b) of ERISA, to an HSA that would be an "employee benefit plan" covered under Title I of ERISA[6] under the principles discussed in the Department's Field Assistance Bulletin (FAB) 2004-01 (April 7, 2004). Further, in such instances, the fiduciary responsibility provisions of Title I would apply to the selection of service providers to the HSA.

In discussing whether, and under what circumstances, HSA's established in connection with employment-based group health plans would be subject to the provisions of Title I of ERISA, FAB 2004-01 states that genearlly such HSAs would not constitute an "employee welfare benefit plan" as defined under section 3(1) of ERISA, if employer involvement with the HSA is limited. Specifically, HSAs meeting the conditions of the safe harbor for group or group-type insurance programs at 29 CFR §2510.3-1(j)(1)–(4) are not considered employee welfare benefit plans within the meaning of section 3(1) of ERISA. However, a finding that an HSA established by an employee is not covered by ERISA does not affect whether an HDHP sponsored by the employer is itself a group health plan subject to Title I. In fact, FAB 2004-01 states that unless otherwise exempt from Title I (e.g., governmental plans, church plans), employer-sponsored HDHPs will be "employee welfare benefit plans" within the meaning of section 3(1) of ERISA and, thus, subject to the fiduciary responsibility provisions of Title I.

---

[4] This distinguishes the arrangement from others that have been found to involve prohibited transactions. See Adv. Op. 89-12A (July 14, 1989) (personal receipt of "free checking" account services by a *customer* from a bank in connection with the investment of assets of the customer's individual retirement account (IRA) in the bank's financial products would constitute a violation of section 4975(c)(1) of the Code.) See also PTE 93-33, 58 Fed. Reg. 31053 (May 28, 1993) (exempting certain arrangements benefiting an IRA account holder).

[5] This advisory opinion does not address payments to the individual account of any person who is a disqualified person for reasons other than as the account holder of an HSA.

[6] Section 3(3) of ERISA defines the term "employee benefit plan" or "plan" as an employee welfare benefit plan (see section 3(1) of ERISA) or an employee pension benefit plan (see section 3(2) of ERISA) or a plan which is both an employee welfare benefit plan and an employee pension benefit plan.

This letter constitutes an advisory opinion under ERISA Procedure 76-1, 41 Fed. Reg. 36281 (Aug. 27, 1976). The letter is issued subject to the provisions of that procedure, including section 10 thereof, relating to the effect of advisory opinions.

Sincerely,

Louis J. Campagna

Chief, Division of Fiduciary Interpretations

Office of Regulations and Interpretations

Field Assistance Bulletin 2004-01

U.S. Department of Labor
Employee Benefits Security Administration

April 7, 2004

Memorandum for: Virginia C. Smith
                    Director of Enforcement, Regional

                    Directors

From: Robert J. Doyle

                    Director of Regulations and

                    Interpretations

Subject: Health Saving Accounts

Issue

Whether Health Savings Accounts established in connection with employment-based group health plans constitute "employee welfare benefit plans" for purposes of Title I of ERISA?

Background

Section 3(1) of the Employee Retirement Income Security Act of 1974 (ERISA) defines the term "employee welfare benefit plan" in relevant part to mean "any plan, fund, or program . . . established or maintained by an employer . . . to the extent that such plan, fund, or program was established or is maintained for the purpose of providing for its participants or their beneficiaries, through the purchase of insurance or otherwise, (A) medical, surgical, or hospital care or benefits, or benefits in the event of sickness . . . ."

Section 1201 of the Medicare Prescription Drug, Improvement, and Modernization Act of 2003, Pub. L. No. 108–173 (the Medicare Modernization Act), added section 223 to the Internal Revenue Code (Code) to permit eligible individuals to establish Health Savings Accounts (HSAs).[7] In general, HSAs are established to receive tax-favored contributions by or on behalf of eligible individuals, and amounts in an HSA may be accumulated over the years or distributed on a tax-free basis to pay or reimburse "qualified medical expenses." In order to establish an HSA, an eligible individual, among other conditions, must be covered under a High Deductible Health Plan (HDHP).[8] Contributions to an HSA established by an eligible individual who is an employee may be made by the employee, the employee's employer or both in a given year.[9] Amounts in an HSA may be rolled over to another HSA.[10] If an employer makes contributions to HSAs, the employer must make available a comparable contribution on behalf of all eligible employees with comparable coverage during the same period.[11] However, employers that make contributions to an employee's HSA are not responsible for determining whether HSAs are used for qualified medical expenses or for investing or managing amounts contributed to an employee's HSA.[12]

It is our understanding that a number of employers that currently sponsor ERISA-covered group health plans may wish to add an HDHP option and offer programs designed to enable employees to establish HSAs to pay for medical expenses not covered by the HDHP. Questions have been raised about whether, and under what circumstances, HSAs established in connection with employment-based programs would constitute "employee welfare benefit plans" within the meaning of section 3(1) of ERISA.

Analysis

Congress, in enacting the Medicare Modernization Act, recognized that HSAs would be established in conjunction with employment-based health plans and specifically provided for employer contributions. However, neither the Medicare Modernization Act nor section 223 of the Code specifically address the application of Title I of ERISA to HSAs. Based on our review of Title I, and taking into account the provisions of the Code as amended by the Medicare Modernization Act, we believe that HSAs generally will not constitute employee welfare benefit plans established or maintained by an employer where employer involvement with the HSA is limited, whether or not the employee's HDHP is sponsored by an employer or obtained as individual coverage.

---

[7] The U.S. Department of the Treasury and the Internal Revenue Service (IRS), which have interpretive and regulatory authority over HSAs under section 223 of the Code, issued general guidance concerning HSAs on December 22, 2003, in I.R.S. Notice 2004-2, and issued additional guidance on March 30, 2004, in I.R.S. Notice 2004-23, I.R.S. Notice 2004-25, Revenue Ruling 2004-38, and Revenue Procedure 2004-22. The Treasury/IRS guidance is available on the Internet at www.treas.gov/offices/public-affairs/hsa.
[8] See I.R.S. Notice 2004-2, Q&A Nos. 1 and 2.
[9] Id. Q&A No. 11.
[10] Id. Q&A No. 23.
[11] Id. Q&A No. 32.
[12] Id. Q&A No. 30.

Specifically, HSAs meeting the conditions of the safe harbor for group or group-type insurance programs at 29 C.F.R. §2510.3-1(j)(1)–(4) would not be employee welfare benefit plans within the meaning of section 3(1) of ERISA.[13] Moreover, although contributions or payment of group insurance premiums by an employer would be a significant consideration in determining whether a group or group-type insurance arrangement is an employee welfare benefit plan under section 3(1), such contributions or payments are not necessarily significant in analyzing the status of HSAs under ERISA. As noted above, HSAs are personal health care savings vehicles rather than a form of group health insurance. For example, funds deposited in an HSA generally may not be used to pay health insurance premiums,[14] and the beneficiaries of the account have sole control and are exclusively responsible for expending the funds in compliance with the requirements of the Code. Because of these differences, we regard court precedent on the significance of employer contributions to group or group-type insurance arrangements as inapposite to HSAs. In the group health insurance context, the employer, whether by choosing an insurance policy or creating a self-funded program, typically establishes the type of benefits provided, the conditions for their receipt, and the manner in which claims will be adjudicated. In the context of HSAs, however, the employer may be doing little more than contributing funds to an account controlled solely by the employee.

Accordingly, we would not find that employer contributions to HSAs give rise to an ERISA-covered plan where the establishment of the HSAs is completely voluntary on the part of the employees and the employer does not: (i) limit the ability of eligible individuals to move their funds to another HSA beyond restrictions imposed by the Code; (ii) impose conditions on utilization of HSA funds beyond those permitted under the Code; (iii) make or influence the investment decisions with respect to funds contributed to an HSA; (iv) represent that the HSAs are an employee welfare benefit plan established or maintained by the employer; or (v) receive any payment or compensation in connection with an HSA.

The mere fact that an employer imposes terms and conditions on contributions that would be required to satisfy tax requirements under the Code or limits the forwarding of contributions through its payroll system to a single HSA provider (or permits only a limited number of HSA providers to advertise or market their HSA products in the workplace) would not affect the above conclusions regarding HSAs funded with employer or employee contributions,

---

[13] Regulation section 2510.3-1(j) excludes from Title I coverage certain group or group-type insurance programs. In general, such programs are excluded from coverage where there are no employer contributions, employee participation is voluntary, the employer does not endorse the program, and the employer receives no consideration in connection with the program, other than reasonable compensation for administrative services actually rendered in connection with payroll deductions. See also 29 C.F.R. § 2509.99-1 relating to payroll deduction IRAs.

[14] Although the Medicare Modernization Act excludes health insurance from the qualified medical expenses that may be paid from an HSA, there are exceptions for the payment of COBRA premiums, certain insurance for individuals over 65, long-term care insurance premiums and health insurance during periods of unemployment. Code section 223(d)(2).

unless the employer or the HSA provider restricts the ability of the employee to move funds to another HSA beyond those restrictions imposed by the Code.

Conclusion

HSAs generally will not constitute "employee welfare benefit plans" for purposes of the provisions of Title I of ERISA. Employer contributions to the HSA of an eligible individual will not result in Title I coverage where, as discussed above, employer involvement with the HSA is limited. Finding that an HSA established by an employee is not covered by ERISA does not, however, affect whether an HDHP sponsored by the employer is itself a group health plan subject to Title I. In fact, unless otherwise exempt from Title I (e.g., governmental plans, church plans) employer-sponsored HDHPs will be employee welfare benefit plans within the meaning of ERISA section 3(1) subject to Title I.

Questions concerning this matter may be directed to Suzanne Adelman, Division of Coverage, Reporting and Disclosure at 202-693-8523.

Annual HSA Limitations

The maximum HSA contribution limits apply to an eligible individual with an HDHP and an HSA for the entire taxable year (see chapters 3 and 4).

	2006		2005		2004		Base Amount[1]	
	Self-Only	*Family*	*Self-Only*	*Family*	*Self-Only*	*Family*	*Self-Only*	*Family*
HSA Maximum Annual Contribution (but not more than deductible under the HDHP associated with the HSA)[2]	$2,700	$5,450	$2,650	$5,250	$2,600	$5,100	$2,250	$4,500
HSA Catch-Up Contributions (age 55 by end of year)	$700		$600		$500		n/a	
HDHP Minimum Annual Deductible[3]	$1,050	$2,100	$1,000	$2,000	$1,000	$2,000	$1,000	$2,000
HDHP Maximum Out-of-Pocket[4]	$5,250	$10,500	$5,100	$10,200	$5,000	$10,000	$5,000	$10,000

[1] These are the base amounts upon which the limits for 2004 and subsequent years are computed. How annual limits are computed and adjusted for inflation (based on the Consumer Price Index (CPI)) is more fully discussed in Q 3:7.

[2] IRC § 223(b)(2)(A)(i). The contribution limit does not apply to rollovers or transfers from an Archer MSA or HSA into an HSA.

[3] To be a HDHP, the plan deductible may not be less than the indexed limit. IRC § 223(c)(2)(A)(i). See Q 3:1.

[4] To be a HDHP, the sum of the annual deductible and other out-of-pocket expenses may not exceed the indexed amount. IRC § 223(c)(2)(A)(ii). See Q 3:1.

Appendix E

State Laws Affecting HSAs: Impediments and Tax Treatment*

(as of July 15, 2006)

Background

The Medicare Prescription Drug, Improvement, and Modernization Act of 2003 included provisions authorizing "tax-favored" health savings accounts (HSAs) for the payment of qualified medical expenses. To be eligible for an HSA, an individual must be covered by a high deductible health plan (HDHP) which meets certain annual minimum deductible and maximum out-of-pocket requirements. In 2006, the minimum deductibles must be at least $1,050 for self-only coverage and $2,100 for family coverage and out-of-pocket expenses must not exceed $5,250 for self-only coverage and $10,500 for family coverage.

Impediments

Some state laws may impede HMOs from offering HDHPs by either specifying the amount of deductibles and copayments or by interpreting requirements for "reasonable" deductibles or copayments as prohibiting these products (IL, MO, and NY). New York issued a bulletin stating that its laws prohibit individual health insurers from offering an individual HDHP intended to be sold in conjunction with an HSA.

The Treasury Department provided "transition relief" for HDHPs that would otherwise qualify for use with HSAs except that they comply with state benefit mandates. Under Treasury Department Notice 2004-43 such plans will be treated as qualified HDHPs until January 1, 2006, if the disqualifying benefits are required by state law in effect on January 1, 2004. On November 17, 2005,

---

* This chart is not intended as a legal opinion regarding the application of state insurance or tax laws or federal tax laws, regulations, or guidelines.

the Treasury Department released Notice 2005-83, that extends the transition relief to allow non-calendar year HDHPs to remain qualified until the renewal date of the policy, but no later than December, 31, 2006.

Tax treatment

Contributions to an HSA by an eligible individual (or by family members on behalf of an eligible individual) may be deducted from the eligible individual's adjusted gross income on their federal income tax return regardless of whether they itemize deductions. Distributions from an HSA for "qualified" medical expenses are excluded from the individual's gross income.

Many states follow the federal tax provisions in determining state tax treat-ment of contributions and allow a deduction for purposes of imposition of state personal income taxes (AZ, CO, CT, DE, DC, GA, HI, ID, IL, IA, LA, MD, MI, MO, MT, NE, NM, NY, NC, ND, OH, OK, OR, RI, SC, UT, VT, and WV). Some states require specific legislation to allow such a deduction. (AL, AR, CA, IN, IA, KY, ME, MA, MN, MS, NJ, PA, and WI). To date, of these latter states, AR, IN, IA, KY, ME, MA, MN, and MS passed such legislation. Other states impose no personal income tax, or impose a tax only on income other than salaries or wages, so the deductibility of contributions is generally not an issue (AK, FL, NV, NH, SD, TN, TX, WA, and WY).

Chart

The following chart shows states with an identified impediment to the offering of an HDHP in conjunction with an HSA. It does not include states with an HMO-type impediment if the department of insurance has approved or indicated it will approve HMO HDHP filings. It also does not include copayment or deductible restrictions applicable to services that are clearly considered "preventive care" (e.g. childhood immunizations) or applicable to well child services. In addition, the chart identifies those states that currently do not permit a deduction for HSA contributions or that impose a tax on interest.

The chart also shows:

- information on insurance department approval of HMO HDHP filings;
- actions taken and bills introduced and regulations proposed to address the identified impediments and tax issues; and
- comments on progress.

State impediments removed and tax laws amended to allow a deduction by passage of legislation or regulations prior to the last update of this chart on January 13, 2005 can be found in AHIP's HSA Impediment or Tax Deduction: Enacted/Adopted HSA Legislation/Regulations chart.
Developments since the last update of this chart on June 16, 2006 appear in red.

State	General Impediment (Y/N - impediment)	HMO-only impediment (Y/N - requirement)	DOI approval of HMO HDHP filings (Y/N)	Tax Issue (Y/N)	Bill /Regulation Status Actions/Comments
Alabama	N	N	Y	Y	Impediment comment: The Health Department indicates it does not believe that HDHPs meet "basic health needs" and HMOs should not offer these products, but DOI has approved HMO HDHP filings. Action: Support DOI position. Tax comment: Budgetary constraints made passage of legislation to allow deduction of HSA contributions impossible during the 2005 session. AHIP will continue its efforts to obtain favorable tax legislation in 2006.
California	N	N	Y	Y	Tax comment: While California conforms its tax code to many IRC provisions, it does not conform for federal HSA provisions. Bills: California AB 115, as amended on 05/02/05, allows a deduction for contributions to an HSA. California AB 2010, introduced 02/09/06, California SB 1584, introduced 02/23/06, and California SB 1787, introduced 02/24/06, allow a deduction in connection with HSAs in conformity with federal law. Status: House passed AB 115 on 06/01/05. In late August, AB 115 was amended to exclude

State	General Impediment (Y/N - impediment)	HMO-only impediment (Y/N - requirement)	DOI approval of HMO HDHP filings (Y/N)	Tax Issue (Y/N)	Bill/Regulation Status Actions/Comments
					application of the federal tax deductions related to HSAs for purposes of computing California income subject to taxation. These amendments survived in the enrolled bill as signed by the governor on 10/07/06. AB 2010 referred to Assembly Committee on Revenue and Taxation On 02/21/06. Committee hearing set 05/15/06. SB 1584 first hearing held 04/26/06. Further hearing to be set. Hearing on SB 1787 set for 04/06/06 canceled at the request of author. Comment: Prospects look doubtful for passage of a favorable tax bill because of consumer advocates opposed to these products.
Illinois	N	Y Limits the combination of deductibles and copayments for basic health care services to 50% of the usual and customary fee of the service and	N	N	Bills: Illinois HB 4293, introduced 01/04/06, amends the Health Maintenance Organization Act and provides that nothing in the powers granted to HMOs should be construed to prohibit a health care plan that qualifies as a high deductible health plan under the Internal Revenue Code from requiring the application of deductibles to benefits provided under the plan.

Missouri — N — N — N

requires a waiver of such deductibles and copayments when they exceed $3000 per enrollee or $6000 per family in a contract year. [50 Ill. Adm. Code 5421.110]

Status: HB 4293 passed House Insurance Committee on 01/31/06. Re-referred to House Rules Committee on 03/03/06.

Prohibits copayments that exceed 50% of the total cost of providing any single service to an enrollee or, in the aggregate, more than 20% of the total cost of providing all basic health services. Prohibits annual copayments for an enrollee for basic health care services in excess of 200% of the total annual premium for that enrollee. [MO ADC T. 20, § 400-7.150]

Y

Bills: Missouri SB 1147, introduced 02/28/06, allows a health insurance policy, contract, or health benefit plan offered by a health carrier in conjunction with an HSA to apply annual deductible amounts as would be required to qualify as a high deductible health plan under federal law.

Status: SB 1147 referred to Senate Pensions, Veterans' Affairs and General Laws Committee on 03/02/06.

Action: Support passage of SB 1147.

New Jersey — N — N — Y

Comment: New Jersey does not conform to federal tax law. While NJ has a state exemption for Archer MSAs, it does not currently provide any HSA relief.

State	General Impediment (Y/N - impediment)	HMO-only impediment (Y/N - requirement)	DOI approval of HMO HDHP filings (Y/N)	Tax Issue (Y/N)	Bill/Regulation Status Actions/Comments
					Bills: New Jersey AB 3583 (SB 2774) introduced on 12/09/04 addresses contribution deductibility. This bill allows gross income tax advantages in connection with Health Savings Accounts in conformity with the federal income tax advantages extended to these accounts under recent federal law. New Jersey AB 724, introduced 01/10/06, provides for favorable tax treatment of HSAs. New Jersey SB 1944, introduced 06/08/06, allows state gross income tax advantages in connection with HSAs in conformity with the federal law. Status: Both Assembly bills remain in committee and carry over to 2006. SB 1944 referred to Senate Commerce Committee on 06/08/06. Actions: Support above current legislative activity. Comments: Passage of the tax legislation appears unlikely.
New York	Y Requires coverage of home health care with a deductible of no more than $50. [Ins.	Y States that HMOs may not offer HDHP coverage because they are prohibited	Y	N	Action: Pursue both the regulatory and legislative activities to address issues. Work with NYHPA on regulatory activity to remove the HMO impediment.

Bills: New York SB 995 (AB 1925), introduced 01/21/05, removes the identified statutory impediments.

New York SB 6609, introduced 02/02/06, requires every insurer and corporation that offers individual and small group policies to also offer a high deductible health plan (HDHP) with an HSA that meets federal requirements. The bill also directs the superintendent of insurance, in his or her discretion, to make, amend, and rescind rules and regulations for the implementation of HSAs and qualified HDHPs.

New York SB 7104, introduced 03/22/06, exempts polices intended for use in an HSA from the following:

• requirements for individual and conversion policies to provide the same benefits as the standardized individual policy (Ins. §§ 3216 (I), 4304,4322);

• prohibitions on the application of deductibles for certain home health and maternity care (Ins. § 3221); and

• requirements for group contracts issued by non-profit medical and dental indemnity, or health and hospital service corporations (§ 4305).

Status: SB 995 was recommitted to Senate Finance Committee on 03/28/05 and carries over to 2006. Senate passed SB 7104 on 06/20/06.

§§ 3216(i)(6)(B) – individual health, 3221(k)(1) – group and blanket health, 4303(a)(3) – nonprofit hospital and health service corporations]

Requires coverage of maternity care or medical care to the same extent that hospital, surgical or medical coverage is provided for 48 hours after childbirth for any delivery other than a caesarean section, and for at least 96 hours after a caesarean section. Gives the mother the option to be discharged earlier than the above time periods and, if she so opts, then requires coverage to include at least one home care visit, in addition to any other home health care coverage. Prohibits the application of

from imposing deductibles on in-network benefits. Provides that the Insurance Department will, after review, offer more guidance as to whether and under what circumstances HMOs will be permitted to offer HDHP coverage. [New York Insurance Department Circular Letter No. 4 (2004)]

State	General Impediment (Y/N - impediment)	HMO-only impediment (Y/N - requirement)	DOI approval of HMO HDHP filings (Y/N)	Tax Issue (Y/N)	Bill/Regulation Status Actions/Comments
	deductibles, coinsurance or copayments to the home health care visit. [Ins. §§ 3216 (10)(A)(i), individual health, 3221(k)(5)(a), group or blanket health, 4303(c)(1)(a) – nonprofit hospital and health service corporations.]				Comments: Anticipated problems in the Assembly with removal of general impediments make chances of passage of any bill that removes the statutory impediments less than fifty–fifty. The NY Insurance Department is approving group, non-HMO HDHPs despite the identified impediments.
	A Department Circular Letter states that there are no statutory or regulatory barriers preventing commercial insurers and Article 43 corporations from offering group coverage that qualifies as high deductible health plan (HDHP) coverage and that the Department is willing to work with insurers to attain approval of such products				

expeditiously. The letter also states that commercial insurers and Article 43 corporations offering major medical, comprehensive, or other comparable individual contracts on a direct payment basis must provide benefits identical to the benefits contained in the standardized individual direct pay contracts governed by § 4322 of the Insurance Law. It further states that because of this prohibition, insurers and Article 43 corporations are limited to offering HDHPs that do not provide major medical, comprehensive, or comparable benefits. [*New York Insurance Department Circular Letter No. 4 (2004)*]

State	General Impediment (Y/N - impediment)	HMO-only impediment (Y/N - requirement)	DOI approval of HMO HDHP filings (Y/N)	Tax Issue (Y/N)	Bill /Regulation Status Actions/Comments
Pennsylvania	N http://www.ins.state.ny.us/cl04_04.htm	N	Y	Y	Comment: Pennsylvania does not conform to federal tax law and has not enacted legislation to allow for pre-tax contributions to HSAs. See PA Letter Ruling PIT 04-005 (Mar 12, 2004).
					Bills: Pennsylvania HB 107, introduced on 01/25/05, and Pennsylvania SB 300, introduced on 02/15/05, address both the impediment and the tax issues. Pennsylvania SB 854, introduced on 09/14/05, addresses the tax issue. As amended, Pennsylvania HB 2125 allows a deduction of HSA contributions for purposes of state income taxation.
					Status: HB 107 was amended to remove provisions allowing an exclusion for contributions by a beneficiary or an employer to an HSA. As passed, the bill removed the mandated benefit impediment and provided for an exclusion from taxation for income on and amounts paid out of an HSA. The governor signed HB 107 on 07/14/05. (Act No. 48)
					Governor signed SB 300 on 07/06/06.
					Action: Continue to seek full, favorable tax treatment for HSAs.

Wisconsin	N	N	Y	Y	Bills: Wisconsin AB 100, the budget bill, amended to conform Wisconsin tax code to the federal code on 06/06/05.
					Wisconsin SB 7, introduced 01/13/05, conformed Wisconsin tax code to the federal tax code for HSAs.
					Wisconsin AB 1140, introduced 03/21/06, adopts federal law as it relates to HSAs for state income and franchise tax purposes.
					Status: The legislature passed AB 100 and reported it correctly enrolled on 07/12/2005. The governor vetoed HSA provisions on 07/25/05. A legislative attempt to override the veto failed on 09/27/05. SB 7 carried over to 2006. SB 7 failed to pass pursuant to Senate Joint Resolution on 05/18/06. AB 1140 failed to pass pursuant to Senate Joint Resolution 1 on 05/11/06.
					Action: AHIP will continue efforts to address the tax issue. Passage is unlikely during Governor Doyle's term.

Appendix F

HSA Impediment or Tax Deduction Enacted/Adopted HSA Legislation/ Regulations*

(as of July 15, 2006)

State/Bill	Status	Summary
Arizona SB 1416	Signed: 04/18/05 Chapter: 111	SB 1416 provides that a corporation, health care services organization, disability insurer, or group or blanket disability insurer may offer one or more subscription contracts, health care plans, or disability insurance policies that contain deductibles, coinsurance or copayments without any restriction or limitation on those deductibles, coinsurance or copayments or without any limits on the level of reimbursement for contracted health care providers. The bill also provides that a health benefit plan intended to qualify as high deductible plan as defined in the federal tax code may apply deductibles, copayments and coinsurance to benefits provided under the health benefit plan.
Arkansas HB 1064	Effective: 02/10/05 Public Act: 94	HB 1064 exempts a health savings account from tax and excludes an

* This chart includes only those enacted laws that remove an impediment to the offering of a high deductible health plan in conjunction with an HSA and laws that allow a tax deduction in states that require such a law to allow the deduction. For information on states with current impediments or tax issues see the chart "State Laws Affecting HSAs: Impediments and Tax Treatment".

State/Bill	Status	Summary
		employer's contributions to an employee's health savings account from an employee's gross income.
Colorado **SB 94**	Signed: 05/17/04 Effective: 07/01/04 Public Act: 230	SB 94, as amended on March 2 and March 18, 2004, modifies the implementation of health savings accounts (HSAs). The bill converts the existing state law provisions for income tax deductions and credits for medical savings accounts to deductions and credits for HSAs. This bill eliminates the requirement that certain basic health benefit plans for small employers be offered in conjunction with a medical savings account, and substitutes a requirement that such plans be offered in conjunction with an HSA. The bill also provides that carriers offering a high deductible health plan in conjunction with an HSA may apply the deductible to the mandatory health benefits mammography, prostate screening, and child supervision services if such mandatory benefits are not considered preventive by the federal department of treasury. The bill also requires an evaluation of the feasibility of offering a high deductible health plan that would qualify for an HSA for state employees. SB 94 also provides that a basic plan that is a high deductible health plan qualifying for an HSA may be implemented beginning July 1, 2004 and is to be implemented by all small employer carriers no later than July 1, 2005.
Connecticut **HB 5204**	Signed: 06/01/04 Effective: 10/1/04 Public Act: 174	HB 5204 stipulates that HSAs are not subject to the annual limit on deductibles for home health care benefits.
Florida **HB 811**	Signed: 06/14/05 Effective: 07/01/05 Public Act: 231	HB 811 provides a general override to any provision of the Florida Insurance Code that is in conflict with federal requirements for an HSA-qualified HDHP. The bill specifically allows an insurer or HMO which is authorized to

State/Bill	Status	Summary
		issue health insurance to offer for sale an individual or group policy or contract that provides for an HDHP that meets the federal requirements of an HSA and which is offered in conjunction with an HSA.
Georgia **HB 291**	Signed: 05/02/05 Effective: 07/01/05 Public Act: 82	HB 291, among other provisions, makes an exception to a requirement for a carry-over deductible for policies or plans designed and issued to be compatible with a health savings account as set out in 26 U.S.C. Section 223.
Indiana **HB 1001**	Signed: 05/13/05 Public Act: 246	HB 1001, the 2005 budget bill, includes provisions conforming Indiana's tax code to the federal code.
Iowa **HB 186**	Signed: 04/13/05	HB 186 brings Iowa's deduction into conformity with the federal code and applies retroactively to January 1, 2003, for tax years beginning on or after that date.
Kansas **HB 2545**	Signed: 05/13/04 Effective: 7/01/04 Public Act: 128	HB 2545, as amended on March 23, 2004, includes the provisions of four Senate bills previously passed by the Senate, including SB 348, which addresses HSAs. The bill allows the offering of HSAs in Kansas by including them, in addition to medical savings accounts, as exempt from the first-dollar coverage provisions of current law related to accident and health insurance policies.
Kentucky **HB 272**	Signed: 03/18/05 Effective: 03/18/05 Public Act: 168	HB 272, among other provisions, conforms Kentucky's tax code to post-2001 federal tax legislation.
Maine LD **1916** (HP 1418)	Effective: 04/29/04 Public Act: 688	LD 1916 provides that benefits for prosthetic devices under health plans issued for use in connection with HSAs may be subject to the same deductibles and out-of-pocket limits that apply to overall benefits under the contract.
Maine LD **1968** (HP 1378)	Signed: 03/29/05 Effective for tax years beginning after January 1, 2006.	The budget bill, LD 1968, contains language conforming Maine income tax law to federal law regarding contribution to HSAs.

State/Bill	Status	Summary
Chapter 750 (Adopted rule number 2005-263) 02-031 CMR Ch. 750, § 12 Notice of rulemaking Text of proposed rulemaking Notice of adopted rules	Chapter: 750, § 12 Effective: 07/28/05	The amended regulation gives the Superintendent authority to waive provisions of the Product Design Guidelines for HMO Plans to the extent necessary to permit HMOs to offer health plans that qualify as high deductible health plans (HDHPs) offered in conjunction with HSAs. The regulation also specifically exempts HDHPs offered with an HSA from the following design requirements: • an annual deductible limitation of $1,000 per individual or $2,000 per family; and • no deductible for primary care physician services, preventive services, ambulance services, emergency room care, or metabolic formula.
Maryland SB 521	Signed: 5/10/05 Public Act: 316	SB 521 exempts high deductible health plans sold in conjunction with an HSA from the prohibition of the application of a deductible for certain home visits to mothers and newborns.
Massachusetts http://www. mass.gov/ legis/laws/ mgl/62-1.htm	Signed: 12/08/05 Chapter: 163	HB 4169 conforms the Massachusetts personal income statute to the federal code.
Minnesota HB 138	Signed: 07/13/05 Chapter: 4 (1st special session)	HB 138 includes provisions allowing a deduction of HSA contributions for purposes of state income taxes.
Mississippi HB 1213	Signed: 03/29/05	HB 1213, among other provisions, provides tax exempt status for HSA contributions and interest thereon.
Mississippi SB 2633	Signed: 04/6/05	SB 2633, as amended March 31, 2005, permits the establishment and maintenance of health savings accounts and exempts contributions from gross income under the state income tax law. The bill states that

State/Bill	Status	Summary
		money withdrawn from an HSA for any other reason than a medical or health related expense will be counted as gross income.
New Jersey		
Notice of proposed amendments, revised - March 2005 Standard Policy Plan C Standard Policy Plan D Explanation of Brackets (Exhibit T)	Adopted: 04/12/05 Filed and effective: 04/22/05	Adopted amendments to N.J.A.C. 11:20-3.1, 11:20-12.5 and 11:20 Appendix Exhibits C, D and T allow a standard plan in the individual health coverage (IHC) market to qualify as a HDHP. The amendments also address the dollar amounts of the deductible and out-of-pocket maximums under the provisions of Plans C and D, as they appear in Appendix Exhibits C and D of N.J.A.C. 11:20.
New Jersey **AB 4543** **(SB 2574)**	Signed: 12/21/05 Effective: 12/31/05	Makes an exception to the prohibition on the application of a deductible for coverage for treatment of blood lead poisoning under high deductible health plans HDHPs sold in conjunction with an HSA. Requires health care facilities and providers to give all necessary medical follow-up treatment to lead-poisoned children and, for families whose income does not exceed 400% of the federal poverty level, prohibits the providers from seeking reimbursement from either the insured or under the HDHP if the deductible limits have not been exceeded. The bill also prohibits the use of HDHPs with respect to the administration of Medicaid in this State and the NJ Family Care Program. In addition, the bill requires the application for an HDHP to include a declaration of understanding that explains the HDHP, which the applicant must sign. Further, all health insurance carriers offering HDHPs complete biannual surveys

State/Bill	Status	Summary
		intended to gather information concerning the impact of HDHPS on the individuals covered by such plans. Finally, the bill limits small employer carriers to offering HDHPS to only those small employers that: • currently offer health benefits plans other than an HDHP; • previously offered health benefits plans other than a HDHP, but have not offered any such plan for a period of five years; or • never offered any type of health benefits plan.
Ohio HB 193	Signed: 08/17/05	HB 193 removes the limitation on health insuring corporations to an annual deductible of no more than $1,000/enrollee or $2,000/family.
Oklahoma HB 1535	Signed: 05/02/05	Although Oklahoma has no current statutory impediments, HB 1535 provides a general override to mandated benefit laws that may not allow the offering of a high deductible benefit plan in conjunction with an HSA.
North Dakota HB 1208	Filed with Secretary of State: 03/16/05	HB 1208 prohibits an insurance company, nonprofit health service corporation, or health maintenance organization from applying a deductible limitation to a high-deductible health plan used to establish a health savings account.
Pennsylvania HB 107	Signed: 07/14/05	HB 107 exempts a health insurance policy that would qualify as a high deductible health plan, when offered in conjunction with an HSA, from any provision which restricts of limited deductible for mandated benefits, except for preventive care, as determined by the standards set forth by the IRS. (Prior to passage of the bill, Pennsylvania law required coverage of medical foods for the treatment of phenylketonuria, branched-chain ketonuria, galactosemia, and homocystinuria and certain home health

State/Bill	Status	Summary
		care visits without application of a deductible.)
Rhode Island HB 5228 (SB 423)	Governor signed: 06/28/05 General override sunsets: 07/01/10	HB 5228 provides that mandated coverage for early intervention services without application of a deductible does not apply to high deductible health plans issued in conjunction with an HSA. The bill also provides a general override to any deductible and/or other cost-sharing requirements for a high deductible health plan purchased for use with an HSA.
Texas HB 1602	Signed: 05/24/05	HB 1602 amends the definition of high deductible health plan under the Insurance Code and provides that no other provision of law may be construed to prevent an insurer, HMO, or other entity issuing a health insurance policy or certificate of coverage from applying deductibles or co-payment requirements to benefits, including state mandated benefits, in order to qualify the policy or certificate of coverage as a high deductible health plan.
Utah HB 85	Signed: 03/17/04 Effective: 05/03/04 Public Act: 98	HB 85 amends the health insurance adoption indemnity benefit to: • remove the requirement for the commissioner to review the adoption indemnity benefit every two years; • increase the adoption indemnity benefit to $4,000; and • clarify that a single adoption benefit is payable to an insured adopting multiple children from one birth. The bill states that this provision does not prevent an accident and health insurer from adjusting the benefit payable under this section for cost sharing measures imposed under the policy or contract.

Source: America's Health Insurance Plans (AHIP), Washington, DC. Reprinted with permission.

Appendix G

State HSA Market Impediments and Tax Issues
(as of July 15, 2006)

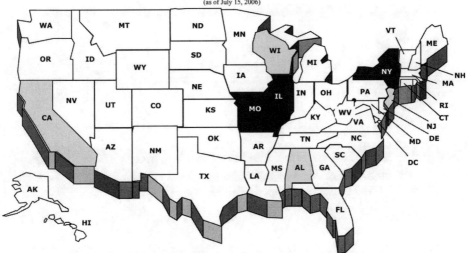

■ **States with an HMO deductible limitation and/or mandated benefit impediment to offering a high deductible health plan in conjunction with an HSA:** Illinois, Missouri, New York
▨ **States with a tax issue:** Alabama, California, New Jersey, Wisconsin

Source: America's Health Insurance Plans.   July 2006

Appendix H

How Health Savings Accounts[1] Compare to Health Flexible Spending Arrangements (FSAs) and Health Reimbursement Arrangements (HRAs)

[1] Health Savings Accounts (HSAs) were passed by Congress as part of the Medicare Prescription Drug, Improvement and Modernization Act of 2003 (Act), which President George W. Bush signed into law on December 8, 2003. HSAs are effective for years beginning after December 31, 2003.

	Health Savings Account (HSA)	Flexible Spending Arrangement (FSA)	Health Reimbursement Arrangement (HRA)
General Description	• Trust or custodial account used to accumulate funds on a tax-preferred basis to pay for certain medical expenses under Code section 213(d), as described below. • Available to individuals covered by a high deductible health plan and no other health plan that is not a high deductible health plan, except for certain "permitted" insurance or coverage. • Contributions may be made by an employer, eligible individual, or both. Contributions may also be made by any other individual (and would be deductible by the account holder). • An HSA may be offered through a cafeteria plan.	• Employer-sponsored benefit program under which employees receive reimbursement for certain medical expenses under Code Section 213(d), as described below. • Generally offered as part of an employer's cafeteria plan, but not in conjunction with any other insurance policy. • Contributions typically made by employees through salary reduction.	• Employer-sponsored benefit program under which employees may receive reimbursement for medical expenses under Code section 213(d), as described below. • May be offered in conjunction with a high deductible or other type of health plan, but this is not required. • Contributions must be solely from the employer.
Expenses Eligible for Tax-Free Reimbursement	• Amounts distributed for medical expenses (generally defined under Code section 213 (d)[2] incurred by the account holder and the account holder's	• Amounts may be distributed to reimburse an employee for medical expenses (generally defined under Code section 213(d)) incurred by the employee and the employee's spouse	• Amounts may be distributed to reimburse an employee for medical expenses (generally defined under Code section 213(d)) incurred by the employee and the employee's spouse

spouse or dependents (as defined in Code section 152, without regard to gross income limitations under Code section 152(d)(1)(B)) are excludable from income, except for amounts distributed to pay health insurance premiums.

• However, distributions for expenses of the following types of health insurance premiums are excludable from income: (i) retiree health insurance premiums (other than Medicare supplemental policies) for individuals who have reached Medicare eligibility, (ii) premiums for COBRA coverage, (iii) premiums for a qualified long-term care insurance contract, or (iv) premiums for a health plan during a period in which an individual is receiving unemployment compensation.

or dependents, except for: (i) expenses for any type of health insurance premiums and, (ii) expenses for long-term care services.

or dependents, except for expenses for qualified long-term care services. (Note that premiums for qualified long-term care insurance are reimbursable.)

[2] Code section 213(d) provides that the term "medical care" means amounts paid (A) for the diagnosis, cure, mitigation, treatment, or prevention of disease, or for the purpose of affecting any structure or function of the body; (B) for transportation primarily for and essential to medical care referred to in subparagraph (A); (C) for qualified long-term care services (as defined in section 7702B(c)); or (D) for insurance (including amounts paid as premiums under part B of title XVIII of the Social Security Act, relating to supplementary medical insurance for the aged) covering medical care referred to in subparagraphs (A) and (B) or for any qualified long-term care insurance contract (as defined in section 7702B(b)).

	Health Savings Account (HSA)	Flexible Spending Arrangement (FSA)	Health Reimbursement Arrangement (HRA)
Distributions for Non-Medical Expenses	• Distributions that are not used for medical expenses are includible in income and subject to a 10 percent additional tax. • The 10 percent additional tax does not apply to amounts distributed in the event of death, disability, or after an individual reaches Medicare eligibility. • If amounts that would otherwise be taxable HSA distributions are rolled over into another HSA within 60 days, there is no tax consequence associated with the distribution (so long as there have been no other such rollovers in the last 12 months).	• Distributions may not be made for non-medical expenses.	• Distributions may not be made for non-medical expenses.
Eligibility	• An individual (or spouse) who is covered by a high deductible health plan and no other non-high deductible health plan that provides benefits covered under the high deductible plan, unless the non-high deductible health plan provides coverage for	• An employee who satisfies the eligibility criteria of the employer and who has made an election under the employer's cafeteria plan.	• An employee who satisfies the eligibility criteria of the employer.

accidents, disability, dental care, vision care, long-term care or other types of "permitted insurance," as defined below.

- A high deductible health plan is a health plan that has an annual deductible of not less than $1,050 for self-only coverage, and $2,100 for family coverage, with a cap on out-of-pocket expenses (including the deductible) of $5,250 self and $10,500 family (all indexed for inflation in $50 increments), with the following exceptions related to preventive care and out-of-network expenses.

- Preventive Care: a plan shall not fail to be treated as a high deductible health plan by reason of failing to have a deductible for preventive care.

- Network plans: a plan shall not fail to be treated as a high deductible health plan by reason of having an out-of-pocket limitation for services provided outside of such network which

Health Savings Account (HSA)	Flexible Spending Arrangement (FSA)	Health Reimbursement Arrangement (HRA)
exceeds the applicable limitations. In addition, such plan's annual deductible for services provided outside of the network is not taken into account in determining the annual contribution limit. • "Permitted Insurance" is defined as: (A) insurance if substantially all of the coverage provided under such insurance relates to (i) liabilities incurred under workers' compensation laws, (ii) tort liabilities, (iii) liabilities relating to ownership or use of property, or (iv) such other similar liabilities as the Secretary may specify by regulations, (B) insurance for a specified disease or illness, and (C) insurance paying a fixed amount per day (or other period) of hospitalization. • Individuals who are entitled to benefits under Medicare are not eligible to make contributions.		

Funding/ Tax Aspects	• Account is funded. Earnings grow tax-free. • Contributions may be made either by the employer or the employee, or both, and may be made through a cafeteria plan. • Subject to certain limits, employer contributions are excludable from gross income, and contributions by an eligible individual are deductible in computing adjusted gross income. Contributions are not subject to employment taxes. • Rollovers are permitted from both MSAs and other HSAs, but not from FSAs or HRAs.	• Account is generally not funded. Rather, reimbursements are paid from the employer's general assets. • Contributions are typically made by employees through salary reduction, are excludable from income, and are not subject to employment taxes. • There is no statutory limit to the amount of contributions that may be made; any limits are by plan design.	• Account is generally not funded. Rather, reimbursements are paid from the employer's general assets. • Contributions must be solely employer-paid, are excludable from income, and are not subject to employment taxes. • There is no statutory limit to the amount of contributions that may be made; any limits are by plan design.
Contribution Limits	• Maximum contributions (computed on a monthly basis based on the individual's health coverage) are the lesser of: (i) the annual deductible under the high deductible policy, or (ii) $2,700 (in the case of self-only coverage) or $5,450 (in the case of family coverage); indexed in $50 increments thereafter.	• There are no contribution limits.	• There are no contribution limits.

	Health Savings Account (HSA)	Flexible Spending Arrangement (FSA)	Health Reimbursement Arrangement (HRA)
	• Maximum contribution amounts are decreased by the aggregate amount, if any, paid into an Archer Medical Savings Account (MSA) or another HSA.		
	• The maximum contribution amount is increased for individuals who are age 55 or older (again computed on a monthly basis). These individuals may contribute an additional $700 in 2006, increasing by $100 increments each year until the limit reaches $1,000 in 2009.		
Nondiscrimination Rules	• Nondiscrimination rules require an employer who makes contributions into an HSA for any employee to make comparable contributions to HSAs of all comparable participating employees. Failure to do so subjects the employer to an excise tax.	• Nondiscrimination rules prohibit discrimination in favor of highly compensated individuals with respect to eligibility or benefits. (Code sec. 105(h)). • Also may be subject to cafeteria plan non-discrimination rules.	• Nondiscrimination rules prohibit discrimination in favor of highly compensated individuals with respect to eligibility or benefits. (Code sec. 105(h)).

Carryover of Funds	• Amounts not used for medical expenses by the end of the year may be carried over to future years, and are non-forfeitable.	• Amounts not used for medical expenses by the end of the year are subject to a "use it or lose it" rule that prevents carryover to future years.	• Amounts not used for medical expenses by the end of the year may be carried over to future years. Limits may be imposed by plan design.
Death of Account Holder	• If the surviving spouse is the designated beneficiary of the account, the HSA will be treated as if the spouse is the account holder. • If any person other than the surviving spouse is the designated beneficiary, the HSA will cease to be an HSA as of the date of death, and an amount equal to the fair market value of the assets in the account on such date will be includible in the gross income of that person or, in the absence of a designated beneficiary, in the account holder's estate. • A deduction is permitted for qualified medical expenses incurred by the decedent before death if paid within one year of death.	• The only amounts that may be distributed upon the employee's death are reimbursements for medical expenses incurred by the employee or by the employee's spouse or eligible dependents prior to the date of the employee's death.	• Upon the account holder's death, the account may continue to be used by a spouse or eligible dependents for reimbursement of medical expenses. • When there is no longer a spouse or eligible dependents, the account must be forfeited.

Source: Groom Law Group. Reprinted with permission.

Appendix I

Administrative Forms

The forms in the appendix are provided by PenServ, Inc., a pension consulting firm with offices across the country. It is not known which forms will change and to what extent as a result of future guidance. For the most current version of any form herein, please call PenServ, Inc., at (215) 444-9812.

ADDITIONAL CONTRIBUTION/DEPOSIT TO EXISTING HSA

GENERAL INFORMATION ━━━━━━━━━━━━━━━━━━━━━━━━━━━━━━━

Organization: _____

Participant: _____ SSN: _____ Account No: _____

Residence Address: _____

DEPOSIT INFORMATION ━━━━━━━━━━━━━━━━━━━━━━━━━━━━━

Type of Deposit (Check one):   **Amount of this Deposit: $** _____

☐ HSA regular contribution (including spousal) for tax year : _____

☐ Rollover from another HSA or Archer MSA.

☐ Transfer from another HSA.

   Transfer received from: _____

Investment(s) Requested:

☐ Regular Savings: $ _____ ☐ Certificate: $ _____ Term _____ Rate _____ % Maturity Date: _____

☐ Other: $ _____ Please specify: _____

Add to existing investment Account No.: _____

   Deposit Date: _____ Total Deposit Amount: $ _____

   Deposit accepted by (initials): _____

Authorization ━━━━━━━━━━━━━━━━━━━━━━━━━━━━━━━━━━━
I authorize and direct the Trustee/Custodian to place this contribution in my HSA. I acknowledge that I am solely responsible for determining my eligibility to make HSA contributions and that I will not make annual contributions in excess of my maximum allowable amount. If this is a rollover contribution, I certify that this deposit is being made within 60 days of my receipt of the HSA distribution that I am depositing and that this amount is eligible to be rolled over. I understand that contributions to my HSA will be reported to the Internal Revenue Service.

Participant's Signature: _____ Date: _____

Reprinted with permisssion.
Control 03114.doc (04/26/04)

HSA DISTRIBUTION REQUEST

GENERAL INFORMATION

Organization: _____ Account Number: _____

Participant: _____ SSN: _____ Birthdate: _____

Residence Address: _____ Phone: _____

For death distributions, complete the following. Beneficiary's Name: _____

SSN: _____ Relationship: _____ Birthdate: _____

Residence Address: _____ Phone: _____

DISTRIBUTION REASON

☐ 1. Distribution used to pay or reimburse for qualified medical expenses (2)
☐ 2. Distribution *not* used to pay or reimburse for qualified medical expenses and no other exception applies (1)
☐ 3. Distribution after becoming eligible for Medicare (age 65) (7)
☐ 4. Permanent Disability (if you are disabled within the meaning of section 72(m)(7) of the Internal Revenue Code) (3)
☐ 5. Death (If you are a Designated Beneficiary of this account and can furnish a certified copy of the Death Certificate) (4)
☐ 6. Removal of Excess plus earnings before tax filing deadline: Excess amount: $ _____ Earnings: $ _____
       Earnings on excess contributions are taxed in the year of distribution.
☐ 7. Transfer (including Transfer Incident To Divorce, Legal Separation, or to a Surviving Spouse). Payable to: _____
☐ 8. Other (specify reason not listed above): _____

FINANCIAL INFORMATION

I instruct the Custodian or Trustee to distribute from the above account. Choose either 1 or 2:

Amount Requested $ _____

Administrative Fees (including CD penalty)   (-) _____
☐ check this box if fees and/or CD penalty
paid from remaining HSA assets.

☐ 1. The entire account balance.
☐ 2. Partial distribution

Amount Withdrawn (reported to IRS) $ _____

Payment Instructions:
☐ Issue check to Participant/Beneficiary
☐ Distribute funds to Account #: _____
☐ In-kind. _____ Shares; Name of Security: _____
☐ Other: _____

Federal Income Tax Withheld   (-) _____
State Income Tax Withheld   (-) _____
Net Amount Paid to Recipient or Transferred
to another Organization. $ _____

METHOD OF PAYMENT

Until I give written instructions to the contrary, I direct the Custodian or Trustee to distribute the amount requested as follows:
1. Date payment(s) to commence(s): _____
2. Distribution(s) to be made: ☐ one time ☐ monthly ☐ quarterly ☐ semi-annually ☐ annually ☐ other _____
3. Make payments(s) to ☐ me directly ☐ account # _____ ☐ other: _____

SIGNATURES

I certify that I am the proper party to receive payment(s) from this HSA, and that all information provided by me is true and accurate. I understand that although HSAs are not subject to withholding, I am still liable for the payment of Federal income tax on the taxable amount of any distribution. I understand that any amounts withdrawn that are not used to pay or reimburse for qualified medical expenses may be subject to income taxes and penalties. I also understand that I may be subject to tax penalties under the estimated tax payment rules if my payments of estimated tax are not adequate. I certify that no tax advice has been given to me by the Custodian or Trustee, that distributions are reported to the IRS, and that all decisions regarding this withdrawal are my own. The Account Beneficiary is solely responsible for determining the taxability or non-taxability of any distribution from this HSA. I expressly assume the responsibility for any adverse consequences which may arise from this withdrawal and I agree that the Custodian or Trustee shall in no way be responsible for those consequences.

Participant's or Beneficiary's Signature: _____ Date: _____

Reprinted with permisssion.
Control 03115.doc (04/26/04)

HSA BENEFICIARY DESIGNATION OR CHANGE FORM

GENERAL INFORMATION

Organization: _____ Account No.: _____

Participant: _____ SSN: _____ Birthdate: _____

Address: _____ Phone No: _____

DESIGNATION OF BENEFICIARY(IES)

I hereby revoke any prior beneficiary designation made by me and designate the individuals named below as my Primary and Contingent Beneficiaries of this HSA. If the Primary or Contingent Beneficiary box is not checked for a beneficiary, the beneficiary will be deemed to be a Primary Beneficiary.

In the event of my death, the balance in the account shall be paid to the Primary Beneficiaries who survive me in equal shares (or in the specified shares, if indicated). If none of the Primary Beneficiaries survive me, the balance in the account shall be paid to the Contingent Beneficiaries who survive me in equal shares (or in the specified shares, if indicated). If any Primary or Contingent Beneficiary does not survive me, such beneficiary's interest and the interest of such beneficiary's heirs shall terminate completely, and the share for any remaining Primary or Contingent Beneficiary shall be increased on a pro rata basis.

Primary   Contingent   Name: _____ SSN: _____ Birthdate: _____

☐   ☐   Address: _____ Relationship: _____ Share: _____ %

Primary   Contingent   Name: _____ SSN: _____ Birthdate: _____

☐   ☐   Address: _____ Relationship: _____ Share: _____ %

Primary   Contingent   Name: _____ SSN: _____ Birthdate: _____

☐   ☐   Address: _____ Relationship: _____ Share: _____ %

Primary   Contingent   Name: _____ SSN: _____ Birthdate: _____

☐   ☐   Address: _____ Relationship: _____ Share: _____ %

Primary   Contingent   Name: _____ SSN: _____ Birthdate: _____

☐   ☐   Address: _____ Relationship: _____ Share: _____ %

If I named a Beneficiary which is a Trust, I understand I must complete the Trust Beneficiary Certification Form.

PARTICIPANT'S SIGNATURE

I understand that I may change or add beneficiaries at any time by completing and delivering the proper form to the Custodian or Trustee.

Signature of Participant: _____ Date: _____

CONSENT OF SPOUSE

I consent to the above Beneficiary Designation.

Signature of Spouse: _____ Date: _____
      (Note: Consent of the Participant's Spouse may be required in a community property or marital property state to effectively designate a beneficiary other than or in addition to the Participant's Spouse.)

Disclaimer For Community and Marital Property States: The Participant's Spouse may have a property interest in the account and the right to dispose of the interest by will. Therefore, the Trustee or Custodian disclaims any warranty as to the effectiveness of the Participant's beneficiary designation or as to the ownership of the account after the death of the Participant's Spouse. For additional information, please consult your legal advisor.

ACCEPTANCE

The Custodian/Trustee acknowledges and accepts receipt of this HSA Beneficiary Designation or Change Form.

Authorized Signature Of Custodian/Trustee: _____ Date Accepted: _____

Reprinted with permission.
Control 03111.doc (04/26/04)

HSA TRUST BENEFICIARY CERTIFICATION FORM

GENERAL INFORMATION ━━━━━━━━━━━━━━━━━━━━━━━━━━━━━━

Organization: _____   Account No: _____

Participant:_____   SSN:_____

If the Account Owner is deceased, the following must be completed:

Name of Trustee(s) of Trust:_____   Trust EIN:_____

                                                          Date of Death:_____

TRUST BENEFICIARY(IES) ━━━━━━━━━━━━━━━━━━━━━━━━━━━━━━

I certify that I am either the Participant or the Trustee of the Trust and I have either:

☐ provided the Trustee/Custodian with a copy of the Trust; or
☐ listed below the beneficiary(ies) of the Trust.

Primary	Contingent			
☐	☐	Name:_____ SSN:_____ Birthdate:_____		
		Address:_____ Relationship:_____ Share:____ %		
		Conditions on entitlement: _____		
☐	☐	Name:_____ SSN:_____ Birthdate:_____		
		Address:_____ Relationship:_____ Share:____ %		
		Conditions on entitlement: _____		
☐	☐	Name:_____ SSN:_____ Birthdate:_____		
		Address:_____ Relationship:_____ Share:____ %		
		Conditions on entitlement: _____		

SIGNATURES ━━━━━━━━━━━━━━━━━━━━━━━━━━━━━━

I understand if the Trust instrument is amended at any time in the future I must, within a reasonable time, provide a copy of such amendment or a corrected certification form to the Trustee/Custodian. I also agree to provide a copy of the trust instrument to the Trustee/Custodian upon demand; and upon the death of the Participant, provide a final list of all beneficiary(ies) or an actual copy of the Trust no later than October 31st of the year following the year of the participant's death.

Signature: _____   Date:_____

Signature of: ☐ Participant   ☐ Trustee of Trust
(check one)

ACCEPTANCE ━━━━━━━━━━━━━━━━━━━━━━━━━━━━━━

The Trustee/Custodian acknowledges and accepts receipt of this Trust Beneficiary Certification Form.

Signature: _____   Date Accepted:_____

Reprinted with permission
Control 03126.doc (04/26/04)

HSA ROLLOVER CONTRIBUTION DOCUMENTATION

HSA PARTICIPANT INFORMATION

Participant's Name: _____ Account No: _____

Residence Address: _____

SSN: _____ Birthdate: _____ Home Phone #: _____ Bus. Phone #: _____

Form of Rollover/Direct Rollover: ☐ In Cash $ _____ ☐ In Kind (Specify): _____

ROLLOVER FROM ANOTHER HSA OR AN ARCHER MSA

☐   I certify that the following statements are true and correct.

1.   This rollover contribution is being made within 60 days after my receipt of funds from another HSA or an Archer MSA, in which I was either the participant or surviving spouse beneficiary.
2.   During the 12-month period prior to my receipt of the distribution being rolled over, I have not received a distribution from the same HSA which was subsequently rolled over to another HSA, and the distribution being rolled over has not been part of a distribution from another HSA that was subsequently rolled over.

SIGNATURE OF HSA PARTICIPANT

The undersigned hereby irrevocably elects to treat this contribution as a rollover contribution. I understand that this will not be a valid HSA rollover unless the statements above are true and correct. I understand that rollover contributions are reported to the IRS. I hereby release the Trustee/Custodian from any claim for damages on account of the failure of this transaction to qualify as a valid rollover.

Date: _____ Signature of Participant: _____

Reprinted with permission.
Control 03113.doc (04/26/04)

HSA TO HSA TRANSFER DOCUMENTATION

GENERAL INFORMATION

Present Custodian or Trustee: _____

Participant: _____ SSN: _____ Account No: _____

Residence Address: _____ Phone: _____

TRANSFER INSTRUCTIONS

Directly transfer all or part of my present HSA with your organization in the manner indicated below.

1. Please make a check payable as follows:

_____, as the ☐ Custodian   ☐ Trustee
            Name of Accepting Organization

for_____
            Participant's Name and Account Number
                                                            Account No:

2. Transfer the assets in the manner prescribed below:

Asset Description	Quantity In HSA	Quantity To Be Transferred	Liquidate Immediately	At Maturity	In Kind
_____	_____	_____		☐	☐
_____	_____	_____		☐	☐
_____	_____	_____		☐	☐

This transfer will (Check one) ☐ completely ☐ partially close my HSA. I am aware that penalties may be incurred if time deposits are liquidated prior to their maturity date.

3. Delivery instructions - Mail check to:

_____
_____
_____

4. If DTC eligible, DTC #: _____

SIGNATURES

The transfer amount ☐ should ☐ should not be placed in a separate HSA. New HSA Account: _____

Participant's Signature: _____ Date: _____

Accepting Organization - Our organization agrees to serve as the new Custodian or Trustee for the HSA account of the above-named individual, and as Custodian or Trustee, we agree to accept the assets being transferred.

New Custodian or Trustee: _____ EIN #: _____

Address: _____

Authorized Signature for Accepting Organization: _____ Date: _____

Reprinted with permission.
Control 03112.doc (04/26/04)

Table of Internal Revenue Code Sections

[References are to question numbers and appendices.]

Table of IRS Announcements and Notices

[References are to question numbers and appendices.]

Index

[References are to question numbers and appendices.]

S

T

U

V

W